ethics

bju press®

Greenville, South Carolina

Note: The fact that materials produced by other publishers may be referred to in this volume does not constitute an endorsement of the content or theological position of materials produced by such publishers. Any references and ancillary materials are listed as an aid to the student or the teacher and in an attempt to maintain the accepted academic standards of the publishing industry.

ETHICS Student Edition

Writers
Kevin M. Collins, MDiv
Paul Hornor, MDiv
Bruce Ostrom, PhD
Thomas Parr, ThM

Writer Consultants
Christa G. Habegger, MA
Manuel Mendoza, Jr., MDiv
L. Michelle Rosier
Martie Spurgeon
A. Charles Ware, DD

Biblical Worldview
Brian C. Collins, PhD
Bryan Smith, PhD

Academic Integrity
Jeff Heath, EdD

Instructional Design
Rachel Santopietro, MEd
Michael Winningham, MA

Editors
Miguel del Toro, MABTS
Kyle J. Keesling Jr., ThM
Kristian Römer, PhD (cand.)
James Zemke, MA

Editorial Assistant
Pam Evans

Designer
Alayna Rowan

Cover and Book Design
Emily Rush

Illustrators
Jonathan Andrews
Seb Camagajevac (Beehive Illustration)
Jullianna Eckardt
B. Taylor Harrison
Roy Hermelin (Beehive Illustration)
David Lompe
János Orban (Beehive Illustration)

Brenna Short
Augusto Zambonato

Production Designer
Sherry McCollough

DesignOps Coordinator
Kaitlyn Quevedo

Permissions
Ruth Bartholomew
Sharon Belknap
Sylvia Gass
Hannah Labadorf
Jennifer Walton

Project Coordinator
Heather Chisholm

Postproduction Liaison
Peggy Hargis

Indexer
Jennifer Weers

Photo credits appear on page 296.

Text acknowledgments appear within the notes, which begin on page 266.

The text for this book is set in Abril Display by TypeTogether, Adobe Hebrew, Adobe Minion Pro, Adobe Myriad Pro, Adobe Text Pro, Arial Bold MT, Calibri by Monotype, Chelsea Market Pro by Crystal Kluge, DIN 2014 by Vasily Biryukov, Felt Tip Woman by Mark Simonson, Free 3 of 9 by Matthew Welch, Freight by Joshua Darden, Freight Sans Pro by Joshua Darden, Futura PT by Paratype, Helvetica Neue, Noto Sans by Google, Sketchnote Text by Mike Rohde, Skippy Sharp by Chank Diesel, Times New Roman PSMT, and Trade Gothic Next LT Pro by Monotype.

© 2024 BJU Press
Greenville, South Carolina 29609

Printed in the United States of America

ISBN 978-1-64626-389-9

15 14 13 12 11 10 9 8 7 6 5 4 3 2 1

content.

foreword

When I was a senior in high school, what I wanted most was to be done with school. I didn't hate school. I liked learning, and I liked my friends. But I was ready to start enjoying the independence of adulthood. I got my wish. Before I knew it, I was walking across the stage to receive my diploma.

I found that adulthood did indeed come with a lot of independence. I had my own car, my own job, and my own bank account. I was able to choose the college I went to, and I chose my own major. But independence, I soon learned, was a two-edged sword. It allowed me to make my own decisions, but it also forced me to take responsibility for my actions. My decisions were my own now, not my parents'. If my car broke down, I paid for it. If I fell behind in my schoolwork, I had to reach out to my professor—he wasn't going to contact me.

Of course, I wasn't alone. Everyone I graduated with had to learn this lesson too. And some didn't learn it very well. Some of my friends managed to cram into the first three months after high school every bad decision a person could make in three months. That's when I learned another lesson: the decisions you make after high school are high-stakes decisions. When you make a bad choice at 10 years old, it doesn't follow you, not usually. When you make a bad choice at 18 or 22, it does. Bad decisions about relationships, substance use, marriage, conflict—these can destroy your life.

That's the reason we produced this course on ethics. Ethics is the study of right and wrong. It helps people make decisions that are morally good and shows them how to avoid the ones that are not. Our world is complex and messy. Doing the right thing is not always obvious. In fact, very often it's not. God has not left us to sort out such questions on our own. He has given us His Word and His Spirit. But we must learn how to make use of what He has given. That's what this course is meant to do for you—to show you how to make right decisions based on the wisdom of God in the Bible.

There are many books on ethics. But this one is different. It's focused on what the Bible teaches about ethics, and it gives a great deal of attention to being the right kind of person. God is interested in more than our decisions. It isn't just what we do that matters to Him; it's also who we are. That's why this course isn't just about issues—issues like abortion, euthanasia, racism, and cloning. It's also about virtues: love, righteousness, patience, and hope. The best way to learn how to make good decisions is to first learn to be a good person. Virtuous people tend to make virtuous decisions.

Of course, no textbook can make you a virtuous person. It takes the grace of God to do that. But a textbook can require you to reckon with God's grace by reading about it, meditating on it, and praying for it. It's my prayer that as you do these things this year, God will in His grace take hold of your life and do something wonderful in you and through you. Here's what I'm praying:

> That ye might be filled with the knowledge of [God's] will in all wisdom and spiritual understanding; that ye might walk worthy of the Lord unto all pleasing, being fruitful in every good work, and increasing in the knowledge of God; strengthened with all might, according to his glorious power, unto all patience and longsuffering with joyfulness. (Col. 1:9–11)

Bryan Smith, PhD
Assistant Director
Biblical Worldview Formation
BJU Press

ethics

Introduction to Ethics

Why is studying ethics relevant to me?

What Is Ethics?

Just do the right thing. Is that sufficient for you to be considered an ethical person? Or is ethics about something more than just making the right choices? How about one's motive, like seeking to please God? What about the standard that guides one's choices, like adhering to the Bible in obedience? Certainly, we have all done wrong things, made wrong choices, displeased God, and disobeyed the Bible's teaching. So we all have to come to grips with this topic—ethics. Is an ethical decision the same thing as a moral or right decision? Before this question can be answered, there needs to be a greater understanding of what ethics is and what the standard for ethics is. We'll get to those things in the foundations for ethics in Chapter 1. Ethics sounds like a good thing. But we'll need to start with some definitions to begin understanding everything that is involved in ethics.

FOUNDATIONAL DEFINITIONS

Ethics is the branch of philosophy that studies how man ought to live. Ethics concerns itself with determining what is right and what is wrong. Ethics seeks to identify what is objectively good. Chapter 2 will provide a brief overview and critique of various secular ethical systems. As can be expected, there are right and wrong approaches to ethics.

The focus of this textbook's discussion of ethics will be Christian, not secular. Even though the term used is *ethics*, the emphasis is on ethics from a Christian viewpoint—one flowing from a biblical worldview. To truly know how to live in this world, we need a knowledge of God and His wisdom as revealed in His Word (Prov. 2:6; 9:10). Any morality* that people rely on to govern themselves is based on something. Only Christian ethics, based on understanding God and His ways through Scripture, is truly ethical.

You will learn in subsequent chapters that ethics has to do with acts (actions that conform to God's Word), agents (individuals who exemplify virtues and have certain motives), and ends (consequences).[1] In addition to these three elements, one must consider the circumstances of the ethical decision that must be made. More elaboration on this ethical model will be presented in Chapter 8.

Christian ethics seeks to determine how man ought to live in particular circumstances through studying God's Word, discerning God's creational norms,* and using moral reasoning. For the ethics to be truly Christian, a thorough consideration of the acts, agents, ends, and specific situation is necessary.

ETHICS

situation

agents
(*person, motivation*)

ends
(*ultimate goal*)

acts
(*principle*)

morality: often used synonymously with ethics, but can also refer more specifically to a society's conclusions regarding what is right and what is wrong

creational norms: the design of God's created order (the way things ought to be) translated into divine laws that govern the way human individuals and cultures ought to operate

What is ethics all about?

THREE KEY RELATIONSHIPS

Now that we have defined ethics, let's consider three key relationships that will help you understand how ethics fits with related areas of study.

First, consider how ethics relates to a biblical worldview. Developing a Christian ethic can only follow from the worldview framework found in God's Word: its presentation of reality in its Creation, Fall, Redemption storyline. The application of a Christian ethic follows from a careful consideration of the three ingredients of a biblical worldview: (1) the metanarrative,* (2) beliefs and values, and (3) personal and group behavior, which form culture. Your personal behavior and cultural engagement will be enhanced by your current study of ethics if you have already studied biblical doctrines and developed a biblical worldview. Unless you are grounded in the teachings of the Bible and you embrace a biblical worldview, you won't be able to consistently make ethical decisions. All ethical systems come from and reflect a worldview.

Second, consider how ethics relates to philosophy. *Philosophy* has been described as "the pursuit of a comprehensive understanding of all the world."[2] Philosophy uses reason to answer questions about the world and life. There are at least four main branches of philosophical study: metaphysics, epistemology, ethics, and aesthetics. You will learn more about these four branches in Chapter 2, but for now notice that ethics is one of philosophy's main concerns. Ancient Greek philosophers tried to figure out the meaning of life and how to live in the world without appealing to God or His Word. Even pagan philosophers realized that wisdom was needed to make good applications from reality to life. Christian philosophers have contributed to this discipline; so, as philosophy developed, it didn't remain totally godless. Each philosophical tradition has its own version of an ethical system.

Most secular philosophers maintain that wisdom can be obtained through reason and intellect alone, rejecting God's revelation. But man cannot be the final authority in his search for wisdom (Jer. 17:7–9; Mark 7:21–23). One of the problems with secular philosophy is its inability to explain truth, reality, and morality apart from God's revelation and thus its failure to consis-

tently employ Christian ethics. Nevertheless, philosophy has had a major impact on ethics, using reason to arrive at some good answers to challenging scenarios. But a strict reliance on secular approaches to philosophy isn't an option for believers who want to develop a Christian ethic. Nonetheless, Christians shouldn't fear the helpful tools philosophy has harnessed (e.g., syllogisms, deductive and inductive reasoning, epistemological reflection, and math).

Third, ethics relates to world religions in that the teachings and practices of a religion influence the ethic that flows from those beliefs and traditions. Ethics is a component of religion as well as of philosophy. For example, Hindus in a high caste live "ethically" according to their religious worldview when they refuse to help Hindus who are part of lower castes. The high-caste Hindus' religion guides their beliefs and behavior. An ethic based on biblical Christianity, however, compels believers to be compassionate to others and to love all people indiscriminately (Luke 10:29–37). In this example, Scripture informs the religious practice which then forms the ethic of biblical Christians. The expression of one's ethics and the practice of one's religion are closely tied together.

metanarrative: an overarching storyline that attempts to explain all reality

RECURRING BIBLICAL WORLDVIEW THEMES

A biblical worldview is foundational to all your studies, not just to Bible class. In this course specifically, your attention will be drawn to various biblical worldview themes that impact your understanding of ethics. What follows is a brief summary of these themes.

1 Authority

There is only one God who made all things, and He is the ultimate authority. Fallen humans replace the true God and His revelation of Himself in His Word with other authorities such as reason, intuition, feelings, or religious texts. Truly ethical behavior can come only from submission to God and His Word.

2 Creational Order

God created not only the physical universe but also the moral norms by which people and societies function. Fallen humans twist God's moral order, and they make this twisted perspective seem normal. Christians should demonstrate why Christian ethics make better sense of the world God made than the alternatives.

3 Man's Chief End

God created mankind with many purposes that can be summed up in one "chief end," namely, "to glorify God, and to enjoy Him for ever."[3] Fallen humans replace this true goal for life with many false alternatives that leave the true God out. Christians demonstrate that right behavior is only found when one makes God the center of all motivations.

4 Virtue

God's goal is not merely for people to do the right thing but also to become the right kind of people. Fallen humans tend toward either external adherence to manmade rules or to displaying an "authentic" self, free from all constraints. The development of true virtue can only happen when the Holy Spirit regenerates a person and begins the work of sanctification.

5 Wisdom

Wisdom is the ability to discern creational norms, communicate them to others, and live by them. The fool lives against the grain of the creational order and develops sophisticated defenses for why he or she does so. The Christian grows in wisdom by learning how to apply the Bible and creational norms to situations the Bible does not explicitly address.

These worldview emphases constitute a helpful way to apply ethics to your life: Recognize God as the ultimate authority in all things. Align your way of thinking with God's creational design of the world. Seek to glorify God now and look forward to enjoying Him forever. Develop virtuous character that reflects God's character. And grow in wisdom, so you can make ethical decisions and be a productive contributor to society and to God's kingdom.

Thinking It Through: What Is Ethics?

1. Define *ethics*.
2. Define *Christian ethics*.
3. How does ethics relate to biblical worldview, philosophy, and world religions?
4. Summarize the five biblical worldview themes that are woven into this textbook.

Why Study Ethics?

At the end of the day, everything you do is motivated by one thing or another. You do some things because you want to. You put on a jacket because you are cold. Or you wear a coat because your shirt underneath is dirty or wrinkled. And maybe you pull on a hoodie just because hoodies are comfy. But many things you just have to do, whether you like it or not. Helping pull weeds in the flower beds around your house and brushing your teeth before bed might fit this category. These things simply need to be done. Pulling the weeds may be motivated by the consequences of disobeying your parents' instructions. And brushing your teeth before bed is a habit, thanks to your parents and the dentist's drill.

What are the personal benefits of studying ethics?

Do you need to be properly motivated to study ethics? Technically you don't need to be; perhaps you study it simply because you have to. But you will get so much more out of this course if you want to study it. The same can be said if you have a "meh" attitude toward your driving lessons. But if you don't pay attention and you don't put some effort into them, you might not pass your driving tests! You know you will personally benefit from being well-motivated for both driving lessons and this course. And the end results of both are very rewarding.

No one wants to be ill-prepared. Sure, there is skill in adapting, but no one wants to plan to be ill-prepared on purpose. Expanding your knowledge, growing spiritually, and improving your Christian testimony are all good reasons to study this material. But there are even more benefits of learning about ethics. Below is a brief elaboration on these good reasons for and benefits of studying this subject.

YOUR KNOWLEDGE

You should be motivated to study this textbook not only to be prepared for all the tests that will be coming your way but also to be prepared for life. Yes, life is full of ethical questions. Questions like whether doing a "greater good" justifies committing a "lesser sin." Or questions about who you should vote for in local or national elections. You will encounter an untold number of ethical situations that are difficult to untangle. You won't have straightforward answers for every ethical curiosity, but you will have a background in Christian ethics and a biblical framework at your disposal. Learning about faulty ethical approaches will also help you identify them and avoid them as you try to use a solid ethical model.

Knowing about ethics has another benefit. Studying ethics will familiarize you with commandments and principles from Scripture used to construct the Christian ethic, which contrasts with the secular ethics you will study. As you learn what God requires of His children, you will be challenged to align your life with what brings God glory (1 Cor. 10:31).

There is much knowledge to be learned in this course, but it is not knowledge merely for its own sake. Without insightful, accurate knowledge of ethical principles, ethical models, and ethical issues, your ability to make ethical decisions would be severely limited.

YOUR PERSONAL GROWTH

Another good reason to take this course seriously (and a benefit of doing so) is personal spiritual growth. Unit 2 is dedicated to growth in Christlikeness and specific virtues as the key to ethical Christian living. Every ethical decision is tied to Scripture and to the character of the person making the decision. Learning how to apply what you learn about ethics directly to your Christian living is both a goal and a blessing of this course. Thinking through issues like abortion, civil disobedience, racial discrimination, stem cell research, and homosexuality allows you to apply biblical truth and wisdom for spiritual growth in your life. This course is a tool to help believers be "fruitful in every good work" and increase "in the knowledge of God" (Col. 1:10). If you know the Lord, this course will also help you be more prepared to speak "the truth in love" (Eph. 4:15) with everyone you encounter.

YOUR TESTIMONY

One more motivation to pay close attention to the content of this textbook is to develop a better Christian testimony before a watching world. Yes, the world loves to draw attention to the inconsistencies and sins of Christians. Believers are called to be "the salt of the earth" (Matt. 5:13). One effect of salt is preservation. When a society is left to its own devices, man's sinfulness sends that society on a downward trajectory (Gen. 6:5; Rom. 1:24–32). Believers who seek to live their lives according to a Christian ethical system showcase the value of what is right and shine light on the damage done by what is wrong. And Christians who are strong in their faith can remain faithful to the gospel message of Christ in the face of philosophical and religious opposition (Acts 5:40–42). This kind of testimony lifts high the name of Christ and draws attention to His unique and authoritative claims (John 14:6). Strong Christian testimonies—deeply rooted in Christian ethics—can continue to preserve a society even when most oppose God and His will.

Believers are also called to be "the light of the world" (Matt. 5:14). The "good works" (Matt. 5:16) this passage speaks of include behavior that is tied to a decidedly Christian ethic. Neither your own smarts nor your own feelings, no matter how much you trust them, qualify as an arbiter* in your ethical decision-making. Jesus is *the* Light of the World, and it is the message of His gospel that shines light into the darkened hearts of sinful people (John 8:12; 2 Cor. 4:4). Believers are commissioned to reflect Christ's light and make an impact on this dark world. Consider your own testimony and how you can improve it through studying ethics.

arbiter: a person who settles disputes

ETHICAL CHOICES, WISDOM, AND PLEASING GOD

We just looked at some reasons to study ethics and the benefits of doing so. In fact, every subject you study benefits you in some way. English—so you can communicate well. Math—so you can create things and understand much of God's orderly universe. History—so you aren't ignorant of the people and events that have led up to the present. Bible—in part, so you can learn how to live for God. Believers usually learn early after their conversion that they no longer live for themselves but for their Lord (1 Cor. 6:18–20). As we saw above, the more knowledge you have of God and His Word, the more opportunity you have to obey Him. And the purpose of knowledge is to gain wisdom for life, a life that is lived to glorify God (Prov. 1:1–7).

A key passage for the study of ethics is Colossians 1:9–12. The main goal for believers in this passage is found in verse 10: "walk worthy of the Lord." This one phrase is where the rubber meets the road for Christians. What someone thinks and believes directly affects their actions. But what someone thinks and believes is directly tied to what verse 9 says about believers being "filled with the knowledge of his will in all wisdom and spiritual understanding." Believers can't do the right thing (that is, make the ethical choice) without knowing how to arrive at that choice. Have you ever noticed that the Bible doesn't come out and give you answers to common yet high-impact life decisions—questions like where to go to college, what career to pursue, who to marry, how many children to have, what neighborhood to move into, or what church to join. Knowledge, wisdom, and spiritual understanding are not just about having information. Christians need the Holy Spirit to give them wisdom and understanding so that they can move from what they know generally about God's will from Scripture to making the best choice in a given situation. When Christians have spiritual wisdom and understanding, they will be able to truly "walk worthy of the Lord" (Col. 1:10).[4]

THE RIGHT APPROACH TO STUDYING ETHICS

It is important to reiterate what is foundational to the study of ethics—the Bible. The right approach to these subjects is to keep the Bible's teaching on anything related to ethics front and center. We need Scripture to saturate our minds, hearts, and choices (Col. 3:16–17). Psalm 19:7–11 and the whole of Psalm 119 declare the necessity of Scripture for all of life, including when we are determining our ethics (see also 2 Pet. 1:3).

We have already covered *why* you should study ethics. Before embarking on the first chapter in our study of ethics, we want to look at *how* you should study ethics.

"Let the word of Christ dwell in you richly in all wisdom."
Colossians 3:16

> *The basic reason that we should study ethics is to better know God's will for us.* WAYNE GRUDEM[5]

There's an old saying that when you're trying to do something correctly, you have to hold your mouth the right way. The saying is slightly humorous because it combines the reality of the effort required to do something right with the whimsical idea that the way you position your lips and tongue has a direct impact on accomplishing a task. This ironic saying is communicating in a light-hearted way that having the right posture helps get the job done. This is actually the case for many things in life. For example, posture is everything when it comes to your golf swing. The positioning of your shoulders, arms, hands, back, hips, and feet plays a huge role in a successful drive or putt. If you slouch or carelessly swing the club, the ball won't go where you want it to. The same principle applies to your study of ethics. The way you "carry yourself" as you approach your studies will have a lot to do with how successful you are.

Prayer[6]

If you are like many, prayer can be one of the last resources you use when you tackle your work. Maybe you rely on your brainpower and willpower entirely—or at least way before you consider praying about your work. Hopefully, you pray regularly for understanding and efficient learning as you study. If not, it isn't too late to start a new habit. And praying for wisdom as you learn to grapple with ethical choices will be essential! Believers have an advantage that unbelievers don't—the Spirit of God works in Christians and helps them understand matters that are spiritually discerned (1 Cor. 2:14–16). Starting now, get in the routine of praying before, during, and after your studies of ethics and ethical issues. And as you gain knowledge and grow from your studies, pray that God will establish the truth deep in your heart, so you can face college and the workplace convinced of the value of Christian ethics.

Humility

Humility is a Christian virtue that isn't highly sought after; by its very nature, it is not often publicly rewarded. Christians who are loving, kind, patient, or disciplined seem to be more readily acknowledged. But a humble person manifests meekness, confidence rooted in faith, and an absence of pride. You will gain a lot of knowledge this year. You will figure out things that many people much older than you don't know because they have never studied ethics. So here is a timely caution: stay humble, and don't let your new knowledge puff you up (1 Cor. 8:1). Humility can be one of your first requests as you pray for your efforts to learn and use this material.

Reason

Human reason rightly has a bad reputation when it is held up as the ultimate standard for determining what's true. Reason that is not submitted to God and not viewed as deficient due to man's finiteness and fallenness is reason misused. But reason is a necessary tool for developing and communicating conclusions. Jesus and Paul used reason appropriately (Matt. 22:42–45; 1 Tim. 5:17–18). And that is because reason as a tool of thinking and communication isn't a boogeyman. You must be careful, though, that your "reasonable" extensions of what Scripture explicitly says don't go against other statements of Scripture. In ethics, this is key so you don't arrive at seemingly justified conclusions that in reality contradict clear biblical teaching. Use reason well, and use it submitted to the authority of God's revelation in His Word.

Effort

Anything worth having requires effort. This saying applies to almost everything and most certainly to the subject at hand. You will need to be engaged and focused on the material as you work through each section and chapter. Of course, completing the assignments is part of the requirements for this course. But going beyond the classroom and homework, you will need to continue to work at coming to the best ethical decisions for countless situations. Consulting with others who are wise, mature

Christians or who are knowledgeable on this subject will be key to your growth in these areas. Don't limit your study of what the Bible has to say on a given ethical topic to what this textbook presents. Search the Scriptures for answers and guidance in all subjects of study and areas of life (Acts 17:11; 2 Tim. 3:16–17).

Praise

A final part of your approach to studying ethics should be praise and rejoicing. Just having a Bible class in school is a blessing and a privilege. God is the giver of all good things that we receive (James 1:17). To rejoice and praise God for His goodness, His care, and His love is a practice that should characterize every believer (Deut. 6:5; Ps. 146:2). Do you praise God for and rejoice over the material things you have? Do you thank God for your family and friends? One of the most helpful ways to begin this course is with praise to God for the opportunity to study ethics. To learn about ethics is to learn how to better please God with your motives, decisions, and actions.

As you embark on this journey, keep in mind that ethical issues constantly swirl around you. Be prepared to stop and think hard about what the Bible says about any given topic or situation—what your motives should be, what your goals should be, and what virtues you should emulate in choosing what you choose. It will be well worth it.

Thinking It Through: Why Study Ethics?

1. Summarize the reasons to study ethics.

2. Summarize the benefits of studying ethics.

3. Explain the value of gaining spiritual wisdom in order to please God in making ethical choices.

4. How can you study ethics in a wise and godly manner?

Creational Foundations for Ethics

01

Who decides what's right and what's wrong?

ROMANS 1:18–20

1.1 God's Character as a Foundation for Ethics

Soccer, which is called football by most of the global population, originated in England. A meeting in Cambridge in 1848 marks the official birth of soccer as an organized sport. The official rules for soccer have changed dramatically in its over one hundred seventy years of history. Take a look at this sample of rule changes or additions through the years:[7]

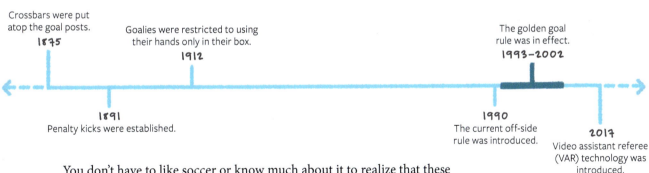

Crossbars were put atop the goal posts.
1875

Goalies were restricted to using their hands only in their box.
1912

The golden goal rule was in effect.
1993–2002

1891
Penalty kicks were established.

1990
The current off-side rule was introduced.

2017
Video assistant referee (VAR) technology was introduced.

You don't have to like soccer or know much about it to realize that these rule changes significantly modified the way the game is played. Why weren't the rules just established and never messed with again? Is there any guarantee that soccer as it is currently played will look the same fifty years from now?

The foundation for soccer has had an interesting progression. You will soon see that, unlike the foundation for soccer, the foundation for ethics does not fluctuate. When discussing something as important as ethics, to start by examining its foundations is not only logically important but also practically helpful. Any foundation you can think of, whether it be for a physical structure or an academic subject, can be damaged or undermined. And damaging or undermining a foundation affects everything above it. Let's begin examining the foundation for ethics.

What is the basis for determining what's right and what's wrong?

THE BASIS FOR ETHICS

Thankfully, the foundation for ethics is not based on something subjective, arbitrary, or susceptible to damage. God Himself, His character more precisely, is the basis for ethics. Why should God be a part of the conversation about ethics? And why must ethics be based on God's character? Follow along closely. God is self-existent and has always existed (Ps. 90:2; Isa. 40:28; John 8:58). God is Creator (Gen. 1:1; Heb. 11:3). God doesn't change; He is the same all the time (Mal. 3:6; James 1:17; Heb. 13:8). God is also infinite in power, knowledge, and wisdom. He is present everywhere all the time.

If you have studied *BIBLE DOCTRINES*, you probably realize we have described God's aseity,* eternality, immutability,* omnipotence, omniscience, and omnipresence. We have also affirmed that He is Creator of all things. God, therefore, is the sovereign ruler over all things everywhere at all times (Neh. 9:6; Isa. 37:16; Col. 1:16–17). There are no other contenders.

But God is not just powerful. He is also holy, just, and loving; He is good. Indeed, God's unchanging holiness, justice, love, and goodness define what those attributes mean. God's character is the standard by which such virtues are measured. There is no sure basis for ethics without God.

And God's character is not hidden. Scripture reveals God's nature and character, but creation itself also reveals to every person what God is like (Rom. 1:18–20, 32). And His character, as revealed in general and special revelation, gives us the standard for ethics. Who God is and how He acts determines what is right and what is wrong, and His character and work are known to some extent by all people.

As Creator and Sustainer of all things, God is also the supreme Judge of all (Gen. 18:25; John 5:22–27; 2 Cor. 5:10). The reality of an ultimate Judge who makes judgments informs us about the realities of right and wrong. Only God is capable of drawing up the boundaries for good and evil. Ken Magnuson summarizes this principle by saying,

> The ultimate source of morality is God, who created the universe with moral order—determined by his character, purposes, and will—and graciously reveals to human beings not only the reality of that order but also how to live according to that reality.[8]

So, God is the one who establishes the universal standards by which to make judgments. His holy character is the measure by which all else is measured (1 Pet. 1:15–16). God's character is the touchstone to achieve clarity on whether something is ethical.

What would happen to society if God's perfect and unchanging character weren't the basis for ethics? Chapter 2 will explain various faulty positions on ethics that people have come up with through the years. But imagine if the majority opinion of the masses determined what was ethically right. Or what if those in power—financially, politically, militarily, religiously—called the shots on what constituted right and wrong? The immorality, chaos, injustice, and subjectivity that could result from either of these options should be apparent. Grab a history book, or just read some news headlines, and you can see the horrible results of making anything but God the basis for ethics—results such as suffering, oppression, hatred, death, and celebration of sin and its consequences (Rom. 1:28–32).

aseity: self-existence

immutability: unchangeability

> *"God is a Spirit, infinite, eternal, and unchangeable, in his being, wisdom, power, holiness, justice, goodness, and truth. . . . God's works of providence are, his most holy, wise, and powerful preserving and governing all his creatures, and all their actions."*[9]
>
> Westminster Shorter Catechism

Is Too Much Authority a Bad Thing?

The fact that the God of the Bible is the one sovereign Lord over the entire universe, including ethics, frustrates many people. Granted, not all agree with the notion of God's universal lordship. But that is what the Bible teaches, and God's people should embrace the clear teaching of Scripture. A popular saying attributed to John Dalberg, Lord Acton, however, might come to mind when contemplating God's absolute authority over all things: "Power tends to corrupt and absolute power corrupts absolutely." Could this apply to God, even in the smallest way? Does the idea that "the guy with the biggest stick is the biggest bully" apply to God?

Continue reading this section to develop your answer more fully.

ATTRIBUTES OF GOD

God's character is inseparable from His nature. We just looked at some attributes of God that describe His unique nature. Any ethical system that presumes to be based on any other grounds is faulty, deficient, and misleading. Let's consider more carefully some key attributes that lay the foundation for ethics.

Holiness

God is holy (Isa. 6:3). God is altogether perfect—in His self-existing triunity (transcendence) and in His interaction with all He created (immanence). God is pure and separate from any form of sin (Heb. 7:26). Holiness isn't only for God. God's people are called to live holy lives (Exod. 19:6; 1 Pet. 2:9). This God-imitating holiness is central to Christian virtue and ethics and comes to bear on challenging ethical situations we face.

Love

"God is love" (1 John 4:8). The love displayed and described by God is the love all ethical systems should imitate (1 John 4:9–11). Christ summarized what obedience to the law of God looks like in one word—love (Matt. 22:37–40). You would be hard-pressed to find a system of ethics that doesn't emphasize love—be it for nature, for others, or for oneself. But God has established what love is, what love does, and how people are supposed to love God and others.

Goodness

God is good (Mark 10:18). The God who is entirely good and delights in giving good gifts defines what goodness looks like (James 1:17). The ultimate display of God's goodness is sending Jesus to be sacrificed for undeserving sinners (Titus 3:4–5). The goodness of God is similar to His mercy. Mercy in lieu of justice can be ethical because of God's good and kind character (Rom. 11:22; James 2:13) and because Christ ultimately paid the price justice demands for those saved by mercy (Rom. 3:25–26).

Righteousness

Discussions of ethics always touch on the topic of right versus wrong, righteousness versus evil. God is righteous (Jer. 9:24). This attribute goes back to the idea mentioned above that God is Judge. And as Judge, God keeps His promises and judges righteously—always (Deut. 7:9; 32:4). The revelation of the God who declares and does the right thing in every instance gives biblical Christianity the only true starting point for ethics.

Trustworthiness

God is trustworthy (Isa. 12:2). This means that God is faithful and reliable. God's character is stable, permanent, and steadfast. Only God is unchanging. He will always be true to the righteous standard of His own character. The foundation for Christian ethics cannot be damaged because God can be trusted. Circumstances can change. We will face the consequences of bad decisions. But God is a rock (2 Sam. 22:31–33). Jesus called those who build their lives on His Word "wise" (Matt. 7:24–27). Only God can be trusted to order our decisions and behaviors (Prov. 3:5–7).

Since God is holy, loving, good, righteous, and trustworthy, anything in our lives that is contrary to these attributes is due to our fallenness. To live in a manner that doesn't reflect God's character is sinful (Exod. 34:6–9). This includes every unholy thought, every unloving motive, every bad consequence, and every unrighteous action.

God's character is the basis for ethics. There are two other related and complementary foundations for ethics that we will now turn to consider. Whereas this section presented *who God is* as the basis for ethics, the following sections will touch on aspects of *what God has done* to round out the foundations for ethics.

Thinking It Through 1.1

1. Explain the basis for ethics.

2. What is the basis for determining right and wrong?

3. Why is God the ultimate authority over all things, including ethics?

4. Summarize the attributes of God that form the basis for ethics.

1.2 The Created Order as a Foundation for Ethics

What do robins, butterflies, airplanes, and drones have in common? They all fly, obviously. Who made the robin and the butterfly? God did, of course (Gen. 1:20–21, 24–25). Who makes airplanes and drones? Well, people do, but they borrow from God's creation to make them. The flight of airplanes involves certain physical materials like metal, fiberglass, and fuel. But flight also involves properties such as lift, propulsion, drag, and aerodynamic design. A more challenging question is, Did God make flight, or did man invent it? Birds and insects have flown since the day they were created by God. So man hardly invented flight or came up with the required elements for it. The Wright brothers' predecessor George Cayley actually used birds in his research of how to form and use the wings of a glider or plane.[10] We can truly say that the pioneers of manned flight used the created order as a foundation for achieving sustained flight. Man tapped into certain laws of God's creation in order to create things that fly.

Flying a plane isn't the same as making ethical decisions—such as telling the truth on your income taxes or protecting the life of the unborn—is it? No, it's not. Scripture directly addresses these two ethical issues. Nevertheless, how God designed mankind also speaks to these scenarios. Christian ethics rightly starts with God's character as revealed in Scripture as a foundation for ethics. But Christian ethics also appeals to the created order and how it reflects the character of the one who created all things. And just as God created all the creatures that fly, He also established the physical principles of lift, propulsion, drag, and aerodynamic design required for flight. And just as God created a world in which governments necessarily exist and the unborn are persons who bear His image, He also established the ethical principles, like honesty and the protection of the vulnerable, required for people and societies to flourish. Such governing principles of God's creation are what we mean by creational norms. **Creational norms** are standards for how life in God's creation works, discerned by observing the design of the created order in light of Scripture's teaching. Creational norms can be found in Scripture explicitly or can be discovered by viewing the world through the lens of Scripture.

THE REALITY OF CREATIONAL NORMS

Scientists might speak of the laws of nature being constant and predictable. Scientists readily recognize that there are natural laws that govern our planet and the entire universe. Just think of the laws of thermodynamics. Scientists have observed certain behaviors and properties in nature that are predictable and consistent. For example, scientists have quantified and described the laws of thermodynamics. Or to reference something more familiar, a physical "law" of this world is that water boils at 212 degrees Fahrenheit at sea level. To mention the laws of nature is to identify certain constants or rules God built into His universe for it to function properly. Nature isn't some collection of random events! God made all things, and that includes how those things work underground, underwater, at sea level, on a high mountain, in the air, or in outer space.

Have you ever realized that attempting to violate natural laws has consequences? Have you ever tried to boil pasta at 175 degrees Fahrenheit? Of course not—unless you wanted to eat crunchy pasta. And if you ignore the law of gravity on a visit to the Grand Canyon or decide the laws of motion don't apply to you when crossing the street, you will soon find the consequences painful or fatal!

God's laws of creation, however, don't just include material things and their relationships. Other laws of creation—creational norms—come to bear on ethics because, in personal and interpersonal relationships, certain virtues and attitudes have been appointed by God for the well-being of individuals and societies.

Genesis 1 and 2 detail God's creation of the earth and the universe. Included in that creation account, though neither explicit nor detailed, are the natural laws that govern the physical world and the creational norms that govern the social world. Albert Wolters explains the breadth of God's design and purpose in everything He created by saying the following:

> All of human life, in all its vast array of cultural, societal, and personal relationships, is *normed* in this sense. The almighty Creator lays claim to it all; the universal Sovereign lays down his laws for it all; the absolute King requires his will to be discerned in it all.[11]

God employed His immeasurable wisdom and understanding in creating all things, including how all things relate to one another (Prov. 3:19–20). Before mankind fell and the plague of sin infected the world, God's creation perfectly aligned itself to God's design and purpose (Gen. 1:31). But in the Fall and the resulting Curse, sin brought confusion, corruption, and a twisting of God's holy and righteous standards among humans (Gen. 3:1–19).

Nevertheless, God's creational norms remain normative for His universe. God's laws that govern both the physical world and the social world are enduring. So before and after the Fall, the earth rotates on its axis and orbits the sun. And before and after the Fall, loving others is good, and unfounded and unjust hatred is evil. Loving others is the standard, the creational norm.

This enduring nature of creational norms can be seen in the fact that people have an innate sense of right and wrong. Various religions attempt to communicate this (faulty though their descriptions may be) in notions such as yin/yang, karma, and positive versus negative energy. God has made man in His image, and part of that design is that everyone has a sense of right and wrong within themselves as well as the sense that the world ought to operate a certain way (Rom. 2:15). You can observe how people have an instinct to pull someone out of harm's way with barely a moment's notice. You can observe how most people have an innate sense that compassion for the needy is praiseworthy. These are just two examples of how God has designed people to respond to and interact with one another.

Don't you want to build it the way it was designed?

DISCOVERING CREATIONAL NORMS

How do you figure out how to do things you don't know how to do? YouTube! Prerecorded instruction is easier and quicker to get than finding someone and asking them for help. Before the advent of the internet, people used almanacs, manuals, and books in general to gain knowledge or learn a skill. Oral tradition has also been an important means of passing down insights and ways of doing things. Keep in mind the principle we are unpacking: creational norms are the built-in principles that reflect God's wise design of how all things should work. Wolters helps us again by saying it this way:

> Human civilization is *normed* throughout. Everywhere we discover limits and proprieties, standards and criteria: in every field of human affairs there are right and wrong ways of doing things. There is nothing in human life that does not belong to the created order.[12]

The question is, how should we, God's creatures, figure out how to align ourselves with the Creator's design of all things?

Let's consider how creational norms are related to farming. Farming must be learned to some degree. When God created the earth, He established how plants would grow, seed, and reproduce (Gen. 1:11–12). Man must discern and submit himself to the creational norms of agriculture in order to provide for himself, his family, and society as a whole. Who taught Adam how to tend to the Garden of Eden and subsequently to farm? God gave Adam and Eve certain tasks, so He, therefore, enabled them to accomplish those tasks (Gen. 1:26–28). After the Fall, Adam and Eve had to struggle with a cursed earth to get what they needed from it (Gen. 3:17–19). God's judgment even extended to how the creation worked. But they still were responsible to fulfill God's mandate and purposes. God's creational norms are still in operation, and we still need to find them out.

Scripture sheds light on how man learns to farm (Isa. 28:24–29). In sum, man is able to discover how to farm due to the creational norms God designed in man and nature. God teaches man how to farm! But God doesn't use specific Scripture passages to do this. A good farmer is a wise farmer because he taps into God's wisdom in how He designed certain plants and animals. This is a large part of God's common grace* that He gives to all. Common grace includes rain and sunshine as well as access to God's creational norms (Matt. 5:45; Acts 14:17).

But the teaching of the Bible can't be totally ignored either. Wisdom calls out to man for him to listen and reap the rewards of acquiring it (Prov. 1:20–23, 33; 3:13–18). Ignoring wisdom, which God offers to all and manifests in both Scripture and creation, is the result of sin and results in suffering (Prov. 1:22, 24–32). Read through Proverbs and notice how the miserable consequences of foolishness are due to violating both the laws of God's Word and the laws of God's creation (especially what we are calling creational norms).

The Difference the Fear of the Lord Makes

In the realm of ethics, not just in the physical world, man needs to discover creational norms; that is, man needs to discover God's *wisdom* built into the design of the world. Creational norms are discoverable. Various psalms affirm that the heavens and the heavenly bodies (19:1–4), man's body (94:9–10), and man's work (104:23–24) display God's knowledge and wisdom in establishing creational norms. As these physical things speak this way, they speak of their proper function.

Solomon's wisdom was displayed in how well he subdued creation and got the best out of every aspect of his kingdom (2 Chron. 9:3–6). Solomon's wisdom surely reached into the realm of ethics, as described in one of the most amazing accounts of Solomon's insight (1 Kings 3:16–28). In the example of Solomon, we see how God-given wisdom can enable a person to discover creational norms, put those norms to good use, and thereby achieve great things (1 Kings 3:5–13).

But there is no wisdom without the fear of the Lord (Prov. 9:10). If God isn't feared (reverenced) for who He is and for how He relates to man, then man will

common grace: God's grace to all humans, both believers and unbelievers, which includes God's restraint on man's sin and God's provision of general creation blessings have a skewed perception of reality. God determines reality and governs all the laws He has set in place. So, if He is not part of a person's worldview, then that person's cultivation of the world will be limited and will lack the wisdom necessary to flourish. And even though unbelievers, who refuse to fear the Lord, can send man to the moon and take part in managing the global economy, their partial mastery of some creational norms doesn't lead to their spiritual and eternal well-being (Rom. 1:24–25, 32). The fear of the Lord precedes any measure of true wisdom and God-pleasing morality.

And the fear of the Lord is learned in Scripture. Notice the close relationship between the fear of the Lord and Scripture (Ps. 112:1; Eccles. 12:13). We've already established that God's character is the basis for ethics. To gain the wisdom we need to live ethically, we need more than creational norms. We need the Word to learn of God's character and to thereby know how to fear the Lord for who He is. Scripture is the lens that clarifies which path to take from the fear of the Lord to discerning and using creational norms.

The Difference the Spirit Makes

Whereas all people are hardwired to be able to seek and find creational norms, it is believers who seek and find wisdom that comes from fearing God (Prov. 1:7; Job 28:28). Remember, wisdom is measured in part by how well you discern and align yourself to creational norms. Fleming James says it this way:

> Wisdom therefore was wrought into the constitution of the universe. It was independent of men, though in a real sense it existed specially for them. . . .
>
> In human life therefore wisdom meant conforming to the divine constitution of the world. One must find out what it is, then order himself accordingly. Of course this was but another way of saying that one must do the will of God.[13]

James helps us see the reality of creational norms and how we use wisdom to discover and apply them to our ethical living.

Believers should readily admit they lack wisdom in life in general and need God to give it to them (James 1:5)—not so much to figure out how to fly and farm, but to figure out how to live well with their neighbors and love other believers as they ought (Rom. 12:9–10; 1 Thess. 4:9). Having wisdom is connected with having the Spirit work in and guide your life (Acts 6:3, 10). Followers of Christ can claim God's promise that He will guide them as they walk by faith and seek to honor God with their ethical living (Prov. 3:5–6).

Read how Solomon used his God-given wisdom and recognition of creational norms in 1 Kings 3:16–28. What creational norms are displayed in this passage?

THE ROLE OF CREATIONAL NORMS

When you video call a friend who isn't in the same room as you, you aren't actually with that friend. Makes sense, right? You are using a device that has a camera, screen, and internet connection to imitate an in-person meeting. A video call lets you see and hear your friend, but the image on the screen isn't your friend. A face-to-face conversation would definitely be more direct and personal. But no one would say that you didn't interact and communicate with your friend on the video call. Using God's creation to discern God's will for a given situation is similar to a video call. Creation reflects and proclaims the character of the Designer. Much of what God desires for humans can be found in how He has set up our world. In our illustration above, the face-to-face conversation is akin to knowing God and His will through special revelation. It is definitely more direct and personal; it is a clearer and more explicit kind of communication of God's design for humanity. But the creational norms we find do reveal God's design and purpose for how all things should work, and they complement what is revealed in the Scriptures.

> **What do creational norms have to do with ethics?**

	SPECIAL REVELATION	GENERAL REVELATION
Role	helps accurately interpret creational norms	God's design reveals creational norms
Type of Communication	direct	indirect, implied
Found in	Scripture	creation

Let's turn now to look at the role creational norms play. Consider the following creational norms.

- Creator-creature distinction
- Two genders, male and female
- Marriage, husband and wife
- Work-rest-work-rest rhythm
- Harmony and peace

Each of these norms directly impacts ethics. We read in God's Word and observe in God's creation what *ought* to be the ideal—the right and the good thing. On this side of the Fall, we experience how the *is* so often contradicts the *ought*. For example, according to God's character, the Bible's teaching, and what is generally observed in creation, the preservation of life and protecting the vulnerable is the *ought* in our world. (We find it natural for parents to protect and nurture their helpless young, for instance.) But in the natural world, some animals and even some plants eat or harm one another, and we find even some human parents who hurt or destroy their own children (what *is,* though it seems unnatural). Much of ethics tries to discover the *ought* when it comes to preserving life and protecting the vulnerable. This is because, unfortunately, the *is* contains so much hatred and mistreatment of people. This is true around the world and can be seen in many practices: murder, abortion, euthanasia, suicide, abuse, and torture. Repeatedly, the *is* as it plays out in society doesn't match the *ought* that creational norms teach in these situations. The *ought* reflects the divine creational norms. The *is* in the fallen world doesn't automatically match up with the *ought*.

Let's look at the items from the bulleted list above and see how the creational norms they teach serve as a foundation for our ethical considerations.

- Creator-creature distinction

    This governs how we relate to God and to one another. We aren't God; we are fallen, finite, and fallible creatures. God, therefore, should be feared. And we should show patience toward one another and love each other despite all our shortcomings.

- Two genders, male and female

  This norm is seen in nature as well as in the creation of Adam and Eve. There are men and there are women. Transgenderism and any other gender fluidity are counter to God's good design of mankind.

- Marriage, husband and wife

  God made Eve for Adam and Adam for Eve, and together they formed a family unit for life. Adultery, polygamy, polyamory, fornication, homosexuality, and bisexuality are all contrary to God's good design of marriage and sexuality.

- Work-rest-work-rest rhythm

  God created the world in six days and rested on the seventh. God ordained that humans work but also that they rest. Work is good. Rest is good. Workaholism and laziness are both contrary to God's good design for people in His world.

- Harmony and peace

  At the end of the creation account in Scripture, prior to the Fall, harmony and peace pervaded all creation. This included Adam and Eve's relationship with God and with one another. This also included the whole of the natural world—the planets, sun, moon, and stars as well as the oceans, rivers, and animals. Violence, vandalism, irresponsible pollution, and unjust wars are all contrary to God's good design of this world.

You will encounter people who reject the authority of Scripture, and their lives won't align with God's will. They base their ethical system on something other than God and His Word. But God has hardwired creational norms into every aspect of life. All people are without excuse when it comes to seeing the divine design in all things (Rom. 1:19–20; 2:1–2). Ethics is founded on the truths that creational norms reveal and which reflect God's character.

Thinking It Through 1.2

1. Define *creational norms*.
2. Defend the existence of creational norms.
3. How are creational norms discovered?
4. How are creational norms related to ethics?
5. Give two examples of creational norms and explain how they relate to ethical issues.

1.3 The Image of God in Man as a Foundation for Ethics

Growing up, you most likely drew pictures, rode a bike, and climbed all over the playgrounds you would visit. Statistically, however, it is unlikely you are an artist or a competitive cyclist or a professional climber. It is easy to see the difference between dabbling in artistic expression, riding a bike around the neighborhood, and climbing playground equipment and their professional counterparts. Expressed more philosophically, there is a difference between *doing* an activity and *being* someone whose whole identity is wrapped up in that activity.

This principle illustrates what it means to *be* human. You don't merely do human things, perform human activities, or act in human ways. You *are* a human, and everything you do is done as a human. The image of God in man is as fundamental to who you are as your humanity. Just as human beings are human from conception and forever more, every human being is also made in God's image (Gen. 1:26–27).

THE IMAGE OF GOD IN MAN

But what does it mean for man to be made in the image of God? This question has been the subject of much theological debate. Let's face it, it's an intriguing topic! Scholars and theologians throughout history have singled out various aspects of the image of God in man—man's body; man's relational abilities; man's mind, will, and emotions; and man's ability to work and create. Right away we can point out the deficiencies in elevating one aspect of man as *the* image of God in man. Man has a body, but he also has a soul. And God is spirit, so to hold that the image of God in man is merely related to man's physical body is unconvincing. Man is hardwired to be relational, but animals and angels also share certain aspects of this trait. Man thinks, decides, and feels, but so do angels and animals. Man (imperfectly) carries out God's original command to work, create, and maintain the natural environment where God placed him (known as the Creation Mandate [Gen. 1:28–30]). But this is one thing man *does* as a human; it isn't who he *is* as a person. In each case, singling out one manifestation of the image of God in man is too limiting.

The **image of God in man**, therefore, is the essence of being human, a status God bestows upon man whereby the whole person is made to be "like God in everything in which a creature can be like God."[14] God's image in man is comprehensive, encompassing all that man is, which directly relates to all that he does. As mentioned, man alone (both male and female) is specifically created in God's image (Gen. 5:1–2; 9:6). Not animals. Not angels. Adam and Eve were made in God's image, in His likeness, and were the king and queen (notice the lowercase) of the whole earth. God had endowed them with all their abilities, faculties, strengths, intelligence, and potential. Nevertheless, they were creatures with limited resources and capabilities. The Creator-creature distinction existed from the beginning, even before the Fall. Following the Creator-creature distinction, Herman Bavinck notes,

> God is the archetype, the exemplar, the original. We are only truly human to the extent that we display God, also in our daily lives. The human person, therefore, has to be viewed theologically, and also in ethics. Morality, too, finds its principle and standard in the relation in which a human being stands to God.[15]

So, man is made in God's image; he isn't God, nor can he become God. Even after the Fall, man retains the image of God, though the image is marred (Gen. 9:6). All the descendants of Adam and Eve are created in the image of God—there are no exceptions (Gen. 5:3).

Being made in the image of God is a status that nobody can lose.

"So God created man in his own image, in the image of God created he him."

GENESIS 1:27

GOD

THE IMAGE OF GOD IN MAN AS A KEY CREATIONAL NORM

A master key is a key that can open multiple locks. The doctrine of the image of God in man is like a master key that can unlock both creational norms and ethics. On the one hand, the image of God in man is the creational norm foundational to all other creational norms. And on the other hand, the image of God in man is also important to ethics itself. Indeed, the image of God in man is the foundational creational norm for ethics. The natural next question is, How so?

What does the image of God in man have to do with ethics?

All people are "people-persons" to some extent. In other words, God not only created man with relational abilities but relational affinities (Gen. 2:18). Even introverts and loners need people. And the reality is, God designed the world for humans; so we interact with people. Even if you took a submarine to the bottom of the ocean or a rocket to outer space, chances are you would go with a few other people, and you would be dependent on a whole team of people! Our ethics, our moral decision-making and living, impacts people directly and constantly. Sure, you can live alone on the side of a mountain or on a deserted island, but your thoughts and actions are still ethical—you are a person created in the image of God.

The image of God in man is important and valuable—and not just because that is how God made man, but because God is to be praised and glorified for all His works (Ps. 145:3–4). The image of God in man is what gives man dignity, a dignity that sets him apart from the angels, animals, plants, and rocks. This is why murdering a person is such a high offense; God Himself is being affronted (Gen. 9:5–6). The person who was murdered was made in the very image and likeness of God. God places high value on how we treat people (Lev. 19:18; Mark 12:31). The ethical treatment of people made in God's image even includes how we talk about or to them (James 3:9). We practice Christian ethics with one another because man's dignity and value come from being made in the image of God.

Remember, you should locate your authority and ethical standards in the Scriptures and in the creational norms imbedded in creation. The image of God in man is to be the *north* on your compass of creational norms. The other creational norms make sense in light of the fact that man is created in the image of God. Unbelievers are also image-bearers and so are able to recognize man's unique status and value in God's created order. Whether or not they are willing to admit it, the golden rule in Scripture makes sense to them (Matt. 7:12). They actually can appreciate and respect that standard. That doesn't mean unbelievers will practice the golden rule out of fear of the Lord and love for God and their neighbor.

Consider any number of ethical situations if people didn't know that man has great dignity and value. (In man's sinful state, he often chooses to ignore or bury this truth [Rom. 1:25, 32]. But the truth is that man has great dignity and value because he is made in God's image.) Otherwise there would be no difference between a human, a bumblebee, and a frog. Any form of mistreatment, abuse, or murder of humans could be allowed under this paradigm. It is precisely because man is made in God's image that we must live ethically with each other.

Remember also that God's character is the basis for ethics. Even fallen man mirrors some of that character because only he is created in the image of God. So the ethics God lays out for man and has revealed to man is wrapped up in the image of God in man. The image of God in man directs all the creational norms as they relate to ethics.

THE IMAGE OF GOD IN MAN AS KEY FOR HUMAN VIRTUE

Finally, consider that the image of God in man is key for human virtue. When considering ethical decisions, virtue is always part of the discussion. Augustine* briefly defined virtue as "rightly ordered love."[16] Virtue is morally commendable

Augustine: early church father of the fourth and fifth centuries motives for behavior. Virtue has less to do with *what* you do than it does with *why* you do what you do. Ultimately, we do what we love. Behaviors are directed by some form of virtue or lack thereof. Virtues and vices account for why you are acting the way you are acting—they explain who you are being, essentially. In a few chapters, it will become more apparent that virtue is an integral part of Christian ethics.

Man, made in the image of God, behaves either virtuously (according to God's character) or unvirtuously (utterly unlike God's character). A quick glance at two passages that list various Christian virtues (Gal. 5:22–23; Col. 3:12–15) shows how many correspond to the character of God. We can readily see the relationship between virtue and the image of God in man.

In Section 1.1 of this chapter, we discussed various attributes of God that form the basis of ethics. Fallen and sinful man can live according to God's holiness, love, goodness, righteousness, and trustworthiness only because he is created in God's image. Believers seek to be transformed into Christ's image (Rom. 8:29–30; 2 Cor. 3:18). People live ethically when they are conformed to God's attributes, to the virtues that are patterned after God's character. Unbelievers are also made in God's image. Anytime they display a form of virtue, any behavior that even slightly conforms to God's character, it is due to their nature as image-bearers and to common grace at work in their lives.

You might say your unsaved family members, neighbors, and friends are good people because they are kind, hard-working, compassionate, and self-disciplined. They might show a little mercy here and have a little hope there. But no one is good like God is good—*good* as in free from sin and *good* as in being incredibly generous because of His graciousness—including Christians (Mark 10:18; Rom. 3:10–12; 1 John 1:8). Nevertheless, every single person at times imitates aspects of virtue, because every human is created in the image of God. But only believers in Christ are indwelt by the Holy Spirit and are, therefore, able to conform their lives to the character of God and truly practice the virtues (Phil. 2:1–5).

THE CREATIONAL FOUNDATIONS FOR ETHICS

We have looked at three foundations for ethics—God's character, the created order, and the image of God in man. God Himself and His creation give us the foundation on which to build ethical conclusions. God's character is revealed in His Word and in creation. The created order displays God's good design for human life and flourishing. And the image of God in man provides the central creational norm for even aspiring to live ethically. In the next two chapters, you will learn about the Fall's effects on ethics and the role of redemption in ethics. The creational foundations are incredibly important as you start down the path of learning about ethics. But they are just that—the start.

Thinking It Through 1.3

1. Define the *image of God in man*.

2. Explain why the image of God in man is a fundamental creational norm for ethics.

3. Define *virtue*.

4. Explain why the image of God in man is key for human virtue.

5. What does the image of God in man have to do with ethics?

Terms to Remember

- ethics
- Christian ethics
- creational norms
- image of God in man

Scripture Memory

Romans 1:18–20

Understanding Ethics

1. What is the value of studying ethics?
2. What is the basis for ethics?
3. What is the relationship of God to ethics?
4. What is the relationship of man to ethics?

Practicing Ethical Decision-Making

5. What explanation would you give an atheist to explain why you both agree that murder is wrong?
6. Suppose you are on a town council and your vote will decide whether to use your town's limited funding on infrastructure improvements or renovating an old shopping mall. Which project would you choose? Explain why you made that choice from a biblical perspective.

Analyzing and Evaluating Ethical Claims

7. What would you say to someone who defines ethical behavior as that which the majority of a society determines works best for the success of individuals in that society? Explain.

8. Defend the continuing role of creational norms as a foundation for ethics even after man's fall into sin.
9. Why does the image of God in man affect all our ethical decisions?

Creating My Own Position Statements on Ethics

10. Suppose a friend says to you that there are no benefits to studying ethics. List the reasons why studying ethics is so beneficial.
11. Why should we approach ethics from a Christian perspective? Defend the understanding and implementation of ethics from a Christian, biblical worldview.

The Fall's Effects on Ethics

02

ROMANS 3:10–12

How can I identify problematic approaches to ethics?

2.1 The Root Cause of All Ethical Difficulties

Have you ever played with magnets, seeing how far away one magnet could be from another before—SNAP!—they were inescapably drawn together? When you were a child, it was rather fun to play with magnets.

You might be amazed to know the strength of a magnet used for industrial purposes. For instance, a Neodymium Iron Boron (NIB) magnet is the strongest class of magnets on earth. They are extremely powerful because of their energy density. An NIB magnet is so strong that, if attracted to something, it could fly across the room, and its high speed and momentum could shatter your bones if you put your hand in its path.[1]

Have you ever known the right thing to do, and yet felt yourself strongly pulled in the opposite direction? You may have even had a clear idea of the negative consequences of doing the wrong thing. You may have had a definite understanding of why choosing right would be the best thing for you and others. And yet, within, you still found yourself yearning to fulfill desires that you knew were wrong and destructive. In the end, you gave in and satisfied your desires.

Apart from the grace of God, our fleshly desires draw us with a force greater than that of an NIB magnet to give into temptations. Whether it comes out in the media we consume or the pictures we view online or the things we find spewing out of our mouths in response to our classmates, siblings, or parents, we feel in us this strong pull to do the opposite of what we know to be right (Rom. 7:7–25).

Are we excused for our responses, then, because something within seemed to inescapably pull us to feel, desire, think, do, or say something? No, but this answer can only be properly understood from a biblical understanding of the Creation, Fall, Redemption storyline. More specifically, a sound understanding of the difficulty of making ethical choices comes from a sound understanding of the biblical doctrines of man, sin, and salvation—all grounded in the reality of that biblical storyline. In other words, we must be grounded in the biblical presentation of truth and reality before we can understand why ethical living is so difficult. The truth and reality of the Fall's effects explain why it is so hard to make ethical decisions and why so many people have embraced fallible ethical systems.

THE FALL'S EFFECTS ON THE CREATED ORDER

Scripture highlights the Fall's effects on the created order in two key passages: Genesis 3:16–19 and Romans 8:18–23. Both passages remind us that the world we live in is not the way creation was designed to be. We live in a world full of physical problems, causing all kinds of ethical difficulties. Solutions to those problems are elusive—some proposed solutions are wrong while others are difficult to accept. For example, why do the fields of bioethics and medical ethics exist? The Fall's effects on our physical world have led to the need for such fields of study.

Genesis 3:16–19

Let's consider the significance of Genesis 3:16–19 in the larger context of the creation narrative. Genesis 1:31 affirms that God made our world *very* good. As defined by God's own goodness, this means that everything in the created world was free from the slightest taint of badness. No aspect of the world was in decline or disrepair. All the natural laws* that governed the physical universe were fully functioning according to God's perfect design. Not only that, but all the processes for *our* functioning within this world were built into the created order, conformed to the perfect wisdom of God (Prov. 3:19; 8:22–31). In other words, God built norms into His creation for living wisely based on how He designed us to function in it.

These original realities—natural laws and creational norms in a perfectly good world—are immensely valuable for ethics; they give us the standard for how things *ought* to be (pointing to the basis for our ethic). God designed the world to work in a moral way that conforms to His character. Both the structures for the physical world and the structures for society in that world find an absolute and ultimate basis in God's character, which is reflected in His design.

But Genesis 3 reveals a major problem that intrudes into this perfect world. Sin entered the world when Adam and Eve chose to disobey God in the garden. And that sin had far-reaching effects on the rest of humanity and on the rest of the world. Its effects extend as "far as the curse is found," which is to say, throughout creation. That Curse is summarized in Genesis 3:16–19. The effects of the Fall ruin the human ability to function according to creational norms, according to God's law, according to God's wisdom, and according to God's righteous character. Humans still image their Creator, but they do so in a distorted, marred, and twisted way.

In Genesis 1:28, God gave humans the task of the Creation Mandate: to fill and subdue the earth. In Genesis 3:16–19, God frustrated that task by making childbirth painful, marriage difficult, and work laborious. This was God's just judgment for humans choosing to live life apart from Him. He gave them a taste of what life is like apart from Him fully upholding the world. Therefore, the world as it operates now cannot be the most accurate guide for our ethic. It is broken.

natural laws: moral norms rooted in God's character, which God established in the creation

Creation

The Fall

A biblical worldview recognizes the distinction between God's creational norms and the warped reality resulting from the Fall.

God's standard for creation

The function of the world

The secular worldview interprets warped reality as the norm.

Those who fail to take into account the brokenness of this world can fall into an error called the **naturalistic fallacy**. This fallacy assumes that what is natural is good. In other words, it assumes that if a behavior is found in nature, it must be morally acceptable. In a secular evolutionary worldview, there can be no transcendent* basis for morality, no authority greater than the consensus of human authorities. Without a transcendent, external authority revealing what is right and wrong, secularists can appeal only to nature. Christians, on the other hand, rely on what God's revelation has prescribed. God's revelation interprets the world, helping Christians to discern what is creational and what is fallen. Because Scripture tells Christians how the world ought to be, Christians may appeal to natural law, a subset of creational norms. However, they must discern such creational norms or natural law in light of special revelation.

The naturalistic fallacy is on full display in some recent claims that homosexual behavior is justified because we observe that behavior in the animal kingdom. You have to wonder how many other animal behaviors these people would appeal to as the basis for their morality. Certainly they wouldn't recommend eating one's mate, killing a competitor, or stealing another's offspring—all commonly observed behaviors in a cursed natural world. The naturalistic fallacy leads to people living like animals. But in the biblical worldview, people are not animals, nor should they behave as such (Gen. 1:26–27).[2]

Indeed, Christians should appeal to the natural world in their ethical reasoning. But they must also take into account that the world is not the way it should be. The Christian ethic stands firmly in the created order's design. But Christians must distinguish between the created order and the Fall's effects on that created order. God's special revelation helps Christians discern these things so that natural law can be more accurately understood. Yet, by God's common grace, even unbelievers may glean some moral grounding by their observations of God's design in this fallen world (Prov. 8:4). They may be inconsistent in their understanding and application of the morality ingrained into the design of this world, but even those without the benefit of God's special revelation have the witness of their own consciences (Rom. 2:14–15). Natural law may be a starting point for a Christian's appeal to an unbeliever. But the Christian must ultimately appeal to the special revelation of God's Word to properly interpret that natural law.

Romans 8:18–23

One final word on the Fall's effects on the created order. Romans 8:18–23 reveals the reason for humankind's desperate efforts to alleviate the ethical difficulties of living in a fallen world. We (and the created order) groan under God's judgment, the Curse, which affects all creation (Rom. 8:20–22). We long for redemption, for restoration. The problems that come from living in a fallen world bring us great discomfort (and worse). Since God's Creation Mandate has tasked us with the stewardship of creation, it is good and right to work against the effects of the Fall by seeking to solve or to better cope with these effects. Ultimately, only Christ's final redemption will rescue us. And these effects of the Fall (including the Curse) point people to the need for a Savior. Yet, God would have us show love and compassion by ameliorating* the effects of the Fall in the lives of our families and neighbors.

Still, *what* should be identified as an effect of the Fall and *how* those effects should be addressed is subject to ethical debate. Should humans be

You wouldn't pull a broken lamp out of a package and assume that's the way it was designed to be. God did not create imperfection; sin has marred His perfect design.

transcendent: pertaining to the things of God beyond the earthly human experience

ameliorating: making better

attempting to do gene therapy? Should they be doing gene therapy to fix genetic diseases like Down syndrome and muscular dystrophy so that one day these diseases no longer exist in our world? Should they be doing gene therapy to produce babies with blue eyes rather than brown eyes? These and many other issues will be addressed in Unit 3.

Structure and Direction

One helpful paradigm for understanding the Fall's effects on the creational order is called structure and direction. Structure refers to the creational norms, the way God wisely designed the world to function. Direction refers to the use of a created thing either toward or away from its God-given creational norm or design.[3] When doing ethics, we don't want to confuse fallen direction with creational structure.

Bad Direction
Bending toward fallen human nature

Structure
God's created order

Good Direction
Bending back toward the intended order

THE FALL'S EFFECTS ON HUMAN NATURE

The Fall's effects on human nature are all-encompassing and inescapable. Every part of every human has been affected by the Fall. The Fall's effects are as pervasive as the air we breathe. "Who can say, I have made my heart clean, I am pure from my sin?" (Prov. 20:9). "If we say that we have no sin, we deceive ourselves, and the truth is not in us. . . . If we say that we have not sinned, we make him a liar, and his word is not in us" (1 John 1:8, 10). Not even the most righteous person on earth is free from sinning (Eccles. 7:20). It is a given that all people succumb to sin (1 Kings 8:46). The law of God was designed to shut the mouths of those who think they could claim to be without sin (Rom. 3:19–20; 7:7; Gal. 3:22). In fact, "all we like sheep have gone astray; we have turned every one to his own way; and the LORD hath laid on him the iniquity of us all" (Isa. 53:6). Even our best works don't come close to an acceptable standard (Isa. 64:6). The reality of our sin nature within us evidences itself in our actions (Rom. 3:10–18). And all of this is due to our standing "in Adam" (Rom. 5:12; see also Ps. 51:5), which imputes guilt and transmits corruption.

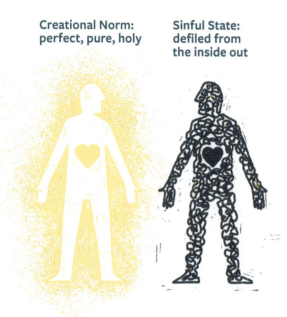

Creational Norm:
perfect, pure, holy

Sinful State:
defiled from the inside out

The Fall's Effects on the Mind

Has the mind of every person been affected by the Fall? Yes! Apart from the glorious gospel, regeneration and illumination by the Holy Spirit, and spiritual union with Christ, all people have their minds blinded by "the god of this world" (2 Cor. 4:4; see also 1 Cor. 2:14; Eph. 1:17). In rebellion, they suppress the truth (Rom. 1:18–25; see also John 8:45). Before salvation, people are characterized by ignorance and a darkened mind because of their desire to justify their sin (Eph. 4:17–19; Titus 1:15). For example, some of the most "enlightened" cultures have tried to intellectually justify mistreating fellow human beings.

The Fall's Effects on the Will

Has the will of every person been affected by the Fall? Yes! Everything a person chooses to do comes from the heart (Prov. 4:23; Matt. 15:17–20). And before God makes us alive to Himself, the condition of the heart is completely dead, unresponsive to God and His righteousness (Eph. 2:1–3). Apart from God's saving grace, all people are slaves to sin (John 8:34; Rom. 3:10–18; 6:16; 8:5–8).

For example, many people with addictions know what they ought to do, but they do not have the willpower within themselves to say no.

The Fall's Effects on the Emotions

Have the emotions of every person been affected by the Fall? Yes! We delight in sin (Prov. 2:14; Rom. 1:32). We become unrighteous in our anger (Prov. 14:29; James 1:19). We love and lust after the things of the flesh—even Christians must put these desires to death (Col. 3:5–10; 1 John 2:15–17). For example, even David, "a man after [God's] own heart" (1 Sam. 13:14), was drawn into impurity by desires he felt compelled to satisfy.

The mind, will, and emotions all work together simultaneously according to the affections that drive them. Our affections are the inclinations (formed by our values) that drive all we are and do because they are like the control center of our hearts. Either they are submitted to Christ's lordship or they are idolatrous. Before salvation, humans are idolatrous to the core (Jer. 17:9; Rom. 1:25). The fear of God is a holy affection, but instead of fearing God, unbelievers scorn His commandments and instruction so they can continue in their sin (Prov. 1:7).

Common Grace: The Spirit's Restraint on the Fall's Effects

If every part of every person has been affected by the Fall, then does this mean that every person is as bad as he or she could be? No! But no person can credit themselves for doing better than the worst he or she *could* do (1 Cor. 10:12–13; 2 Tim. 3:13). Not all people manifest badness in the same way or to the same extent. But that's due to God's gracious restraint through a variety of means: conscience, fear of consequences, the undeniable design of this world and how it works, the influence of God's people for the good of society, and the direct restraint of the Holy Spirit (Ezra 5:3–5; 6:6–12; Esther 2:21–23; 4:14; 8:7–14; Dan. 3:28–29; Matt. 7:9–11).

THE FALL'S EFFECTS AND THE DIFFICULTY OF MAKING ETHICAL CHOICES

When you think of making difficult ethical choices, you may be thinking of things like capital punishment, stem cell research, and immigration laws. These things may seem distant and irrelevant to your personal life. But ethical decision-making has as much to do with our daily lives as it has to do with the major debatable issues of the day.

"Should I break a school rule because I think that it doesn't make sense? I could give an intellectual explanation for why it's an unnecessary rule. My friends all agree with me."

"Should I deliberately choose to cheat on a test even though I know it's wrong? I need to get a decent grade to go on the school's mission trip. I'm sure I can do some great spiritual good that will make up for cheating on an insignificant test."

"Should I date the guy or girl my parents disapprove of? I just can't help but like him or her. My parents' reasons for disapproving are so unconvincing."

Do you see how the Fall affects our minds (intellectual justifications), wills (the end justifies the means we choose), and emotions (forbidden desires)? We have to make ethical choices all the time. The effects of the Fall on the created order and on human nature make it difficult to make ethical choices. The issues in this world, in every aspect of life, can be complex. And the people trying to solve problems are plagued by rebellion (fallenness) or by limited understanding (finiteness). Even saved people are still affected by the Fall—they are not yet perfected and glorified. Saved people are still finite—they don't have all the facts (with absolute certainty) as they seek to make the right decisions.

The effects of the Fall on individuals have ramifications for the cultures and sub-cultures of groups of individuals who interact together—in families, churches, friend

Why is it so hard to make right decisions?

groups, societies, governments, educational institutions, businesses, art guilds, and the list could go on. These groups are affected by the fallen understandings, choices, and feelings of people who work together. All this fallenness and finiteness make it a struggle to properly answer important questions: How should they behave? How should they solve problems?

Ethical decision-making relates to both our responses to issues or problems in this world and the desires of our hearts. Our belief and value system should direct our responses. But too often we ignore or manipulate our belief and value system to justify wrong responses. We can be ignorant of what our own professed belief and value system would demand (we're finite). But we can also violate our own professed belief and value system (we're fallen). If we're Christians, we should desire to better match what we say we believe and value with the reality of our ethical choices and our daily lives.

Even if we ourselves are determined to live right, we have to respond to a sinful world around us that often won't cooperate with our desires to live ethically. We live in a sinful world that is bent on fulfilling its own idolatrous rebellion—people doing things their own way, prioritizing the wrong things, and not wanting to admit that their separation from God is the cause of many of the world's problems. This world system has developed a number of faulty approaches to practicing ethics. Believers need to understand what these approaches are and why they are faulty so that they don't end up conforming themselves to unbiblical ethical systems.

Thinking It Through 2.1

1. a. Identify two key passages about the Fall's effects on creation.
   b. According to one of the key passages, how does the Fall affect our ability to fulfill our responsibilities?
   c. According to the other key passage, how do the Fall's effects on the created order impact ethics?
2. a. Define the naturalistic fallacy.
   b. Explain how the naturalistic fallacy relates to ethics.
3. Should Christians appeal to the natural world or to natural laws to forward their ethical positions? Explain your answer.
4. Identify the areas in which the Fall has had an effect on human nature. Provide at least one supporting Scripture reference for each of the areas.
5. Why is it so hard to make right decisions?

2.2 Faulty Approaches to Ethics

What do you think of the soldier who throws himself on a grenade to save the lives of others? He lives by a duty to a principle greater than himself and his own happiness. But what would you think of a soldier who continued to fight decades after he was informed that an official surrender had been declared? Should his commitment to his own ideals and his own perception of duty make no concession to other factors whatsoever? What about you? Should you make choices based on self-sacrificial duty to absolute principles, even if that means negative consequences to yourself or to society as a whole?

What do you think of a politician who takes bribes? He lives by doing whatever he can get away with while most benefiting himself. But what if the bribes resulted in saving thousands from being executed by an authoritarian dictator? The politician might justify benefiting from the bribes because of the risk he was taking and because he was benefiting many others in the end. What about you? Should you make choices based on what brings you the most happiness? Should you make choices based on what brings the most happiness to society as a whole—regardless of the means used to achieve that end?

What do you think of a professional athlete who skips practice and hogs the ball because she is by far the best player? She says, "I can't help being that way—that's just who I am." But what do you think of an Olympic athlete who helps up a fallen runner—even though it means losing the race? She explains the action to reporters this way: "That's just who I am and how I was raised." What about you? Should you make choices based on being true to yourself?

Do you generally live by strictly adhering to unbendable rules? Do you generally live by trying to achieve the best results—relative to your own desires, situations, or cultural expectations? Or do you generally live by attempting to be your most authentic self—whether that's who you are naturally or who you ideally want to be?

Of course, people are complex and will act according to a combination of approaches. Still, formal secular philosophers tend to operate according to one of four overall approaches. These four approaches to ethics can be labeled deontological ethics, consequentialist ethics, virtue ethics, and existentialist ethics.

How Does Ethics Relate to Philosophy?

If you take an Introduction to Philosophy class in college, you will probably learn that philosophy entails four branches:

1. **metaphysics** (including ontology and cosmology): the study of nature and reality itself (including the essence of existence as well as the nature and origin of the universe)

2. **epistemology**: the study of knowledge—how we know what is true and how we know what we know

3. **ethics**: the study of what *ought* to direct behavior, attitudes, and character (what makes something right or wrong)

4. **aesthetics**: the study of beauty

Since ethics is one major branch of study within the larger discipline of philosophy, it is something that most philosophers have

wrestled with through the centuries. The four major ethical systems outlined in this chapter can be matched with proponents* who were major philosophical thinkers. These philosophers represent the human quest to discover a solid basis for knowing how to live life well or rightly. Due to the image of God in man and the human conscience, many have been concerned about ensuring moral living. God built this need into us. But this quest has been misdirected by human sinfulness. The biggest failure of most philosophers is that they don't rely on special revelation. Instead, they locate a basis for ethics in their reason, personal intuitions, or observations of the world. Therefore, they can never find a sure standard. Apart from God and His revelation, philosophers stumble in the dark, run into dead ends, and fall off cliffs in a fruitless

quest for truth and righteousness. The problem isn't with the quest for better decision-making. And philosophers sometimes do stumble upon some truth. But half-truths lead to faulty systems and conclusions too.

The seeming futility of trying to find a sure standard has led to some giving up and not caring about ethics. But this too is an effect of the Fall. Christians should certainly care about how to live. They should be concerned about the destructive behavior in their own lives as well as in society. They should lead the way in knowing and practicing right behavior. Will you be such a leader? This textbook equips and enables you to be that much-needed leader in your areas of influence.

	Deontological	Consequentialist	Virtue Ethics	Existentialist
CORE APPROACH[4]	Driven by objective, absolute, universal rules or principles	Driven by results or goals (for the individual or society)	Driven by inward virtue or character (ideals)	Driven by just being who one is naturally (authenticity)
MAJOR PHILOSOPHICAL PROPONENT(S)	Immanuel Kant (1724–1804)	Jeremy Bentham (1748–1832) and John Stuart Mill (1806–73)	Alasdair MacIntyre (1929–) and Stanley Hauerwas (1940–)	Jean-Paul Sartre (1905–80)

proponent: a person who advocates for something

What are some wrong ways to practice ethics?

THE DEONTOLOGICAL APPROACH

In general, **deontological ethics*** is governed by objective, absolute, universal rules or principles. *Objective* means that these rules are true regardless of what a person thinks of them or whether he or she understands them. They must be discovered. *Absolute* means that these rules are binding (with few if any exceptions). They are founded on definite, unchanging principles regardless of the circumstances. *Universal* means that these rules apply to everyone, everywhere, and at all times. They are to be enforced without partiality.

Immanuel Kant is one of the most famous and influential philosophers to this day who promoted this approach to ethics. Someone who is driven by a Kantian deontological ethic is driven by duty above all else. This duty may even require self-sacrifice. It entails not only doing the right thing but being motivated to do it with the purest of motives. The purest of motives requires disinterest in benefiting oneself by the outcome of one's actions. One's own desires may need to be set aside. Positive or negative outcomes don't determine the goodness or badness of an act. Abiding by the principle is what matters. The ends (the ultimate goals or outcomes) do not justify the means (the method used to achieve the outcomes).

Immanuel Kant

None of this means that specific, different situations don't matter. People may act in a variety of ways in different situations, but the underlying principle must not be violated. In other words, a single principle (like keeping one's promises) can have multiple, varying applications so long as the principle is not violated in any situation.

One of the major questions for this approach is how to discover these rules or principles. The secular philosopher rejects God and His Word as a source for absolute rules of morality. So, without special revelation, philosophers are left with their observations of the natural world. They seek to discover, by reason and observation alone, natural law principles for how this world operates and how everyone in this world must operate in all times and all places. They ask, "Do we want _____ to be a universal norm (regardless of potential outcomes at certain times)?" For example, do we want permissibility of lying to be a universal norm (even if in some circumstances it might benefit me)? What would it do to society as a whole if all kinds of people could come up with all kinds of justifications for lying? The world would spin out of control! (So, consequences are not completely left out of consideration, but the principle is what *determines* morality regardless of the consequences.)

Immanuel Kant is famous for stating the following as the fundamental basis for the ethic that he promoted: "Act only according to that maxim by which you can at the same time will that it should become a universal law."[5] Kant sought to discover whether there was anything good at all times, regardless of circumstances. He concluded that a good will was the answer, for it was never criticized in any circumstance.[6] But how should one define and describe a good will? He defined a good will as one that does its duty for the sake of duty itself. In other words, you don't make ethical decisions as a means to benefit yourself. Your ultimate commitment is to abide by principles of duty.[7]

But how do we know what our duties are? Kant's answer has become known as the categorical imperative. A **categorical imperative** is something that all people must do if they are acting according to a maxim (or principle) that they believe would guide all people to do the right thing. This maxim is true no matter the circum-

deontological ethics:
ethical model which says that ethical choices are governed by objective, absolute, universal rules or principles and a selfless commitment to duty

stances. In other words, the duty to the principles is not a *hypothetical* imperative (if this, then you must do this). How does one find out a categorical imperative? By asking, "What if everybody did it?"[8] More specifically, Kant used three ideas to identify a categorical imperative:

1. Act according to ethical principles that you can will to be universally followed.

2. Act according to principles that you could will to be universal laws of nature.

3. Act so as to treat human beings always as ends, never as mere means.[9]

Today, this kind of ethic is used by many different religious and secular people. They tend to be moralists (or legalists) who rely on their own goodness and good works. They ground their morality in their own reason and in observation of the natural world. Some may appeal to the Bible, but typically not as the inerrant, sufficient, and absolute special revelation of God. Other sources of absolutes must be appealed to over and above the Bible: church dogma, other religious books, false prophets, or other scientific and philosophical reasoning.

THE CONSEQUENTIALIST APPROACH

Consequentialist ethics* is a teleological approach (from the Greek word *telos*, meaning "end"). In general, this approach allows for judgments and choices based on goals or results ultimately determined to be good by the desires of either the individual or society. Self-determination (or social determination)—and not discoverable rules—dictate how one should live. Every situation calls for a new evaluation of what the individual (or society) would most like to achieve in the end (sometimes regardless of the means used to get there). The best choices will bring the most happiness to the individual or to society as a whole; this defines what is good.

People who are driven by a consequentialist ethic are driven by results. They must do whatever they foresee will bring about the greatest happiness or the highest good. In this approach, the acts themselves are never in and of themselves good or evil, right or wrong. They are determined by their outcomes or consequences. Sometimes the outcomes can be viewed as one's fate. If good things happen to you, then you know that the universe is happy with you and you made the right choice. If bad things happen to you, then you know that the universe is angry with you and you made the wrong choice.

This approach rejects the inflexible rules of absolute, universal moral norms (the deontological approach). It rejects the idea of intrinsic good and evil. But most consequentialists also reject the complete subjectivity of existentialism—that a person can live out his or her own behavior regardless of the outcomes that affect others. However, some consequentialists end up going that route in the end.

Of all the approaches, this one has the most variations in how it is actually understood and practiced. For example, everyone in this category believes that humans ultimately seek happiness or pleasure (the highest good and the end goal). But from ancient times, groups differed on what this meant and how it was achieved. The Cyrenaic school of hedonists believed that the most intense, immediate pleasures were the best. In contrast, the Epicurean hedonists believed they needed to look for what would produce the most pleasure *and* the least amount of pain in the long run. They sought calmness without disturbance. Still another version comes from Aristotle, who defined the highest good as simple well-being—what everyone wants.

The most common version of the consequentialist approach is **utilitarianism**. Jeremy Bentham and John Stuart Mill are two famous and influential philosophers who promoted it. This view teaches that the utility, or usefulness, of an action in bringing about an intended, helpful end determines what is right or best. The idea that the end justifies the means or the rule of thumb that we should do the greatest good for the greatest number of people is a classic way of expressing utilitarianism.

consequentialist ethics: ethical model which says that ethical choices are governed by the results or ends they will achieve. The proper end is that which achieves the greatest amount of good. The good is often happiness, as defined by the individual or by society

BEST COURSE OF ACTION

Undesirable Results

Desirable Results

Bentham and Mill emphasized doing the most possible good for society as a whole. Bentham believed that achieving the best for all would benefit the individual self the most too. Mill believed that achieving the best for all was just a necessary part of being a social being. Regardless of the motives for doing the best for all, they both represent the utilitarian version of consequentialist ethics.

To clarify, not everyone who is a consequentialist ignores the means to the end (how the result is achieved). Ken Magnuson clarifies that "it might be more accurate to say that acts that produce a balance of desirable over undesirable results are right, while acts that produce a balance of undesirable over desirable results are wrong."[10] Some consideration is given to whether it is worth doing such and such to achieve a given end. How valuable is that end compared to the cost it takes to get there? But this is simply a pragmatic consideration.

Another version of the consequentialist ethic is known as **situation ethics**, a form of ethical relativism. Joseph Fletcher is the most famous proponent of this approach. Fletcher argued that the only governing principle for determining what is ethical is that of love. And this principle isn't defined absolutely. A person must figure out what love would look like in every new situation, and people's conclusions may legitimately differ. What's right for me is right for me, and what's right for you is right for you. No authority governs anyone.

Yet another version of the consequentialist ethic is known as **ethical egoism**. This version can be defined as pure, individual self-interest. This often comes with a bare admission that a person couldn't care less about others. The only thing that matters is the self-fulfillment of what the individual most desires for happiness. This philosophy has been happily embraced by totalitarian dictators like Mao Zedong. This kind of ethic has been, and continues to be, used by many different religious and secular people. Summarizing ethical thought, "especially from the eighteenth century to the middle of the twentieth century," ethicist Ken Magnuson opines:

> Moral philosophy has been dominated by deontology and consequentialism, as the two main frameworks for ethics. It has seemed that either ethics is about doing the right thing, regardless of the consequences, or doing whatever it takes to make sure things turn out right. . . . While recognizing that a number of smaller trails have been made, two of the main paths have been the deontological commitment to principles and rules, and the consequentialist focus on result.[11]

Today those religious and secular people tend to be libertines (given to license and lawlessness) or pragmatists (not lawless, but with a subjective basis for the laws they want to impose to achieve their version of the greatest good). They ground their morality in self-interest or in a supposed omniscience of what will turn out to be good for everyone else. Some may appeal to the Bible's ethic of love, but that term is usually gutted of any meaning given in the concrete commands of God's Word. Subjective desires reshape the Bible to fit one's own desired goals.

THE VIRTUE ETHICS APPROACH

The goal of **virtue ethics*** is to work a value system into people thoroughly—in other words, to build character. In general, this approach relies on ancient Greek and medieval Christian definitions of virtue. When faced with an ethical question, the moral intuition of the virtuous person takes over so that he or she will almost automatically know what to do because of who he or she is. Such a person can be guided by virtuous character rather than considering principles (the deontological approach) or outcomes (the consequentialist approach) at the crux of a decision.

The idea is that a person of good character, someone who is virtuous, will choose the best course of action when confronted with an issue. This approach presumes that people know what it is to be virtuous either by their own contemplation of virtue or from being taught to be virtuous within a particular community. Through one of these two means, a person's character can be formed as virtuous. This approach minimizes the focus on the issues (doing what I should do) and maximizes the focus on the person (being who I should be).

virtue ethics: an approach to ethics that focuses on discerning what virtues lead to a flourishing life and on developing those virtues so that they become habitual

People who are driven by the virtue ethics approach often focus on cultivating ideal character traits so that, when confronted with a situation, they will choose the best course of action. Figuring out the character traits to cultivate could depend on the individual or the community to which a person belongs. Magnuson puts it this way:

> Rather than speaking of our duty to a universal moral principle or of the responsibility to make sure things turn out right, we might say that moral obligation is derived from the nature of virtue (what virtue demands) or from community expectations (what a virtuous community demands).[12]

The more a virtuous person is in tune with himself or herself (or with the expectations of the community), the more that person will know what to do in any given situation. The key is to become who you ought to be (character) on the basis of either virtue itself or what the community demands, and then let your actions flow out of who you are.

Aristotle emphasized ideal character as a basis for ethics (as well as consequentialist outcomes). But some of the most influential representatives of the virtue ethics approach (in terms of living up to ideal character within a community) would be the more recent philosophers Alasdair MacIntyre and Stanley Hauerwas. They emphasize what it means to live a good life in community: displaying virtuous character in the unfolding story of this world. As such, they are critical of what they perceive to be poor character traits that degrade a flourishing community.

Versions of this approach have grown in popularity today. Many who reject traditional and conservative morality attack the social norms of previous generations by critiquing them through the lens of a new morality under the guise of virtue. The tables have turned, and those who once promoted virtue are now told that they are the ones who are not virtuous. Good is called evil, and evil is called good.

Virtue ethics says that good character can be cultivated and internalized so that it becomes one's nature.

THE EXISTENTIALIST APPROACH

Existentialist ethics* grounds ethics in the individual person. The existentialist looks at habits and customs and cultures and deems them to be shams. Instead of conforming to others' expectations, the existentialist must choose the right way to exist in this world. And in doing so, the existentialist defines existence. Existentialists were concerned that many people mindlessly conformed to conventional morality without having personal integrity. The existentialist wanted people to feel the weight of the choices they made and for which they alone were responsible.

Jean-Paul Sartre is the best, or perhaps the worst, representative of an existentialist approach to ethics. He believed in absolute human freedom—individuals must create for themselves their own identities (or essences) by the choices they make and thus can be whatever they want to be. (There is no inherent human nature or natural law that a person must conform himself to.) His view seems very triumphalist in that humans can achieve who they want to become. But each individual also bears sole responsibility for failure. Therefore, there is no objective meaning to existence, only the meaning the individual creates. This view can lead to great despair. Sartre's view also teaches that no outside constraints should inhibit people from being who they wish to become. There are no moral restraints. In the end, this ethic mirrors ethical egoism. But the route to living for absolute self-interest is cerebral (introspection on being one's true self) rather than pragmatic (what works).

Although pure existentialist philosophy is less popular than it used to be, our postmodern culture is overrun by those who live according to self-defined identity and who throw off all moral constraint. Radically subjective notions of truth, meaning, and goodness abound. The self-determined ethics of existentialism is very much alive.

This cord is holding me back.

Do divers need safety lines? "Let us break their bands asunder, and cast away their cords from us." Psalm 2:3

existentialist ethics: ethical model which says that ethical choices are determined by the freely choosing individual; in the absence of absolute truth or meaning, the individual creates his or her own meaning and essence by the choices he or she makes and must take full responsibility for the outcome of these choices

CONCLUSION

The common denominator in each of these faulty approaches is that they tend to look for the origin and basis of morality in humans or in this world (what is). They leave the discovery of ethical norms to man's own reasoning or observations. Even many of those who use a holy book tend to look elsewhere for ethical foundations. Many believe that the holy book or religion resulted from an evolutionary process, such that society developed and constructed the religion for pragmatic reasons (such as survival).

So far, we have only described the faulty approaches to ethics by summarizing what they teach. In the next section, we will critique them, exposing their central errors. In Chapter 8, we'll attempt to construct the best Christian methodology for ethical decision-making.

Thinking It Through 2.2

1. How does ethics relate to philosophy?
2. a. Identify the four major ethical systems outlined in this chapter.
   b. Explain the basis for each ethic.
   c. Explain what drives people in each ethic.
3. Identify at least one major proponent who best represents each of the major ethical systems.
4. a. Explain how utilitarianism, situation ethics (ethical relativism), and ethical egoism are all similar.
   b. Explain how utilitarianism, situation ethics (ethical relativism), and ethical egoism differ.
5. What is a categorical imperative in the view of Immanuel Kant?

2.3 Evaluating the Faulty Approaches to Ethics

Have you ever committed to something that sounded good when you first heard about it, only to find out in the end that you hadn't really understood what you were committing to? Certainly, some part of what you had heard sounded beneficial or attractive. But another part was hidden or obscure. Once that part was revealed or made clear, you realized your obvious mistake. Maybe an advertiser pulled you into a bad purchase by using a gimmick or a friend tricked you into some lousy work or a raw deal of a trade. Or maybe it was something far more serious. Our sinful thinking and desires can also take us further than we want to go, and the price we pay is far greater than advertised by our self-deceived hearts.

Each faulty ethical approach has something within it that sounds beneficial or attractive. One piece of it may be right. But overall, each system is misdirected. If you found yourself drawn toward one ethical approach or another outlined in the last section, then you need to step back and consider what's really being sold by each system.

How do you step back and consider each system? Here are three rules of thumb to help you.

- Look for **internal consistency**—that is, does the ethical system contradict or undermine itself?
- Look for **external coherence**—that is, does the ethical system match up with how things work in real life (according to the wisdom of God's creational design)?
- Look to God's Word—that is, does the ethical system in any way contradict the explicit teachings or underlying principles and clear implications of God's Word?

The last rule of thumb presupposes that you are a Christian who trusts God's mind over your own. God's revelation is the ultimate and clearest lens for evaluating all things, for we are finite and fallen. However, the other two rules of thumb are helpful tools. Perhaps the unbeliever will not listen to the correct presuppositions found in God's Word for interpreting the evidence in this world. The other two rules of thumb can remove the unbeliever's confidence in faulty ethical systems, leaving him or her helpless and in need of something else (Prov. 26:4–5; 2 Cor. 10:5). Then you can present the biblical truth.

PROBLEMS WITH THE DEONTOLOGICAL APPROACH

Don't Christians commit themselves to a self-sacrificial duty to obey objective, absolute, universal moral principles or rules? Don't Christians believe that motives and means to an end are just as important as the outcome? Don't Christians believe it's wrong to live for pleasure or to use people to achieve selfish ends? Yes! These questions highlight some of the strengths of the deontological approach. But a one-dimensional deontological approach is also filled with weaknesses, making the approach problematic overall.

The deontological approach (if it is not grounded in Scripture) has no sure *basis* for determining objective, absolute, universal moral principles because it rejects (or supplements) the all-sufficient Word of God and replaces it with human reason. God is replaced and humans are given independent authority to determine which maxims *they* wish were universal laws. This approach is contrary to the Word of God. Our only source of *authority* for universal absolutes is Scripture itself.

Human logic is limited and fallible. Trying to find a universal absolute principle outside oneself without a transcendent, personal Being (and His revelation) becomes impossible. This is made more obvious by observing the futile efforts of those who have tried to operate according to the deontological approach without God and His Word. On the one hand, they struggle to come up with very many unarguable categorical imperatives (universal absolutes everyone must obey regardless of the time or situation) even among themselves. When a supposed categorical imperative is settled on (for example, Kant's idea of acting from a good will, which always does its duty without self-interest), the imperative is usually so generalized and non-specific that it is hardly useful, because people may apply it in contradictory ways in a specific situation. (Does a good will, which selflessly fulfills its duty, mean prioritizing my duty to my wife or to my children in this situation?) It is difficult to get this approach to cohere with or at least be useful in real life.

On the other hand, the deontological approach can devolve into making tons of specific rules into categorical imperatives. (Never go over the speed limit! In any situation?) So what might be a good rule in most specific situations becomes unbending

Why are secular approaches to ethics wrong?

in any and all situations regardless of other factors. And this leaves people weighed down under heavy, restrictive burdens. The impersonal rule becomes senseless, and the people who legalistically follow the rule may reveal themselves to be uncaring (by following the letter of the law over the spirit and intended purpose of the law, at the expense of others). Again, it is difficult to get this approach to cohere with real life.

Other criticisms have been leveled against the deontological approach. While duty is a laudable motive, is it the only acceptable motive? Which duty do I follow when I have equal, competing duties? Who gets to determine my duties? Must I always be completely disinterested in receiving any benefit from what I do, or else I become an immoral person? Isn't there a difference between using someone only for self-interest and benefiting from someone (finding mutual benefit agreed upon by both parties)? Isn't it possible to pursue and achieve happiness (the end goal of the consequentialist approach) by fulfilling my duties? Is happiness at odds with fulfilling duty? Does God's Word teach me to shun happiness or to find happiness in the right source?

In sum, only divine revelation (without other competing authorities) can provide the basis for universal moral absolutes. Appeals to other sources of authority for absolute moral rules can lead to burdensome, legalistic human traditions (Matt. 15:1–20; 23:1–33). John Frame critiques this lack of internal consistency:

> Kant claims to avoid any appeal to consequences (the teleological approach) or inclination (the existential approach). But he tests the universality of maxims precisely by showing the consequences of their universal affirmation. And in the end he judges these consequences according to his inclinations: his desire to live in a world in which promises exist, but cruelty does not, and everyone treats everyone else as an end.[13]

Even with the benefit of receiving the Bible's own universal absolutes, Christians don't use these alone in ethical decision-making. Biblical absolutes ground and direct the Christian. But other complementary* considerations must factor in as well.

PROBLEMS WITH THE CONSEQUENTIALIST APPROACH

Don't Christians calculate the cost and consider how their actions affect others? Aren't they driven by doing the most loving thing in any given situation? Aren't all people inescapably bound to aim at accomplishing some goal or purpose in all that they do? Isn't it natural (by God's design) that humans normally seek self-preservation and seek to find delight in what they do in life? Yes! One might even argue that it is best to attempt to do the greatest good for the greatest number of people due to human limitations. These questions highlight some of the strengths of teleological considerations. But a one-dimensional consequentialist approach (the consequences becoming the basis of the ethic and not just one consideration among several) is also filled with weaknesses, making the approach problematic overall.

The consequentialist approach makes results the absolute measure of what is right and wrong. Although the consequences should be considered as a factor, they should not ultimately determine what a person ought to do in a situation. Can finite human beings always accurately predict the outcome of actions—especially when there is a whole web of decisions involved and many people making those many decisions over many years with billions of factors at play across a whole society? Making choices based on an obvious-enough outcome can only take place in very simple, limited situations. So the approach might work out sometimes, but it's not usually a workable approach in much of real life since nobody can truly predict all the effects in the long run. It lacks external coherence.

Who gets to decide (and when) whose perspective is most accurately judging whether an outcome will bring about the greatest good for an individual or society in the long run? One generation may be confident that certain choices are right and good. So those choices are judged to be moral in that generation. But then the next generation observes that the outcomes of those choices actually produced all kinds of harm (or at least what the next generation defines as harm). The next generation

complementary: completing by adding benefit without contradicting or undermining judges the previous generation as immoral (even if the previous generation never purposed to cause harm). There is no sure standard of right and wrong—only perspective (postmodernism embraces this as true rather than seeing it as a problem). A person can be a hero in one generation and demonized in the next. This approach is internally inconsistent; it undermines itself as a consistent guide for ethical choices.

Here's another problem: How would you like to be in a minority population that doesn't matter to a majority population that operates according to the greatest good for the greatest number of people? Wouldn't you cry foul when you yourself suffered? The idea that "might makes right" has led to many atrocities throughout history. More than that, the Bible supports the intrinsic worth and proper treatment of every individual because all people are made in God's image. It is possible to do the greatest good for the greatest number of people as long as nothing immoral is being done to individuals (administrative rules often work this way). But as soon as the minority are suffering due to immoral actions (which can only be determined outside a consequentialist approach, by the way), then the utilitarian approach becomes problematic to the Christian.

Other criticisms have been leveled against the consequentialist approach. While people may find it attractive to live for pure self-interest (ethical egoism), the pleasurable results are usually short-lived. Their immoral living will produce painful consequences in the end. But consequentialists have a very difficult time measuring the balance between pain and pleasure in order to determine what to do. There are too many factors, and the judgments are too subjective. Even if they were to agree on a course of action, the judgment would boil down to agreed-upon preferences. Consequentialism can never tell someone what is actually right or wrong in and of itself. Situation ethics suffers from all these problems as well. It sounds good that we should operate by the rule of love in all situations. But how is love defined, and what does it actually look like without any direction from God's moral law? "Love" turns out to be nothing more than a person's subjective preferences.

In sum, only God's glory can be our ultimate end. And only God's commands in God's Word can describe what it actually looks like to pursue that end. God's commands describe what it looks like to love God and others—the two Great Commandments that sum up what ought to motivate us and how we can glorify God in all of life (Matt. 22:37–40). We need the specific direction of God's Word to guide us in our judgments. Both the means we use and the ends we achieve are important to God.

PROBLEMS WITH THE VIRTUE ETHICS APPROACH

Don't Christians need to focus on being the right kind of people so that what they do flows out of who they are? Shouldn't Christians cultivate virtues? Aren't some ethical difficulties easy to resolve once a person becomes virtuous and thus sees the situations with clarity? Yes! These questions highlight some of the strengths of the virtue ethics approach.

Another strength of the virtue ethics approach is that it shifts the focus from the most difficult ethical choices that few people ever face in life (or that people rarely face) to focus on the moral choices we all have to make every day. The study of ethics should not be reduced to hard-to-solve ethical difficulties. The study of ethics should relate to basic growth in Christlikeness or sanctification (see Chapter 4). The hard cases should indeed be better resolved by the spiritually mature who have developed virtuous character (although even then the course of action isn't automatic—based simplistically on who I am). The Bible emphasizes that actions flow from the heart and that hypocrisy makes even right actions wrong.

But a one-dimensional virtue ethic has significant weaknesses as well. Virtue ethics tends to avoid evaluating specific acts and can neglect the reality of universal moral norms. Different groups of people will define what is virtuous differently. For instance, Aristotle thought the most virtuous man was "the one who thinks himself worthy of great things and really is worthy of them."[14] But Jesus said, "Blessed are the poor in spirit" (Matt. 5:3). Virtue ethics alone cannot decide what is truly a virtue and thus worth pursuing. If this decision is made on the basis of a community's values rather than upon universal moral norms, then virtue ethics becomes relative to that community.

In addition, even if everyone could agree on what a virtue is and what it looks like and how it should be applied, how does a person *become* inwardly virtuous? John Frame observes the problem that non-Christian virtue ethicists have with this question:

> Aristotle teaches that we need to have virtuous dispositions to perform virtuous acts; but we need to perform moral acts in order to form the habits that produce virtuous dispositions. Aristotle is aware of this circularity and counsels readers to begin the process by doing things that "resemble" virtuous acts. But how one gets from resemblance to actuality is a mystery.[15]

One of the possible strengths of virtue ethics can also be one of its greatest weaknesses. Many who make use of virtue ethics make use of storytelling with model characters in order to inspire students to build character in their own lives. They may even use the Bible for character-building. But this moralistic approach to the Bible can reduce the Bible to a book of fairy tales with moral lessons that are simply useful to instill character into people—much like Aesop's fables.

The Bible does recount historical narratives with biblical persons who can be held up as examples (both negative and positive) to learn from. But the Bible is much more than this; it is not merely an ethical guidebook. The Bible explains truth and reality according to the historical unfolding of one overarching redemptive plan that all the individual historical accounts plug into. The Bible is primarily about God and His redemptive plan. Many of the biblical stories are meant to point us to our own inability to produce virtuous character within ourselves. The source of character must be the transforming work of Christ (see Chapter 4). Many virtue ethicists (even those in a broadly "Christian" tradition) miss or minimize the gospel.

PROBLEMS WITH THE EXISTENTIALIST ETHICS APPROACH

Don't Christians need to avoid mere external adherence to conventional morality? Don't Christians need to be who they really are, avoiding hypocrisy? Don't they need to examine their hearts to ensure that they have integrity, that their inner persons and their outward actions are not at odds with each other? Don't they need to take responsibility for their own choices? Yes! There are even some strengths in the existentialist approach. However, this approach tends to be worse than the others because it explicitly denies an objective moral order outside the individual. The existentialist approach can lead to the absolute anarchy of the individual who wants freedom to become whoever he or she wishes to become (in the name of authenticity). When many such people wish to become all that is antithetical to virtue, their society becomes less and less moral, and existentialism provides no mechanism or basis for restraining the disorder and immorality. Eventually that society will implode upon itself. God has not called us to be people of authenticity (in contrast to hypocrisy); God has called us to be people of integrity.

"You do you."

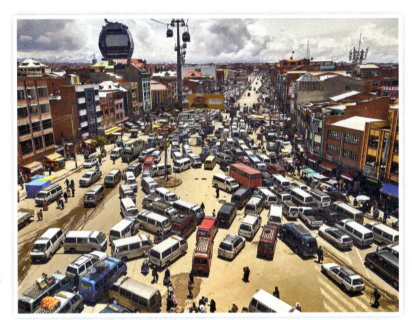

In sum, virtue (who I am on the inside) must be defined, described, and applied according to moral norms found in the Bible and in the design of God's creation. A person's ethical choices will reveal the fruit of true virtue versus hypocritical claims to virtue. Without any moral restraint from external absolutes or inward virtue, a society is doomed to self-destruction.

Less-structured rules of the road can lead to more chaotic driving. How does this image illustrate the ideology and outcome of the existential worldview?

CONCLUSION

Chapter 8 will present a biblical approach, or methodology, for making ethical decisions. This approach brings together the need to act according to absolute principles (acts) by rightly motivated virtuous people (agents) to the glory of God (ends). In other words, elements seen in the deontological, consequentialist, and virtue ethics approaches must all be put together and rightly prioritized in a biblical approach to ethics.[16]

Thinking It Through 2.3

1. List and explain three rules of thumb for critiquing the ethical approaches.

2. Summarize at least two strengths of the deontological approach.

3. Summarize at least two weaknesses of the deontological approach.

4. Summarize at least two strengths of the consequentialist approach.

5. Summarize at least two weaknesses of the consequentialist approach.

6. Summarize at least two strengths of the virtue ethics approach.

7. Summarize at least two weaknesses of the virtue ethics approach.

8. Summarize at least one strength of the existentialist approach.

9. Summarize at least one weakness of the existentialist approach.

Terms to Remember

- naturalistic fallacy
- deontological ethics
- categorical imperative
- consequentialist ethics
- utilitarianism
- situation ethics
- ethical egoism
- virtue ethics
- existentialist ethics
- internal consistency
- external coherence

Scripture Memory

Romans 3:10–12

Understanding Ethics

1. What is the value of living in a world with natural laws and creational norms?
2. Based on the Fall's effects on the created order and human nature, explain why it is so hard to make right decisions.
3. Summarize each of the four faulty approaches to ethics. Identify the major proponent(s) of each approach.
4. What do most philosophers who are driven by results identify as the ultimate goal of all people (or the highest good)? How would you differentiate Cyrenaic hedonists and Epicurean hedonists who followed this line of thinking?

Practicing Ethical Decision-Making

5. Summarize how each of the four faulty ethical approaches would respond to the scenario below, and briefly explain the reasoning behind each.

   A store manager asks you to set aside some extra inventory without documenting it because he wants to give the product to charity without receiving any recognition for doing so.

6. Summarize how each of the four faulty ethical approaches would respond to the scenario below, and briefly explain the reasoning behind each.

   Your best friend asks you to help him or her cheat on a test.

Analyzing and Evaluating Ethical Claims

7. How would you respond to someone who claims that the family unit can be defined however one wishes (two dads, two moms, marriage is unnecessary for a couple, and so on) because society is no longer bound by the traditional family setup? What fallacy has this person embraced?
8. How would you respond to a claim that a soldier cannot confiscate an enemy's weapons because stealing is wrong? What fallacy has this person embraced?
9. How would you respond to a claim that you can steal a computer because you have been disadvantaged in life and this tool will help you to graduate from college and do a lot of good for others in return one day? What fallacy has this person embraced?
10. How would you respond to a claim that all virtuous people will know by intuition (without needing to evaluate the complexities of the situation in the light of moral absolutes) whether the law should force the descendants of American slaveholders to compensate the descendants of American slaves for loss and disadvantage? What fallacy has this person embraced?

Creating My Own Position Statements on Ethics

11. Summarize your own position on the effects of the Fall on the created order and on human nature.
12. Summarize your own position on the best approach to ethics.

COLOSSIANS 3:1–3, 12

The Role of Redemption in Ethics

How can I live according to a Christian ethic?

ⓍⓍ Redemption and the Law

Christian ethics addresses us as whole persons—our character, motivations, actions, and relationships. It aims to restore the image of God in man through the redemptive work of Jesus Christ. It neither minimizes outward conduct nor does it reduce morality to outward conduct. It transforms heart motivations. It recognizes the reciprocal relationship between character and actions (actions flow from character and also shape character). And it provides the universal moral norms necessary for determining right and wrong.

Without the universal moral norms of God's law, individuals and societies are bereft of an objective standard for assessing right and wrong. What is moral becomes a matter of personal preference or the consensus of a particular society. But these are ever-changing standards. The unchanging norms of Scripture provide us with the reliable compass we need to navigate the ethical currents of life.

covenantal structure: the scaffolding for the biblical storyline formed by a series of covenants between God and certain individuals in redemptive history, beginning with the Adamic Covenant and concluding with the New Covenant

Christians approach the task of ethics with an awareness of God's character revealed in creation, in His law (summarized in the Ten Commandments), and in the person and work of Jesus Christ. We follow the Bible's storyline so that our ethic is built according to the covenantal structure* of redemptive history. Then we draw on our new identity in Christ to apply ethics to our lives.

GOD COVENANTS MAN

ADAMIC · NOAHIC · ABRAHAMIC · MOSAIC · DAVIDIC · NEW

GOD'S CHARACTER AND GOD'S LAW

God's moral law is a reflection of His holy character. It is not an abstract code of ethics found in His personal library. Human judges are under the law by which they adjudicate* legal disputes. In this case the law exists outside the judge. But if God's law existed outside Himself, it would not be a reflection of His own character. It's important to understand that God does not declare, for example, murder and adultery wrong because that's what the moral universe imposes on Him.

But if universal moral norms are not independent of God, does this mean that God's law is arbitrary? In other words, could God have made up an entirely different set of laws from the ones He has given to us? Instead of declaring murder and adultery wrong, could He have declared these things to be right? This faulty view is known as the **volunteerist perspective**. It maintains that God's law is whatever God wills it to be. We need to understand that even though this view seems to elevate the sovereignty of God, it makes ethical behavior arbitrary.

Contrary to volunteerism, biblical Christianity maintains that God only wills that which is consistent with His holy character. When God's law is divorced from His good character, ethics loses its grounding. Ethics is not arbitrary; it could not be other than it is because God's character could not be other than it is. Nor is there some moral standard external to God; right and wrong are established by God's character. His commands to not murder and to not commit adultery reflect who He is. He is the God of life, and therefore murder is always wrong. He is the God of faithfulness, and therefore adultery is always wrong.

The Two Great Commandments

There are a lot of laws in the Mosaic code, so God in His wisdom boils them down into two Great Commandments: to love God supremely and to love others as oneself (Lev. 19:18; Deut. 6:5; Matt. 22:36–40). The ethical implications of the two Great Commandments are obvious. If we loved God perfectly, we would seek to please Him in our thoughts, motives, and actions. If we loved people perfectly, we would seek their good in every situation. Though no one does this perfectly, this is the standard to which we are called.

There is a great simplicity in being able to boil down all ethical choices to these two laws. And yet, the two Great Commandments are so broad that we might be tempted to fill the love commands with our own fallen concepts of what love should look like. The Ten Commandments define what it means to love God and others, and other laws in the Pentateuch explain them further and apply them to specific situations.

How can I delight in God's law?

Christian love for God and for others is predicated on God's love for us. As the apostle John wrote, "Herein is love, not that we loved God, but that he loved us, and sent his Son to be the propitiation for our sins. . . . We love him, because he first loved us." (1 John 4:10, 19). Redemption does not come at the expense of God's law; it comes at the expense of God's own Son. The plan of redemption accomplishes two things: it deals with the penalty of the law hanging over us for our sin, and it gives us a new power to delight in the law. God is not only the standard of love; His love for us also enables our love for Him and for others.

The Ten Commandments

We can relate the two Great Commandments to the Ten Commandments by asking two questions: What does love for God look like? Answer: having no other gods before Him, not making an image of Him and bowing before it, honoring His name, and honoring His day of worship (Exod. 20:3–11). What does love for people look like? Answer: put in positive form, the commandments teach us to honor our parents, respect human life, remain faithful in marriage, respect people's property, speak the truth, and rejoice in our neighbor's blessings (Exod. 20:12–17). But even the Ten Commandments are broad statements. God's people need further help knowing how to apply these commands to their lives. Many of the commands in the rest of the Pentateuch seek to do this.

---

adjudicate: to come to a judicial decision; to act as judge

As the moral standard for human society, the Ten Commandments reflect the creational norms given to Adam, which in turn reflect God's character. After mankind fell into sin and God moved the plan of redemption forward by calling Israel to be His people, God gave Israel the law, which was a statement of creational norms and their applications. Even though some people read the Mosaic law as if it is arbitrary, it is not. The creational norms that it expounds are rooted in God's own character.

THE CHRISTIAN AND THE MOSAIC LAW

The ethical nature of the Ten Commandments must not be abstracted from its redemptive-historical context. The Mosaic law was given shortly after God delivered Israel from Egyptian bondage (Exod. 20:1). The laws that God gave through Moses reflect that historical context. One author says, "The Mosaic law was the divinely accredited implementation of creational law for ancient Israel."[1] This means that God took creational norms and applied them to Israel's particular time and place. For instance, in Israel's time and place, the flat roofs of houses were places where people lived. The law required the Israelites to build a low wall around the rooftops so that people would not accidentally fall off the roof and die or injure themselves (Deut. 22:8). This was God's specific application of the fifth commandment, which concerns itself with the protection of human life.

The New Covenant and the Law

Despite Israel's privilege of receiving the law, its moral failure was evident from the start and therefore hinted at the need for a better covenant (Deut. 31:20, 27; Jer. 31:31–34). Israel's problem with disobedience was not unique to that nation. Violating God's creational norms, which are reflected in His moral law, is a universal problem. We are all guilty and therefore deserving of the death and curses threatened in the law. Humanity's long-awaited hope rested on God's promised Messiah.

By fulfilling the Old Covenant law, Christ ushered in the New Covenant and thereby changed the way His people relate to the law (Rom. 7:1–6; 8:3–4). Christians are not under the Mosiac law as a covenant; that was Israel's relationship to the law. Christ was born under the law-covenant in order to fulfill its demands and its penalties (Gal. 4:4). Because Christ fulfilled the law for us, we can enjoy through faith in Him the undeserved life and blessings promised in the law. God's people no longer receive His law from the thunder of Sinai, causing them to shrink back in fear; they now receive it from the hand of Christ on lovely Mount Zion, causing them to walk in loving obedience (Heb. 12:18–24; 1 Cor. 9:21).

But this does not mean the Mosaic law has no relevance for the Christian today. There is much the Christian can learn by observing how God made specific application of creational norms to Israel's particular time and place. As Wolters puts it,

> Insofar as the Mosaic law is addressed to a particular phase of the history of God's people it has lost its validity, but insofar as it points to the enduring normativity of God's creation order it retains its validity. . . .
>
> . . . In the Old Testament the explanations [God] gave included detailed instructions for the implementation of the blueprint; that was by way of apprenticeship. In Christ we are journeyman builders—still bound to the architect's explicit directions, but with considerable freedom of implementation as new situations arise.[2]

God's applications for Israel help Christians understand how to apply general laws like the Ten Commandments or the two Great Commandments to their own time and place.

Christians must ask when reading the Mosaic law, What part is universally normative because it is rooted in creation? What part is an application to Israel's time and place? And what can we learn from how God applied creational norms to Israel that should inform how we apply creational norms to our own situation? Thus, while Christians are not under the Mosaic law as their covenant, they are not released from all of God's laws either. Instead, Christ has fulfilled the law on our behalf to save us and then enable us to obey His law.

The Holy Spirit and the Law

Though Christians are not saved by keeping the law of God, they're not without the law of God (Rom. 3:20, 31). Christians refusing to obey God's law because they are under grace is incompatible with the New Covenant promise of the Spirit. The Old Testament prophets summed up God's promise this way: "I will put my spirit within you, and cause you to walk in my statutes" (Ezek. 36:27), and "I will put my law in their inward parts, and write it in their hearts" (Jer. 31:33).

Though a believer be less under the power of the law than others...
[h]e sees more of its spirituality and holiness. JOHN OWEN[3]

God's promise to put His Spirit within His people corresponds with His promise to put His law within them. This law refers to the moral norms written in creation, then written on tablets of stone for Israel, and now written in the believer's heart. The difference now is that believers have the Spirit to empower them: "I will . . . cause you to walk in my statutes" (Ezek. 36:27). The Spirit is the wind in our sails of faith, enabling us to choose what is pleasing in His eyes. This is a blood-bought gift because Christ purchased our Spirit-enabled obedience by His death (2 Cor. 1:20). Therefore, the reality of the indwelling Spirit assures believers that they can keep His law as they yield to the Spirit.

OBEDIENCE AND THE LAW OF CHRIST

Christian ethics does for our moral reasoning what other ethical systems cannot. It provides moral sanity in a morally insane world. At the same time, it offers hope for people who have fallen short of God's moral law and are looking for help.

Indicatives and Imperatives

Believers are often conscious of their weaknesses. The high ethical demands of God's moral law leave many feeling overwhelmed. Where can they find help to obey? The Spirit's work in them, as we noted, is one answer. Learning "the grammar of the gospel"[4] is another.

We learned in our English grammar studies the difference between the indicative mood and the imperative mood. The indicative mood refers to a factual statement, something that is true. The sentence "I am crucified with Christ" (Gal. 2:20) is in the indicative mood. The imperative mood refers to a command, something we must do. The sentence "Present your bodies a living sacrifice, holy, acceptable unto God" (Rom. 12:1) is in the imperative mood.

With respect to the gospel, the indicatives refer to what Christ has done, is doing, and will do for us, while the imperatives refer to what we must do as His redeemed people. The indicatives always precede and serve as the incentive for the imperatives. In other words, the love of Christ for us, expressed in our costly redemption, results in our love for Him, expressed in our joyful obedience. The fact that Christ has liberated His people to live righteously means that they really can live righteously (in dependence upon Him). Freedom to obey does not mean it's easy or that Christians can obey without a fight. It means that, for all the obstacles in their pathway, they can have ever-increasing victories in the fight for faith and obedience (1 Tim. 6:12; Rom. 8:37).

Christian Identity and Christian Ethics

Ethical living is the outworking of a believer's new identity in Christ. It's not a self-help strategy for improving our moral character. Nor is it merely a matter of imitating Christ's life. Imitation is not possible without identification. In other words, we must be united to Christ by faith in order to become like Him.

Identification flows in two directions. First, Christ identified with sinners by taking on the likeness of sinful flesh and nailing it to the cross (Rom. 8:3). Second, those who trust in Christ are identified with Him in His life, death, and resurrection (Rom. 5:17; 6:4–5). This is a covenantal identity. Our old identity in Adam (sin and death) has been replaced with our new identity in Christ (righteousness and life).

Ethical systems that ignore the biblical teaching of **covenantal identity*** are doomed to failure. The current crisis in our world is a crisis of identity. People no longer know who they are. Burdened with the unbiblical notion that they can create their own identity, people are floundering to make sense of life and of their place in the world. Popular culture says, "Be true to yourself" (an expression of ethical egoism or existentialist ethics). Although this mantra is trumpeted as individual freedom, the despair of so many who follow it is evidence that it isn't freedom.

Freedom doesn't come from rejecting the fundamental nature of our humanity—namely, that we are the very image of God. It comes from being restored to this noble dignity, becoming what we were created to be as mirrors of God's holy character. The mystery of Christian ethics is that believers are gradually being restored in Christ to this original design as they trust and obey.

It takes biblical wisdom to resist the deceptive appeal of other ethical systems and believe that Christian ethics is the right way because it is God's way. Implementing the Christian ethic boils down to this simple principle: become what you are in Christ. In other words, know who you are, Christian. You are one who has been raised with Christ and seated with Him in heaven. Now, live in the light of this glorious fact (Col. 3:1–17)!

Thinking It Through 3.1

1. What is the proper way to think of God's law in relationship to His character?
2. What would our ethics look like if we obeyed the two Great Commandments?
3. How do the Ten Commandments relate to the ethic of loving God and loving people?
4. How does Christ's fulfillment of the Mosaic law change the way Christians relate to it?
5. How does the grammar of the gospel help Christians keep God's law?

3.2 Redemption and Wisdom

How does wisdom help me live ethically?

Christian ethics is more than just following a list of detailed rules. Especially in the New Testament, God wants Christians to understand the laws He has revealed and then reason the specific applications needed in their own situation. And already in the Old Testament Wisdom Literature, God was preparing His people for this task. Wisdom and law are closely connected because both are based on creational norms. Wisdom is the ability to discern those norms and live by them out of a heart of love for the Creator. It is also the ability "to summarize those principles in a succinct and memorable fashion."[5]

Since these norms are rooted in creation, the wise person is a careful observer of creation to see how God designed it to work. However, to rightly understand what

covenantal identity: who a person is—based not on individual characteristics but based on his or her relationship to a representative head whom God established, either Adam or Christ he or she is seeing, the wise person needs the corrective lenses of Scripture. Thus law and wisdom focus on the same thing. But, while in the Mosaic law God made the applications, the wise person needs to work those applications out using wisdom—still looking to the law for further guidance. Wisdom in applying creational norms is a fundamental task of the Christian life. It is something we do every day as well as when we are faced with hard ethical choices.

As we progress in this section, we'll consider how observing creational norms relates to gaining wisdom, how God's law relates to wisdom, and how creational norms apply to the Christian life.

WISDOM AND DISCERNING CREATIONAL NORMS

Other ethical systems are like a Picasso painting; their secular attempts to reassemble the broken pieces of our lives are unsuccessful. If you've seen many Picasso paintings, you know that the artist often portrayed people as fractured and disjointed. Fallen people are not always as they appear. They strive to give the appearance of a life put together, but the pieces of their lives are in the wrong place. Picasso's fractured people appear foolish and bizarre, and in a way they are a parable of the foolish and sometimes bizarre results of man's efforts to repair himself apart from Christian redemption.[6]

If we could obtain wisdom on our own, we wouldn't need the Lord Jesus Christ. Sadly, many people approach wisdom the way they approach salvation. Trusting in themselves, they exalt the wisdom of man above the wisdom of God. But those who trust in the person and work of Christ discover in Him the fountain of all wisdom (1 Cor. 1:30). It is through Him that Christians become wise.

To be wise is to be discerning, prudent, and virtuous (among other attributes). Discernment is the ability to determine the best course of action in a given situation. Prudence is the ability to be reasonable and cautious in addressing difficulties. And to be virtuous is to be righteous and just in dealing with others. We will not possess wisdom without possessing these qualities in some measure.[7]

Weeping Woman by Picasso

Yet there is no quick and easy formula for acquiring wisdom. Wisdom is an art that Christians develop over time as they walk with God. We may define **wisdom** as the art of living well by observing creational norms through the lenses of Scripture, by listening to the counsel of the wise, and by being conscious that all life is lived before the face of God.

Wisdom is living out the whole of life with a constant awareness of accountability before a loving, gracious, and just Creator and Redeemer. O. PALMER ROBERTSON[8]

Wisdom and the Observation of God's Creation

True wisdom begins with a humble reverence for God (Prov. 9:10). This includes the recognition that He is an infinitely wise Creator who has purposefully ordered His creation. When God fashioned the world in its physical and moral dimensions, wisdom was by His side (Prov. 8:30). Therefore, pursuing wisdom in our lives "offers us the key to interpreting our world: its beginnings, its purpose, its shape and its direction."[9] To correctly interpret the world, we must assume the right posture before God. We have to be teachable and willing to learn God's viewpoint.

When you purchase a new piece of technology, such as a smartphone, you recognize that the device is created to operate according to the design of its creator. An insightful operator learns the device's proper function and uses it as its creator intended. God's creation is similar in that He designed it to function one way and not another. Our job is to carefully observe what God has written into creation. When we do, we gain wisdom.

Let's consider the following examples: money, sex, and power. We choose these examples because people have strong ethical disagreements about them. So we start with a basic question: Who determines how these things should function? What is the good, right, and just way for people to utilize these things? Do human beings get to arbitrarily decide, or has God structured His creation such that money, sex, and power are to be handled according to His wise purposes? How you answer these questions indicates whether you have insight.

Wisdom and the Corrective Lenses of Scripture

Wisdom is more than affirming that God has ordered creation; it's a matter of being attuned to that order and conforming our lives to it. God's intention has always been that people would do this in dependence upon Him. But we now live in an upside-down world, meaning people interpret reality according to their own imaginations. Everything is backward: the wisdom of God is made to appear foolish, and the foolishness of the world is made to appear wise (Rom. 1:22; James 3:14–16). Sin has impaired our ethical vision so that we don't perceive reality as it is.

Reading God's ethical intentions for society off the pages of creation requires the corrective lenses of Scripture. By looking at the world *through* Scripture, we see God's creational norms more clearly, but we also see how sin has distorted these things. For example, with a biblical lens we see the goodness of work and of building wealth, but we also see workaholism, laziness, and greed for the distortions they are. Similarly, we see God's purposeful distinction of men and women, but we also see gender confusion and the abuse or reversal of gender roles. Likewise, we see the goodness of humans exercising dominion over creation, but we also see animal abuse and poor stewardship of natural resources. The question is, How do we get back on track with creational norms?

The answer points us back to the important concepts of *structure* and *direction*. Recall that structure has to do with creational norms, the way God wisely designed the world to function. Direction has to do with what humans do with a created thing, bending it either toward or away from its creational design.[10] In the Fall, humans pushed creation in the wrong direction, which is one of the reasons we need the corrective lenses of Scripture to guide our observations of creation. One mistake many people make is to identify bad direction with structure. For instance, people assume that if they have a desire for something, that desire must indicate something about the way God made them. But they don't stop to ask whether their desires are consistent with God's structure or are the result of pushing God's structure in a fallen direction. Pushing structure in a good direction requires wisdom, because it is often not easy to undo the way bad direction has twisted things and to move back toward creational structure.

Wisdom and the Law of God

God's law is an explicit revelation of God's wisdom. We can inductively gain some wisdom by observing God's world. But we can also deductively receive wisdom by listening to God directly telling us what we ought to understand when we observe God's world. The Wisdom Literature takes us a step beyond the law of Moses. In the New Testament, God's people have to make their own applications of God's law to their time and place. Wisdom Literature is an Old Testament preparation for that task.

As we carefully listen to the voice of wisdom, we will hear the same truth we hear in God's law. In other words, the moral substance of the Bible's Wisdom Literature echoes the moral substance of God's law. Both share the same purpose and goal: to realign God's people with creational norms so that they can flourish as individuals and as a community of believers.

A few examples from the Ten Commandments and the book of Proverbs will make this clear. First, God's law reaffirms man's subordinate position before his sovereign Creator (Exod. 20:2–3). Wisdom echoes the Creator/creature distinction. It instructs us to not be wise in our own eyes but to trust God and acknowledge Him in all our ways (Prov. 3:5–7). Second, God's law harkens back to the creational norm of marriage as the appointed realm for human sexuality (Gen. 2:18–25; Exod. 20:14). Wisdom raises her voice in agreement: sexual immorality is a fire that burns, but sexual faithfulness in marriage is a satisfying fountain (Prov. 5:15–19; 6:27–29). Third, God's law reiterates the work/rest rhythm of life that we see at the beginning of creation (Gen. 1:31–2:3; Exod. 20:8–11). Wisdom lends her voice to this commandment, reminding us that work brings profit, but we should discern when to cease from work and should not put our trust in wealth (Prov. 14:23; 24:4–5).

WISDOM AND APPLYING CREATIONAL NORMS

Redemption does not rewrite creational norms; it reorients people to those norms. It restores the Christian's capacity for discernment, prudence, and virtue so that he or she can go with the grain of creation instead of against it. It redirects us to our gracious Redeemer who beckons, "If any of you lack wisdom, let him ask of God, that giveth to all men liberally, and upbraideth not; and it shall be given him" (James 1:5).

It pleases God when we trust Him for what we lack. He will not hold our foolishness against us when we exchange it for His wisdom. After all, one of the ways we gain wisdom is by learning from our poor choices and changing our conduct as a result.[11] Learning how to apply creational norms in the context of a fallen world is a necessary part of the Christian life. Although the Bible is sufficient for providing us with wisdom, it doesn't provide simple solutions to every problem we encounter. That's why we need the Holy Spirit to make us wise and to enable us to live wisely.

Consider the application of creational norms to making decisions about what to purchase with our money. Every decision we make with money is an ethical decision. Scripture has a lot to say about money, but it doesn't tell us whether we should purchase one brand of tennis shoes or another. But what if you discover that one company is using slave labor to manufacture their tennis shoes while another company has a volunteer workforce that is well compensated? Should these factors influence your purchasing decision?

How might you apply creational norms to this situation? You could point to the fact that slavery is a distortion of the Creation Mandate, a result of the Fall. You could point to the fact that we are responsible to steward our possessions in a way that leads to human flourishing. These are wisdom issues, and they directly relate to how you should respond to the above scenario.

Although the Fall has complicated our decisions in life, Christians can respond to these challenges by paying attention to God's creational norms. We will need Scripture to help us correctly interpret creational norms, and we will need wisdom to sort through the various issues that arise. Redemption means that Christians possess the resources to grow in wisdom and push further and further toward God's creational norms.

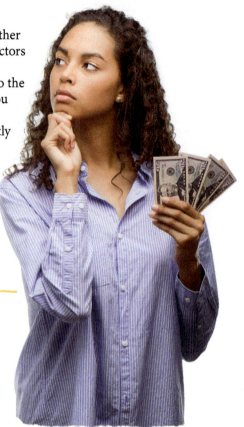

Thinking It Through 3.2

1. How is wisdom defined?

2. How does a Christian's reverence for God impact his or her interpreting of creational norms and increasing in wisdom?

3. Why do people need the corrective lenses of Scripture to correctly discern creational norms?

4. How does the Bible's Wisdom Literature relate to God's law?

5. How does growing in wisdom enable Christians to realign with creational norms?

3.3 Redemption and Man's Chief End

A biblical ethic is not only about following the right rules. It is also about having the right goals and acting in such a way that those goals are furthered. Scripture gives Christians many goals, but these can all be boiled down to the one goal of glorifying God. God's glory is His excellence put on display, and when we glorify God, we honor and praise God for His excellence and seek to make His excellence visible to everybody.

One way to glorify God is by pursuing Christlikeness. God created humans originally as bearers of His image. This is a foundational truth, one which undergirds much of ethics. Sin has twisted that image of God in man. But Christ is the image of God, and the image of God in man is restored in us as we become more and more Christlike.

Similarly, God created man to rule over the earth under His greater rule. In and after the Fall, man has attempted to rule the world apart from God. The kingdom of God is the reign of man over the world under God's greater rule. This is ultimately fulfilled in the man Christ Jesus, but all those in Him are also to reign with Him and so fulfill God's plan for creation.

When humans pursue these goals, the result is blessedness—happiness in the richest sense of the word—human flourishing. Everybody is pursuing happiness, but when it is pursued apart from the glory of God, it is a shallow and fleeting happiness. The Christian who pursues God's way may suffer much now, but in the end he or she will flourish "like a tree planted by rivers of water" (Ps. 1:3). So in making ethical choices, the Christian should ask: Is this choice going to glorify God? Will it make me more Christlike? Will it advance God's kingdom? And will it make me a person who is happy in God?

GOD'S GLORY AND MAN'S CHIEF END

The Bible provides a number of purposes for which God made man: to be conformed to God's image and to rule over creation under God's greater rule (Gen. 1:26–28); to delight in God's law (Ps. 1:1–3); to fear God (Prov. 1:7); to trust in God with all one's being and acknowledge Him in all one's ways (Prov. 3:5–6); to be blessed or to flourish (Ps. 1:1; Matt. 5:3–12); to walk worthy of God and do good works, which glorify the Father (Matt. 5:16; Col. 1:9–12); to seek first God's kingdom and righteousness and enter that kingdom (Matt. 5:20; 6:33); to be conformed to the Son's image for the Son's glory (Rom. 8:29); to be holy, blameless, pure, and righteous so that God receives glory (Eph. 1:3–4; Phil. 1:9–11); to be mature in Christ (Col. 1:28–29); to attain the Sabbath rest (Heb. 3–4). These various purposes are often summed up as "to glorify God, and to enjoy him forever."[12] According to Scripture, an action is considered morally good when it springs from a motive to glorify God (Matt. 5:16; 1 Cor. 10:31; 1 Pet. 4:11).

Knowing and enjoying God are essential to glorifying God. The tendency of the fallen human heart is to reduce morality to mere duty as though joy in God were irrelevant in the performing of our duty. But this is to rob God of His glory. A person who dutifully serves God without gladness of heart communicates that God is not worthy of service. Thus, God told the Israelites that He would hand them over to their enemies if they did not serve Him "with joyfulness, and with gladness of heart" (Deut. 28:47). That's how seriously God takes His glory and our happiness in Him.

Therefore, duty without delight is an insufficient motive for Christian ethics. It is by our delights that we show what is valuable to us, and it is by our greatest delight that we show what is most valuable to us. Since God is the most valuable being in the universe, it is only fitting that He be our greatest delight. To act morally includes acting from a genuine delight in God and His worth, which is the same as glorifying God. This is the teleology* of Christian ethics. In other words, God is not a means to some other good. He is our greatest good, and therefore He is the chief end for which we live, move, and have our being (Ps. 73:25; Acts 17:28).

Why do I do what I do?

Thou madest us for Thyself, and our heart is restless, until it repose* in Thee.

AUGUSTINE[13]

teleology: referring to the end goal
repose: to lie or be at rest

CHRISTLIKENESS AND THE KINGDOM OF GOD

Christian ethics measures the good by considering what leads to the honor and glory of God. For our purposes, we'll consider two ways Christians are called to honor God. The first is by being conformed to the likeness of Christ, and the second is by pursuing Christ's kingdom instead of the values of the world. Honoring God is not limited to these two areas, but these are two important areas that relate to man's chief end.

Christlikeness

As God's image-bearers, we were created to prioritize the glory of God above everything. Since Christ is "the image of the invisible God" (Col. 1:15), He is well suited to restore human beings to their original purpose. Christians are gradually restored as God's image-bearers by regularly beholding God's glory in the face of His Son (2 Cor. 3:18; 4:5–6).

To be like Christ is to find satisfaction in doing the will of God (John 4:34). This points to a vital principle in Christian ethics. Walking the path of obedience will at times be costly to our personal comfort. The degree to which Christians are motivated by the glory of God is the degree to which they will gladly sacrifice personal comfort in doing the will of God.

Being satisfied in God doesn't mean that we avoid the path of pain; it means that we draw strength to endure adversity from our satisfaction in God. Even Jesus chose to endure crucifixion "for the joy that was set before him" (Heb. 12:2). He likewise motivated His disciples to endure temporary hardships with the promise of everlasting joy (Matt. 5:10–12).

Therefore, pursuing Christlikeness entails following Him in His humiliation* in the assurance of one day sharing in His exaltation* (Matt. 16:24; Rom. 8:17). When faced with the choice between personal comfort and faithfulness to God, we should choose faithfulness to God (Luke 9:58; Rev. 2:10). This response glorifies God because it reflects the way Christ responded throughout His earthly life.

The Kingdom of God

Part of the challenge of Christian ethics is learning how to live in the world without adopting the values of the world (John 17:14–17). An ethical person is one who correctly perceives the true value of things based on a biblical evaluation. He or she understands that not everything in the world that glitters is gold and that the things of God appear unattractive to the undiscerning. While the things of this world can be deceptively attractive, Christians can—by the grace of God—resist their allure because they've discovered in the kingdom of God the "pearl of great price" (Matt. 13:46).

humiliation: the appointed path of suffering that Christ endured as His people's representative head and the pattern of life to which Christians are called as His faithful followers

exaltation: the triumphant end to an obedient life of humiliation, which Christ experienced in His resurrection and enthronement and which He secured as the destiny for His believing people

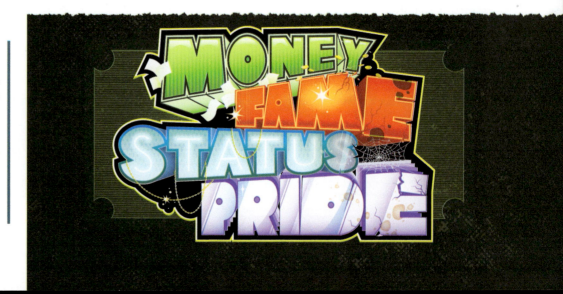

The **kingdom of God** refers to the reign of the risen and enthroned Lord Jesus Christ. The kingdom of God includes Christ bringing the saints to fulfill the Creation Mandate as well so that they rule the creation as God intended. In 1 John 2:15, the phrase "things that are in the world" refers to the various forms of thinking and living that are in opposition to Christ's reign. These include "the lust of the flesh, and the lust of the eyes, and the pride of life" (1 John 2:16), all of which describe a life dominated by the senses and the pursuit of self-centered pleasure. Since glorifying God means making much of Him, what better way for us to make much of God than by pursuing His kingdom over the fleeting pleasures of this world?

Entrance into the kingdom through faith in Christ is the beginning of a lifelong pursuit of the kingdom of God (Matt. 6:33). Learning how to live as citizens of the kingdom does not happen all at once. The ethics of the kingdom are counterintuitive to our fallen nature. For instance, those who are blessed in the eyes of heaven are poor in spirit, they mourn their sin, and they hunger and thirst for righteousness (Matt. 5:3–4, 6). Known as the Beatitudes,* the sayings of Jesus in Matthew 5:3–12 exalt character traits that are the opposite of what the world esteems. And yet, what makes these character traits attractive in believers is that they draw attention to the worth of Christ and His redemptive work.

"But lay up for yourselves treasures in heaven, where neither moth nor rust doth corrupt, and where thieves do not break through nor steal: for where your treasure is, there will your heart be also."

Matthew 6:20–21

BLESSEDNESS AND MAN'S CHIEF END

It's interesting to observe how Jesus motivated ethical living. He wasn't reticent to warn people of the dangers of an unethical life, yet His preference seemed to have been setting before believers the unfathomable blessings awaiting those who live for the kingdom of God rather than for the lusts of the world. "Blessed are the meek: for they shall inherit the earth," He said (Matt. 5:5). And "Blessed are the pure in heart: for they shall see God" (Matt. 5:8).

The word translated *blessed* can also be translated as *happy*, and it refers to God's favor upon His people, which is the source of all their happiness. The biblical perspective on happiness includes human flourishing in the physical world. As the above Beatitudes indicate, the chief privilege of the redeemed will be to behold God's glory in the new creation as they rule with Christ.

Blessedness: Inheriting the Earth

Christ has promised that His people will inherit the earth, which means they will rule forever with Him in the new creation. This future state of blessedness is the spiritual birthright of every believer (Gal. 3:29; 4:7), and it directly relates to man's chief end. God's original purpose was for His image-bearers to glorify Him by ruling the earth under His sovereign reign and provision (Gen. 1:26–28). Despite the disruptive impact of the Fall on man's rule, God's purpose will be fully restored when Christ returns to be glorified in His people (2 Thess. 1:10).

Meanwhile, our current situation is one in which Christians suffer many wrongs. When this happens, it doesn't feel like a state of blessedness; it feels more like being on the losing side of history. Instead of retaliating against those who wrong us, the Christian ethic challenges us to respond with meekness.

Meekness is the ethical virtue that Jesus commends in the third beatitude. It refers to the "moral quality of humility and gentleness, usually exhibited during suffering or difficulty and accompanied by faith in God."[14] Although it currently looks as though the earth goes to the ruthlessly ambitious, the surprising turnabout is that it eventually goes to the meek. Jesus guarantees it. Therefore, Christians can experience blessedness here and now as they await that coming day.

Beatitudes: the supreme blessings that Jesus pronounced upon His believing people in the Sermon on the Mount

Blessedness: Seeing God

The restoration of all things in Jesus Christ is the theme of redemptive history, and the consummation of redemption is when believers see God face-to-face (Rev. 22:4). Instead of hiding from Him as Adam and Eve did after they sinned in the garden (Gen. 3:8), Christians will dwell in the holy presence of God and never feel the slightest inclination to hide from Him (Rev. 21:3; 22:3–4). This is all the more stunning when we recall that God told Moses that no man can see His face and live (Exod. 33:20).

By faith Christians currently behold the glory of God in the face of Christ (2 Cor. 3:18). But one day faith will give way to sight. Then our eyes will look upon Him with the greatest satisfaction, and we will experience what Christians call the **beatific vision.*** We cannot imagine what this immediate sight of God will be like, but we do know that Jesus Christ is central to the beatific vision. There's no sight of God apart from Him (John 14:8–9; Col. 1:15).[15]

beatific vision: "the sight that makes happy,"[16] specifically the direct sight of God Himself, which believers will experience in their glorified state

If ever there was a motivation to pursue purity of heart, the beatific vision is it (Matt. 5:8). Nothing will compare to visually beholding the glory of God in Christ, because that alone will meet the deepest longing of the human heart. The perfect rest and wholeness that man enjoyed at the beginning of creation in the presence of God will be realized once again (Heb. 4:9–11; Rev. 14:13). But this inheritance, according to Jesus, belongs to the pure in heart.

God is the believer's greatest inheritance for now and for eternity (Pss. 16:5; 73:26). Seeking to be Christlike, to advance God's kingdom, and to flourish (now and eternally)—all for the glory of God—these are essential parts of ethical decision-making. This is the blessed life for which we were made but then lost because of our sin. Christ has come and recovered all of this for us.

Thinking It Through 3.3

1. According to Scripture, what motive is necessary in order for an action to be morally good?
2. Why is it impossible to dutifully serve God without also delighting in Him?
3. How does God's glory revealed in Christ help to restore Christians as God's image-bearers?
4. How does being motivated by the glory of God and the enjoyment of God enable Christians to be like Christ?
5. How does being motivated by the glory of God and the enjoyment of God enable Christians to pursue the kingdom of God over the things of the world?
6. How do the character traits commended in the Beatitudes glorify God when they are manifested in a believer's life?
7. Based on the Beatitudes regarding the meek and the pure in heart, what will be the chief privilege of the redeemed?
8. How does the redemption accomplished by Christ relate to the blessing of seeing God?

Review 03

Terms to Remember

- volunteerist perspective
- covenantal identity
- wisdom
- kingdom of God
- beatific vision

Scripture Memory

Colossians 3:1–3, 12

Understanding Ethics

1. Summarize how God's character and God's law should inform our ethics.
2. Explain why redemption is necessary for ethical living.
3. Explain why humility before the Creator is necessary to wisely discern creational norms.
4. Summarize how the New Covenant promise of the Spirit and the grammar of the gospel help Christians to obey God's law.

Practicing Ethical Decision-Making

5. Scripture has a lot to say about money, but it doesn't tell us whether we should purchase one brand of tennis shoes or another. How would you respond in the following situation?

   You're interested in purchasing a new pair of tennis shoes, but the ones you want are manufactured by a company that uses slave labor.

6. How might you utilize the biblical teaching regarding the Christian's new identity in Christ to address the following situation?

   Suppose a new Christian is tempted to lie to his parents. He used to lie to them regularly because he feared their rejection. He comes to you for advice on how he can be truthful with them.

Analyzing and Evaluating Ethical Claims

7. How would you respond to the claim that God's law is too restrictive of human freedom and that the only reason God imposes His law is because He wants to withhold good things from people?
8. How would you respond to the claim that Christians are not obligated to keep God's law because they are under grace?
9. How would you respond to the claim that a desire to help people is the only motive necessary for a deed to be considered morally good?
10. How would you respond to the claim that a blessed life only relates to spiritual blessings and does not have anything to do with Christians ruling on the earth?

Creating My Own Position Statements on Ethics

11. Summarize your own position on whether people need Scripture to accurately discern creational norms for ethical living.
12. Summarize your own position on the best way to motivate ethical living.

04

What makes Christian ethics unique?

Becoming Like Christ

2 PETER 1:3, 5–7

4.1 Virtues and Vices

DEFINING VIRTUE

Has anyone ever told you that patience is a virtue? Perhaps someone said it in jest because you were grumbling about having to wait longer than expected. But what does that saying even mean? What is a virtue?

The Greek word for virtue (*aretē*) can be found five times (in three passages) in the New Testament (Phil. 4:8; 1 Pet. 2:9; 2 Pet. 1:3, 5). But the *concept* is found throughout Scripture (see Gal. 5:19–23). The Bible calls us to be virtuous by emphasizing that a virtuous person is one of excellent moral character[1]—being righteous, godly, and Christlike. In fact, the two Great Commandments—to love God and to love others—are commands to be virtuous by reflecting God's character, the source of all virtue.

Originally, the word *virtue* related to a person excelling in any number of ways, including accomplishing a task such as a well-built (virtuous) boat. Eventually, one of the most common uses of the word had to do with mastering or achieving excellence in particular character qualities. In the ancient Greek culture, this moral excellence was usually understood as the result of a person's own effort to produce these qualities in himself or herself; thus, the person merited praise for being so excellent or virtuous. A person became renowned (obtained glory) for being virtuous (excelling in good character).[2]

In contrast, Christians look to God in order to become virtuous. God, through the gracious working of the Spirit (who unites us to Christ and lives in us), gets all the credit for anything good about who Christians *are* or what they *do* (Phil. 2:13; Gal. 2:20). Nevertheless, Christians are exhorted to diligently and actively make every effort to cultivate excellent (virtuous) character traits. God gets the credit for enabling our efforts (2 Pet. 1:5; see also Phil. 2:12). When the Holy Spirit was granted to us, transforming our nature, we were given all that we needed for godliness. In fact, our calling is to reflect "the praises" (*aretē*: excellencies) of our God to a watching world (1 Pet. 2:9; see also Matt. 5:16). All this is in the context of being distinct from a world driven by lust for vices (Phil. 4:8; 1 Pet. 2:11–12).

For the Christian, **virtue** can be defined as rightly ordered love.[3] Everything we do is motivated by love (properly directed or misdirected). What we love directs our commitments. If we are committed to the right things according to the right priorities, then we are virtuous. Since Christ is the source and enabler of our virtue, virtuous character entails reflecting Christ, motivated by a love for Him. And this sums up the ultimate goal of every Christian: to glorify God by being like Christ (Rom. 8:29; see also Matt. 22:37–40).

> *A virtue ethic that is Christian will focus on a description of the regenerate heart.*
>
> JOHN FRAME[4]

This ultimate goal should direct all Christian ethics. What we do must be directed by who we are. Becoming *who we ought to be* can only be accomplished by the internal transformation resulting from Christ in us. And "Christ in us" comes through the redemptive work of God when we accept the gospel. The gospel works itself out in ethical living (Eph. 2:10; 4:13, 20; Phil. 2:12–13; James 2:14–26) because true repentance (stemming from true transformation) bears fruit (Luke 3:8). Just as the fruit of a tree evidences what kind of tree it is, so also our actions evidence what kind of people we are (Prov. 20:11; Matt. 7:16–17; 12:35).

A true Christian will be motivated by a whole web of virtues, reflecting Christlikeness. It is not enough to do the right thing outwardly; God examines the heart motivations as well (Deut. 6:5–6; Matt. 22:37; 23:5). Apart from Christ, the unbeliever will lack the power to be consistently and genuinely virtuous. When the unbeliever is in some sense virtuous, all credit goes to the restraining work of the Holy Spirit (God's common grace) and the image of God remaining in that person.

DEFINING VICE

The word **vice** generally refers to a character trait or behavior that is recognizably wicked or immoral. Someone who is characterized by a vice has been overcome by a particular destructive habit. When bad behavior characterizes a person, those actions evidence the internal heart of that person (just as virtue is a matter of the heart). Vice is a deviation from God's upright standard (Gal. 6:1). The Bible speaks of the crooked person (Prov. 3:32; 11:3, 6; 21:8). This is the person characterized by vice—the opposite of the upright person.

A vice could be the exact opposite of a virtue. But it could also be the twisting of a virtue into something that appears like a virtue at first but in the end is a counterfeit. Often, "the prince of the power of the air" (Eph. 2:2) takes the second, more deceptive, approach; this world's system touts a virtue (like love, justice, or compassion) but misdefines or misapplies it. Or someone accomplishes a moral end but does so for the wrong reason. If someone has selfish motives for doing the right thing, is that person virtuous (Prov. 15:8; Matt. 6:1–8)?

In Chapters 5–7, you will be studying various virtues and vices. You will have to carefully examine the meaning, motives, and ends associated with each virtue in order to rightly understand each and to avoid vices that are portrayed as virtues. Then in Chapters 9–13, you will be grappling with specific ethical issues. When you do, one key will be to evaluate the motives of people in various situations. Are they truly motivated by virtue? Or do they portray themselves as virtuous while succumbing to vice?

At this juncture you may be wondering to yourself why one character trait or action should be considered a virtue and another a vice. Why is "good" good and "bad" bad? Is it random? Do societies choose (and change the definitions in each new generation)? Is it all just perspective? Maybe you do believe that God decides. But could God have chosen the opposite to be good?

The Bible gives clear answers to all the above questions. Virtue and vice are determined by God's own unchanging righteous character. Good matches up with who God is and with His design for this world. His design was created for our well-being. So, to behave badly is to be destructive to ourselves, to hurt others, and to blaspheme God through our selfish and prideful idolatry (which is what all sin is at its root). There is no virtue in choosing to be a person of vice. You will only destroy yourself and others in your rebellion. And God, the righteous Judge, will be victorious in the end. You should tremble in fear to even consider glorying in vice (Prov. 1:22–33; Heb. 10:26–31; 12:29; see also 2 Cor. 5:11).

IDENTIFYING VIRTUES AND VICES

How can we find out what the virtues are? Where do we look to obtain such knowledge? Identifying the virtues comes through knowing God and His Word. He has revealed Himself, His character, through His self-revelation. The Old Testament remains important for ethics as a revelation of the unchanging God and His dealings with a particular people in a particular place. The Old Testament provides a value system. The Gospels emphasize the need for inward transformation to internalize that value system into our character. And the Epistles provide doctrinal explanations and direct instruction on how to behave in the church age. But above all, God has revealed Himself (His character) through His Son, Jesus Christ. God has supplied all that we need to be virtuous in Christ Jesus (2 Pet. 1:3). The promise found in 2 Peter 1:10–11 is the climax to the exhortations to put on the virtues in 2 Peter 1:5–8.

In Chapters 5–7, you will survey some of the virtues identified in God's Word. You will also encounter many vices, which contrast with these virtues. This survey is not exhaustive. But these virtues and vices play a major role in ethical decision-making. Thus, when you grapple with the issues in Chapters 9–13, these virtues and vices will play a major role in your analysis of what should be done in a situation.

VIRTUES	VICES
faith	unbelief
love	lust, hate
hope	despair
righteousness	ungodliness
goodness	corruption
prudence	rashness, cunning
diligence	sloth, laziness
faithfulness	disloyalty
courage	recklessness, cowardice
self-control	self-indulgence, addiction
temperance	addiction, asceticism
patience	strife
humility	pride
meekness	anger
gentleness	harshness
kindness	cruelty
compassion	indifference
gratitude	ingratitude
joy	despair
peace	worry
honesty	dishonesty, falsehood

UNDERSTANDING THE IMPORTANCE OF VIRTUE IN CHRISTIAN ETHICS

Why do virtues matter?

In Section 2.2 you learned about virtue ethics, and in Section 2.3 you learned about the problems with certain forms of the virtue-ethics approach. But the problems with that approach should not lead us to reject the important place for Christian virtue ethics. The problems that can arise in virtue ethics are removed when the virtues are properly defined, described, and applied by moral norms found in the Bible and in the design of God's creation. The problems are removed when the source of virtue is the transforming work of the gospel (Christ in us).

GRAPPLING WITH ETHICAL ISSUES

Can Evil People Do Good Things?

Would it surprise you if you were told that Adolf Hitler had a great affection for his dogs? How could such a cold-hearted individual warm-heartedly and cheerfully love anything?

On the other hand, can good people do evil things? Would it surprise you if you were told that the man after God's own heart committed adultery—and murder to cover up that adultery? How could a person with such a passion to love God fall into such gross sin?

If a very bad person can do good things and a very good person can do bad things, then does virtuous character matter?

Ethicist Ken Magnuson highlights the importance of virtue in ethics by emphasizing that this approach to ethics

> deals better with the majority of ethical choices in part because such everyday situations are more common than quandaries, and require virtues that direct the will to do what we ought to do, rather than intellectual problem-solving skills that settle moral dilemmas. . . . As we learn what to do in everyday situations, we develop virtue and character, along with wisdom, that helps to prepare us even for moral quandaries.[5]

Therefore, the study of ethics should not be reduced to hard-to-solve ethical difficulties. The study of ethics should relate to basic growth in Christlikeness or sanctification. We will turn our attention to this in the next section. This focus is a much-needed corrective regarding a much-neglected piece of ethics. The study of ethics has most often focused on what people *do*, especially in difficult scenarios where the right choice is not obvious. But most of life relates to moral decision-making in everyday-living scenarios. These scenarios are the focus of the Wisdom Books (especially the book of Proverbs). The Bible makes a concerted effort to connect what we *do* to who we *are* inwardly (our character). The important place for virtue in Christian ethics is this: God's goal is not merely for people to do the right things. God's goal is for people to be the right kind of people.

Christians do need to focus on being the right kind of people so that what they do flows out of who they are. Christians do need to cultivate virtues. Some ethical difficulties are indeed very easy to resolve once a person becomes virtuous and thus sees the situation with clarity. However, virtue in a truly biblical ethic will contrast greatly with the notion and application of "virtue" in non-Christian (or pseudo*-Christian) ethics. That's why it is so important to place one's understanding and application of virtue in the context of the gospel, in the context of the redemptive storyline of Scripture.

> [A Christian virtue ethic] provides a window into the soul. JOHN FRAME[6]

Thinking It Through 4.1

1. Define *virtue*.
2. Define *vice*.
3. Identify one virtue and the counterpart vice(s).
4. Why is the Old Testament still valuable to the study of ethics?
5. Why does virtue matter in Christian ethics?

4.2 Christlikeness and Counterfeits

In the last section we asked, What is virtue? How should it be defined or understood? Why is it important to Christian ethics? In this section we ask, Why should a person want to be virtuous? Where can a person turn for power to be virtuous? How can a person take the necessary steps to become virtuous?

Have you ever been trying to accomplish something only to find yourself failing over and over again? You just couldn't figure out the key to success. Then perhaps someone came alongside and pointed out that you would never succeed until you changed one key ingredient. When that person revealed the key ingredient that was missing, everything clicked.

How important is Christ to growing in virtue? He is the key ingredient. Christ is at the center of it all—not as a magic potion or formula to gain power. A life that is

pseudo: false, counterfeit, pretended, spurious

truly wrapped up in Him, relying on Him, and guided by Him can be transformed little by little into more and more virtuousness—Christlikeness (2 Cor. 3:18).

You can be filled with hope and confidence that you can grow in virtue when Christ is at the center of your efforts (rather than trying to grow through self-effort). You can know that calls to virtuous living are on track when those exhortations are Christ-centered and gospel-driven. Our growth in virtue comes from focusing on Christ (aim), drawing from the wellspring that is in Christ (source), and depending on the gracious work of the Holy Spirit to grow us in Christ (means).

SEEKING TO BE VIRTUOUS: CHRISTLIKENESS (THE AIM)

Perhaps you've had the opportunity to learn about target shooting—whether at a camp, from a family member, or from a certified instructor. If so, one of the first and fundamental lessons you learned (after range safety) was how to take aim. Even a slight misadjustment, breathing at the wrong time, or the way you hold your equipment can ruin your aim. Taking aim requires careful concentration, avoiding all other distractions. But above all, you should make sure all that effort is aimed at the right target in the first place!

Why should a person want to be virtuous? Is that person aiming at the right target? Many people seek to be virtuous (or at least to be seen by others as virtuous). But far too many seek to do so for the wrong reasons. They're aiming to achieve something other than what they should. Does the motive or the goal matter as long as a person does the right thing?

The Bible has a lot to say about the inward heart motivations for why we do what we do (1 Sam. 16:7; Ps. 44:21; Prov. 4:23). Are people aiming at the right target when they go through the motions of empty religious ritual (Isa. 1:10–18)? What do they think they're accomplishing? The problem of aiming to look good on the outside comes to a head in the Gospels. Jesus repeatedly confronted the religious leaders' hypocrisy (Matt. 6:1–8, 16–18; 15:8–20; 23:3–7, 23–27). They weren't aiming to love God and others; they wanted power and prestige.

The Bible warns against being deceived by those who flatter with their seemingly virtuous words and actions but whose hearts are wicked (Prov. 23:6–8). Lots of people say they desire to be virtuous, but few people arrive at the right destination. Their goal, purposes, motives, desires, and focus are misdirected. They are seeking to be righteous in the eyes of others (leading to moralism). Or maybe they are seeking to be culturally accepted, conformed to the spirit of the age; in our age, that often means heeding the call to "just be who you are" (leading to lawless "authenticity"). Externally living up to ideals (being a moralist) and redefining vice as virtue (being an authentic lawless person) both aim at fulfilling a person's (or society's) idolatry, and thus the aim turns out to be self-serving.

In contrast, the Christian aims to be like Christ (Rom. 8:29; 2 Cor. 3:18) to the glory of God (1 Cor. 10:31). Christians live to please God (Eph. 4:1; Col. 1:10) and to love others (1 John 4:7–8). God's goal for Christians is to restore the image of God by renewing them in the image of Christ (Col. 3:10). Christians should be motivated to act ethically because their desire to glorify God conforms them to His image, encouraging them to obey His law and advance His kingdom. This is the life they believe will truly flourish (Ps. 1:1–6). Aiming for something other than Christlikeness will result in being off target for becoming a truly virtuous person. Becoming virtuous cannot truly happen apart from being conformed to the likeness of Christ.

How can I become a virtuous person?

ENABLED TO BE VIRTUOUS: CHRIST (THE SOURCE)

Have you ever heard the retort, "Consider the source"? Maybe you were repeating some claim or opinion that you had heard. Then your friend asked you, "Who told you that?" When you revealed where you had gotten your information, your friend responded, "Consider the source." Your friend was implying that you got bogus information from a poor source.

Where can people turn to enable themselves to be virtuous? The Old Testament law demonstrated that people needed to be changed from the inside out because they had no ability within themselves to keep the law, to be virtuous (Deut. 30:6; Acts 15:10; Gal. 3:21–22). The New Covenant provides for this needed inward heart change (Jer. 31:31–34). Only in a believer's new life in Jesus can this heart transformation occur (John 3:3). The source for virtue comes from Christ in us (Gal. 2:20). Lots of people claim to have discovered the secret to success or to spirituality, but few of them are drawing from the wellspring of living water offered by Christ (John 4:10–14). The basis of their morality is something other than Christ.

The Christian relies on his or her union with Christ (1 Cor. 12:13). At salvation, the believer is united to Christ and regenerated by the Holy Spirit, transforming his or her inward character (2 Cor. 5:17). Regeneration fundamentally changes the orientation of the believer, releasing the believer from slavery to sin (Rom. 6:1–23). Regeneration and the Spirit's indwelling provide the Holy Spirit's empowerment to overcome sin rather than remain enslaved to its pull. If you have been born again, the source of virtue, righteousness, and godliness is Christ living in you (Gal. 2:20). And if He lives in you, the evidence will work itself out in how you live (Phil. 2:12–13; Eph. 2:10).

A person cannot only have a desire to be like Christ (the aim); he or she must be connected to Christ (the source) to make that desire a reality. Developing Christlike virtue flows from union with Christ (John 15:1–14). There is no other way to properly develop virtue than to be connected to Christ by regeneration and saving faith.

> In . . . **Pilgrim's Progress**, *John Bunyan did a masterful job of portraying our ongoing reliance on Christ's ministry for the maintenance of the work of grace in our soul.*
> ANDREW DAVIS[7]

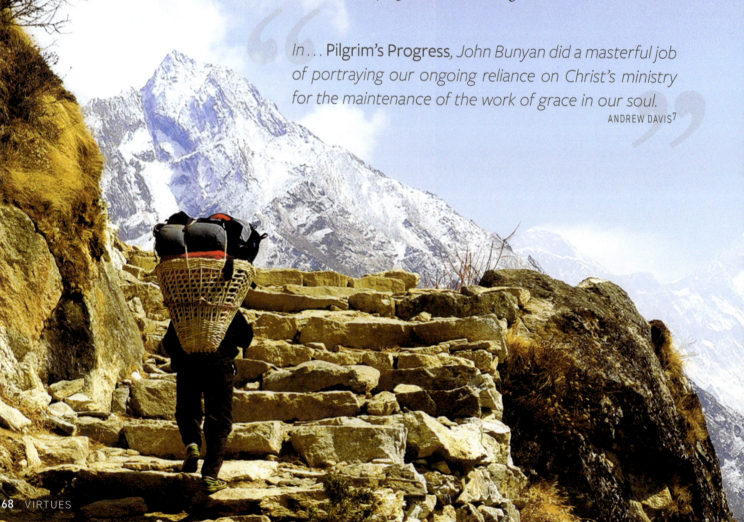

BECOMING VIRTUOUS: THE SPIRIT'S WORK (THE MEANS)

Have you traveled around the country or even internationally? Getting from point A to point B could happen in any number of ways—different modes of transportation and different routes. It doesn't matter how you get to some places as long as you reach your destination. But some places require a specific route. Sherpas guide mountain climbers because they know the path to take.

Growing in virtue requires one definite means to get to that end. Sure, different people will be in different situations, have various trials, and have varying stories of how God has worked in their lives. But ultimately, all believers share in common the one and only means of growing in virtue through those various circumstances: the work of the Holy Spirit in their lives (Rom. 8:2–5, 13). In fact, living virtuously is one and the same as displaying the fruit that comes from the Spirit (Gal. 5:22–23).

How can a person take the necessary steps to become virtuous? There's no formulaic shortcut; there's no earning brownie points with God by going through ritualistic motions. Rather, Christians live out a loving relationship with God by carefully discerning what is pleasing to the Lord (Eph. 5:1–2, 10, 15). And Christians do this in the power and by the guidance of the Holy Spirit.

The work of the Holy Spirit is the instrument God uses in our lives to sanctify us. Even though we ourselves have an active role to play in yielding ourselves to be filled or controlled by the Spirit (Eph. 5:1, 18; see also Rom. 12:1–2; 2 Cor. 7:1; Phil. 2:12–13; 1 Thess. 4:3; Heb. 12:14), the Spirit plays the central role in empowering us so that Christ lives through us (Gal. 5:16–17, 25; see also Eph. 4:16–24). The Bible's descriptions of the Holy Spirit's role in sanctification are all-encompassing: the Holy Spirit leads the believer (Rom. 8:13–14, 26), imparts virtues (Gal. 5:22–23), bestows gifts (Rom. 12:6; 1 Cor. 12:4), prompts and guides to live by a new law— "the law of the Spirit of life in Christ Jesus" (Rom. 8:2; see also Rom. 8:4; Gal. 5:6; 6:2)—and renews the intellect and will (1 Cor. 2:10; 2 Cor. 5:17; 1 Thess. 5:23). Believers should be characterized by living and walking in the Spirit (Rom. 8:1, 4, 9–11; 1 Cor. 6:19; Gal. 4:6).

Christian growth (growing in virtue by the Spirit's work) takes place gradually and progressively through the habits of the spiritual disciplines: Bible reading, prayer, communion with the saints in the work of the church, and consistently battling against our still-present sin nature as well as the temptations all around us in the world. Indeed, the flesh, the Devil, and the world will always be with us until we are present with the Lord and glorified in heaven (Gal. 5:16–17; 1 Pet. 5:8; 1 John 2:15–17). And no Christian enters the kingdom of God by skipping suffering, which includes having to reckon with the unethical acts of others against them (Acts 14:22; 2 Thess. 1:4–5).

COUNTERFEITS OF VIRTUE: MORALISM AND AUTHENTICITY

The importance of the correct aim, source, and method is that they determine the true achievement of genuine virtue, keeping us on the path of growth in true holiness. This is well illustrated in John Bunyan's *Pilgrim's Progress*. The main character, Christian, soon finds out that Worldly Wiseman misdirected him to the Village of Morality. Evangelist has to redirect Christian to the Wicket Gate so that he will find true relief from his burden of sin at the foot of the cross. Later, Christian encounters Formalist and Hypocrisy, who are convinced they have a better path than the straight and narrow way up the Hill of Difficulty. Their "easier" routes lead to Danger and Destruction, where they wander lost in the woods and mountains. Only the straight and narrow path up the Hill of Difficulty can lead Christian to his eternal destiny with God.

People are always looking for an easy and happy way to both look good to others and enjoy their own idolatrous ends. Three of the most common ways to appear virtuous while remaining idolatrous are the pathways of legalism, moralism, and authenticity.

Christian climbing the Hill of Difficulty

Legalism

Legalism involves trying to earn a right standing with God (justification) through works. It can also refer to trying to earn a higher standing with God by the performance of works or rituals—as if going through external motions automatically brings about inward spirituality that would be acceptable to God. It minimizes or ignores horizontal relationships in the here and now to focus on vertical efforts to win God's favor. However, it tends toward pride and hypocrisy or guilt and hopelessness.

Moralism

Moralism involves trying to be a good, upstanding person through one's own good works. Although this is similar to legalism, it is more focused on social acceptability. The moralist is less concerned with right standing before God than with being approved as a good person by others. The focus is on the horizontal relationship with other people rather than the vertical relationship with God.

Moralism can sometimes be observed in a person who focuses on doing good works in the community: serving in soup kitchens, doing volunteer work in hospitals, raising awareness about human trafficking, funding projects in third-world countries for clean water, becoming a political activist to fight injustice—the list could go on. Moralism can sometimes also be observed in a person who dutifully attends church, prays piously, and puts money in the offering plate. If you were to observe this person, he or she might appear to be a very upright person (particularly when compared with many others in this world who live openly vile lives). But could you spot a moralistic person as a counterfeit? Could you spot the wrong aim, source, and means in your own attempts to be a virtuous person?

It's not as though Bible-believing Christians shouldn't participate in these kinds of works. But what's missing from the moralist's efforts? What is it about what the moralist does that makes his or her works misdirected, prioritized incorrectly, and insufficient? Is the moralist truly aiming at Christlikeness, drawing from the resources found in Christ, and being guided and transformed by the Holy Spirit? When outwardly good works are disconnected from the gospel, done for the wrong reasons, empowered by the wrong source, and misguided to achieve some self-serving purpose, then this is all self-righteousness, not virtue. Ultimately, the moralist is a hypocrite, because whether he or she realizes it or will admit it, he or she behaves "morally" for self-serving or merely horizontal purposes. Don't be a moralist; don't be a hypocrite.

Authenticity

In reaction to hypocrisy, **authenticity** has become very popular. You're told to be yourself, to be true to yourself, to be real, to be transparent, to follow your heart, to fulfill all your dreams. But the rage for authenticity is a counterfeit contrast to hypocrisy. Yes, Jesus called on the Pharisees not to be hypocrites. But His solution was far from calling on them to be themselves. He called on people to deny themselves (Matt. 16:24). His solution was far from calling on the Pharisees to become authentically or transparently sinful. Rather, He called on them to come to Him for genuine, inward transformation (Matt. 5:17–20).

Our natural desires are sinful because we are sinful beings by nature: our minds, wills, and emotions are driven by the fallen desires of our affections. To let go of any inhibitions in order to "be true to ourselves" would be the surest way to embrace what's most vile. Having to say no to our sinful desires, having to discipline ourselves to be obedient, has nothing to do with hypocrisy (unless such efforts focus on the wrong aim, draw from the wrong source, and make use of the wrong means). Hypocrisy would be pretending our obedience to Christ were entirely our own or pretending to be obedient while secretly finding a way to be disobedient (Acts 5:1–11). Working hard toward godliness is not the same as hypocritical lying (1 Tim. 4:7).

Jesus calls on us to have integrity. The difference between *authenticity* and *integrity* couldn't be greater. Instead of "just being ourselves," Jesus calls us to become, by God's grace, who we ought to be.

integrity = being who God wants me to be

authenticity = being "my true self"

CONCLUSION

Our culture redefines virtue as vice and vice as virtue. It also cancels or shames those who transgress its notions of virtue. In such times, nothing is needed more than our Creator's law and our Redeemer's gospel. Our Creator's law can restore moral sanity by showing us what actual virtue is. But that same law also exposes our own *lack* of true virtue. For such self-destructive rebels, the gospel provides the hope-giving forgiveness for the most unvirtuous, hypocritical people—truly good news. Wretches like you and me can be redeemed to live a life of integrity. Judah, the man who was ready to burn Tamar to death for prostitution when in fact he was the one who had gone to her for immoral relations (Gen. 38:24–26), later demonstrated profound virtue and a changed life when he was willing to sacrifice himself for Benjamin (Gen. 44:18–34). He, rather than his firstborn brother, was exalted by God and became the father of the kingly tribe from which the Davidic Messiah would come (Gen. 49:8–12).

Becoming a virtuous person is at the heart of Christian ethics. You can only realistically plan to live virtuously once you have been transformed by the power of the gospel and united to Christ. But your regeneration and conversion are the starting line, not the finish line. Planning to be a virtuous person begins by rightly understanding the virtues and how they relate to practical issues of life. By God's grace, the Holy Spirit will begin to sanctify you as you seek to grow through the spiritual disciplines and look to Him for wisdom in applying the Word of God to your circumstances. Plan to be in God's Word; to pray; to learn from your pastors, teachers, and other spiritual mentors in the church; and to engage in the fight against sin day in and day out.

As you study the virtues in the next three chapters and apply those virtues to ethical decision-making (in Unit 3 on ethical issues), remember the dangers of misdefining virtue, having inappropriate aims, relying on incorrect sources, and using wrong means for achieving virtue. These are common mistakes not only in non-Christian ethical systems but even among Christians, who are subject to missteps along the way as they seek to be virtuous.

Thinking It Through 4.2

1. Why should a Christian seek to be virtuous? (What's the correct aim?)
2. How is a person enabled to be virtuous? (What's the correct source?)
3. How can a person take the necessary steps to become virtuous? (What's the correct means?)
4. a. Identify three counterfeits of true virtue.
   b. Describe each counterfeit and explain what makes each a counterfeit.
   c. What is the end result of each counterfeit?
5. What is Jesus' solution to hypocrisy?
6. How can you plan to become virtuous?

Review

Terms to Remember

- virtue
- vice
- legalism
- moralism
- authenticity

Scripture Memory

2 Peter 1:3, 5–7

Understanding Ethics

1. Contrast the biblical concept of virtue to that of Greek culture.
2. Identify at least three virtues and the contrasting vices.
3. Why shouldn't the study of ethics be reduced to hard-to-solve ethical difficulties?
4. What three elements necessary for growing in true virtue can lead to virtue counterfeits when wrongly oriented?
5. How does the life of Judah illustrate the hope for forgiveness and true transformation offered in the gospel?

Practicing Ethical Decision-Making

6. Analyze the scenario below to determine where virtue could be subtly twisted into a vice.

   A college student works diligently to achieve a 4.0. He or she focuses all attention on studies and will not allow any other activity to interrupt those studies.

7. Analyze the scenario below to determine where virtue could be subtly twisted into a vice.

   Even though you know your sibling is sneaking out of the house at night, you cover for him or her because you believe in staying loyal to your closest sibling.

8. Analyze the scenario below to determine how a virtue could be wrongly accused of being a vice.

   A pastor confronts sinful, unethical practices in the culture. He calls on people to repent to receive God's forgiveness.

Analyzing and Evaluating Ethical Claims

9. How would you respond to the following claim? The greatest heroes in movies and literature are not the simplistically virtuous personalities. The greatest heroes are the complicated personalities who choose to do good despite having major flaws. This proves that inward character is far less important than some people make it out to be.
10. How would you respond to the following claim? Jesus was a great man who showed us how to be better people. We should follow his example by overturning unjust systems and doing good to the oppressed in society.

Creating My Own Position Statements on Ethics

11. Write a position statement on the aim, source, and means that you would like to be your own in pursuing virtue. Personalize it and make it more specifically applicable to your own life situation.
12. Write a biblically based position statement on the concept of being authentic.

Three Central Virtues

Why are faith, love, and hope the central virtues?

05

I CORINTHIANS 13:13

Developing Christlike virtues for the glory of God is an essential goal of Christian ethics. Each virtue is like a distinct thread in a multicolored garment that adorns believers with the enduring beauty of the gospel (1 Pet. 3:3–4). It's no accident that our culture's overemphasis on outward beauty coincides with a neglect of the New Testament virtues. When the true beauty of the inner person—with the virtues of faith, love, and hope—disappears from a culture, all that is left is a shallow fixation on outward appearance. Yet there is something exceedingly attractive about a genuinely faithful, loving, and hopeful Christian.

A survey of the New Testament reveals that faith, love, and hope are purposefully integrated, suggesting that this triad of virtues is foundational to all other biblical virtues. The earliest grouping of these three virtues appears in 1 Thessalonians, where the apostle Paul commended the believers for their work of *faith*, labor of *love*, and steadfastness of *hope* (1 Thess. 1:3).[1] A couple of observations about this passage are worth noting.

First, while all three virtues are distinct from one another, they're like a threefold cord that cannot be broken. Christian living in the present is bound by all three. It's inconceivable that a Christian could have faith without also possessing love and hope and vice versa. Second, an argument can be made that the New Testament's usual ordering of the virtues is significant. A Christian first comes to *faith*, then lives on the basis of *love* to God and neighbor, then perseveres through hardship and persecution by *hope* in what is to come.[2] This order will serve as the outline for our present study.

5.1 The Virtue of Faith

From a biblical standpoint, no act is truly ethical unless done from faith (Rom. 14:23; Heb. 11:6). Faith in God is a virtue because it is fitting for dependent creatures to trust their Creator. The word *fitting* refers to something that functions properly. For example, the eye is made for seeing, the ear for hearing, and the nose for smelling. Our senses were fitted to relate to the outside world. Likewise, our human constitution was originally fitted for faith in God. Before sin entered the world, it was natural for human beings to rely on God for their every need. God delights in providing for His believing children as their heavenly Father (Matt. 6:8; Luke 12:32). Faith magnifies God's roles as the Creator and Provider, and this is what makes faith virtuous. We can see this more clearly by contrasting faith with unbelief.

Unbelief in God, His Word, and His promises is a vice because of what it says about God. It says that God is untrustworthy, which is a lie against His holy character. It says that God's Word is unclear and unreliable, which is an insult to His gracious self-revelation. And it says that God's promises are uncertain, which is a slight against His perfect faithfulness. We could multiply the examples, but the important thing to note is how faith and unbelief find their meaning, not in abstraction from God, but in direct relation to God and His revelation.

THE NATURE OF FAITH

One Protestant reformer said, "We shall possess a right definition of **faith** if we call it a firm and certain knowledge of God's benevolence toward us, founded upon the truth of the freely given promise in Christ, both revealed to our minds and sealed upon our hearts through the Holy Spirit."[3] As this definition indicates, biblical faith consists of three inseparable components—knowledge, assent, and confidence. Faith knows something of the content of God's Word (knowledge), agrees that these things are true (assent), and exercises personal reliance on God for the fulfillment of all His promises (confidence).

Faith Includes Knowledge

How can one believe without first knowing what he or she is supposed to believe (Rom. 10:14)? Biblical knowledge is necessary if faith is to be rooted in reality. Those who set faith in opposition to knowledge are equating faith with fantasy, a kind of unfounded wish. But there's no virtue in wishful thinking. Instead, God is honored when we trust Him because we know, based on Scripture, "that he is, and that he is a rewarder of them that diligently seek him" (Heb. 11:6).

Faith Includes Assent

The difference between knowledge and assent is one of agreement. Many unbelievers know the content of Scripture; they simply don't believe it to be true. They know, for example, that the Bible teaches that Christ was crucified and raised from the dead, but they don't agree that Scripture gives an accurate historical account of these things. Faith, on the other hand, accepts the self-authenticating* evidence of Scripture (Heb. 11:1). Faith rightly perceives the divine authorship of Scripture and therefore assents to the truth of what it teaches.

Faith Includes Confidence

Knowledge and assent by themselves, however, are insufficient to constitute a living faith. Even the demons know and assent to the truth of Scripture (James 2:19). They understand the truth about God and His mighty acts in history. After all, they knew that Jesus was the Holy One of God who came to destroy them (Matt. 8:29; Luke 4:34).

Therefore, in order for faith to be genuine, it must include the element of confidence—a heartfelt commitment by which we rest in Christ as a result of the Holy Spirit opening our eyes to see the truth and to sense the glory of it so that our minds are held captive by it. Confidence is faith's capstone to knowledge and assent because it heartily approves of what it knows to be true about God, His Word, and His promises.

If you have faith, you have infinitely more than he who has all the world.

CHARLES SPURGEON[4]

self-authenticating: demonstrating its own truthfulness

THE OBJECT OF FAITH

Where we place our trust is of great ethical significance. As the psalmist wrote, "Some trust in chariots, and some in horses: but we will remember the name of the Lᴏʀᴅ our God" (Ps. 20:7). Chariots and horses were tangible symbols of technological and military strength in the ancient world, and Israel was frequently tempted to trust in these things for its protection. As Isaiah wrote, "Woe to them that . . . trust in chariots, because they are many; and in horsemen, because they are very strong; but they look not unto the Holy One of Israel, neither seek the Lᴏʀᴅ!" (Isa. 31:1). Whether the technology is ancient or modern, the choice remains the same for every generation: Will we trust in our own ingenuity and strength, or will we trust in the Lord?

Trusting God and His Word

Biblical faith has God as its object; it rests on Christ and no other (Rom. 5:1–2; 1 Cor. 2:5). Faith is nothing if it is not directed toward the right person. In the absence of God, secular society has normalized the notion of self-confidence. To have confidence means to firmly trust, or to fully rely upon. Therefore, we should question the wisdom of frail and dependent creatures investing confidence in themselves. This is like telling people to be their own shelter in the midst of a storm. While people may legitimately have a limited confidence in their abilities or in the abilities of others, absolute faith is only valid if the object of faith is self-sufficient and great enough to bear the weight of the world. And since God alone fits this description, He alone is worthy of our complete and unreserved confidence.

To clarify, we cannot separate faith in God from faith in His Word (Rom. 10:17). Building our faith upon the proper authority of Scripture is necessary for faith to be virtuous because it is in the Bible that we learn the things to believe—things that are true and trustworthy and things that feed and fuel our faith (Rom. 1:16–17). Remove the Bible from the Christian faith, and the Christian faith ceases to exist—and with it the virtue of faith itself. Trusting the Bible means receiving it with all the authority that comes from God Himself and then living in its truth and power.

What role does faith play in living ethically?

Taking Hold of God's Promises

As faith leans in to what the Bible says, it is listening to the very voice of God. One way God speaks to us in Scripture is through His promises. A divine promise is an assurance from God that He will act to accomplish His good purposes for those who are in Christ. The promises of God range from supplying our daily needs to completing our salvation when Christ returns (Matt. 6:8, 33; Phil. 1:6). Whether the need is for help in times of distress, strength to act virtuously, or grace to persevere in the Christian life, God supplies the believer's every need. The guarantee that He will do this is found in the "exceeding great and precious promises" of Scripture (2 Pet. 1:4).

But faith must take hold of these promises. It does a person no good to leave the promises dangling in the air. When a particular need arises, faith goes into action by embracing one of God's promises. Trusting in the promises of God is a firm foundation for ethical behavior in the face of present temptations and trials. For example, you may be tempted to retaliate in anger when treated unjustly. Resisting this temptation is possible as you trust God to avenge all wrongs (Rom. 12:19). God has promised to do this. If you trust Him, your ethical response to a personal injustice will not involve taking vengeance into your hands.

THE POWER OF WALKING BY FAITH

In the book of Hebrews, there's an entire catalog of believers who are commended for their faith (Heb. 11). What stands out about them is that their faith in God was not static but active and powerful; it made a practical difference in their lives under very difficult and trying circumstances. They looked beyond their immediate circumstances to God's greater kingdom purposes, trusting that God was with them by working providentially behind the scenes (see Heb. 10:32–39). In other words, they walked by faith in the unseen rather than fixing their eyes on what is seen (2 Cor. 4:18; 5:7).

Christian ethics depends on a clear teleological focus. As a reminder, *teleological* refers to the end goal behind our choices. But we cannot see the end goal except with the eyes of faith. Therefore, it is vital that we cultivate our faith so that we can make ethical choices consistent with a biblical teleology.

Forward-Looking Faith

Faith possesses power largely in its ability to look forward to the unseen future, a future defined by the trajectory of redemptive history, which culminates in the triumphant return of Christ. Whenever Christians face trouble and distress, or even comfort and pleasure, it is tempting to see the present, visible world as all of reality. But faith understands there's an unseen reality with which we must reckon. Faith knows of the coming judgment and the coming rewards, and it lives life in light of those realities.

When God called Abraham to leave his home country for a land that God had promised, Abraham obeyed in faith even though he didn't know where he was going (Heb. 11:8–9). When Abraham's wife, Sarah, was beyond the age to conceive a child, she trusted God to fulfill His promise for a child (Heb. 11:11). They and their descendants lived as exiles in the world, looking forward to that better country God had prepared for them (Heb. 11:13–16). Their forward-looking faith enabled them to act in their present circumstances based on what God would do for them in the future.

This highlights an important lesson about the relationship between faith and ethics. The degree to which a believer is confident God will act exactly as He has promised is the degree to which a believer will base his or her decisions on the promises of God rather than on his or her limited perception.

Acting ethically when pushed to one's limit requires a forward-looking faith. You may find yourself confronted with a situation that is extremely difficult to handle. Faith is often tested not merely by the severity of a trial but also by its duration. Part of you may look for an easy way out, even one that is sinful. But as you look forward to the day when God will deliver you from adversity, you will gain strength to persist in righteousness instead.

Dependent Faith

The most powerful dynamic of faith is the settled conviction that God loves His believing children in Jesus Christ (Rom. 5:8; 8:35; Eph. 1:3–5). As Christians grow in the certainty of the Father's love and care for them, they grow in their dependence upon Him. They readily admit to being little children before an all-powerful and all-wise Father, and they make regular appeals to Him for His enabling grace so as to respond in every situation with faithfulness to Him (Matt. 21:22; Heb. 4:16).

A dependent faith also means being convinced that God's ways are better than our own and that to be "rich toward God" (Luke 12:21) is better than to be rich in this world (Isa. 55:8–9; Prov. 15:16; Matt. 6:19–21). This was precisely the faith-ethic at work in Moses' decision to leave Pharaoh's palace, for he would "rather . . . suffer affliction with the people of God, than . . . enjoy the pleasures of sin for a season" (Heb. 11:25). Faith enabled Moses to make a difficult but rewarding choice. He looked beyond the passing treasures of Egypt to the greater wealth of Christ (Heb. 11:26).

To an unbelieving world, Moses' decision looks foolish. But to the eyes of faith, his decision makes perfect sense. God's love and care for Moses surpassed anything that Egypt could offer, and this belief influenced his ethical choices in practical ways. In a similar way, the biblical virtue of faith can influence our ethical choices as we rest assured of God's unfailing love in Christ.

Thinking It Through 5.1

1. How is faith defined?
2. What are the three essential elements of faith, and what is the significance of each?
3. What does it mean for God to be the object of faith, and why is faith in His Word essential to that?
4. How do God's promises relate to faith and ethical behavior?
5. How does walking by faith and not by sight motivate virtuous living?
6. Why is a phrase such as "Believe in yourself" or "Have faith in yourself" bad advice?

5.2 The Virtue of Love

Love has a unique role among the central virtues. Whereas faith and hope are temporary (for these virtues will cease when the future glory becomes reality), the virtue of love never ends; it continues throughout eternity. This explains why Scripture speaks of love as the greatest virtue (1 Cor. 13:13).

In thinking carefully about the virtue of love, we need to understand that in a fallen world there's no virtue in the word *love* itself. Whether or not our love is a virtue depends on the object of our love. There's no virtue in loving what is evil. One of the most appalling features of fallen human nature is misdirected love, and that's all the more reason for us to rely on God's Word to get our bearings on what true love is. Our capacity for self-deception on this issue is far too great to rely on our feelings and the sentimental lyrics of popular love songs.

The virtue we're seeking to cultivate is not as obvious as people assume. What is love? Is it an emotion? An action? A commitment? All the above? Where does true love originate? What is the standard of love? What does it mean to love God and to love one's neighbor? Are we to love every person in the world equally? Is there a sense in which love and hate can be compatible under certain circumstances? These and many more questions indicate that love is not as simple as people suppose.

CONTRASTING VIEWS OF LOVE

There's a direct connection between the things we love and our ethical choices. If our love is misdirected, then our choices will be also. Erroneous conceptions of love can easily cloud our judgment and lead us to make choices that we mistakenly believe are moral, when in reality they are immoral. Love is commonly misdirected as self-love and as sentimental love. These are in contrast to the spiritual love of biblical Christianity.

Self-Love

Although there's a biblically proper way to think of self-love, the dominant view today involves a self-love that is inward-focused and self-absorbed. The song "Greatest Love of All" (most famously sung by Whitney Houston) is an example of self-love gone horribly wrong:

I found the greatest love of all inside of me.
The greatest love of all is easy to achieve.
Learning to love yourself is the greatest
    love of all.[5]

There are several problems with this line of thinking. First, the idea that people should learn to love themselves assumes that they don't already, when in fact all people fervently love themselves. Second, love is not discovered by a person looking inward. It's a sad irony of our time that the more people turn within to find love the more lonely and unloved they feel. Third, this kind of love is not proper self-love but self-absorbed love. Self-absorbed love is a vice because it never goes any higher than one's private self-interest, never makes any sacrifices for the good of others, and paradoxically never considers its own best interest in an eternal sense. But the most problematic aspect of this thinking is that it elevates self-love above God's love, which is the greatest love of all.

Sentimental Love

Feelings of love are not a reliable measure of whether the love being expressed is appropriate, and yet a great many people make choices based on a certain kind of sentimental love. This is most obvious in the way our culture approaches romantic relationships, but it can manifest itself in any relationship.

The problem with sentimental love is not the fact that emotions are involved; biblical love includes godly emotions. The problem is in making private emotions rather than God's law the standard for what love looks like. Situation ethics, for example, teaches people to do the loving thing while rejecting biblical norms, as if people could somehow intuit on their own what the loving thing is. Unfortunately, many people violate God's law in their relationships, especially romantic relationships, under the guise of love. Despite the trail of misery and broken relationships in our culture, people continue to rely on their fleeting sinful passions, convinced that a relationship must be right if their hearts tell them it is right.

Spiritual Love

We can think of Christian love as spiritual love, which is to be distinguished from natural love. There is a natural affection that family members and friends have for one another, and this kind of love exists among non-Christians as well as Christians. It is called natural love because it springs from natural causes, such as when we love a friend because of his or her kindness toward us. Spiritual affection, however, does not arise from natural causes; it is the fruit of the Holy Spirit (Gal. 5:22). It is spiritual because it is a love that flows from God and thereby enables us to love as He loves (1 John 4:10, 19). To be clear, natural love and spiritual love are not in opposition. Christians should have both. Unbelievers may or may not have natural love, but apart from God's grace they will certainly lack spiritual love.

But there's another sense in which Christian love is spiritual. As Augustine wrote, "I define '**love**' as any movement of the soul to enjoy God for God's own sake, and to enjoy one's self and one's neighbor for God's sake."[6] This alone makes love a true virtue for two reasons: it prioritizes love for God above all else, and it gains its strength to love others from loving God.

Spiritual love for God sets self-love in its proper context, such as when a believer approaches God for the pleasure of His presence and fellowship. And with respect to loving people, those who are most loving are those believers who seek their "*own* happiness in doing good to others."[7] Far from being a non-emotional, disinterested act, true biblical love regards the beloved with such delight that it is even willing to suffer for the good of the beloved. When we love like this, we can say that our love is Godlike (1 John 3:16).

unbeliever   believer

Spiritual love amplifies natural love.

Christian love will never be found except in a heart prepared by the Holy Spirit.

J. C. RYLE[8]

THE CASE FOR CHRISTIAN LOVE

Christian love begins with God because "God is love" (1 John 4:16). Apart from Him, there would be no such thing as love. The greatest demonstration of God's love is the gift of His Son for the salvation of sinners (Rom. 5:8; 1 John 4:10). Loving as God loves is one of the evidences that a person has been born into God's family (1 John 4:7). "We love him, because he first loved us" (1 John 4:19). Similarly, we could say that we love others because God first loved us (1 John 4:11).

The two Great Commandments—love God and love others—speak to the moral obligation upon us to love (Matt. 22:37–39; Mark 12:29–31). The heart, mind, and body are under this obligation, and therefore we cannot limit love to one aspect of our humanity, as if love were only emotional or rational or volitional. As we'll see, Scripture takes a comprehensive view of love.

A Disposition of the Heart

In overreacting to the sentimental love of the world, some Christians have discounted the emotions as an essential part of love. In addition, they reason that a moral obligation cannot extend to the emotions because people cannot control how they feel. "All that matters is doing the right thing," they say. A mother may not feel like sacrificing for the good of her children, but because it's the right thing to do, she makes sacrifices anyway. But is it really the case that the mother's emotional bond with her children plays no role in her sacrifice? She may not feel good about the sacrifice *per se*, but she could feel an affection for her children that would certainly motivate her sacrifice.

If we reduced love merely to a sacrificial action, as some would have it, we would actually contradict Scripture: "Though I bestow all my goods to feed the poor, and though I give my body to be burned, and have not [love], it profiteth me nothing" (1 Cor. 13:3). The logic of this passage is unavoidable; not all sacrificial actions flow from love. The apostle Paul was not making a case for non-sacrificial love; he was making a case for having the right disposition toward the objects of our love. As he wrote to the Thessalonian believers, "So being affectionately desirous of you, we were willing to have imparted unto you . . . our own souls, because ye were dear unto us" (1 Thess. 2:8). This is the disposition of a loving heart.

A Mindful Consideration

Doing good to others presupposes that we know what constitutes the good, and therefore love will be well-informed as to how Scripture defines the good. According to the prophet Micah, God has shown us "what is good," which is "to do justly, and to love mercy, and to walk humbly with [our] God" (Micah 6:8). Therefore, one aspect of love is a mindful consideration of how best to relate to people in diverse situations. This is not as easy as people think. Doing justice and showing mercy take more than good intentions; they also take biblical wisdom and discernment.

For example, how we love victims of injustice will look different from how we love the perpetrators of injustice. Biblical love "rejoiceth not in iniquity, but rejoiceth in the truth" (1 Cor. 13:6). Therefore, it is loving to validate the experience of genuine victims and then to protect them from further abuse. And it is loving to hold perpetrators accountable for their actions and then to call them to repentance. What is good for one is not appropriate for the other. And biblical love understands how to make these important distinctions.

A Joyful Action

Saying "I love you" to the people we love is perfectly normal. However, we understand that sometimes our actions do not match our words. The apostle John wrote, "Let us not love in word, neither in tongue; but in deed and in truth" (1 John 3:18). While John was not prohibiting readers from telling people of their love, he was stressing that actions speak louder than words and that we do well to express genuine love by deeds that meet real needs.

James made the same observation: "If a brother or sister be naked, and destitute of daily food, and one of you say unto them, Depart in peace, be ye warmed and filled," all the while refusing to help them, such words are of no value (James 2:15–16). When the apostle Paul sought to inspire the Corinthian church in their love, he held up the Macedonian believers as an example for them. When the Macedonians gave, "the abundance of their joy and their deep poverty" overflowed in a wealth of generosity (2 Cor. 8:2). Even if we are poor, we should be joyfully eager to support those in need because that's what real love does.

RIGHTLY ORDERED LOVES

Cheerfully giving to those in need when you're in poverty is not natural. It's a strange ethical choice—that is, until we understand the idea of *rightly ordered loves* (remember the definition of virtue from previous chapters). A man who loves money more than God and more than people has wrongly ordered loves. But so does the man who loves people more than he loves God; his loves are also out of order. Therefore, rightly ordered loves are necessary if we are to make right ethical choices.

Loving God above All

The reason the Macedonian believers sacrificed financially for the support of other Christians was because the grace of God was powerfully at work in them (2 Cor. 8:1). Grace empowers believers to love God above all—above their possessions, their lives in this world, and their closest family members. The fact that Jesus calls the command to love God "the first and great commandment" (Matt. 22:38) is a strong argument for prioritizing love for God. Then there is the direct statement from Jesus that we are to prioritize love for Him above "father or mother . . . and . . . son or daughter" (Matt. 10:37).

And yet, when we prioritize love for God, the result is not less love for people but more love for them. Scripture teaches this explicitly. "By this we know that we love the children of God, when we love God, and keep his commandments" (1 John 5:2). It's impossible to truly love people with a biblical ethic without loving God above people.

The reasons for this are many, but here are a few to consider. First, by loving God above all, we do the greatest good for people, which is to set before them the worth and beauty of God for their enjoyment. The psalmist concurs, proclaiming, "My soul shall make her boast in the LORD: the humble shall hear thereof, and be glad" (Ps. 34:2). Second, by loving God above all, we are more scrupulous in keeping His commandments, including the commandments to love our neighbors and our enemies in all the ways God requires. Loving people can be hard, but loving God means having Him with us in the hard places. Third, by loving God above all, we relinquish all we have to His disposal. None are more generous to others than those who are convinced that God is their provider and their great reward. Fourth, by loving God above all, we lean more heavily on the Spirit's leading through the Scriptures and thereby possess the wisdom and grace necessary to do what is best for others. In each of these ways, our love for God releases an aroma of Christ which results in the good of others as they observe and experience His loving character reflected in us.

Loving People Rightly

Having considered how our love for God motivates ethical choices, we now turn our attention to how our love for people motivates our ethical choices. Our focus here is on what it means to love our neighbor as ourselves (Matt. 22:39). Whom we love and how we love are the two main issues before us.

There's a sense in which our love should be broad enough to include every human being, while at the same time we recognize the practical limits of our resources. We are to have a general goodwill toward humanity, desiring what is best for all people in all places. This sets us up to show love to the people within our sphere of influence regardless of who they are. Love shows no partiality based on ethnicity or socioeconomic status (Acts 10:34–43; James 2:1–13). At the same time, Scripture recognizes that our affections for family and friends will be stronger than they are for other people and that our duty to them takes priority (1 Tim. 5:8; Exod. 20:12; Eph. 6:1–4). This is not an absolute rule because there are occasions when our Christian ties take priority over our family ties (Luke 8:21; Gal. 6:10). The main point is that God has placed within our lives specific people for us to serve in real time and in real situations, albeit in various ways and to differing degrees depending on the circumstances.

How do the things I love influence my choices?

natural love

natural love expanded

Rightly ordered spiritual love increases our potential for loving others like a double concave lens refracts light and spreads it over a larger area.

The one constant in our love for people is that we have their best interests in mind, loving them as we love ourselves. We should treat others the way we want to be treated (Matt. 7:12). This includes actively performing deeds that will benefit them and refraining from deeds that would harm them.

With regard to harm, love for neighbor includes hating that which harms them. We must guard against the false dichotomy the world establishes between real love and an appropriate hate. The more we love people the more we will hate anything that ultimately threatens them, including the life-destroying decisions they may make. While people may struggle with the idea of a good hatred, everyone instinctively recognizes that indifference toward evil in the world is unloving. One of the most urgent ethical issues of our day is the protection of vulnerable people, which can be costly to those who stand up for them. But that's what biblical love does. It lays down its life for the good of others (John 15:13).

There are many practical ways to love others. We should not underestimate the power of rejoicing with those who rejoice (Rom. 12:15). For example, suppose a friend receives a new car from his parents, and he shares the good news with you. What is the loving response? Do you inwardly begrudge his new car because you're driving an old car or no car at all? Or do you put aside envy and share in your friend's blessing (1 Cor. 13:4)? The latter response is an ethical expression of Christian love because it flows from a genuine delight in your friend.

Christian love also recognizes and seeks to meet the greatest need that people have, which is spiritual and eternal in nature. As important as it is to feed a hungry person, it is infinitely more important to feed a spiritually hungry person with the Bread who supplies eternal life (John 6:35). We can and should do both. The church, however, has regularly faced challenges regarding its primary mission. As the reality of eternity recedes into the background of society and many temporal needs press upon us with immediate urgency, the church must remember that the gospel of Jesus Christ is what our neighbors need most urgently. The moment we lose sight of this is the moment we lose the Christian virtue of love.

Thinking It Through 5.2

1. How does an unbiblical self-love differ from Christian love?
2. What is the biblical defense for understanding love as a disposition of the heart?
3. What is the biblical defense for understanding love as a joyful action?
4. How does prioritizing love for God motivate ethical choices?
5. How does love for others manifest itself in our ethical choices?

5.3 The Virtue of Hope

How can I be joyful when life is so difficult?

It's encouraging to know that God is actively at work on behalf of those who trust Him. Although God hasn't promised His people an easy life, He has promised that "all things work together for good to them that love God, to them who are the called according to his purpose" (Rom. 8:28). The "all things" includes even the bad things we experience. Everything from daily frustrations to the deepest hurts of life are woven into the fabric of God's redemptive purpose. Knowing this sustains the joy of many Christians in their darkest valleys.

The biblical view is realistic about the sorrows that accompany life. At the same time, it points forward to a day when God will wipe away every tear and restore this broken world (Rev. 21:4). For this reason Christians are able to grieve, not "as others which have no hope" (1 Thess. 4:13), but as those who eagerly anticipate the coming of the Lord (1 Thess. 4:14–18).

The virtue of Christian hope, therefore, reaches back to the past where God has acted redemptively in human history, ensuring that the ravages of sin and death are "swallowed up in [the] victory" of Christ (1 Cor. 15:54). It also reaches forward to the wrapping up of redemptive history when all of God's promises meet their final eschatological goal. Where true Christian hope exists, we find a tenacity among believers to move forward in God's ways even as they patiently wait for the completion of God's work.[9]

THE SOURCE OF CHRISTIAN HOPE

Hope in the Lord rather than in our circumstances is what fuels our joy, and it is joy in the Lord that enables us to abound in hope. The reciprocal relationship between hope and joy is made explicit in Scripture: "Now the God of *hope* fill you with all *joy* and peace in believing, that ye may abound in *hope*, through the power of the Holy Ghost" (Rom. 15:13, emphasis added).

The fact that God is identified as "the God of hope" is a clear indication that He is the source of our hope. The verse above amplifies this point with the additional comment that God's Spirit empowers our hope. The Spirit is the guarantee of our promised inheritance until we acquire possession of it (Eph. 1:14).

Faith is also indispensable for keeping hope alive. Scripture indicates that it is "in believing" that we can "abound in hope" (Rom. 15:13). Only believers can have the true virtue of hope because God's promises of redemption are only given to believers (1 Pet. 1:3; Gal. 5:5).[10]

Hope Defined

Christian **hope** may be defined as "the expectation of the things that faith has believed to be truly promised by God."[11] Oliver O'Donovan describes hope this way: "When we hope, we begin from the problematic character of the present, from its ambiguity and unsatisfying incompleteness, and turn gratefully to the future judgment of God which perfects the imperfections of the present and promises completion."[12] The validity of hope is not based on what a person wishes *might* happen but on the certainty of what God promises *will* happen.

The impact of hopelessness on people's ethical choices can be seen all around us. How many people turn to substance abuse to escape feelings of hopelessness? How many people resort to crime and justify it because they see no other hope to improve their lives? How many marriages end in divorce because of hopelessness? How many people end their own lives in suicide because of hopelessness? And how many people despair from a guilty conscience for lack of hope in the Redeemer? These ethical failures are undeniably connected to the absence of the virtue of hope.

Distinguishing Hope from Faith

The virtue of hope bears a special relationship to the virtue of faith. Though they're similar, we can distinguish the two. As faith lays hold of the promises of God, hope lives in anticipation of their fulfillment. Believers may have to wait many years before seeing the fulfillment of the promises, but hope patiently endures because it understands that God's timing is always perfect. His promises may seem slow to us, but God is never late (Hab. 2:3; 2 Pet. 3:9).

Both faith and hope cling to the promises of God, yet they function differently as believers navigate life in a fallen world. Whereas faith believes God to be true to His promises when surrounded by a skeptical world, hope finds joy in the promises of God when surrounded by a despairing world. Despair directly relates to the erroneous belief that life is fundamentally meaningless. If the world is meaningless, then there's no basis for believing the future will be any better than the present.

Hope Well-Founded

Unless God is capable of making good on His promises, there's no basis for hope. His character and nature must be what Scripture says they are in order for our expectations to be well-grounded. Every divine attribute serves as a certain anchor for hope. For example, God's truthfulness assures us that His promises are not empty, His infinite power guarantees that His promises will not fail, and His unchanging character undergirds the unchanging nature of His promises (Num. 23:19; Titus 1:2; Job 42:2; Mal. 3:6).

As if all this were not enough (when in fact God's character *is* enough), God goes the extra mile just to put our minds at ease. He confirms His promise with an oath (Heb. 6:17–18). God's character and God's oath give believers a double assurance that His promises are irrevocable.

The storms of life may rage against the believer, but the anchor of hope will keep the ship of faith from capsizing. How certain is this hope? It is as certain as the resurrection and ascension of Christ, the one who has entered within the heavenly temple as our "great high priest" (Heb. 4:14; see also 6:19–20). The believer can no more fall short of the promised inheritance than Christ can fail in His priestly work or cease to reign as our risen Lord.

> "To hope is to exist in trust that God's constancy is such that the present is on the way to perfection."
>
> JOHN WEBSTER

THE SUBSTITUTES FOR CHRISTIAN HOPE

Christ is the only hope for a hopeless world (Col. 1:27). Those who reject the hope that God offers in the gospel must find substitutes to combat hopelessness. Money and family are common substitutes. Human progress is another one.

The Myth of Progress

The temptation for the modern world is to place its hope in science, technology, and political structures. Because these things have ameliorated* disease, poverty, and conflict, the assumption is that they will lead humans into a perfect world of peace and prosperity. While science, technology, and good political structures are not the enemy (they are all part of the Creation Mandate), people fail to appreciate their limits. Despite great advancements that have improved the quality of life, hopelessness remains a problem. Some of the most anxious and unsettled people in the world today are those who have benefited the most from mankind's achievements.

But there's an even bigger problem. Hope in human progress undermines the Christian ethic because it promotes a **utopian*** future in direct competition with God's eschatological hope. It is a fantasy to think that humans can usher in a perfect world. A little historical awareness, as well as a biblical doctrine of man, should put this myth to rest. Just think of the utopian leaders of the past who have employed unethical means in their attempts to usher in a "perfect" world—for example, Vladimir Lenin or Mao Zedong. The things sinners do to achieve their supposedly noble goals for a better future often violate God's good law and have resulted in some of the worst atrocities in history.

---

ameliorated: made better

utopian: relating to an ideal society of perfect peace, justice, and prosperity; often intended as a description of an unrealistic hope

The Failure of Pragmatism

A misplaced confidence in human progress goes hand in hand with a utilitarian ethic, also known as pragmatism. For example, few would dispute that hard work and productivity are necessary and good, but when we place our hope in these things, we run afoul of God's will. Neglecting family and church for the sake of career can seem reasonable to people whose hopes in this life depend on their retirement accounts. Fear of the future leads many people to engage in vices like dishonesty and theft for pragmatic purposes. How many people justify their selfishness under the pretense of wise money management? Pragmatism can make sin look respectable.

Without the virtue of Christian hope, people are tempted to use sinful means to achieve desired ends. Even believers can fall prey to a misplaced confidence in self-effort. Impatience with God led Abraham and Sarah to resort to pragmatic means to produce an heir. Instead of waiting on God to provide them with the promised heir, Abraham conceded to Sarah's plan to impregnate her handmaid Hagar (Gen. 16:1–6). And though this momentary failure did not invalidate the overall faith commitment of their lives, it was an unethical attempt at an end run around God's promise. This is what happens when hope wavers in the face of delayed promises.

THE SIGN OF CHRISTIAN HOPE

The virtue of hope is necessary for living in accord with biblical ethics. There are so many obstacles on the journey of faith that require a steadfast hope in order for Christians to prevail. Despair, fear, impatience, and anger are just a few of the ugly vices that can raise their heads when we face obstacles. But hope breeds the opposite—joy, courage, patience, and a peaceable spirit.[14]

Overcoming Obstacles to Hope

The sign that Christians are prevailing in hope is their ability to overcome obstacles on their way to their final destination. We'll consider four obstacles and how to overcome them.

First, to counter the world's tendency to cloud God's promises in our hearts and minds, we need to cultivate greater familiarity with His promises. Hope is only as strong as our grasp of their majesty and appeal.

Second, we must regularly meditate on Christ and the sufficiency of His work in order to keep from despairing of salvation. Sin often leads believers to doubt their salvation and consequently to doubt their future inheritance. When hope falls, it needs the restorative power of the gospel to be able to get back up.

Third, believers may become "weary in well doing" (Gal. 6:9). Hope needs constant reminders of the brevity of this life and the glory that awaits. The storms of life will pass, and the sufferings we experience will only serve to increase our everlasting joy in Christ.

Fourth, the world constantly attempts to undermine the trustworthiness of biblical Christianity. Believers are often tempted to question their beliefs. Hope must resist the sophisticated lies that threaten to sever it from the promises that depend on biblical truth.[15]

Finishing Well through Hope

Believers are not called to "fix" the world; they're called to be faithful to the Lord who rules the world with sovereign might. We cannot fall for the world's imagined perfectibility of life in this fallen creation. The world cannot and will not achieve perfect peace and justice. Christ alone is qualified to realize these things for His people, and He will not do so until He returns. Therefore, hope fixes its eyes on Christ rather than on the hollow promises of political leaders.

This doesn't mean Christians can be inactive or disengaged from the culture. Christian hope is neither passive nor silent in the world; rather, it bears witness to the reign of Christ through a life of love and service. It motivates Christians to do the right thing for the right reasons, especially in difficult circumstances.[16]

One of the most powerful witnesses to the world is when Christians redeem the time by living in this present evil age as citizens of the age to come (Eph. 5:16).[17] Everything that a Christian does in the world will look different from the way the world does things. How Christians go about raising their families, pursuing a career, managing resources, and facing trials should all strike a distinctive note of hope.

Far from engendering complacency in believers, the virtue of hope empowers the most rigorous ethical behavior possible. Avoiding hardships and aspiring to an easy life here and now is not our hope. Our hope reaches for something greater and better. It reaches for God's best, rests in God's promises, and runs toward God's reward. It has one goal in mind—to finish well, hearing the Lord say, "Well done, thou good and faithful servant" (Matt. 25:21).[18]

Thinking It Through 5.3

1. How does the virtue of hope relate to the virtue of faith?
2. How do God's character and nature relate to the virtue of hope?
3. What is wrong with placing our hope in human progress?
4. What can happen when a person lacks biblical hope?
5. What four obstacles do we need to overcome to prevail in hope?

05

Terms to Remember

- faith
- love
- hope
- utopian

Scripture Memory

1 Corinthians 13:13

Understanding Ethics

1. Explain the reason love is the greatest virtue.
2. Summarize the three essential elements of faith.
3. Explain the difference between biblical love and an unbiblical self-love.
4. How are faith and hope related?

Practicing Ethical Decision-Making

5. The virtue of faith enables Christians to make difficult ethical choices. How would you respond in the following situation?

   You're struggling with some financial needs and learn of an opportunity to earn some money, but it involves engaging in sinful activity.

6. How would you apply the virtue of hope in overcoming the following obstacle?

   Suppose you are experiencing a long-term disability, and you're tempted to despair because it seems the suffering will never end.

Analyzing and Evaluating Ethical Claims

7. How would you respond to the claim that the highest love is loving yourself?
8. How would you respond to the claim that mental assent alone is real faith?
9. How would you respond to the claim that biblical love is only an action and does not involve the emotions?
10. How would you respond to the claim that human progress is a sufficient hope for the world?

Creating My Own Position Statements on Ethics

11. Summarize your own position on whether the virtue of love is ever compatible with hate.
12. Summarize your own position on the best way to address feelings of hopelessness.

06

With so many obstacles... how do I... navigate the right path?

Virtues
Part 1

PHILIPPIANS 4:8

6.1 Righteousness and Goodness

Have you ever felt crushed under the weight of your homework? Have you ever been on the brink of despair from trying to figure out how to do that big project? You might have approached your teacher with your frustration only to hear that you have all you need to do the assignments. You just need to sit down and do the work! That doesn't quite remove the feeling of being overwhelmed though, does it?

You should be aware by now that living a life marked by virtue is indeed a challenging task. Identifying virtues will be a helpful step toward living virtuously for God's glory. These three chapters on virtues should make you aware of most virtues, but they should also do much more than that. Our sin nature rebels against God's expectations (Rom. 7:20, 23). Our flesh lusts after complacency or any vice that seems more rewarding than letting virtue motivate our actions. Developing virtue in your heart so that it flows out into your thoughts and actions takes a lot of effort. Thankfully, like the illustration about the homework assignments above, believers have everything they need to develop virtue and live virtuously (2 Pet. 1:3–9). They aren't left to themselves to produce virtue in their lives.

You have learned what is the basis for ethical living and virtuous character—the character of God Himself (Exod. 34:6–7). You have also learned that believers can live ethically and virtuously by means of the Spirit's regenerative work and transformative power (Rom. 12:2; Titus 3:5). The next two virtues we will cover, like all virtues, seem so foreign to man in his natural state. By God's grace, believers are able to exemplify and practice righteousness and goodness. In fact, God commands and expects His children to live according to these two virtues (1 Pet. 1:15–16).

DEFINING RIGHTEOUSNESS AND GOODNESS

Righteousness corresponds to the concepts of *rightness* and *right,* the opposites of wickedness and wrong. That much is easily observable from the root of the term and from looking at its antonyms.[1] Defining righteousness can't be done by simply saying that x is right and y is wrong. If something is to be determined to be right, then there has to be a standard by which to judge its rightness or wrongness. So the virtue of **righteousness** is the conformity of an individual's life to God's standards of moral perfection. If we kept our definition more general, we could say that righteousness is any conformity to any standard. But not all standards are inherently upright, and not all that conforms to those standards is morally acceptable. For example, an exclusionary high school or college club might require prospective members to antagonize someone or deface school property for admittance. A foolish student might humiliate and hurt someone or commit vandalism, therefore meeting the standard to be admitted to the club. But in this case, since the standard itself would be unethical, the immoral conformity to it could not be deemed righteous. By His character, God Himself determines the standard for righteousness (Ps. 71:19; Isa. 5:16).

What Kind of Righteousness?

When you hear the word *righteousness*, what do you think of? Some may think of the righteousness of Christ imputed to sinners who come to Him in repentance and faith. Many passages describe the kind of righteousness that justifies sinful man before a holy and righteous God (Rom. 1:17; 4:3; 2 Cor. 5:21). We might call this *salvific* righteousness, because apart from the righteousness of Christ, no one could be saved from the penalty of sin. This is God's righteousness.

But then there is the kind of righteousness that believers pursue as they seek to conform their lives to God's perfect standards. We might call this *ethical* righteousness. Romans 5:1–5 shows the strong connection between these two aspects of righteousness. Verse 1 says that sinners are "justified by faith"; the peace they now have with God is because of Christ's atonement for their sin and their receiving of His imputed righteousness. But notice the mention in verses 3–5 of various virtues that are produced in the lives of justified believers—faith, joy, hope, patience, and love. Paul also instructed Titus that righteousness should characterize the lives of believers (Titus 2:12). This is believers' ethical righteousness. But even this ability to practice righteousness is given to a believer by God; no believer can produce in himself or herself any amount of righteousness (Phil. 2:13).

Salvific Righteousness *imputed to sinners who believe on Christ*

Ethical Righteousness *lived out as a believer conforms to God's moral standard*

righteousness	goodness
adheres to a moral standard of "rightness"	in its purest form flows from a love for righteousness
character qualities in sync with God's character	rightness in action

Identifying something as righteous or unrighteous communicates whether an individual's actions conform to God's perfect standards. Goodness, on the other hand, flows from a heart that loves righteousness, resulting in generous and kind actions toward others. **Goodness** is generously seeking others' happiness and well-being, as determined by God's righteous standards. Goodness is truly virtuous when both generous motives and generous actions are directed by righteousness (see example in James 3:9–12). For example, unsaved people might have a good motive to protect young people who are driving home drunk or high from clubs, so their solution might be to create more clubs closer to residential areas of town. However, when believers critique this solution against righteousness, they should recognize that the solution falls short of actual goodness, since God condemns what goes on during clubbing as immoral, sinful behavior (Rom. 13:13; 1 Pet. 4:3). Goodness is present only when others benefit from a righteous motive, through moral means, and with upright consequences.

moral means

righteous motives

upright consequences

true goodness

others benefited, God glorified

CONCEPTIONS OF RIGHTEOUSNESS AND GOODNESS

You have probably realized that righteousness and goodness are quite similar. Even though there is some overlap in how the Bible refers to these two virtues (Prov. 2:20; 14:19; Eccles. 9:2; Rom. 5:7), the two terms aren't identical in their meanings and uses. Their distinct-yet-close relationship is seen in passages that describe the righteous as doing good (1 Sam. 24:17; Eccles. 7:20) and in passages that use both words to describe one person or thing (Luke 23:50; Rom. 7:12). So a righteous individual does good things, and good character describes a righteous individual. We can even say that justice, the application of the righteous standard, is good even if the result is painful or sad (Deut. 19:13, 21). When God's standards of morality are upheld, the applications of those standards are good. Righteous justice is good because it meets God's standards and is met with God's approval (Ps. 11:5–7).

Why isn't it sufficient for me to identify what is right and what is good based solely on situations starting and ending well?

Since non-Christians don't appeal to God's standards, how do they determine what is righteous and what is therefore good to do? For many people, whatever they feel is right and good works for them. For many others, whatever the consensus of their society says is right and good sets the standard. Whatever worldview people have manifests itself when they appeal to whatever standard they use (some are conscious of their standard, while others are not). A person can live life according to any number of contradictory standards. Sometimes unbelievers borrow from the Christian worldview that has influenced a society in the past. By God's common grace, unbelievers can demonstrate some measure of apparent righteousness and show apparent goodness to others. Unbelievers, who are made in God's image, can be honest in business transactions, seek to alleviate poverty in their cities, and show love to their children (Matt. 7:11). Nevertheless, a broken foundation is still broken even if the roof doesn't cave in immediately.

An unbeliever might feel righteous ("justified") by arguing that he or she is in the right on the basis of the standard he or she appeals to. Unbelievers might feel they have done something good for someone when they make a philanthropic* gesture. They feel justified when they live in conformity to their self-established standards. But if the standards aren't God's standards, according to His character and how He designed the world, then no true righteousness or goodness is expressed.

True virtue comes out of a right relationship with God, aligns with God's standards, involves a right motive, fits the occasion, and seeks a right outcome.

TWISTING RIGHTEOUSNESS AND GOODNESS

Society has a knack for bending God's structure (the design of His good, created order) in a sinful direction. The language society uses might seem innocent to some. But the ungodly world system we live in has mastered using virtuous-sounding words and redefining or reapplying them in ungodly and corrupt ways. A woman's "choice" becomes synonymous with killing her unborn baby, and "freedom" or "love" might mean living opposed to God's creation of men as men and women as women. These are clear examples of calling "evil good, and good evil" (Isa. 5:20). In the next unit, we will spend five chapters discussing a great variety of issues that require ethical decisions. Included in those chapters are the examples above, plus many more.

Sinners ignore God's design, rejecting that which reflects God's righteousness and goodness (Rom. 1:18, 25, 29, 32). The virtues that all Christians should strive by God's grace to develop can get twisted by a sinful society, which demonizes Christians for working toward true virtue. Vices are approved and virtues are repressed. Righteousness gets traded for ungodliness, and goodness gets traded for corruption.

The vice of **ungodliness** is anything that is contrary to God's nature or opposed to God's ways. The default mode of society, of all unregenerate people, can be summarized by this term. Those who are enslaved to sin and to its master wholly oppose God and His righteous standards (Eph. 2:1–3). Why is society approving of same-sex marriages? To violate God's righteous standards for marriage is to embody unrighteousness, which is ungodliness (Rom. 1:26–27, 29). What corresponds to righteousness is one man and one woman who are faithful to one another and submitted to God's design and purpose for marriage (Gen. 2:22, 24; Eph. 5:22–33).

The vice of **corruption** describes any harm done to God's good design and moral will for His creation. Similar to ungodliness, this term encompasses all the tragic

philanthropic: loving one's fellow men; benevolent; humane consequences of the Fall and the Curse. Corruption twists goodness into a counterfeit. Being kind and helpful to classmates because you want them to vote for you for student council corrupts the virtue of goodness. Goodness is corrupted when there is an ulterior motive. Even something like a "white lie" is unrighteous. Pretending you didn't hear your parents call you corrupts the goodness you should do by acknowledging them. Your inaction shows you're seeking your own convenience over your parents' happiness and well-being, and your deception undermines the well-being of your relationship with them.

Examples of ungodliness and corruption abound. Excessive punishment for a simple infraction or crime is corrupt and ungodly. Even though punishment was applied, it wasn't done in a righteous manner. Therefore, it can't be classified as good. God has revealed His standard for righteous punishments for real offenses: true justice involves punishment that fits the crime committed (Exod. 21:23–25). When wrong is done and it is overlooked or covered up by those responsible for justice, the vices of ungodliness and corruption may also be at play. Punishment is in order when just and good laws are broken. But righteous punishment gets twisted into ungodliness when wrongdoing is either punished too severely or not severely enough. Authority figures who justly enforce righteous standards and laws do good, even to the offender, when they punish the offender appropriately. But failing to do one's duty of enforcing the law is a corruption of one's role.

What do the virtues of righteousness and goodness look like? In many ways they look like the opposite of ungodliness and corruption. Ungodliness and corruption are bent away from God's good creational structure. When believers' lives embody righteousness and goodness, they begin to untwist the mess ungodliness and corruption make.

GROWING IN RIGHTEOUSNESS AND GOODNESS

If you play an instrument or sing, what do you do when your instructor tells you that you need to improve in a specific area? Practice! If you don't practice playing your instrument or singing, you won't improve your skills. You need to know what to do, for sure, but then you really just need to apply what you have learned. Knowledge is important; that much should be obvious. But lots of focused practice is what you need in order to improve. Do you recognize your need to grow in the virtues of righteousness and goodness? Do you have a plan to grow?

Believers don't lack opportunities to practice growing in virtue. Each day contains temptations, challenges, and needs that can be met—all opportunities to practice a virtue rather than a vice by turning to God for help so that Christ lives through you (Gal. 2:20). But you can still neglect practicing virtues, as you might neglect picking up your instrument to practice. You might try to avoid or ignore temptations and difficult situations. But you can't avoid them all. And avoiding uncomfortable situations can reveal cowardice, a vice, rather than potentially displaying courage, a virtue. And just as you need knowledge and skill to perform well musically, you need wisdom in order to live according to righteousness and goodness (Prov. 2:6–9). Virtuous living doesn't just happen. And it doesn't come about in your life without God giving you His wisdom.

Goodness is listed as a fruit of the Spirit (Gal. 5:22). Righteousness can be found in other lists of virtues (Rom. 14:17; Eph. 5:9). On the one hand, God enables believers to grow in these virtues. This growth includes gradually living more in conformity to God's perfect standards and gradually becoming more generous and benevolent in how they treat others. This enablement comes from the nature of salvation and how God works to bring about growth and change in His children (Rom. 8:29–30; Phil. 2:13). On the other hand, believers need to actively do their part in pursuing virtue and avoiding vice (Phil. 2:12).

What do you need to do to take notice of ungodly thought patterns or behaviors in your life (Eph. 5:15–17)? What routines could you set up to remind yourself of God's righteousness and His perfect standards (Ps. 1:1–6)? How can you increase your dependence on the Spirit's empowerment to live by those standards (Rom. 8:12–15; Gal. 5:16, 25)? And what do you need to do to assess your motives, thoughts, and actions to see whether they have been corrupted by selfish or worldly influences (Ps. 139:23–24)? And finally, how might you keep God's goodness fresh in your mind and heart, so you can practice generous, no-strings-attached goodness to others (Gal. 5:14; 1 John 4:10–11)? You need to plan to run away from sin and its tempting trappings and to run after righteousness and the virtues that enable you to imitate God's goodness (1 Tim. 6:11; 2 Tim. 2:22).

Remember, the goodness that should characterize your life flows from your joyful conformity to God's righteous standards (Ps. 119:97). God is powerful enough and gracious enough to grow these two virtues in your life. Trust that God will do so, and enjoy your participation in the Spirit's work in you.

Thinking It Through 6.1

1. Define *righteousness*.
2. Define *goodness*.
3. Compare and contrast Christian and non-Christian conceptions of righteousness and goodness.
4. Contrast the virtues of righteousness and goodness with the vices of ungodliness and corruption.
5. What steps can you take to grow in righteousness and goodness?

6.2 Prudence

There was a time when computers filled entire rooms and had very limited capabilities. As computers gradually got smaller, supercomputers were developed and gained greater and greater capabilities. The smartphones most people carry today are just that: sophisticated supercomputers. Back in 1996, an IBM supercomputer called Deep Blue played chess against the world's number one chess master at that time, Garry Kasparov. The match ended with a victory for the human, but only after the machine had managed to win one of the six games. The tables were turned, though, in the following year's rematch. The final decisive game was won by Deep Blue—and in only nineteen moves. A machine had outplayed, outsmarted, and bested the greatest chess mind in the world. Processing chips had beaten a brain. Artificial intelligence had defeated genuine intelligence.[2]

PRUDENCE DEFINED

The virtue of prudence has much in common with the game of chess, at least the way someone like Garry Kasparov plays. Prudence is related to knowledge and wisdom. But prudence isn't simply having a lot of knowledge, nor is it only knowing the right thing to do. It is also knowing the best way to carry out the right thing. **Prudence** is the ability to choose the best course of action, having considered all the constraints of the situation, to obtain the most righteous and beneficial outcome. There are aspects of past knowledge, present discernment, and future considerations involved in the virtue of prudence. In our illustration above, the human or the computer could be described as more "prudent" than the other when winning a match. Having knowledge of the game of chess, an accurate analysis of the opponent and each move's implications, and foresight to plan out many moves in advance is essentially a version of chess prudence! But machines can't be virtuous; only people can. And the virtue of prudence can't be limited to running data through a predetermined algorithm. Prudence, like wisdom, involves the whole person—head and heart.

PRUDENCE TODAY

What concerns us, however, is the ethical nature of prudence as a virtue. Prudence must be present any time an ethical difficulty arises. We know loving God and loving others are explicit commands of Scripture that apply to all believers at all times (Matt. 22:36–40). *How* to love your neighbor who is an angry, cursing drunk most evenings and weekends requires prudence, among other virtues. You want to protect your family, but you don't want to appear unfriendly. You want to address your concerns about his effect on the neighborhood, but you want to keep the channels open for future, gospel-intentional communication. Both short-term and long-term implications of your decisions must be considered. When working through a difficult situation that requires multiple virtues, you will usually know what the various good options are. But you will need to assess the effects of doing the right thing on the various parties involved in that scenario. And to do all this, you need prudence.

What is the difference between what Christians and non-Christians understand prudence to be? In a moment we will look at multiple passages that teach how believers relate to prudence. But how is prudence viewed from the world's perspective? Some unbelievers may view prudence as overly cautious, such that those who practice it are prudes* or cowards—as if boldly and thoughtlessly doing whatever they want, no matter the consequences, is best for everyone. Prudence to unbelievers could be seen as excessive, unnecessary, and even legalistic—as if considering the situation, assessing how much they know about everything related to the situation, analyzing their motives, and calculating the effects on all involved would usually be unhelpful. But unbelievers don't shun prudence altogether. For those outside Christ who seek their own interests and promote their personal agendas, prudence can come in handy when it serves their best interests. For example, most people want an efficiently run government that makes buying and selling and moving about the nation easy. Christ Himself pointed out how prudent unbelievers can be when it comes to a construction project or military matters (Luke 14:28–32). This type of prudence generally serves their own best interests and isn't necessarily ethically motivated. Remember, God's common grace on all people enables them to imitate virtuous living, though that imitation is hollow.

As for the Christian's understanding, prudence is a biblical Christian virtue and therefore necessary for believers to practice. Prudence is a foundational virtue seen especially in the Wisdom Literature in the Old Testament (particularly Proverbs and Ecclesiastes). The Word of God informs a believer's motivations and conditions his

prude: someone who is excessively proper or modest in the way he or she speaks, dresses, and conducts himself or herself in general or her choices (Ps. 119:97–104). To have ready access to a knowledge of what is pleasing to God, believers need to know what He has communicated in His Word. A prudent person can take this knowledge and determine the best way to apply it to specific situations. As you might expect, Proverbs in various places describes the value of wisdom and the benefits that applying wisdom (prudence) provides (4:7; 9:10; 13:10; 15:22).

A Christian demonstrates prudence by internalizing the wisdom in Scripture and applying it, living it out. Prudence is most needed when there are several goals that are biblical or several paths to reach a biblical goal but only one choice can be made. So, for example, it might be prudent to take a gap year after high school if you need to make some money prior to enrolling in a four-year degree program. But if you were able to secure a scholarship, it might not be prudent to wait a year. Many other ethical issues come up in either scenario though: Is your job conducive to moral living? What ethical issues, if any, come up frequently at your job? Is the college where you got a scholarship going to help you grow as a Christian? How wise is it to go into debt for college, and how much debt could you manage? A prudent person not only raises the questions necessary to make a wise decision; a prudent person is skilled in choosing the best goal from several legitimate alternatives and choosing the best means for reaching a given goal.

Another point that aids the Christian's understanding of prudence is that only believers can truly practice prudence. All the goals unbelievers have are in some way distorted or misplaced because they are not in service to the great goal of glorifying God and enjoying Him forever. So even good goals, like securing a quality education for their children, will be distorted. Instead of wanting their children to be well-educated so that they can serve God more effectively, they may be more concerned about their children's wealth or social status. These non-Christians may be very effective at reaching their goals, but it isn't really prudence if they're pursuing the wrong goals.

Christians might see the non-Christian pragmatic idea of what prudence is and then decide to shun prudence. Or they might think that since their goals are good and right, there is no need to worry about whether the *way* those goals are pursued is wise. However, the Bible teaches that even the Messiah needed the Spirit of the Lord to give Him wisdom and counsel (Isa. 11:2). The Spirit of God is also at work in believers, guiding them into truth and helping them see what good and right choices are (1 Cor. 2:12–13). Believers need to receive God's wisdom (James 3:17). Faithful believers are compared to "a faithful and wise servant" who carries out his master's charge (Matt. 24:45–46) and to the wise virgins who brought extra oil for their lamps (Matt. 25:1–13). Jesus illustrated the necessity of prudence by comparing His twelve disciples to "sheep in the midst of wolves" and urging them to "be . . . wise as serpents, and harmless as doves" (Matt. 10:16). A sheep among wolves must not only be careful, but also smart and wise to navigate life and not be harmed. Turning the appropriate knowledge into applied wisdom requires prudence. Snakes can be dangerous to other creatures, but they are also wise. Doves are weak, but they are also harmless to other creatures. Prudence determines how to apply both the wisdom of snakes and the harmlessness of doves to a given situation. And for believers to be like sheep, snakes, and doves (in appropriate ways) requires submission to the Lord and obedience to His Word, combined with a solid understanding of how the world works.

> In modern ethics, prudence is often reduced to utility or self-interest. The modern view of prudence is derived from a misunderstanding of prudence as pragmatic self-interest.
>
> CLARKE FORSYTHE[3]

PRUDENCE FORGOTTEN

You've heard it said, "The end justifies the means." This sentiment is totally contrary to prudence. The virtue of prudence is evidenced through a combination of (1) the proper knowledge about an issue, (2) the specifics of the situation, and (3) the appropriate foresight—so that the best means available are used to reach the right goals. But does the final outcome really justify whatever has to be done to obtain it? This unethical mentality is widely accepted in our culture. But that thinking is pragmatic, which means that whatever needs to happen to obtain the desired end result is valid. In such thinking, prudence has been ignored. It has been deleted from the equation. Prudence isn't only choosing the most preferable end and getting there by causing the least amount of damage possible. Nor is prudence charting a path that is entirely ethical but landing on an unethical outcome.

1. knowledge of the issue

2. consideration of the situation

3. appropriate foresight

The vice of cunning fills the void that prudence leaves when it is ignored. **Cunning** involves shrewdness as well as deception. Like prudence, cunning employs a thorough analysis of the situation, but it does so to obtain something through immoral means or to an unethical end. Growing up you might have learned some of Aesop's fables. Do you remember the one about the fox and the crow? This fable portrays the fox as cunning and the crow as vain. But more importantly, this fable helps us learn about the difference between prudence and cunning. The fox em-

ployed a devious means to get a snack. It used a pragmatic approach in which cunning was a main ingredient. The fox was hungry, and the crow had cheese. The fox didn't want to go hungry, so he decided to take what wasn't his to take. But in order to do so, he needed smarts—the fox stooped to vice rather than rising to virtue. The fox utilized cunning means by flattering the crow to get it to open its beak and drop the cheese.[4] Cunning only served the fox's interest. This isn't virtuous prudence. This is the vice of cunning.

Do you ever notice your selfish motives for doing something nice for someone? Have you ever felt justified for pursuing a good cause but at the same time felt uncomfortable knowing that the way you were achieving it was wrong? The way of prudence offers a clean conscience as well as God's approval.

The vice of rashness also ignores prudence. But rashness is the opposite of cunning. While cunning uses deceptive yet calculated means to obtain a desired goal, **rashness** acts in the moment with no regard for whether one's actions are the best way, or even a good way, to reach a desired end. Rashness is impulsive and reckless. Rashness usually causes harm in the end because it doesn't take the end into consideration. Rashness works against the fruit of the Spirit and the rest of the virtues. And you can find terms related to rashness in a few of Scripture's lists of vices, often translated by words like *foolish* or *reckless* (Rom. 1:31; 2 Tim. 3:4; Titus 3:3). Sometimes people confuse rashness with boldness for the truth and for what is right. But rashness jumps in prematurely and adds to a problem rather than waiting to hear the whole story and then helping with a solution (Prov. 18:13).

Do you wait to hear both sides of a story? Do you ever stop to consider the short-term effects of your words and the long-term effects of your actions? Prudence demands that you do.

PRUDENCE IN ACTION

Can we rightly say that prudence is necessary for all ethical decision-making? What does prudence look like in action?

Think of prudence like a quality control worker at a factory. You might have seen a video of one of these workers carefully watching a steady stream of product go by on a conveyor belt. This worker must remove defective items, ensure a constant flow of the product, and stop the belt immediately if something goes wrong. In this analogy, the conveyor belt is a complex ethical situation as it develops. The products going by are various virtues that rise to address the situation. Prudence knows what the virtues are and can identify them. When a vice (a virtue made defective) comes down the conveyor belt, prudence can identify it and remove it.

Two Examples

Prudence helps shape our daily habits and helps us make judgment calls. Our habits reveal much about who we are, and they require much effort to develop or change. We need prudence to establish and develop truly virtuous habits. Also, when we decide to do something we usually don't do (or decide not to do something we usually do), prudence comes into the picture if the actions in question are ethically significant. When we aren't choosing between clear vice and clear virtue, prudence helps us discern when exceptions to our normal habits of godly living are necessary and good.

For example, consider this first scenario: You have a friend who is starting to hang out with the wrong crowd. You want to be courageous and confront him about the path he is on because you are truly concerned for him. So, the next time you see him with those friends, you confront him in front of them, tell him he's being an idiot, and let him know those friends will ruin his life because if he continues to hang out with them, he'll most likely start doing drugs and committing small crimes with them. You tell him that, if he were smart, he'd walk away from them right now and cut off further friendship with them. Now, everything you said might have been true, but how you said it, when you said it, and even the words used to say it would have been imprudent.

Consider this alternative approach: You invite him over to your house so the two of you can have a private conversation. You tell him that you're really concerned about his new friends. You point out that, if he continues to spend time with them, he'll come under pressure to do drugs or to commit petty crimes. You let him know that they're likely to be friends only in the short term—but that the impact on his life would likely be long-term. Which approach is more likely to accomplish the goal you are seeking?

Here is a second scenario: You have (prudently) established the habit of not fighting and avoiding situations where you might be drawn into a fight. But one day while you're walking home from school, some guys show up out of nowhere and start harassing you and your friends. You do your best to ignore them, but they get in your face and start pushing you. They do the same to your friends. You ask them multiple times to leave you alone, but they don't. One of your friends is able to run away, and you yell after him to call the cops. At that point, you realize that these thugs are out to give you and your friends a serious beating. So, the prudent thing to do at that moment is to minimize the harm done to you and to your friends by resorting to self-defense; despite your usual habit, you end up in a fight. You aren't sure why these guys are acting so violently toward you and your friends. But you know they have it out for you. You can either get seriously beat up and watch them do the same to your friends, or you can try to forcibly make them stop as you yell for help and try to get to safety.

> *Prudence is at the heart of moral character, for it shapes and directs the whole of our moral lives, and is indispensible to our becoming morally excellent persons.*
>
> W. JAY WOOD[5]

> *Prudence is essential for moral virtue because it provides the ineliminable* sound judgment required to practice any of the virtues in our particular moral circumstances.*
>
> W. JAY WOOD[6]

ineliminable: indispensable

GRAPPLING WITH
ETHICAL ISSUES

Is It Ever Virtuous
to Fight?
How would you explain
the use of prudence in the
second scenario? Work
through your response
and then check with your
teacher for the answer.

In the first scenario, the initial tension is between being courageous by telling a hard truth versus being cowardly by avoiding an uncomfortable conversation that could threaten your relationship (Eph. 4:15). Courage isn't the same as rashness, though, and the need for courage doesn't cancel the need for humility. And prudence should tell you that a gentle, yet direct, private conversation is more likely to achieve a good result than an in-your-face public confrontation. Prudence takes all this into consideration and values the virtue of courage enough to align with it and make an ethical decision (Heb. 3:13)—but acts courageously in the wisest way possible. Paul exhorts believers to be careful as they live for God amid the surrounding culture, which affects and influences them (Eph. 5:15–17). The current world system and those who are part of it go against God and His people. Prudence plays a major role in cutting through the bad motives that we or others might have and in determining the best means to arrive at a good end.

How can prudence help me with my social media usage?

PRUDENCE IN DEVELOPMENT

As you pursue prudence, you will develop more virtues than just prudence. Practicing prudence will also help you identify and avoid certain vices. What steps can you take to develop prudence? Be aware that caution by itself isn't prudence. But prudence often requires you to pause to consider all aspects of the ethical difficulty you have encountered. (Sometimes prudence entails thinking through possible ethical difficulties *before* encountering a crisis—as you can imagine, it would be helpful for our second scenario above!) What follows are various steps you can take toward developing prudence when you encounter your next ethical difficulty. Pray and ask God to give you the wisdom and understanding that He provides for you through Christ and by the Spirit. Only with the Lord's help will these steps help you grow in your exercise of prudence (Ps. 119:73; Eph. 1:16–17; James 1:5).

- Pause to think through all aspects of the challenging ethical situation (thus also practicing patience and humility).
- Mentally check off the virtues that are lacking in the situation or are necessary to help solve it (always remember faith, love, and hope).
- Identify the vices involved in the situation or those that might come up (always watch out for pride and selfishness).
- Don't lose sight of the overall goal, and seek the best outcome given the circumstances (and remember, prudence avoids cunning and rashness).

Thinking It Through 6.2

1. Define *prudence*.
2. How do Christian and non-Christian conceptions of prudence differ?
3. Contrast the virtue of prudence with the vices of rashness and cunning.
4. How does prudence relate to ethical decision-making and ethical living? Give examples other than those given above.
5. What can you do to grow in prudence?

6.3 Diligence, Faithfulness, and Courage

Knights in the Middle Ages were known for their code of chivalry. Think of the stories of King Arthur and the Knights of the Round Table. Not that the men who fought the king's wars were virtuous or moral men, because most weren't. But the code of chivalry was meant to keep them in check and was intended to make them model subjects of the king and model members of the Roman Catholic Church. For example, knights were to defend the weak and vulnerable, respect women, support the Church, and be valiant in battle. Knights were also supposed to exhibit various virtues.

The three virtues presented in this section were included in the medieval knight's code of chivalry. Knights were to be diligent in serving the king, faithful to the Church and to the code, and courageous in battle.[7] As you have recently learned, lofty goals that are reached by unethical means don't qualify as virtuous and neither do ethical means that end with an immoral outcome. Hard work, loyal commitment, and bravery are important character traits, but they aren't virtuous in and of themselves. God's character is the basis and God's glory is the goal of all the virtues, including these three. Diligence, faithfulness, and courage, like all virtues, can fully be practiced only by believers. Only believers seek to glorify God by conforming to His character. So, what exactly are these three virtues?

DEFINING DILIGENCE, FAITHFULNESS, AND COURAGE

Diligence can be defined as *"the exertion of the spiritual and physical powers of a believer whereby he willingly, joyously, and earnestly executes that task which God assigns him, doing so because it is the will of God."*[8] Diligence is more than hard work. Diligence is dedication to do the will of God. And diligence approaches tasks and does them "heartily, as to the Lord" (Col. 3:23; see also Eccles. 9:10). This means that other virtues (honesty, prudence, kindness, etc.) are factored in so that diligence doesn't become consumed with only the work, the timeliness of completing the work, or the amount of effort put into the work. Paul exemplified diligence through his work ethic when he was in Thessalonica (2 Thess. 3:7–9). Paul and his companions worked hard in order not to be a burden to the church but also to set an example of what Christian diligence looks like. The virtue of diligence involves working hard for a good reason with a useful goal in mind.

Faithfulness is steadfast loyalty to that which is morally acceptable and good, despite difficulty and conflict. This virtue is related to faith (as seen in the root of the word) in that we are faithful toward those things that we believe in, that we think are trustworthy. Paul's life is an example of what faithfulness looks like for a believer (Phil. 3:12–21). Faithfulness isn't limited to maintaining faith in God, but it serves as a strong foundation for this virtue.

Courage is spiritual strength to unashamedly do the right thing at the right time even at risk of one's own harm.[9] The ideas of bravery and valor rightfully come to mind when we think of courage. And courage as a virtue, practiced by believers, takes bravery and valor to the spiritual realm of everyday living. Paul teaches about the armor of God, and courage is important for making use of this armor—even though we don't find the term in this passage (Eph. 6:10–20). Here we have a parallel with our knight illustration from above. Paul's encouragement to "be strong in the Lord" (6:10), the references to standing against all that comes against Christians

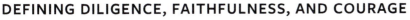

Christlike wholeness requires the courage to do the right thing no matter what.

JIM BERG[10]

(6:11, 13–14), and Paul's desire for personal boldness (6:19–20) all point to the virtue of courage.

RELATIONSHIP BETWEEN DILIGENCE, FAITHFULNESS, AND COURAGE

So how are these three virtues related? Diligence gets something done. Faithfulness maintains a commitment to something. Courage does what's right for the right reasons no matter the cost.

Here is a scenario where all three virtues are required and seamlessly work together: a friend of yours, we'll call her Sandy, goes to a public high school. Sandy has a reputation, a good one, for being a thoughtful and strong Christian. Her teachers, though, are either atheistic or irreligious. As the school year goes on, the pushback from some teachers and classmates over how she practices her Christian faith increases. How should Sandy respond?

First, she needs to diligently study the Word (and maybe some other resources) in order to learn how to defend her faith and have the best possible answers for her detractors while maintaining a bold yet gracious attitude toward them. She can't learn everything in a matter of weeks or months, but she must display *diligence* in learning how to engage in apologetics with those at school (2 Tim. 2:14–15).

Second, Sandy must remain faithful to the Lord amidst the growing pressure against her for her Christian faith. Some unbelievers can be very antagonistic to Christians and even try to get a believer to leave the faith or slip up in their faith. Sandy must demonstrate *faithfulness* in her commitment to Jesus Christ as her Lord and her source of truth and confidence (Rom. 1:16).

And third, Sandy needs to be unashamedly courageous in her defense of the truth of the Bible and of the authority of Christ (Matt. 28:18; Eph. 3:12–13). She might be alone in her efforts or at least feel alone. She might not feel persuasive. But as Sandy trusts the Lord with the outcome, she shows *courage* by speaking up for her faith and not forsaking her beliefs despite harassment from those around her.

In short, Sandy's faithfulness to Christ and His Word leads to diligence in preparation and courage in proclamation as she faces those who oppose the gospel. And it's worth noting that Sandy's diligence (in preparation and in her general way of living) can contribute to courage (confidence in what she has to say and in her testimony) when the moment comes to speak (see 1 Pet. 3:14–16).

MISAPPLICATIONS OF DILIGENCE, FAITHFULNESS, AND COURAGE

What distinguishes an advanced musician from a beginner? Many things undoubtedly, but would you say that both musicians have different knowledge about what to play on their instrument? Not necessarily. An advanced musician might play all the same notes and chords that a beginner has recently learned. But if both the beginner and the advanced musician played the same piece of music, the latter's rendition would be unquestionably better. Why? Because an advanced musician has learned by experience and practice what it means to play skillfully and artfully, beyond simply hitting the right notes.

What distinguishes a mature believer from an immature believer? Often, the difference between the two also comes down to being able to live skillfully and artfully, and this ability too is developed by experience and practice. Both believers are trying to apply the same virtues, but the mature believer has thoroughly internalized the virtues more and developed moral skill in applying them to specific circumstances in a balanced and grace-infused way. When it comes to applying diligence, faithfulness, and courage, such developed moral skill will help you apply each virtue in a careful fashion, with the right goals in mind. Practicing diligence, demonstrating faithfulness, and showing courage fall short of virtue if your goals and means aren't wise and ethical.

Misapplied Diligence

God requires that we be diligent about important issues that affect our lives and relationships—including our relationship with God (Prov. 4:23; Phil. 2:12–13). That means that being diligent at just any task doesn't count for anything unless the goal is godly. For example, you might set for yourself the goal of being as healthy as you can possibly be. To achieve this sort of health and physical fitness will require great diligence. Your diligence might be exemplary in eating healthy foods, staying away from sodas, snacking only on fruits or vegetables, working out consistently, getting plenty of sleep each night, and having annual physicals that include bloodwork. This level of diligence, though it could be commendable, could also be misapplied, since seeking to achieve peak health and fitness can turn into an idolatrous pursuit. God expects us to be healthy so we can be good stewards of the bodies He has given us and so we can be able to fulfill His will for us (inferred from Gen. 1:26, 28, 31 and 1 Tim. 4:8). But God also expects us to diligently do many other things throughout our lifetimes, and these good responsibilities may conflict with such a rigorous health and fitness schedule. If we adjust the goal to rightly accommodate our physical limitations, realistic life stages, ministry opportunities, work responsibilities, spiritual growth, and family demands, then the virtue of diligence can truly be ethical in a measured pursuit of health and wellness. In other words, the fundamental virtue of *prudence* should help us order our responsibilities rightly. Truly living for God's glory involves diligently balancing our time and effort in all our areas of responsibility—not being excessively "diligent" in one area to the neglect of others.

Misapplied Faithfulness

If you get a job at a store or restaurant one day, or already have one, then you should be faithful to your agreement to work there. Your goals are to bring glory to God through your work and to provide for yourself financially. You need to work! Let's say that when you get your job, you and your boss agree that you will work Mondays through Saturdays. But after a few months, your boss schedules you to work on Sunday mornings. What do you do? You want to be faithful to your commitment to work for your employer. You also want to keep your job so you can provide for your needs. These are legitimate goals. Notice how the circumstances of your employment changed, though. Upon accepting the job, you weren't required to work Sunday mornings; now you are. A narrow "faithfulness" to your job for its own sake would cause you to be unfaithful to God's commands and expectations regarding church involvement (Heb. 10:25). The goal of being a faithful follower of Jesus, which includes consistent church involvement, needs to be addressed at this crossroads. This is an example of conflicting goals, both good. Blind faithfulness to one goal that causes unfaithfulness to a greater goal isn't ethical. Again, prudence should help you in ordering your priorities and understanding what faithfulness across the whole of your life's responsibilities would look like.

Misapplied Courage

Consider someone pursuing the goal of consistently confronting all the sin they perceive in their friends and fellow church members. To do this takes courage, lots of it. The goal seems commendable, and the path to achieve it does re-

> *Courage is a Christian duty but also a constant possibility for one who places himself in the almighty hands of God. It shows itself in patient endurance, moral steadfastness and spiritual fidelity.*
>
> H. D. MCDONALD[11]

quire courage. But the goal can be easily misapplied because, first, we are fallible at detecting actual sin in the lives of those we would plan to courageously confront. In observing a friend strictly externally or with little context, there is a chance you are making a judgment based on your own preferences rather than on biblical teaching. Second, the Bible suggests that there may be times when it is appropriate to overlook an offense (Prov. 19:11; Acts 17:30; Rom. 3:25; 1 Pet. 4:8). Third, Christ was clear that it is far easier to see small faults in others than to see large faults in ourselves and that we should address our own sins first (Matt. 7:2–5). The goal of seeing believers repent of sin and pursue godliness is a great goal. Courage is truly ethical when a better goal is set up and followed—a goal for which prudence has balanced love, humility, mercy, concern for holiness, and wise understanding of various particular circumstances. Nonetheless, the goal of confronting clear and grave sin does require courage, and believers should actively seek to do so ethically (Gal. 6:1).

Righteous Motives and Goals, but Bad Outcomes

God is glorified when your motives are in the right place and the goal you are reaching for is righteous. But you can't control all the circumstances that affect the outcome. You are responsible for your motives. You are responsible for how you go about living out the appropriate virtues and how you set the goal. God alone knows how all things will turn out and declares "the end from the beginning" (Isa. 46:10). He knows each of our motives and why we set the goals we set (1 Cor. 4:5). Using the example of diligence from above, let's say someone is diligent and careful to eat well and exercise frequently. This person is also as diligent as can be in all other responsibilities. The goal is right this time. But at age thirty-eight, this person finds out he or she has an aggressive form of cancer. Is this the individual's fault? Is this someone who was not diligent enough with their diet after all? Did God not see his or her just motives and righteous goal?

TWISTING DILIGENCE, FAITHFULNESS, AND COURAGE

The easiest way to twist diligence is to pit the vice of sloth or laziness against a vice in the opposite ditch—workaholism. **Sloth** is laziness, a lack of motivation to do necessary and productive work—the opposite of diligence. One who is slothful is also foolish and ends up hurting him- or herself and others. In the book of Proverbs, the vice of sloth is exposed as destructive (Prov. 6:9–11; 13:4; 18:9; 19:15; 20:4; 21:25; 26:13–16). **Workaholism**, on the other hand, twists diligence, leaving no room for and giving attention to the other good and necessary parts of life that aren't work. It involves making an idol out of work and usually results in overworking one responsibility to the detriment of others. To be diligent at work is a good thing; it isn't workaholism, which twists the virtuousness of diligence.

You have probably faced the temptation to procrastinate getting your schoolwork done. Be careful! Habitual, prolonged procrastination is essentially the vice of sloth. The virtue of diligence would see you work ahead where possible and see you guard your time so as to get your schoolwork done when it's due. On the other hand, you may have been tempted to study all the time, neglecting time with the Lord or with family. That, too, is problematic. Be diligent in what God has called you to do right now. Don't be lazy and don't be a workaholic.

Faithfulness can also be twisted and brought down from its lofty position as a virtue to a lowly and distasteful vice—the vice of disloyalty. **Disloyalty**, the opposite of faithfulness, is when any commitment to remain faithful and loyal to something or someone is disregarded (without a legitimate ethical reason). To answer the question above, where does your primary loyalty lie? To God and His ethical standards (which include not participating in cheating on assignments) or to your friend and your friendship? Actually, to not allow a friend to copy your homework isn't disloyalty to him or her; it is the right, ethical response. Real loyalty to true friendship sometimes means being willing to do or say the hard thing for the good of the other person. Your friend needs to accept the repercussions of not getting his or her homework done, whatever the reason might be.

How should I respond when a friend asks to copy my homework?

While faithfulness says, "Yes, I will be true to a righteous commitment no matter what self-sacrifice there may be," disloyalty says, "I'm out. This isn't convenient for me anymore." Disloyalty should be entirely unattractive to Christians because it stands in such contrast to the loyal faithfulness of God (Lam. 3:22–23).

Engaging in culturally acceptable sins (such as telling small lies or being impatient) and falling into apathy toward the things of the Lord—these mark the path of disloyalty to God. Watch out! It is "the little foxes" (Song of Sol. 2:15), seemingly insignificant displays of willful disloyalty, that wreak havoc on your faithfulness to God. Faithfulness won't let go of what it knows to be true and good. Disloyalty ignores all virtue and selfishly and foolishly settles for vice.

Courage can easily be twisted in two different directions—recklessness or cowardice. **Recklessness** throws all caution to the wind and acts or reacts impulsively. Recklessness parades as courage, but it acts imprudently and therefore doesn't consider the outcome of its rash actions. **Cowardice**, on the other hand, runs away from danger and won't stand up to defend what is true and right when threatened. Cowardice is the polar opposite of courage. The Bible is clear that fools and unbelievers are both reckless and cowardly (Prov. 14:16; Rev. 21:8). There is no worth, no goodness, in the vices.

Whenever you hear a friend answer the question, "Why did you do that?" with, "I wasn't thinking," recklessness is partly to blame. And when you are asked about your response to an immoral situation and you reply, "I just didn't say anything," cowardice likely had a role. Pay attention! Most of us aren't as courageous as we think we are. The test of your courage is how you respond when doing the right thing will be costly. Even with good intentions, a lack of prudence can turn courage into recklessness. And fear can easily cause courage to fail at a crucial moment. Dutch pastor and author Wilhelmus à Brakel illustrated godly courage this way:

> As someone who in a storm finds himself too weak to remain standing takes hold of a post or a tree and remains standing due to its immobility, the courageous person likewise takes hold of the strength of the Lord, and thus remains strong and unyielding.[12]

The truth is, we need the Lord's wisdom and strength to make us what we are not.

PRACTICING DILIGENCE, FAITHFULNESS, AND COURAGE

Overcoming sloth, disloyalty, recklessness, and cowardice is essential to practicing diligence, faithfulness, and courage. Scripture teaches that believers are to put off the old self and then put on the new self (Eph. 4:22–24). Unfortunately, to sin by engaging in the vices rather than the virtues can come all too naturally to us (Rom. 7:15–19). We not only need God's help to practice these three virtues, but we also need a plan to make sure that we do.

Where do you find yourself lacking in diligence? What top priorities in your life are you struggling to be faithful to? In what circumstances do you habitually lack courage? The answers to these questions will help you set up a plan to live ethically. Ask God to help you see where you are lacking in diligence, faithfulness, and courage. And ask God to help you grow in these virtues as you depend on Christ to make them part of how you think and who you are.

1. Define *diligence*, *faithfulness*, and *courage*.
2. In what ways can diligence, faithfulness, and courage be misapplied to wrong goals?
3. Contrast the virtues of diligence, faithfulness, and courage with the vices of sloth/laziness, disloyalty, recklessness, and cowardice.
4. Give examples of how diligence, faithfulness, and courage relate to ethical decision-making and ethical living.
5. Outline a plan for growing in diligence, faithfulness, and courage.

6.4 Self-Control, Temperance, and Patience

What defines a person with a chill personality? Easygoing? Never rushed? Maybe you know someone slightly introverted or shy. They don't get into trouble. They're fairly even-tempered. Is someone who doesn't blow their top at the slightest provocation necessarily practicing self-control, temperance, and patience?

DEFINING SELF-CONTROL, TEMPERANCE, AND PATIENCE

This trio of virtues has to do with a believer's relationship to temptations and handling of hardship. Jerry Bridges explains that "*self-control is the exercise of inner strength under the direction of sound judgment that enables us to do, think, and say the things that are pleasing to God.*"[13] The focus of this definition lies with the ideas of inner strength and sound judgment when a believer is faced with temptation (Gal. 5:23; 1 Cor. 9:25–27; Titus 2:2). **Temperance** is closely related to self-control and refers to one's moral conditioning and the avoidance of excessive behavior. And **patience** is a believer's faithful and hopeful endurance under long-lasting difficult circumstances. Patience carries the idea of steadfastness, longsuffering, and forbearance. A sampling of the New Testament's use of the term for patience demonstrates the expectant waiting and endurance that typifies patience (Rom. 12:12; 2 Thess. 1:4; 2 Tim. 2:10).

MOTIVATING SELF-CONTROL, TEMPERANCE, AND PATIENCE

"Don't give in!" "Don't overdo it!" "Hang in there!" These three exhortations summarize what you might think of when you think of self-control, temperance, and patience respectively. But what motivates you to not give in? It could be pride. It could also be a legalistic mentality. What motivates you to not overdo it? It could be to avoid shame and embarrassment. It could also be to avoid trouble at home or at school. And what motivates you to hang in there? It could just be pride.

All the motives mentioned above might sound natural, but that doesn't mean they're virtuous. In fact, those motives represent what is typical for unbelievers. Refusing to binge on desserts or snacks for the third night in a row is a demonstration of self-control. The result is obviously positive, but what motivated you to show self-control in this area is also important. A general answer might be to be healthy. A non-Christian motive might be solely to look more physically attractive. A Christian motive would be to better worship God with all areas of one's life (Rom. 12:1). Attractiveness, in this case, can be a natural result or bonus, but it should not be the primary or sole motivation.

Moderating how much of your free time in the evenings is consumed by your mobile device or by a streaming platform is a demonstration of temperance. Doing this will help you develop a taste for a better use of your time and a distaste for wasting too much time on social media, videos, or shows. You might set those boundaries and be careful to respect them during the school year just to keep your parents from getting on your case all the time. This would be a limited, even non-Christian, motive. You should, however, be motivated to redeem the time the Lord has given you to accomplish the things He expects you to accomplish (Eph. 5:15–17).

Waiting till some point in college to seriously date someone might be a demonstration of patience. Exercising this virtue in this scenario would require many other virtues as well, but a desire to date and the availability of a good prospect would increase the need for patience. However, you might put off dating seriously because you want to live for yourself, doing whatever you want without having to worry about another's preferences. This seems more like a non-Christian motive. A Christian's motive for patience in this area might be to focus more on his or her walk with the Lord (1 Cor. 7:32–35) or to grow in the maturity necessary for marriage and possible parenthood. Often believers must patiently wait in order to see their hopes fulfilled (Rom. 8:24–25).

OPPOSING SELF-CONTROL, TEMPERANCE, AND PATIENCE

As you have learned by now, the opposites of virtues are vices. Two vices that stand directly opposed to self-control and temperance are self-indulgence and addiction. **Self-indulgence** is having no inhibitions, a total letting go of oneself to do as one pleases. Scripture calls this kind of behavior by various names, but what commonly comes of it are sexual sin and sin related to drunkenness (Rom. 13:13; 1 Pet. 4:3–4). **Addiction** is when an individual has become entirely dependent on getting pleasure from a substance or behavior regardless of the negative consequences. Scripture portrays the folly and danger of this vice in both testaments (Prov. 23:33–35; 1 Cor. 6:12).

Another vice that opposes the virtue of temperance is the seemingly pious vice of **asceticism**, which is the severe denial of the normal physical needs of the body, usually for the purpose of gaining spiritual merit. Rather than being the explicit opposite of temperance, asceticism stretches temperance past its breaking point. Robert Roberts explains the proper and improper use of temperance by saying the following:

> Temperance is an important virtue because food, drink, and sex, if desired improperly, can be sources of disruption, corruption, misery, and ill being both to the intemperate or weak-willed person and to others in his or her social world; but if properly loved and pursued, they can be sources of joy and wellbeing. We all want happiness, and the wise person sees that pleasure without temperance is like money without justice, generosity, and gratitude; it does not bring happiness because it upends an order of values that is normative for human nature. The temperate person is one who understands these connections between bodily pleasures and the larger human good, and whose understanding actually tempers the desires and pleasures.[14]

The issue which separates asceticism from temperance is this: there is a major difference between mortifying* sin (part of the practice of temperance) and refraining from enjoying legitimate physical pleasures (compare Rom. 8:13 with Col. 2:18–23 and 1 Tim. 4:1–5).

Strife works against patience. **Strife** is adversarial contention that leads an individual to verbally disagree with, ideologically break away from, or physically engage the conflicting party. Patience endures hardship and even hostility and doesn't end up in an altercation over every minor disagreement (see Rom. 12:18). Strife is found throughout the New Testament in lists of common sins of godless people (2 Cor. 12:20; Gal. 5:20).

Neither self-indulgence nor addiction supports the Christian's duty to practice consistent self-control (Titus 2:12). And neither self-indulgence nor addiction nor

mortifying: putting to death

asceticism enable the believer's call to a life marked by thoughtful temperance (1 Cor. 9:25). Strife flies in the face of the Christian's grace-infused desire to express his or her faith, love, and hope through patience (1 Cor. 13:7). Be careful not to view the vices as "all or nothing." In other words, a little self-indulgence, a "harmless" addiction, a little experimentation with asceticism, and temporary strife are still sinful and still need to be avoided. You might not be caught up in habitual practice of a vice to the consistent neglect of certain virtues. But every vice starts out slowly and sporadically until it grows into a damaging way of life.

APPLYING SELF-CONTROL, TEMPERANCE, AND PATIENCE

It has been said that buying things on sale is saving money by spending money. If the personal rule is to save money on something you know you need to buy soon anyway, then by all means get it while it is on sale! But if the personal rule is to not spend money, period, then saving by spending isn't even an option. If you are a spender, then this section's virtues can help you. If you are not a spender except for when something is on sale, this section is also for you. And if you are extremely frugal and don't like to spend a dime, you can still learn from these applications.

First, let's spell out a distinction between self-control and temperance, even though the two are interrelated. Self-control is reactive. It is used in the moment. Temperance seeks to avoid reactive situations. When presented with a temptation to sin or to indulge, a believer practicing self-control will resist that temptation and not give in to sin. Notice that the Christian is put under pressure and has to make a quick decision whether to practice self-control or concede to self-indulgence.

The moral conditioning of temperance, however, prepares the believer to be less affected by those same temptations. Temperance often reflects our human, physical appetites (for things like sleep, food, and sex) and passions (strong desires) in general. To temper metal, for example, is to heat it and cool it in such a way that the metal becomes harder and more resistant to bending or breaking. So one's desires, legitimate and illegitimate, can be tempered appropriately so that their direction and use is ethical. Both self-control and temperance are critical for believers. Just think of self-control as adjusting the way you are playing a sport so that you can keep playing even when a cramp seizes your leg. And think of temperance as all the conditioning, warming up, and stretching you do that help prevent your legs from cramping up.

self control vs. temperance

Now, back to our shopping example. Self-control is shopping at one specific store for one specific item and resisting the urge to buy multiple items that you love from the displays in the checkout line. Temperance could result in shopping for the same gift in the same store and not even noticing or being drawn to items that you know you neither need nor have the money for. Think of something more serious, such as blowing up at people online over a political issue or current event topic. You need to practice self-control when tempted to do so, but you also need to grow in temperance to use social media without being incited to even engage with incendiary* topics.

As for applying patience, there is no lack of scenarios that require us to be patient. You have undoubtedly heard many say that patience is a virtue or even the mother of all virtues. Have you ever thought about why that is? Part of our definition of patience is endurance under long-lasting difficult circumstances. The fallen and sin-stricken world we live in affords us with innumerable instances of difficult circumstances. The patience required is often greater than the version of patience needed any time you must wait for something—waiting for your sibling to finish getting ready in the bathroom, driving behind a slow-moving vehicle, or waiting for a friend to return your text.

incendiary: tending to stir up strife

But how does one show patience when the situation is serious? If an unmarried girl gets pregnant and she or the father considers an abortion, what role does patience play? Assuming responsibility for our actions includes patiently accepting the consequences of those actions. Patience is required to endure a less-than-ideal pregnancy and all the hardships that might come in the years following the baby's birth. Getting an abortion isn't just impatience, it is to strive against an innocent life at a lethal level. Another situation that might require patience is our country's current immigration policies. You might strongly disagree with some aspects of those policies and feel that much wrong is being done to our nation or to those trying to enter it. You need patience as you exercise faith in the sovereign God while being hopeful that certain politicians will be voted into office and will commit to improving those policies.

GROWING IN SELF-CONTROL, TEMPERANCE, AND PATIENCE

Every believer needs to grow in these three virtues. Let's look at the beginning of a plan to grow in these virtues.

How do I become an emotionally stable person?

Self-control

Growing in self-control is more than just counting to ten when you get irritated. We need the help of the Holy Spirit to resist the temptation to sin (Gal. 5:16). Do a study on the empowering work of the Spirit in the lives of believers. Study the implications for believers of being united to Christ by the Spirit, positionally justified, and progressively sanctified (Rom. 6:1–4, 6–7, 11–14). Avoiding situations where you will likely self-indulge and feed an addiction is wise, but fortifying your mind and heart with Scripture and gospel-centered resources is also necessary (Rom. 12:2; Phil. 4:8).

Temperance

Think of growth in temperance like consistent, appropriately paced physical conditioning. The Christian life is likened in Scripture to a race (which also requires the virtue of patience). Developing temperance fits right in with this picture of strength and endurance (Heb. 12:1). Saturate yourself in the Word. Pray often. Sit under good preaching of the Word. Seek out encouraging fellowship with mature believers. Temperance cuts off temptations before they start, so thinking biblically about everything in your day is a great step in the right direction.

Patience

A helpful way to grow in patience is to recognize that not all is as it should be. Cultivating a realistic expectation of the world will serve you well in coping with the constant need for patience. When you are conscious of the difficulties and hardships that are common to life, especially life as a believer, your practice of patience will come more easily (James 1:3–4). But everything will be made right by Christ, and the faith and hope for the future that patience is rooted in are among the believer's greatest comforts (2 Cor. 4:17–18).

Thinking It Through 6.4

1. Define *self-control*.
2. Define *temperance*.
3. Define *patience*.
4. List several Christian and non-Christian motives for these virtues.
5. What is the relationship of the virtues of self-control, temperance, and patience to the vices of self-indulgence, addiction, asceticism, and strife?
6. How do these virtues relate to ethical decision-making and living? Give examples.
7. What do you need to include in a plan to grow in self-control, temperance, and patience?

Terms to Remember

- righteousness
- goodness
- ungodliness
- corruption
- prudence
- cunning
- rashness
- diligence
- faithfulness
- courage
- sloth
- workaholism
- disloyalty
- recklessness
- cowardice
- self-control
- temperance
- patience
- self-indulgence
- addiction
- asceticism
- strife

Scripture Memory

Philippians 4:8

Understanding Ethics

1. How do the virtues of righteousness and goodness relate to ethics?
2. How does the virtue of prudence relate to ethics?
3. How do the virtues of diligence, faithfulness, and courage relate to ethics?
4. How do the virtues of self-control, temperance, and patience relate to ethics?

Practicing Ethical Decision-Making

5. What role does prudence play when one turns eighteen, becoming a legal adult?
6. What role does patience play in abiding by the rules set by your parents and by your school administrators?

Analyzing and Evaluating Ethical Claims

7. Why isn't it sufficient for people to identify what is right and what is good based solely on situations starting and ending well?
8. Why does social media use require prudence?
9. Why is it unethical to allow a friend to copy your homework?
10. Does doing what is best for myself mean that I'm an emotionally stable person? Explain.

Creating My Own Position Statements on Ethics

11. Formulate a position regarding the role of the Holy Spirit and regeneration in the proper practice of the virtues. Include scriptural support.
12. Defend your use of the virtues to chart the right path to ethical decisions through all the obstacles of life.

07 Virtues
Part 2

Why does society oppose virtue?

GALATIANS 5:22–23

"Humility opens the way to all other godly character traits. It is the soil in which the other traits of the fruit of the Spirit grow." JERRY BRIDGES

7.1 Humility, Meekness, and Gentleness

Have you ever been to one of those Japanese restaurants where the chef prepares the food in front of you on a teppanyaki grill? The chef shows off and entertains you with various antics while preparing your meal. Compare that experience to a meal prepared in a slow cooker. A slow cooker takes hours and hours to prepare a meal. It simply works in the background. But when the slow cooker has been going all day, the delicious smell of dinner permeates the house.

In a way, the virtues of humility, meekness, and gentleness are like that meal prepared in the slow cooker. Some virtues, such as faith and love, get a lot of attention. Humility, meekness, and gentleness, however, support these and other virtues by being "on," though in the background. These three virtues are godly and should be pursued by all Christians. And they are critical for avoiding one of the oldest and most pervasive of all the vices—pride.

PROPER DEFINITIONS

Meekness and gentleness flow from humility. **Humility** is a lowly view of one's own importance, resulting from "a high view of God's person"[2] and a profound sense of one's own weakness and sinfulness. **Meekness** is a humble and calm disposition in situations that can lead to pride or anger. **Gentleness** is tender care for others even when they are hard to deal with. Jerry Bridges offers a helpful distinction between meekness and gentleness: "Gentleness is an active trait, describing the manner in which we should treat others. Meekness is a passive trait, describing the proper Christian response when others mistreat us."[3]

The Bible gives us examples of these three virtues in action. The best example of humility is seen in Christ's incarnation and crucifixion (Phil. 2:3–8). Meekness takes one's sober estimation of oneself and applies it with the proper restraints and responses to difficult circumstances. Moses exemplifies this virtue in how he endured with the children of Israel from Egypt to the brink of the Promised Land (Num. 12:3). The gentleness of Christ is closely related to His humility and meekness (Matt. 11:29; 2 Cor. 10:1) and is seen in His tender care for His people. A proper view of ourselves that leads to a patient and merciful response to sinful, imperfect people allows us to show others the gentleness of Christ.

Rather than thinking less of yourself, humility leads to thinking less about yourself. BRIAN ROSNER[4]

PROPER CONCEPTIONS

One sure way to verify that society at large is standing on its head morally is to notice what it thinks of Christian virtues. According to many non-Christians, if you are humble, you are naïve; if you are meek, you are weak; if you are gentle, you are cowardly. These three virtues are unpopular among some unbelievers because they appear to them to hinder advancement in the face of opposition. Even Christians can be tempted to minimize or avoid these virtues because of society's influence and because they misunderstand what these virtues really are. Humility, meekness, and gentleness don't get in the way of a successful life. But these virtues definitely don't play into the selfish mindset that many people have.

How do I become great in the eyes of God?

Can Christians also see humility as naïveté, meekness as weakness, and gentleness as cowardice? Unfortunately, yes. Does every achievement and every fashionable outfit or hairstyle need a picture posted to social media? Is there room for humility when you do that? Do you vocally oppose every individual or organization that supports abortion and the LGBTQ agenda? How about your tirades against all those perceived injustices that are your hobbyhorses or soap boxes? Where does meekness fit in? Do you view a gracious, tender heart as contrary to a tough, steely mindset needed for this fallen world? What place does gentleness have in the life of a believer, then?

Consider humility and pride. Whom do you seek recognition from to satisfy your ego? Who must know what you have done and what you possess to give you fulfillment? Receiving due recognition and healthy encouragement is not what we are addressing here. True humility counters any notion of bragging or boasting. A Christian conception of humility considers the fact that believers are sinners saved by grace and anything good about them comes from God's hand (Eph. 2:8–9; James 1:17). Believers should, therefore, constantly point others to God and His goodness rather than themselves.

Does meekness have anything to do with weakness? Not really. The Christian conception of meekness involves a combination of patience and faith. Being hot-headed and getting even with someone flies in the face of true meekness. Meekness sees the believer entrusting the situation and outcome to God while humbly enduring the adverse circumstances (Isa. 11:4; Matt. 21:5; Eph. 4:2). Early church father Chromatius described meekness this way: "The meek are those who are gentle, humble and unassuming, simple in faith and patient in the face of every affront. Imbued with the precepts of the gospel, they imitate the meekness of the Lord, who says, 'Learn from me, for I am meek and humble of heart.'"[5] Remaining meek in the face of adversity is real strength—a far cry from weakness.

Do you enjoy following the rules and making sure everyone else does too? Do you seek justice at any cost? It is challenging to maintain righteous responses and just reactions to evil done to us or to those we care about. Gentleness shouldn't get in the way of justice and courage. But neither can gentleness be forgotten altogether. The Christian conception of gentleness seeks to bring heart and understanding to the implementation of justice. Gentleness is not cowardly; it does the right thing while tenderly caring for the individuals involved in the situation (Gal. 6:1; 2 Tim. 2:24–25).

PERVERTING THE VIRTUES

Pride

If there is one prevalent sin that Christians often fail to identify in their own hearts, it is the vice of pride. **Pride** is an inflated estimation of oneself, which attempts to rob God of His rightful place as sovereign Lord of all. Pride is the nemesis of humility. This can be seen in Scripture's descriptions of the proud being brought low and the humble being raised up (Prov. 29:23; Matt. 23:12; 1 Pet. 5:5–6). God despises the proud (Prov. 6:16–17; Ezek. 28:6–8, 17). It is ironic that pursuing what pride seeks, personal glory and self-exaltation, actually results in the destruction of the proud person (e.g., Nebuchadnezzar [Dan. 4:30–33] and Herod [Acts 12:21–23]). That doesn't always happen in this life. But the vice of pride in unbelievers will surely lead to their eternal demise (Prov. 16:18; 1 John 2:16–17).

Pride fills the void where humility should reside. If autonomy and selfishness rule a person's mind, there is no room left for a humble recognition of frailty and fallibility (Prov. 3:7). The vice of pride cancels any acknowledgement of and submission to God's wisdom, power, and sovereignty.

Anger

The vice of anger stands opposite the virtue of meekness. **Anger** is intense displeasure arising from strong disagreement with a situation. Moses was meek, but not perfectly so. Look at these passages to see examples of Moses' anger, stirred for the right reasons but poorly expressed: Exodus 2:11–12; 32:19; Numbers 11:10–15; 20:2–12. Just as meekness is closely related to humility, anger can be closely connected to pride, as seen in the history of Haman in the book of Esther (for example, see Esther 3:5). It is too easy to let unimportant things get under our skin, and then we unleash anger. Even short outbursts of anger, if they happen often enough, can point to the vice of anger. Proverbs attributes "great understanding" (Prov. 14:29) to those who know how to control their tempers but calls quickness to anger foolish (Prov. 14:17). James memorably conveys the folly of anger by saying, "The wrath of man worketh not the righteousness of God" (James 1:20). James also relates wisdom to meekness (James 3:13). Meekness measures up to God's righteous standards and is the wiser choice over anger.

Harshness

Where gentleness should thrive in the heart of a believer, harshness seeks to assert itself. The vice of **harshness** is to be unpleasant, rough, or mean toward someone. Harshness can come across through spoken or written words and nonverbally through looks and body language—and even through silence when gentleness demands verbal communication. In Scripture, the vice of harshness is described by various terms that stand against gentleness—violence, quarrels, strife, brawling (1 Tim. 3:3; 2 Tim. 2:23–24; Titus 3:2). Whereas gentleness is a fruit of the Spirit (Gal. 5:23), harshness is involved in several of the works of the flesh—"hatred, . . . wrath, strife" (Gal. 5:20). Where curt, rude responses take place, the vice of harshness is present. Gentleness encourages, de-escalates, and soothes. Harshness discourages and aggravates, making problems worse.

PERSONALIZING HUMILITY, MEEKNESS, AND GENTLENESS

All the virtues, but especially these three, are like a cellular network that operates in the background, enabling a device to communicate properly. Just as the network your cell phone uses to communicate with other devices is always active, so must humility, meekness, and gentleness be constantly active in governing your personal interactions. In any conversation, either the virtue of humility is helping the relationship, or the vice of pride is spoiling the relationship. Meekness must counter anger, and gentleness must thrive instead of harshness. Season your success stories with humility. Blend meekness into discussions of frustrating topics. Sprinkle your defense of the truth with gentleness.

God didn't intend humility to be the virtue that squashes all expressions of personal success and accomplishment, but humility will keep such things from being our focus. We all know the individual who wants to give off an appearance of modesty and humility but finds ways to name-drop* or boast in an indirect, nonchalant way. The fact that you have had a 4.0 all through high school or that your new car is way cooler than all your friends' cars doesn't entitle you to bring those things up at any moment in every context. Humility helps us keep everything in perspective—God is the giver of all good things, and we aren't better than anyone else, especially based on our performances or possessions (Luke 18:10–14; 1 Cor. 4:7). Pride infects all of us with great ease. Be motived by humility in all your conversations.

Do you have a short fuse? Do you get angry easily about every single thing that goes against what you believe in and support? Many things should make believers angry, in a righteous way: the far-left agenda shaping educational materials, abortion, the normalization of pornography use, rampant fornication among young people, any sort of abuse against the innocent and vulnerable, and many other expressions of evil in the world. Practicing meekness will help you keep your righteous anger from turning into sinful irritableness and brashness. Meekness is also paramount during times when pride attempts to seduce you to accept flattery. When you feel like someone is flattering you with ulterior motives, meekness will help you duck out of the way of that temptation. All believers are commanded to "put on . . . meekness" (Col. 3:12)—in other words, to practice it.

It's not only muscular or passionate individuals who need to practice the virtue of gentleness. Yes, the six-foot-four pediatrician can and should be extremely gentle with the infant patient he is treating. Gentleness presupposes the power to do damage, to be harmful or harsh. But we are all capable of that, at least with our words.

> Meekness . . . is where humility and self-control meet. It is one of the most attractive and indispensable aspects of truly Christlike character.
>
> JOHN MACARTHUR[6]

Think of your intellectual, athletic, or spiritual opponents. You might think they have it coming to them! You can be tempted to win at any cost because you have the right knowledge, the better team, or the right interpretation of the Word. Practicing gentleness isn't passivity or compromise. Not harming or embarrassing an opponent unnecessarily, even though it would be easy to do, is practicing gentleness. The apostle Paul makes the point that, when dealing with people who present challenging situations in the church, gentleness must reign (Eph. 4:2; 2 Tim. 2:24–25; Titus 3:2). The truth is, God deals with us with perfect gentleness (Ps. 18:35; 2 Cor. 10:1). The Almighty chooses to deal with His people with gentle tenderness (Isa. 40:10–11). These truths must permeate believers' ethical decision-making processes.

PRACTICING HUMILITY, MEEKNESS, AND GENTLENESS

Like many of the virtues, it might seem a daunting task to actually develop these three in your life. Do you find it embarrassing if people know that you are weak in certain areas of the Christian life? Don't be afraid that people might find that out. All believers are in the same boat—all need to grow in their relationship with Christ!

The fruit of the Spirit is just that, *fruit* in the singular. The different aspects of that fruit are distinguishable—meekness and gentleness included (Gal. 5:22–23)—but each fruit comes with the rest as believers respond to the work of the Spirit in their lives. Be encouraged that God's work in the hearts of believers is comprehensive and not limited. The fruit of the Spirit is a single unit, and the virtues are interconnected (2 Pet. 1:5–7).

name-drop: to introduce names of important or famous people into a conversation, implying a personal connection to them

Do you have a plan to grow in these virtues? When was the last time you specifically prayed to God asking for His help to be less proud and more humble, less angry and more meek, or less harsh and more gentle? Praying to grow in humility, meekness, and gentleness is the right place to start. Praying taps into the Lord's power and cultivates an awareness of your need for these virtues. If you aren't aware of these virtues and their vices, then you won't be thinking of ways to practice the virtues like you should.

Another aspect of a plan to grow in these three virtues is to ask a friend, perhaps an older mentor who knows you well, to assess your humility, meekness, and gentleness. Be honest and then submissive to the report the friend gives about you. You can practice humility by graciously accepting what he or she says and repenting, if necessary, from any traces of pride, anger, and harshness in your life. Thank your friend and ask him or her to keep you accountable in these areas.

We all need God's grace to be humble, practice meekness, and treat others gently. Look to Christ, who is the supreme model of humility, meekness, and gentleness (Matt. 12:20).

Thinking It Through 7.1

1. Define *humility*.

2. Define *meekness*.

3. Define *gentleness*.

4. How do Christian and non-Christian conceptions of humility, meekness, and gentleness differ?

5. How do the vices of pride, anger, and harshness contrast with humility, meekness, and gentleness, respectively?

6. Give examples of how humility, meekness, and gentleness relate to ethical decision-making and ethical living.

7. What are some actions you can take that can help you grow in humility, meekness, and gentleness?

7.2 Kindness and Compassion

You have been told to smile for the camera since you were a child wrinkling your nose in a cheesy grin. Your parents constantly reminded you to say, "Thank you" and "Please." They also taught you not to laugh at someone if they tripped or got hurt. Were all those smiles, words, and acts genuine? If you only look and sound nice at the appointed times, are you truly kind? And can compassion be faked?

True kindness is much more than being nice or polite, and compassion is much more than feeling sorry for someone.

DEFINING KINDNESS AND COMPASSION

Kindness is an internal sentiment, cultivated by the Holy Spirit, that motivates believers to indiscriminately do good to others. **Compassion** is an external manifestation of loving-kindness that sympathetically and indiscriminately meets a need. Whereas kindness is primarily a disposition of one's character, compassion activates that kindness by sympathizing with someone and meeting their need.

Can you identify which central virtue (faith, love, or hope) is most at work behind kindness and compassion? Kindness and compassion are an outflow, a demonstration, of love. Believers can love because of God's love for them (Eph. 2:4–5; 1 John 4:19). It is also the case, then, that believers can show kindness and compassion to others because that is how God has dealt with them (Rom. 2:4; Eph. 4:32). Love always plays a role when kindness and compassion are shown.

MOTIVATING KINDNESS AND COMPASSION

When discussing ethical difficulties, we should pause to consider why we do what we do. When do you stop to carefully think through decisions? Maybe it's when you stand in front of your closet or dresser deciding what to wear. Maybe it's when you decide what to spend your birthday or Christmas money on. These types of decisions may have ethical ramifications involving any number of virtues, but even then, you probably don't contemplate your motives too extensively. Determining whether the virtues of kindness and compassion are part of your normal, everyday motives as you interact with people is well worth your consideration.

A great scriptural description of these virtues motivating righteous actions is Christ's parable of the Good Samaritan (Luke 10:30–37). Though Jesus used this teaching to make a point about how to love our neighbors, it is clear that neither the priest nor the Levite showed compassion for their fellow Jew. Only the Samaritan, a non-Jew, "had compassion" (Luke 10:33) and "shewed mercy" (Luke 10:37) (which flows from compassion). Do you think we can infer from this text that the priest and Levite were kind men? What kindness did they feel that then translated into helping the man in desperate need? None. A kind heart, a disposition of kindness, leads a person to demonstrate compassion to the needy (Luke 6:45).

Kindness and compassion treat people with dignity—recognizing the enormous value of humans created in the image of God. Do you refuse to say "Hi," "I'm sorry," or "Thank you" to friends or classmates? Do you hear of physical or spiritual needs of people within your community and immediately shift your thoughts elsewhere? If you help some people out of self-interest and refuse to help others out of prejudice, then you are no different than the partial, indifferent priest and Levite in Christ's parable of the Good Samaritan.

1. The Holy Spirit plants the seed of love.

2. Kindness of character grows.

3. Kindness shows itself through acts of compassion.

Brotherly kindness is not limited strictly to physical siblings and spiritual brethren. . . . [The Bible] commands us to show kindness to strangers.
JOHN MACARTHUR[7]

Christians should be motivated—compelled even—to be aware of situations that require kindness in their area of influence. If a new student joins your class or a new kid moves onto your street, realizing that you need to be kind to him or her should be automatic. As a rule—the golden rule—as well as by conscious choice, Christians should show kindness to others (Matt. 7:12). Christians should be motivated by a desire to live according to the new life they have in Christ and according to the fruit that the Spirit produces in them (2 Cor. 5:17; Gal. 5:22).

Believers should be motivated to demonstrate compassion based on an honest examination of their own need for God's compassion. Where would sinful, rebellious humans be if it weren't for God's merciful and generous compassion (Lam. 3:22–23, 32)? Practical compassion, in which one sympathetically cares for someone in need, is expected of believers (James 1:27). Faithful obedience to the Savior is a strong motivation and should be the primary one.

There are also non-Christian motives to be kind and compassionate. Unfortunately, most of them are self-serving. For instance, you might make a kind comment on a friend's post on social media even though your friend's post was flaunting selfish, vain, or proud characteristics. Your affirmation of a friend's problematic post does not actually help him or her; the result of your action is wrong and harmful. And if your comment was motivated by the expectation that your friend will also affirm your posts, then your motive was selfish too. True kindness never uses selfish means to an end, nor does it affirm someone in their sin.

Social media can fuel non-Christian motives to display compassion. Take the young person doing inner-city community work or foreign missions work who chronicles every activity on his or her social media. These pictures and videos show this individual doing compassionate things for down-and-out people. But the sheer volume of media shared and the captions that accompany each post betray a proud and self-interested motive for showing compassion. Those posts can be therapeutic to this person's self-esteem while crafting an endearing image to friends, family, and even potential future employers. True compassion doesn't plan for people to be watching its works, nor does true compassion serve an ulterior motive (Matt. 6:1–4).

OBSTRUCTING KINDNESS AND COMPASSION: CRUELTY AND INDIFFERENCE

If someone isn't nice, we say they are mean. If someone isn't loving, we say they are coldhearted. How mean does someone have to be to be considered cruel? How coldhearted does someone have to be to be considered indifferent? The virtues of kindness and compassion have corresponding vices of cruelty and indifference, respectively. These vices go further down the path of ungodliness than merely being mean or coldhearted. The vice of **cruelty** is the willful causation of distress or discomfort in others. The vice of **indifference** is apathy toward others and utter lack of concern for the ethical good of a situation. Cruelty enjoys being mean. Indifference finds comfort in coldheartedness.

It isn't just psychopathic criminals and totalitarian dictators who are cruel. Cruelty, like all vices, can find ways to sneak into believers' hearts and actions. Although you might not have been the one to cause someone pain or embarrassment, if you see it and could alleviate it but don't because it's entertaining, that is being cruel. It might be a little uncomfortable to let someone know about an unnoticed wardrobe malfunction or a dirty spot on his or her clothes. But it would be cruel to see either of these and chuckle to yourself or laugh with your friends about it, not making the person aware of the situation. Even more patently cruel is the killing of unborn babies or being racist against another human being. It's also sometimes tempting to make fun of the way people look, but people come in a variety of shapes and sizes; it is cruel to make fun of someone for the way God made them. There is zero room for cruelty in the heart and actions of a Christian (Eph. 4:29–32).

The vice of indifference is a blind spot for many Christians. Believers can all too easily excuse inaction due to indifference by saying, "I have too much going on to help," or "I'm not prepared, so I won't be of any real help." Have you found your heart turning to those excuses rather than warming up to act compassionately? Indifference can too easily be passed off as legitimate or even righteous. God warns us in His Word not to be deceived by our own reasoning, which so easily leads to sin (James 1:13–16)—reasoning that can drive us to a lack of compassion. What do you first think when you hear of a request at school or church for volunteers to help with a need in your school, church, or community? Your Saturdays are generally free, and the need requires someone with your profile—young, available, and able. The virtue of compassion and the vice of indifference lock horns as you contemplate how to respond to that call. There is a danger in saying no to showing compassion. You don't want to create a habit so that it becomes automatic for you to be indifferent when you need to be compassionate.

Sympathy Tethered to Truth Versus Sympathy Severed from Truth

So far, we have established that, to display the virtue of compassion, you must possess sympathy. Sympathy is to emotionally suffer with someone who is suffering. The term itself conveys this, but Scripture further illustrates its meaning: Christ's incarnation, life, death, and ongoing priestly work are the greatest expression of true sympathy (Phil. 2:7–8; Heb. 2:17–18; 4:15).

The use of sympathy becomes problematic when someone's reactions to a situation and the resultant feelings are placed above determining the morality of the situation. For instance, if you know someone who is angry, sad, frustrated, or offended, a wrong use of sympathy would tell you to join them in their experience without asking any questions. That would be like jumping in to save someone who is drowning without considering the depth of the water or the strength of the current or size of the waves. The person in need desperately wants someone to sympathize with how they are feeling. But leaving the stability and safety of the shore leaves the one joining the person in need without a solid foundation from which to help. To truly help the one drowning would mean safely rescuing the person from the shore or at least carefully entering into the situation with wisdom, vigilance, and skill. A successful rescue produces zero casualties, not two. And to truly help someone spiritually, your sympathy and compassion must be guided by the truth of God's Word, not mere emotion. Wisdom, vigilance, and the skillful application of truth can keep both you and your struggling friend from disaster, even as you sympathize with his or her suffering.

You have seen that kindness and compassion require sympathy. Yet all virtues are tied to the character of God as revealed in Scripture. If someone is wallowing in self-pity and selfishly seeking approval of unbiblical behaviors or reactions, is sympathy the ethical approach? Simply affirming how someone is feeling is not necessarily helping them. Believers must maintain their practice of sympathetic compassion (1 Pet. 3:8) while applying the truth of God's Word to someone's situation (Gal. 6:1). How can we "rejoice with them that do rejoice, and weep with them that weep" (Rom. 12:15) and also be truthful? In what ways can sympathy severed from truth actually be harmful?

PRACTICING KINDNESS AND COMPASSION

It's easy to be kind to those who are kind to you. This social phenomenon can be observed in the drive-through when a long chain of customers "pay it forward." You weren't expecting the person ahead of you to pay for your order, but it feels great. That kindness you were shown usually motivates you to follow suit and pay for the person behind you. This example, however, doesn't necessarily involve the Christian virtue of kindness. It is a form of kindness or generosity, but it is hard to know the motives or goals of each person who participates. The Christian virtue of kindness manifests itself when you politely and calmly interact with the drive-through workers who get your order wrong and drag their feet to fix it. Kindness is watching your words and tone when you express your disappointment about a decision your parents made. Kindness looks like respect and honor for your parents even when deep down you feel tempted to be unkind to them.

Compassion comes more easily to those who have developed a genuine kindness and love for others. But whereas kindness is a virtue you express every day, compassionate acts aren't necessarily daily activities. We can assume that the Good Samaritan didn't find mugged Jewish men alongside the road every day. But if he did, it would be unethical for him to choose indifference on some days and compassion on others. The fact that kindness is more of a constant whereas compassion is demonstrated occasionally when needs arise doesn't mean that compassion is not as big a deal as kindness. No, all virtues are important for believers and are necessary for them to live ethically (2 Pet. 1:5–10).

If one of your classmates suffered a loss in the family, reaching out to him or her with a note would be an act of compassion. Compassion would also motivate you to pray for the student and his or her family. If you were really close to this person, compassion would motivate you to support and care for your friend in even more tangible ways.

While biblical compassion is tender-hearted (it feels deeply the distress others are in), it is never sentimental (governed by emotionality rather than spiritual purposefulness). JIM BERG[8]

How should I
respond to those
who are hurting?

Ask yourself the question, How should I respond to those who are hurting? Let's take a few steps back to consider how growing in kindness and compassion can answer this question. You can't give what you don't have. This is an extremely basic principle! You might have a desire to get a gift for a friend. Your friend won't get a gift from you based on your desire alone. You must make it or buy it before you can give it. The same principle applies to the virtues—in this case to kindness and compassion. You must have a tree of kindness and compassion planted in your heart before you can pick its fruit and give it to others who need it.

By following these guidelines to engage those who are hurting, you will be well prepared to show true kindness and demonstrate genuine compassion:

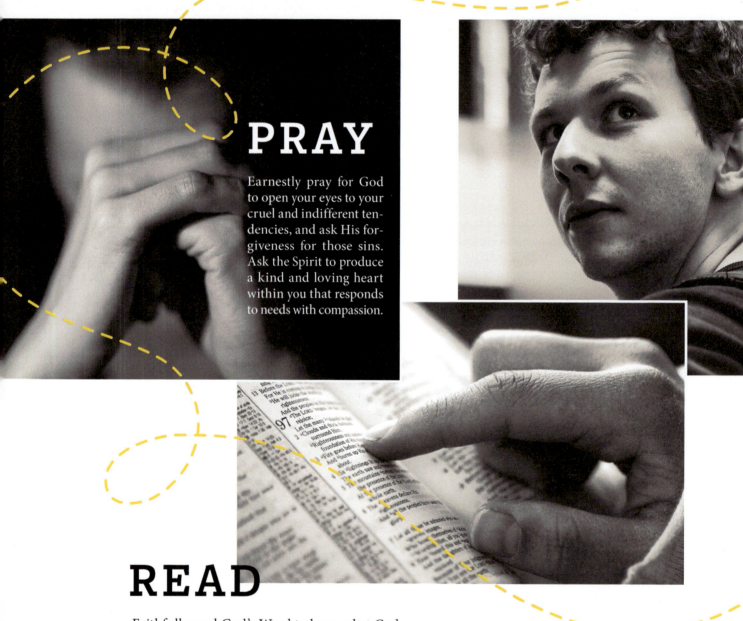

PRAY

Earnestly pray for God to open your eyes to your cruel and indifferent tendencies, and ask His forgiveness for those sins. Ask the Spirit to produce a kind and loving heart within you that responds to needs with compassion.

READ

Faithfully read God's Word to learn what God is like and learn more about godly kindness and compassion. Find specific verses and passages to read and study that will help you grow in kindness and compassion.

PRACTICE

This is where the rubber meets the road. This is where you have to step up and show kindness and compassion, even if you are nervous or uncertain how you will be received. Include those who wouldn't expect kindness or compassion from you.

LOOK

Consciously look around for opportunities to be kind and compassionate. Purposefully look for new ways to be kind, ways you haven't shown kindness in the past. Look for a meaningful way to demonstrate compassion to someone in need, even if it is a very small way.

REPEAT

Keep practicing kindness and compassion. Stay aware of needs around you. Continue reading and studying the Word. And keep praying for God to increase your desire to be motivated by kindness and compassion in all you do.

Allow the virtues of kindness and compassion to influence your ethical decisions. Love has many manifestations and applications. But kindness is a virtue that takes a little love and makes it go a long way. And compassion comes from a deep-seated and sympathetic love that reflects the heart of God Himself (Exod. 34:6–7; Matt. 11:28–30; Titus 3:4). What a privilege and what an opportunity!

Thinking It Through 7.2

1. Define *kindness*.

2. Define *compassion*.

3. List various Christian and non-Christian motives for kindness and compassion.

4. Contrast the virtues of kindness and compassion with the vices of cruelty and indifference.

5. List several examples of how kindness and compassion relate to ethical living.

6. What is the difference between sympathy tethered to truth and sympathy severed from truth? Why does this difference matter?

7. List aspects of a plan for growing in kindness and compassion.

7.3 Gratitude, Joy, and Peace

Do you know Steady Freddy? How about Roller Coaster Roger? Roger is all over the place emotionally. Some call him moody. The weather, how many hours of sleep he got the night before, whether he has food in his stomach or not, and how he did on his last test all greatly influence his current temperament. Freddy, on the other hand, is calm, cool, and collected. He is nice to be around, and he even lifts the spirits of those he interacts with.

The virtues of gratitude, joy, and peace have much in common with Freddy. Gratitude should be a natural and consistent trait for believers because Christians are the most blessed people on the planet (Eph. 2:1–7). Joy looks to God and to the reasons believers have to rejoice in His salvation and provision (Eph. 1:3–8). And peace comes from God, who Himself is "the Lord of peace" (2 Thess. 3:16). If He can and will give peace, then His people can experience it. Gratitude, joy, and peace offer believers a steady outlook on life—something Roger lacks and desperately needs. A firm understanding of gratitude, joy, and peace contributes to a steady, vibrant faith.

DEFINING GRATITUDE, JOY, AND PEACE

Another common term for the Christian virtue of gratitude is *thankfulness*. The two terms, though, are essentially interchangeable. **Gratitude** is an attitude of thanksgiving to God for His provision and governance of all things. Gratitude requires faith and hope for Christians, the only ones who fully express this virtue, to believe God's promises and trust in His care for them. Gratitude goes beyond being thankful for just the good or pleasant things in life. Believers know that God knows best, He knows all things, and His will is perfect for their lives (Rom. 8:28). This virtue is as much a mindset as it is individual instances of thanking God for His marvelous ways.

life

trials

suffering

joy

peace

God and His promises

The Christian virtue of joy isn't the same thing as happiness. **Joy** is a confident delight in God's sovereign work in all of life's circumstances. Joy is more of a governing mindset than a fleeting emotion. In other words, joy doesn't ebb and flow as happiness and sadness do. Joy is firmly rooted outside the circumstances of life; joy is rooted in God, in His provision of salvation, and in His sovereign purposes (Rom. 5:1–5). Joy, for believers, coexists with trials and suffering (Acts 5:21; Heb. 10:34). In many cases, joy isn't put to the test in the life of a Christian *until* the arrival of difficult circumstances (James 1:2–4).

The Christian virtue of peace is much more than the absence of war or conflict. Peace also goes beyond a mere personal internal tranquility.[9] **Peace** is a harmonious wholeness produced when God's design of the world, including human relationships, is rightly ordered. There is no peace outside of God because any peace we can have with God and with others comes through Christ (Rom. 5:1; Eph. 2:13–19). Just like joy, peace coexists with trials and sufferings (John 16:33). The virtue of peace describes the mindset and character of a believer, even during difficult and unpleasant circumstances.

CHRISTIAN GRATITUDE, JOY, AND PEACE

How can I be a biblically happy person?

At least fifteen countries including America commemorate their own version of Thanksgiving.[10] However, the United States of America's celebration of it is the best-known to most of us. Can unbelievers express gratitude? Sure they can. Everyone is thankful, or at least happy, for good weather, for not getting badly injured in an accident, and for babies that sleep through the night. The objects of gratitude for unbelievers and for believers are very different though. But as with the original Thanksgiving Day in the United States, the primary object of gratitude should be God. Non-Christians, who refuse to come to the Creator and Sustainer of all on His terms, can't be properly grateful to Him. They simply enjoy the abundance that God graciously provides (Matt. 5:45; Acts 14:17). Sadly, unbelievers don't recognize who God is and what He does for them: "They glorified him not as God, neither were thankful" (Rom. 1:21). Non-Christians attribute the good things in their lives to things like luck, fate, destiny, cosmic energy, science, the evolutionary process, or themselves. How empty and unfulfilling!

> *Thanksgiving is a normal result of a vital union with Christ, and a direct measure of the extent to which we are experiencing the reality of that union in our daily lives.*
> JERRY BRIDGES[11]

But Christians have endless reasons to be grateful, reasons that include but go well beyond physical blessings. When was the last time you considered how much you have to be grateful for? How is a Christian's gratitude for life, health, good friends, or the opportunity to go to college different from a non-Christian's gratitude for the same things? Knowing that God is the giver of all these things, plus all the spiritual blessings in Christ, makes all the difference (Eph. 1:3; James 1:17)! Gratitude breeds more gratitude. Once you begin to thank God for His work in your life in so many ways and on so many levels, you find more and more reasons to continue to be grateful. Christians and non-Christians can be grateful for a good job and steady income. But a Christian recognizes that both of those are from God. He or she, therefore, is generous with that income and gives to his or her church and helps to meet other needs out of sheer gratitude for all that God has done on his or her behalf.

When you investigate the sourcing of a product, you are looking to see not only where a product comes from but how it is produced. In our culture, people are interested in sourcing products for a variety of reasons: allergies to certain ingredients, dietary preferences (organic, vegetarian, vegan),

Biblical Peace

שָׁלוֹם

When it comes to the idea of peace in Scripture, both Testaments have helpful terms that aid our understanding of what biblical peace is. The Hebrew word for peace is *shalom*, and it has a rich and broad meaning. *Wholeness*, *blessing*, and *prosperity* are some terms that help explain *shalom*. Three passages in Isaiah illustrate what *shalom* encompasses. First, the Messiah is called the "Prince of Peace" in Isaiah 9:6, and peace will characterize the reign of His kingdom (9:7). Second, Isaiah 32:15–18 relates peace to righteousness, quietness, and rest in God's kingdom. And third, Isaiah 52:7 describes the announcement of God's kingdom; notice how peace is a key part of that reign along with good news, happiness, and salvation.[13] When God reigns in the hearts of His people and humans live for their King, there is peace.

εἰρήνη

In the New Testament, the Greek term *eirēnē* is used for peace in a similar way to its Old Testament counterpart.[14] *Rest* and *harmony* are two terms that help explain *eirēnē*. Jesus is introduced at His incarnation as one whose coming signaled peace (Luke 2:14). Jesus not only spoke peace, He brought peace (Luke 7:48–50). God grants peace to those He saves (Col. 1:20). And believers can live lives of peace because of the work of Christ and the Spirit (Rom. 14:17; Phil. 4:9).[15] How divine is this biblical peace, and how necessary! Peace with God, which results in peace with others and oneself, can only come from God Himself.

> *We can go through life bored, glum and complaining, or we can rejoice in the Lord, in our names being written in heaven, in the hope of an eternal inheritance.* JERRY BRIDGES[12]

or maybe the labor involved (child workers or inhumane conditions). What if we "sourced" our virtues? What are the differences between non-Christian and Christian sources of joy and peace? Non-Christians unashamedly look within themselves to find joy and peace. There is so much focus on self-care, self-worth, and being true to oneself that it comes as no surprise that most people look to themselves to find their joy and peace. On the one hand, Christians can look at this and agree that looking to circumstances outside ourselves is a shaky and unsteady source for true joy and peace. But on the other hand, looking to ourselves is just as bad a source for joy and peace as looking to the sin-twisted and curse-afflicted world (Gen. 3:14–19; Ps. 51:5; Jer. 17:9). When the mantras of the day are "Be true to yourself" and "You create your own happiness," then the unstable source of any joy and peace is readily apparent. How can someone create joy or peace when their lives are in shambles and they are relying on themselves (or their circumstances) for joy or peace?

> *[Joy] is a deep gladness that comes from within, and it's prompted partly by the knowledge that God has accepted us in Christ and partly by the delight and satisfaction we find in him.*
>
> JOHN MACARTHUR[16]

The source of true joy and true peace is God (Rom. 15:13; Gal. 5:22). It is abundantly clear from Scripture that God is the ultimate possessor and giver of joy and peace (Pss. 16:11; 51:12; Isa. 52:7–9; Rom. 5:10–11). The virtues of joy and peace are crucial for Christian living. This can be seen by their inclusion in the fruit of the Spirit (Gal. 5:22) and by Paul's frequent mention of joy and peace when greeting or saying farewell to the recipients of his epistles (Rom. 15:32–33; Phil. 1:2, 4; 1 Thess. 1:1, 6; 5:16, 23). Since God is the source of these virtues, Christians can be confident not only that they can be joyful and experience peace but also that joy and peace can't be permanently taken away from them (John 14:27; 15:11). A bad grade shouldn't take away your joy in the Lord. A broken relationship can't take away your peace with God. Sin is the real joy-killer and peace-stealer (Ps. 32:3–4). But repentance renews joy and peace in believers (Ps. 32:5–7). God's joy is greater than your adverse circumstances (and even your sin), and God's peace is overwhelmingly comforting (Phil. 4:7; 1 Pet. 1:8).

> *The starting point for authentic peace is peace with God.*
>
> JOHN MACARTHUR[17]

FORSAKING GRATITUDE, JOY, AND PEACE

In the absence of virtue, there is vice. Out of a lack of gratitude comes ingratitude. Where there is no joy, there is despair. And no peace leads to worry. Just as the virtues are related, you should be able to see the relation between these three vices. He who thinks he has nothing to be thankful for begins to despair. This despair results from a lack of rejoicing and giving thanks for what one has. And then worry sets in because the despair builds and worsens. (Sadly, worry is often in the background of the lives of many Christians. But when despair is also present, worry comes to the fore.)

Ingratitude is taking things for granted, overlooking what is clearly worthy of thanks, and being unthankful for all the good one has. **Despair** is synonymous with hopelessness and describes giving up and being pessimistic about the outcome of a situation. **Worry** is emotional instability where someone rehearses all the what-ifs about a given situation and fails to trust God and His Word.

You'll recall that pride is a common vice that doesn't necessarily get called out too frequently. The same can be said for the vices of ingratitude and worry. If the average high school student rarely expresses gratitude, then the average high school student's norm is essentially ingratitude. Unchecked ingratitude can lead to a mindset of entitlement. That is a step in a very wrong direction. With entitlement comes an expectation of certain things or special treatment and then the temptation to demand what's expected. Where is the heart of gratitude in that? Stay clear of ingratitude. Express thanksgiving to God for the big and the little things in your life.

And worry is all too commonplace. In one sense it follows that unbelievers would be anxious, but worry doesn't make sense for believers (Matt. 6:25–34; Eph. 4:17). A worrisome individual thinks and acts as if God doesn't exist or at least as if He is incapable of handling a trying situation. It's easy to see how worry is also an opposite to one of the three central virtues: faith. Faith leads to hope and peace. Unbelief leads to despair and worry. What does worry accomplish? Worry is a vortex that sucks you into ungodly thinking and unbiblical behavior. God gives peace to His children for them to have and enjoy (2 Cor. 13:11). Don't settle for worry when God provides peace.

What brings you down? What causes you to despair? Life is full of one disappointing and depressing situation after another. Some are able to hold up and resist most temptations to despair when their own personal circumstances are grim. Others succumb to despair. But even when circumstances are at their worst, things like contemplating suicide or cutting oneself are sinful expressions of despair. During these times of extreme solitude, pain, sadness, and frustration, don't trade in the virtue of joy for the vice of despair. At the foundation of a Christian's joy is Christ's powerful presence (Rom. 8:31; 1 John 4:4). Believers are never without hope—Christ is willing and able to give you joy in the midst of overwhelming circumstances (Rom. 15:13). Repeated personal sin, or sin by others against you, can gnaw at you and can tempt you to despair. The vice of despair can still be crushed by the virtue of joy because you can rejoice that "where sin abounded, grace did much more abound" (Rom. 5:20).

PRACTICING GRATITUDE, JOY, AND PEACE

Have you ever been told, "Say it like you mean it," when apologizing? Children hear this often when forced to ask their sibling for forgiveness. Words come out of their mouths, but neither their tones nor their facial expressions communicate remorse. When you are confronted with a significant ethical choice, just nodding to the pertinent virtues while operating with selfish motives for prideful gain does not equal an ethical decision. Gratitude, joy, and peace need to be deeply embedded in your head and in your heart, so those virtues can influence and guide you as you make ethical decisions.

Consider when you are tempted to cheat on a test. Cheating is dishonest and can sometimes involve stealing too, depending on how it is done. "But I need to pass this test" doesn't cut it as an excuse. That is simply pragmatic, the ends justifying the means. A believer who cheats on a test is bound to experience the following: worry that he or she will be found out, despair or regret due to resorting to cheating, and ingratitude because one can't be thankful for the results of work that isn't one's own. Doing your best on a test you haven't been able to study for, without cheating, might try your gratitude, joy, and peace. But honoring God is the virtuous choice. And it is always the right choice.

What is the difference between a troublemaker and a peacemaker? One obvious answer is that peacemaking is a biblically ethical lifestyle, unlike troublemaking (Matt. 5:9). Peacemaking isn't the same thing as avoiding all confrontation; that is cowardice. If you are grateful for and rejoice in the fulfilling blessings of life in Christ, then you want others who are opposed to God to come to peaceful terms with Him. Calling others to peace with God is the duty of all believers, by the way (2 Cor. 5:18–20). And believers who are controlled by gratitude, joy, and peace will seek to return broken and disrupted relationships back to the order God created them for. When you've had a conflict with someone, do you either humbly seek forgiveness for yourself or seek reconciliation if the person wronged you? Or do you hold grudges and let the conflict remain unresolved?

Pursue growth in these three virtues through Bible reading and study, other resources (books, messages, podcasts, articles, devotionals), prayer, and encouragement from a mentor or close friend. Remember, you can't practice ethical living without a Spirit-dependent pursuit of gratitude, joy, and peace.

Thinking It Through 7.3

1. Find a definition of *gratitude* online. How does that definition differ from the definition of gratitude found in this chapter?
2. Find a definition of *joy* online. How does that definition differ from the definition of joy found in this chapter?
3. Find a definition of *peace* online. How does that definition differ from the definition of peace found in this chapter?
4. Do an online search for "how to be happy." Look for non-Christian ideas of happiness and contrast them with the Christ-focused virtues of joy, peace, and gratitude.
5. Contrast the virtues of gratitude, joy, and peace with the vices of ingratitude, despair, and worry.
6. List a few examples of how gratitude, joy, and peace relate to ethical decision-making and ethical living.
7. What would you include in a plan for growing in gratitude, joy, and peace?

7.4 Honesty

What do Abraham Lincoln, a courtroom, and the best policy all have in common? Honesty! You might have heard of "Honest Abe"; you're probably familiar with the courtroom oath to "tell the truth, the whole truth, and nothing but the truth"; and you may know the adage about honesty being "the best policy." Honesty is telling the truth, but this virtue is much more than that for Christians.

Out of all the virtues covered thus far, which virtues were practiced as far back as the Garden of Eden? What vices were present in Genesis 3 when the serpent deceived Eve and humanity fell into sin? We can identify faith, love, righteousness, faithfulness, self-control, unbelief, lust, ungodliness, cunning, disloyalty, and pride as being part of Adam and Eve's time in the garden. The vice of falsehood played a large role in the Fall. After all, the Devil is called the father of lies (John 8:44), and his first interaction with man involved his blatant lie to deceive Eve into rebellion against God (Gen. 3:4–5). The rest is history, literally.

DEFINING THE TERMS

Examining this first lie in human history helps us begin to define honesty as well as lying. Satan knew what God had commanded Adam, and he knew what the consequences were if the human king and queen of creation disobeyed God's clear command. The serpent was crafty and cunning, after all (Gen. 3:1). By this time Satan had already fallen from his angelic position near the throne of God (Ezek. 28:13–17). Wallowing in his hurt pride and seething with anger, Satan retaliated against God by attacking His premier creation—man. God and man were in perfect communion, and the only way Satan could interrupt that communion was by causing man to doubt God and disobey Him. As long as man trusted and followed God's commands, life in Eden was perfect. That is why Satan resorted to his original trick—lying to cause the woman to doubt God's love and care for them. Satan spoke a false assertion that he knew was untrue, contradicting God's very words. So **lying** is verbally declaring something that one knows to be false.[18] **Honesty**, on the other hand, is a devotion to truthfulness where one affirms and acts in accord with what is true and righteous. Honesty governs speech, as in truth telling instead of lying, but it also governs actions that are fair, just, and righteous. And the vice of **falsehood** is endorsing untruths to harm someone else or for one's personal gain. Ripping someone off in a transaction, slander,* and stretching the truth to one's advantage are all examples of falsehood.

WHAT A LIE ISN'T

We need to make room for normal types of communication that aren't violations of the virtue of honesty. An accurate understanding of honesty and falsehood is extremely important. The categories below fall outside our definition of lying.

- **Silence**
  If nothing is expressly said, then neither truth nor falsehood is stated.

- **Certain nonverbals**
  Using a noisemaker that sounds like a rainstorm to help a baby sleep isn't lying to the baby. (On the other hand, pointing to written language, like "yes" or "no," in order to deceive someone would be the same as writing or speaking it—a false verbal declaration and therefore a lie.)

- **Irony or humor**
  Jokes by their nature are fictional or made-up scenarios. (It would be lying to intentionally deceive someone and only after the fact try to excuse it by saying that it was all just a joke. That would be two lies.)

- **Fictional storytelling**
  Much literature involves telling stories that are known to be false. Parables fall under this category. Theater and filmmaking are also legitimate forms of fictional storytelling.

- **Hyperbole**
  Exaggeration to deceive or with no hint that actual hyperbole is intended is lying. But hyperbole is common in speech and is not falsehood. You might exclaim to your friends, "I'm starving! I could eat a horse!" Both sentences are instances of hyperbole.

- **Accidental misspeaking**
  There are times that we will be mistaken or share something that we didn't believe to be false information. But later what we said turns out to be false. You need to be more careful, but you didn't lie as such. For example, you might tell a friend that the game is next Monday night (you misremembered), but it actually is two Mondays away.[19]

slander: maliciously false accusations against someone's character and person

SOURCES OF FALSEHOOD AND TRUTH

We have already briefly seen how falsehood intrinsically stems from Satan. He is the original liar, deceiver, and counterfeiter (Job 1:9–11; Rev. 3:9; 12:9–10). Peter tied Satan to this sin in his rebuke of Ananias (Acts 5:3). For Ananias and his wife, Sapphira, the consequence for lying to the Holy Spirit was extreme (Acts 5:5–6, 9–10). The book of Revelation has three lists of various sins that typify people who are hell-bound; included are lying and the vice of falsehood (Rev. 21:8, 27; 22:15). Falsehood runs in Satan's veins. Deceit oozes out of his pores (see Acts 13:10). Lying and falsehood belong to the darkness, not to the light. And the Devil's home base is the darkness (2 Cor. 11:13–15; 1 John 1:6). Falsehood and lying, categorically so, are one and the same with Satan's character and with everything that opposes God, truth, and righteousness.

It is clear from Scripture that those who are children of the Devil will live the way he lives (1 John 3:8–10). They share the same character. Just as babies imitate and look like their parents, so the children of disobedience and wrath (Eph. 2:2–3) imitate their "father the devil" (John 8:44). Should any sin that is characteristic of the lives of those outside of Christ characterize the lives of those who are in Christ? Of course not. Salvation involves an entire transformation of those who come to Christ (2 Cor. 5:17; Titus 3:5). No aspect of a believer's life is out of the Spirit's reach to conform him or her to the image of Christ (Rom. 8:29; 12:2).

So why is honesty so important for believers? What makes this virtue so valuable for Christians to pursue? Because all virtues, and therefore honesty and truth, are grounded in the character of God. God doesn't dabble in falsehoods (Heb. 6:17–18). God cannot lie (Num. 23:19; Titus 1:2). God is perfect and just in all His ways (Rev. 15:3). When God speaks, decrees, and acts, He is totally trustworthy (Prov. 30:5). In concord with such affirmations about God in general, the Scriptures also record the character of truthfulness that the Son and the Spirit exhibit (John 14:6, 17). The triune God is the source of truth and is always truthful.

In summary, the Bible clearly connects the character of Satan to falsehood and the character of God to truth. Believers, therefore, must speak the truth. Believers must be honest because truth characterizes God Himself. Lies are typically told to allow one to sin (Did you really do what you told your parents you were going to do at the place you said you were going to be?) or to cover up someone else's sin (Did you vouch for your friend who disobeyed his parents so he wouldn't get in trouble?).

Christlikeness and lying don't mix.

THE BIBLE ON FALSEHOOD AND TRUTH

Before considering a few passages in Scripture where deception is employed for a commendable end, we want to look at an overall picture of the Bible's teaching on lying, falsehood, honesty, and truth telling. Doing this will allow us to get a feel for the overall tone and message of the Bible on these subjects. There are dozens of passages that mention the sinfulness and dangers and consequences of lying, deceit, and falsehood. There are also many passages that praise and commend honesty, truth telling, and righteous dealings with others. Below is a mere sampling.

Truth and Falsehood Contrasted

PSALM 119:163

I hate and abhor lying: but thy law do I love.

PROVERBS 11:1

A false balance is abomination to the LORD: but a just weight is his delight.

PROVERBS 14:5

A faithful witness will not lie: but a false witness will utter lies.

EPHESIANS 4:25

Wherefore putting away lying, speak every man truth with his neighbour: for we are members one of another.

EPHESIANS 4:29

Let no corrupt communication proceed out of your mouth, but that which is good to the use of edifying, that it may minister grace unto the hearers.

Prohibitions of Falsehood

EXODUS 20:16

Thou shalt not bear false witness against thy neighbour.

LEVITICUS 19:11-12

Ye shall not steal, neither deal falsely, neither lie one to another. And ye shall not swear by my name falsely, neither shalt thou profane the name of thy God: I am the LORD.

EPHESIANS 4:31

Let all bitterness, and wrath, and anger, and clamour, and evil speaking, be put away from you, with all malice.

COLOSSIANS 3:9-10

Lie not one to another, seeing that ye have put off the old man with his deeds; and have put on the new man, which is renewed in knowledge after the image of him that created him.

The Value of Truth

PSALM 15:1-2

LORD, who shall abide in thy tabernacle? Who shall dwell in thy holy hill? He that walketh uprightly, and worketh righteousness, and speaketh the truth in his heart.

PSALM 19:14

Let the words of my mouth, and the meditation of my heart, be acceptable in thy sight, O LORD, my strength, and my redeemer.

PSALM 120:2

Deliver my soul, O LORD, from lying lips, and from a deceitful tongue.

JOHN 8:31-32

Then said Jesus to those Jews which believed on him, If ye continue in my word, then are ye my disciples indeed; and ye shall know the truth, and the truth shall make you free.

The Evil of Falsehood

PROVERBS 6:16-17, 19

These six things doth the LORD hate: yea, seven are an abomination unto him: a proud look, a lying tongue, and hands that shed innocent blood, . . . a false witness that speaketh lies, and he that soweth discord among brethren.

MATTHEW 15:19

For out of the heart proceed evil thoughts, murders, adulteries, fornications, thefts, false witness, blasphemies.

ROMANS 1:25

Who changed the truth of God into a lie, and worshipped and served the creature more than the Creator, who is blessed for ever. Amen.

ROMANS 1:29

Being filled with all unrighteousness, fornication, wickedness, covetousness, maliciousness; full of envy, murder, debate, deceit, malignity; whisperers.

1 JOHN 2:21-22

I have not written unto you because ye know not the truth, but because ye know it, and that no lie is of the truth. Who is a liar but he that denieth that Jesus is the Christ? He is antichrist, that denieth the Father and the Son.

Is there any doubt about God's approval of honesty and truth and His denunciation of lying and falsehood? Some of these passages about lying, deception, and falsehood are set within descriptions of the lifestyle of the wicked and those that oppose God. Habitual cheating, deceiving, slandering, and lying are clearly condemned as the practice of the ungodly lost. Speaking the truth, being honest, and dealing fairly with others are what Christians do. But don't believers occasionally cheat, deceive, slander, and lie, thus forsaking the truth and honesty? To answer yes (and we must because believers are not-yet-glorified sinners saved by grace) is not to approve or make the sins of lying and falsehood any less serious than they are. Christians who fall into these sins should immediately seek forgiveness from all the offended parties (Matt. 5:23–24; 1 John 1:9). Be careful about dishonest behavior you might be tempted to justify. The fact that you deceived your parents once before doesn't make it acceptable or any less sinful to do so again in the future, just as one lustful thought that you quickly repented of doesn't make future lustful thoughts less sinful. Love truth telling. Hate lying. If you are a believer but have fallen into bad patterns in this area, don't excuse yourself or give up on becoming a truthful person. Instead, repent and move forward with hope in the power of the Spirit to transform you into the image of Christ.

CHALLENGING BIBLICAL EXAMPLES

At this juncture, you might have begun to wonder about instances in Scripture where deception or lying is used to do much good. For example, Samuel had a main purpose to go to Bethlehem to anoint David as the future king of Israel. But God told him to say he was there to offer a sacrifice, which was also true (1 Sam. 16:1–5). Samuel didn't lie, nor was he guilty of falsehood for not divulging all the details of his visit—he obeyed God's direct order! God had already rejected Saul as king, and since God was the ultimate King of Israel, neither God nor His prophet was obligated to reveal all that was in God's mind regarding a successor for Saul. There are some occasions when the saying, "A partial truth is a whole lie," holds true, such as when a parent or teacher is asking for a full accounting of your wrongdoing. But there are many people who do not have a right to the whole truth, usually because of the evil they would do if they knew it.

One other initial example in which deception seems to be part of God's plan is God's judgment on the wicked in the end times. Paul records how the Antichrist will, empowered by Satan himself, lie to and deceive the wicked (2 Thess. 2:8–10). God will providentially ensure that all the wicked who loved falsehood believe what is false, sealing their judgment (2 Thess. 2:11–12). God is always above reproach, and though deception or lies will be employed by Satan and believed by wicked people, God will not be, nor is He ever, the author of evil (James 1:13). This situation is similar to how God judged Pharaoh for his hardened heart. God continued to harden Pharaoh's hardened heart (Exod. 7:3–5; 8:15).

The Hebrew Midwives

Let's turn our attention now to a seeming case of deception by two Hebrew midwives. God was blessing the Hebrew people in Egypt after the time of Joseph, but the Egyptians, fearing them, devised ways to keep them submissive to their rule (Exod. 1:8–14). A genocidal command was given to Hebrew midwives in the land— kill all the Hebrew baby boys the moment they were born (Exod. 1:15–16). Given this evil, immoral command, the midwives disobeyed the Pharaoh because they feared God. They did all in their power to save the threatened Hebrew babies (Exod. 1:17). Word got back to Pharaoh that Shiphrah and Puah were not killing the babies as commanded. When called on to explain themselves, the women didn't reveal to Pharaoh their reasons for not killing the babies (Exod. 1:18–19). What they told him might have been at least partially true. Either way, it seemed Pharaoh believed them. But Pharaoh didn't give up his desire to see the male babies killed and turned to his own people to carry out the slaughter (Exod. 1:22). All things considered, God blessed the outcome of what these women did out of fear for Him, despite the nature of their possible deception, not because of it (Exod. 1:20–21).[20]

Rahab and the Spies

And now to the most well-known passage in Scripture where God used a lie to further His sovereign will. The context of Joshua 2 is Israel's taking possession of the Promised Land. God appointed Israel to judge the wicked people who were living in the land, and Israel was supposed to clear them out and move in (Josh. 1:6, 11). Before attacking the walled city of Jericho, Joshua sent two spies into the city to do reconnaissance work (Josh. 2:1). God had apparently been graciously working in the heart of Rahab because she took the spies in and hid them rather than turn them over to the city's authorities (Josh. 2:1–11). When soldiers came to her door looking for them, Rahab lied to save the lives of the two spies and to support the attack of Israel on Jericho. She aligned herself with Israel and Israel's God and in doing so essentially put herself in the position of fighting alongside the Israelites against her own people, including the men who were looking for the spies. The passage finishes with everything working out—the spies were saved, Rahab and her family's lives would be preserved, and Joshua got the information he needed (Josh. 2:12–24).

Rahab's protection of the spies is commended in the New Testament (Heb. 11:31; James 2:25), and God sovereignly included Rahab in the direct line of the ancestry of Jesus (Matt. 1:5). The New Testament commends Rahab's faith, and her true faith showed through her works—she hid the spies. But her lie, her claim that the spies had already left Jericho, is never approved anywhere in Scripture.

What can be concluded from these challenging biblical examples above? As seen from the passages presented and considered earlier, the Bible is clear on God's approval of truthfulness and honesty. These virtues reflect God's character. And we have also seen that lying and deception are rooted in the devil and reflect his nature. The Bible contains several narratives that portray believers in God who lie or deceive. The Bible never once praises the lies or the deception as such; Scripture praises honesty and truth telling. God uses imperfect sinners saved by grace to accomplish His purposes. So, we must emulate honesty, and we must practice truth telling.

YOUR HONESTY PUT TO THE TEST

Truth be told, you most likely won't find yourself in a work situation where you are commanded to commit infanticide. Neither will you probably ever need to hide righteous spies from a wicked government that would kill them if they found them. So there can be no case made to justify lying based on the passages examined in the previous section, since the motives, circumstances, and outcomes presented in those passages are entirely distinct from your own. Add to that the fact that the Bible never once explicitly condones lying, even in extreme circumstances. And God's Word is crystal clear on the relationship of truth to God's character and on lying's relation to evil.

The temptation to be dishonest comes at you from every direction. Sharing information known to be false that fits with your personal views is to endorse falsehood. Fact-checking has a legitimate place, especially for Christians who don't want to be dishonest. When your parents ask you whether you've completed *all* your homework and you say yes but you are actually planning to finish your last assignment on the way to school tomorrow, it is still a lie. When you are asked how you did on a test or how many points you scored in the game, and you embellish the answer, that is lying. When you minimally know someone yet you make assumptions about their character and then accuse them of some sort of wrongdoing, you are not only being mean, but you are also engaging in slander. Slander survives on falsehood. And when you peek at the answer sheet while doing your homework, even though your teacher expressly said to use it only *after* you have finished the assignment, you are cheating.

What these examples have in common is that they are normal situations you could easily find yourself in, and the actions in question are all dishonest. They all dishonor God because of the deception and falsehood involved in them. The goal or the reason why dishonesty or falsehood is used does not justify the rejection of the virtue for the acceptance of the vice. These are the everyday kinds of challenges to honesty you are likely to face. But if you ever *do* find yourself in a dire situation where a lie wouldn't cover up someone else's sin nor selfishly benefit you but could potentially save innocent life, pray that God will give you grace to do what is right.

Thinking It Through 7.4

1. Define *honesty*.
2. How does the character of God relate to truth, and how does the character of Satan relate to falsehood?
3. What is the Bible's direct teaching on truth and falsehood?
4. How are we to understand passages in the Bible that seem to approve of deception?
5. In what ways can you apply the biblical teaching about truth and falsehood to difficult ethical choices?

Terms to Remember

- humility
- meekness
- gentleness
- pride
- anger
- harshness
- kindness
- compassion
- cruelty
- indifference
- gratitude
- joy
- peace
- ingratitude
- despair
- worry
- lying
- honesty
- falsehood

Scripture Memory

Galatians 5:22–23

Understanding Ethics

1. How do the virtues of humility, meekness, and gentleness relate to ethics?
2. How do the virtues of kindness and compassion relate to ethics?
3. How do the virtues of gratitude, joy, and peace relate to ethics?
4. How does the virtue of honesty relate to ethics?

Practicing Ethical Decision-Making

5. How do you become great in the eyes of God? Give an example of pursuing humility rather than pride.
6. How should you respond to those who are hurting? Give an example of showing kindness and compassion to someone in need rather than cruelty or indifference.

Analyzing and Evaluating Ethical Claims

7. How would you respond to those who say that humility, meekness, and gentleness are for the weak?
8. How would you respond to those who say that kindness and compassion require us to accept someone no matter what and that Christians are required to sympathize with anybody's discomfort no matter the nature of it?
9. How would you respond to those who say that joy and peace can't be had if the circumstances are hard and discouraging?
10. Why is a "little white lie" still a lie? Defend your answer.

Creating My Own Position Statements on Ethics

11. Formulate your own position on whether believers should constantly express gratitude. Then make a list of thirty things you are thankful for.
12. How is deception sometimes distinct from lying? What are the differences between ethical and unethical deception?

A Method for Handling Ethical Issues

08

How do I make ethical decisions?

8.1 The Components of a Sound Ethical Method

"Show me how to do it." "Coach me." When you're starting a new job or when you're learning a new skill—whether you're learning to play a sport, play a musical instrument, or use new technology—you need someone to show you the ropes. A good mentor will direct you step-by-step until you can begin working more independently. Then that person will coach you as you take more ownership. Eventually he or she will simply be in the background for support if you need it. And maybe one day you'll be the leader who takes over and mentors someone else.

Have you ever been in a position where you were given a task and nobody was there to direct you, coach you, or support you? You can feel lost when that happens. Even if you know the end result you're supposed to achieve, you have no idea how to get there. Imagine having to cook a high-class catered meal for over five hundred people. Most high-class restaurants have a hierarchy of chefs from the executive chef to the sous-chef to a host of support cooks. An executive chef can cater a high-class meal to hundreds of people only after years of experience under the guidance of others.

Ethical decision-making begins with knowledge, but it requires more than that. Even for those with a heart to please Christ, ethical decision-making is a learned skill requiring mentoring. That mentoring begins with someone showing you the ropes: the components to a sound ethical method. Then you can start practicing the skill of applying this method to issues (see Chapters 9–13).

What do I need to know to make the right decisions?

Numerous books on Christian ethics lay out similar methods. But the most helpful method and the one we'll follow is provided by Ken Magnuson. He brings three aspects of ethics together to form a biblically based Christian ethic:

> Deontology rightly draws attention to moral acts that are grounded in moral principles. Virtue ethics rightly draws attention to moral agents, and to the communities to which they belong, and the narratives—and grand narrative—that provide the context or story of the moral life. Teleology rightly draws attention to the end or purpose of our lives, which orders and provides meaning for both acts and agents.[1]

> **Remember...**
>
> *In Chapter 2 we learned that*
> **Deontology** focuses on duty.
> **Teleology** focuses on results.
> **Virtue ethics** focuses on one's character.

Magnuson recognizes how the deontological, teleological, and virtue ethics methods all pick up on needed aspects of ethics (see Sections 2.2 and 2.3).

First, God's law, especially as presented in the Ten Commandments, provides moral principles (universals) to guide moral action. Second, the Bible is a grand story that is going somewhere; there are ends (goals). God's goal is to glorify Himself through the establishment of His kingdom, and His goal for each person is that they glorify Him by being conformed to the image of Christ. Third, Jesus also made clear that mere external obedience without internal transformation (virtue) falls short of what God requires. The components to a Christian ethical method then, following Magnuson's lead, can be summarized in three words: *acts*, *ends*, and *agents*.

↻ Remember...

ETHICS

situation

agents
(person, motivation)

ends
(ultimate goal)

acts
(principle)

ACTS: WHAT'S THE STANDARD?

This component most closely resembles the deontological method, which focuses on rules that guide actions. However, the secular approach seeks in vain to find an absolute principle that can bind all people in all times and places. That's because the secularist is trying to do the impossible: find a basis for a transcendent* standard in a finite world—a basis discovered by human logic. But God alone can provide such a standard. (It's worth noting here that this component of a Christian ethical method also contrasts sharply with the existentialist ethic and its call to be true only to oneself with no transcendent standard at all.)

↻ Remember...

*In Chapter 2 we learned that the **existential** ethic focuses on one's true self.*

A standard is that by which something can be measured or used for comparison. If you draw a straight line freehanded and compare it to the standard of a ruler, is it perfectly straight?

Unlike the secular approach, Christians have a sure and clear transcendent standard given to them in the Bible. Since God has revealed Himself in His Word, we can know His character, we can rightly discern His wise design in creation, and we can recognize when humans are reflecting their Creator. Biblical truth (reflecting the created order) provides the authoritative, universal moral absolutes that humans need to govern themselves in this world.

First, the Bible is full of direct commands for how to live ethically in obedience to God out of love for Him and others (see Exod. 20:1–17; Matt. 22:37–40; Eph. 4:25–5:16; Col. 3:1–14). Second, the Bible contains numerous general principles that can be applied by all people in all times to a variety of situations (see Prov. 14:16; 27:6; Luke 10:27–37). Third, there are many implications to what the Bible explicitly says, meaning that believers need to make careful inferences that connect to their lives, applying the intent of God's Word to new situations (see Matt. 5:21–48). God expects believers to mature to the point that they can discern what is pleasing to the Lord (Eph. 5:10; Heb. 5:11–14) based on the guidance of the Holy Spirit who helps them make proper inferences and applications (Rom. 8:13–14). Finally, the Bible is full of descriptions and demonstrations of God's character (see 1 Sam. 12:7; Neh. 9:32–33; Dan. 9:14). The whole Bible is a rich resource for a Christian's understanding of right and wrong.

God's general revelation is also a rich resource for a Christian's understanding of right and wrong. God designed creation, including the social dimension, so that it functions a certain way. We call these principles of design *creational norms* (see Sec-

transcendent: pertaining to the things of God beyond the earthly human experience tions 1.2 and 2.1). If you read the Bible carefully, you will see that the biblical writers sometimes grounded their arguments in the authority of the created order, which is just as authoritative as a direct command from God (Matt. 19:4; 1 Cor. 11:14–15; 1 Tim. 2:13). You'll also notice in the Wisdom Literature that wise men observed God's world, seeking to discern these creational norms. Yet because we are finite and fallen, our observations of God's world must always take place in connection with what God has more clearly revealed in His written Word.

The acts of the ethical person need to align with both the creational order and God's commands to the New Covenant believer—neither of which are subject to cultural changes.

You'll notice that both God's wise design in the created order and God's commands are being undermined by the world around you (see Chapters 9–13 on various issues). You will have to decide where your allegiance lies if you are going to take a courageous biblical stand (Josh. 24:15). Can you trust God enough to be faithful to Him while waiting on Him to triumph in the end? Or will you twist the Bible's meaning or outright reject its clear statements to remain in step with the world around you?

ENDS: WHAT'S THE GOAL?

This component of a Christian ethical method most closely resembles the teleological method, which focuses on the goals or results (the ends) of a given decision or action (see Sections 2.2 and 2.3). However, the secular approach generally locates the ultimate goal of all people in themselves—in their own happiness (or freedom from pain).

Unlike the secular approach, Christians have a God-given goal: to glorify God by loving God and others. Determining exactly what this means and looks like comes from understanding the objective commands that set the standard for us. You cannot separate the goal from the standard. They work hand-in-hand. Rather than seeking self-serving happiness, Christians will even endure persecution and suffering for the sake of a greater end goal (Matt. 10:28; 2 Cor. 4:7–18). The happiness they do pursue is found in God and in His good will for them rather than in fleshly pleasures. To persevere in such commitment to God's commands in order to achieve a higher end requires the formation of inward character.

The goal of any ethical action must ultimately be to glorify God and enjoy Him through holy conformity to the image of Christ and the advancement of His kingdom.

Why are God's commands not burdensome to the believer (1 John 5:3)? The believer knows that God's commands are not arbitrary. God's commands have a purpose, an excellent end: God's glory and our greatest good. God's commands are not designed to get in the way of our fun; they are designed to uphold our greatest flourishing. God's commands describe what it means to love Him and others, upholding God's wise design for our best life.

The Ends for Which Believers Live

Why do believers do what they do? The Bible identifies many ends for which believers live:

- to be conformed to God's image (Gen. 1:26–28)
- to rule over creation under God's greater rule (Gen. 1:26–28)
- to delight in God's law (Ps. 1:1–3)
- to fear God (Prov. 1:7)
- to trust in God with all their hearts and to know Him in all their ways (Prov. 3:5–6)

- to be blessed or to flourish (Ps. 1:1; Matt. 5:3–12)
- to walk worthy of God and do good works that glorify the Father (Matt. 5:16; Col. 1:9–12)
- to seek first God's kingdom and righteousness and to enter that kingdom (Matt. 5:20; 6:33)

- to be conformed to the Son's image for the Son's glory (Rom. 8:29)
- to be holy, blameless, pure, and righteous so that God receives glory (Eph. 1:4; Phil. 1:9–11)
- to be mature in Christ (Col. 1:28–29)
- to attain the Sabbath rest (Heb. 3–4).

All these ends can be summed up as the ultimate goal or "chief end . . . to glorify God, and to enjoy him for ever."[2]

Therefore, believers should consider the consequences of their actions (Gal. 6:7). You can only push so hard against God's norms, God's wise design, before the consequences become devastating (Prov. 1:20–33; 26:27). Although God is patient with rebellious mankind (Gen. 8:21–22; 2 Pet. 3:3–9), in the end His blessing or His judgment will be brought to bear on people's actions (Rom. 12:19; 2 Pet. 3:10–11; Rev. 20:13). The biblical worldview does allow for the suffering of the righteous and the temporary flourishing of evil people in a fallen world (Job 1:1, 8; 42:7; Ps. 73:2–14). And the Bible's teaching on grace and forgiveness (Ps. 103:10) differentiates the biblical worldview from the simplistic and fatalistic idea of karma. Nevertheless, the general principles found in the book of Proverbs hold true. Behaving a certain way does lead, in general, to good or ill because God's world generally works a certain way by His wise design and blessing.

AGENTS: WHAT'S THE MOTIVE?

This component of a Christian ethical method must correspond to virtue ethics, which focuses on the person or agent (see Sections 2.2 and 2.3). However, unbiblical approaches to virtue ethics misdefine virtue or pass off vice as virtue. Or they misapply virtue, making it fit an agenda that is at odds with the biblical ethic. (And then there is the existentialist approach, which knows *only* the agent, divorced from any virtue besides what the agent wishes to become.)

Christians' motives and virtuous characters must be governed by biblical standards (God's commands, best understood within the larger Creation, Fall, Redemption metanarrative of Scripture). And Christians' motives and virtuous characters must be evaluated in light of their ultimate purpose (to glorify and enjoy God) and mission (to carry out the Great Commission).

When biblically defined and understood, the character and motives of the agent acting to accomplish an end undergird everything else in ethics. Virtuous character is foundational to carrying out God's commands to His glory. How could God's commands be rightly followed by a person whose inward character has not been transformed? Commands mean nothing to the person who disdains authority and presumes he or she can escape consequences. On the other hand, people who imagine themselves to be inherently good can make a good show of following commands, but for all the wrong reasons. People's character determines the effectiveness of commands. More than a few countries have good laws written on paper, but the general character of the politicians and the people makes those laws next to meaningless (or by application turns the intent of those laws on its head).

To act ethically is not merely to do the right thing; it is to be the right kind of person doing the right thing for the right reasons.

Ethical decision-making may relate to hard-to-solve issues. But often the issue isn't difficult to understand. Depraved people are unwilling to do the right thing. The problem isn't with their intellects but with their wills and desires. Sometimes people try to do the right thing, but they have no power to do the right thing for the right reasons and no grace toward others who fall short. They become unforgiving, perfectionistic legalists with no mercy (James 2:12–13; 4:11–12). Virtuous character and motives are vital to carrying out God's commands to His glory.

CONTEXT: WHAT'S THE SITUATION?

The three main components—acts, ends, and agents—must all be applied to a specific ethical situation. Context is the additional element to making an ethical decision. What is the ethical issue that demands ethical decision-making? The importance of fully understanding the situation is best stated in Proverbs 18:13: "He that answereth a matter before he heareth it, it is folly and shame unto him." You must have an accurate understanding of all the factors to rightly apply God's Word and to rightly discern the proper motives and goals.

In Chapters 9–13, each section will raise an ethical difficulty (an issue or scenario). Then each section will direct you to consider the Bible's teaching on how one ought to *act*. Each section will direct you to consider the *end* consequences to an individual or a society that does or does not conform to the biblical standard. And each section will direct you to consider the virtues and vices that motivate an *agent's* (a person's or society's) response. Because we live in a world that is full of sinful responses (both your own and others' responses that affect you), each section will conclude with how to biblically respond to troubling situations you may find yourself in.

Because of their character, persons (agents) apply norms (acts) to situations (context) for reasons (ends).

The Bible provides the help we need to situate acts, ends, and agents in a context. The Bible isn't a dry book of rules disconnected from real-life situations. The Bible is full of narratives and parables that illustrate what is and what is not acceptable behavior in various situations. Our situation may not be identical to a situation we find in the Bible, but there are bountiful situations that we can draw analogies from in order to find guidance for our own current situation. Soaking yourself in the Word of God, from the Old Testament narratives to the New Testament imperatives, will equip you for ethical behavior (2 Tim. 3:16–17; 2 Pet. 1:3).

CONCLUSION

All the components must work together. Magnuson summarizes the necessity and usefulness of all the components by saying the following:

> The nature and character of God (corresponding to virtue ethics) is the source from which God's commands are given (corresponding to a form of deontology), and God's purposes or ends (corresponding to teleology) flow from his character and are indicated by his commands. Likewise, a person's character (virtue ethics) provides the foundation for keeping God's commands (deontology), which work together to fulfill the purposes for which human beings are created (teleology).[3]

The faulty ethical systems overviewed and critiqued in Chapter 2 were all deficient because humans tend toward one emphasis to the neglect of others. Even if they do stumble on one aspect of the truth, people tend to misuse the truth they do have by ignoring or minimizing other truths. A Christian should seek to avoid extremes by pulling all the components together.

Good intentions or goals don't justify violating God's commands (1 Sam. 15:22–23; 2 Sam. 6:1–8; Exod. 25:14). Carrying out God's commands as He has instructed is all-important (Num. 26:61; Mal. 1:6–8). And obeying God's commands with the wrong motives is not acceptable in the eyes of God (Isa. 1:11–18). A biblical ethic requires meeting God's standards to achieve the right goals with right motives—in all of life.

Thinking It Through 8.1

1. Explain the component labeled *acts* in a Christian ethical method.

2. Explain the component labeled *ends* in a Christian ethical method.

3. Explain the component labeled *agents* in a Christian ethical method.

4. Explain why one must understand the context of a given situation in order to properly apply the three components of a Christian ethical method.

5. Explain why acts, ends, and agents must all work together.

8.2 Using a Sound Ethical Method

Imagine having practiced particular skills to prepare for a big performance or a big game. Your teacher or coach assures you that you are ready. You know what you need to do, and you know how to do it. You've demonstrated it in practice. But the day arrives, and you're so nervous you're not sure you can follow through. But you finally muster up the courage and step up to the task.

How did you do? Maybe you performed well. Maybe you didn't. That's all right. That just means you get up, dust off, practice more, grow your skills, and try again. Eventually, with more dedicated effort, you are ready for the next big performance. That middle school student who forgot all his or her lines at the fine arts competition can be that high schooler who places several years later.

At this point in the year, you're ready to begin practicing the use of a sound ethical method. You'll continue to practice this method repeatedly in Chapters 9–13. And yes, you'll be tested. But the real test comes in life outside the classroom. You'll need to seek wisdom from above through prayer to put into practice what you've learned. And hopefully you'll grow into a leader who can influence others to live ethically in your church, family, workplace, and society. Today you are preparing yourself for your future—both your near and distant future.

What questions should I ask to make an ethical decision?

A PRACTICAL METHOD FOR ETHICAL DECISION-MAKING

In the last section, you overviewed the basic components of a biblically sound ethical method. Now it's time to put that method into use. One way to make it more useful is to boil everything down to a few basic questions to ask every time you need to make an ethical decision:[4]

The first question relates to the situation that raises an issue. The second question relates to the standard for one's actions. The third question relates to the ends or goals being aimed at. The fourth question relates to the agents involved—their character and motives. Persons (agents) apply norms (acts) to situations (context) to achieve goals (ends). Those four basic questions encompass all that is involved in ethical decision-making.

Those questions are very general. But they break things down so you can focus on one thing at a time. They'll get you started, pointed in the right direction. They're also ordered in a way that will help guide your investigation down the right path. Then you can start filling in the details and asking more specific questions.

For example, once you ask the four major questions, you can start digging into more specifics:

You could probably think of a few more questions to ask under each step. And once a topic or issue is specifically identified, then your questions and research can become even more specific.

A TEST CASE

Are you ready to practice with a test case? As you're walking across the parking lot to school one day, you notice a wallet on the ground. Should you walk past it or pick it up? If you pick it up, should you look inside? If you find money and an ID in it, should you turn it in? To whom should you turn it in? What if there's no ID?

Let's change the scenario a little bit. As you're walking across the parking lot to the grocery store one day, you notice a ten-dollar bill near the gutter. Should you walk past it or pick it up? If you pick it up, should you pocket it or turn it in? To whom should you turn it in? How do you know that person won't just pocket it? Do you have a responsibility for what that person might do with it?

What if it were a hundred-dollar bill? What if it were more money than that? How much money would it have to be to turn it in? What if it were only a penny or a quarter? Could you just pocket it then? Why?

Before reading any more, use the four basic questions to help you make an ethical decision and discuss it. Then you can read some of the suggested answers below.

ANSWERING THE TEST CASE

The Basic Scenario

Let's think through the differences in the scenarios that might factor into different responses. Does your responsibility heighten when you can find an ID? Certainly. And does your responsibility heighten when you have a trustworthy authority at your school (who also has accountability to other staff members) to whom you can turn in that wallet? Absolutely. You have no excuse.

The Bible is clear on this matter (Exod. 20:15; 23:4; Deut. 22:1–4; Eph. 4:28). You certainly should pick up the wallet and return it to its owner or turn it in to the school office. There's no question that stealing is wrong. And there's no question that you would be stealing if you kept the wallet or took anything from the wallet before turning it in.

Even many unsaved people know in their consciences that taking something that doesn't belong to them and that someone else worked hard for is just plain wrong. They know that society as a whole is better off with honest people who do unto others as they would like others to do unto them (a creational norm and a biblical principle they borrow from a Christian worldview). Nevertheless, people's greed can cause them to do what they know is wrong (1 Tim. 6:9–10).

Additionally, there's no need to leave the wallet there in the parking lot, tempting someone else to do the wrong thing. (In fact, simply bypassing the lost item is probably not a biblical option [Deut. 22:1–3].) You may choose not to open the wallet to look inside, thus avoiding a temptation to swipe any money. You could look for an ID in the presence of the staff when you bring it in to the office, or you could let the school office staff look for the ID themselves after you turn it in to them.

Before moving on to the alternative scenarios, can you locate the four basic questions that are being answered in the above paragraphs? The first and last paragraphs are analyzing factors in the context (the first question). The second paragraph is stating what the Bible clearly says about stealing (the second question). The third paragraph is analyzing the consequences to society (the third question) and the motives of people (the fourth question). All these components fit naturally into thinking through all the factors in an ethical issue.

The Scenario with Changed Factors

Now let us consider the scenario with some of the factors changed. The buying power of an amount of money would probably determine the value lost money had

EVALUATING
CONTEMPORARY EVENTS

[NEW]

Can you find a news story involving the return of lost money or property? What took place? How did people respond? What explanations were given for why people responded the ways they did? Evaluate what took place and why. Can you spot some or all of the ethical components?

to the person who lost it—which would determine the likelihood of the person returning to look for that lost money. And a person who lost any significant amount of money would expect that an honest person would seek to return that money. If someone lost just ten dollars, that amount of money has enough buying power for some small items. And an honest person would seek to locate the owner. (If you get excited over finding some money because you know it would give you buying power, then that's a clue that you should probably turn the money in so the owner can get the money back.)

However, few people would be distressed enough over one lost penny or quarter (or a handful of pocket change) to search a random grocery store parking lot. And turning a few coins in to the store manager would likely be nothing more than a contribution to that store (or to that individual) rather than a return of the coins to the person who dropped them. Someone's conscience could be constrained to turn in every penny found, based on an absolute commitment to a biblical principle not to steal. And people shouldn't violate their consciences (Rom. 14:23). Nevertheless, a God-fearing Christian could argue that the biblical principle (the letter of the law) was being pushed to the limits by the person who turned in pennies—without consideration of the context, motive, and ends. (And Deuteronomy 22:1–4 recognizes something must be of enough value that a person would come looking for it.) A rightly formed conscience should take into consideration all those elements when seeking to fulfill the spirit or purpose of God's law.

Let's say you found $100 (or more) near the gutter in a grocery store parking lot. You know it is likely that the person who lost it would want it back. But you didn't find the money in a wallet with an ID. How would you locate the person? And what if the store clerk or even the manager would be likely to pocket the money? Do these concerns justify you pocketing the money rather than

turning it in? No! You have an obligation to show good faith* by trying to locate the proper authority, seeking to make sure that authority itself will be accountable, and giving an opportunity to the person who lost the money to locate it. Depending on the amount of money, this might require a police report and then communication to the community to inform them that money has been found. Then that person would have to provide some explanation or knowledge (for example, the exact amount and in what bills) of the items lost to prove ownership.

Sometimes honest people have been rewarded by the person who was able to recover a lost item(s). And sometimes when a large amount of money is never claimed after months of concerted effort by the authorities, the honest person gets to keep the money. But with or without hope for a gracious reward (which you're not entitled to), you should want to do the right thing in order to love others, obey the Lord, and be a good testimony to God's glory.

The conclusion of the matter is that you should always make a good faith effort to return lost items of value to their owner or an accountable authority. Some discernment may be required for items that have little to no intrinsic value. The context may determine what you do. Finding a quarter in a random parking lot is different from finding a quarter in the chair that your five-year-old sibling just sat in while counting piggy bank money. You have an obligation to give the money back since it has value (buying power) to your sibling and since you have enough contextual information to know who it likely belongs to and how to give it back.

Circumstances like these will reveal your character, motives, goals, and commitment to God and His Word. The issues in the coming chapters will challenge you to evaluate all these components as you make more and more ethical decisions.

GRAPPLING WITH ETHICAL ISSUES

What if you realize that, in the distant past, you're guilty of having taken something that did not belong to you and that you should have returned it or turned it in? What are your obligations? What if an ancestor stole something in the distant past? What are your obligations?

Thinking It Through 8.2

1. List the four basic questions you should ask yourself in ethical decision-making.

2. Match the three ethical components and the additional element to the four questions.

3. Practice using the ethical method you've learned in this chapter by explaining the appropriate response to a friend who wants to gossip about a classmate who has been annoying you.

good faith: a sincere intent to do the right thing, be honest, fulfill commitments, or carry out legal obligations

Scripture Memory

Psalm 119:97, 101–4

Understanding Ethics

1. Identify the three components of a Christian ethical method. Identify one additional element that must be considered alongside those components.
2. Explain the meaning of each of the components and the additional element.
3. List the four main questions you should ask yourself in ethical decision-making, matching the ethical components and the additional element to the appropriate questions.
4. Why must all three components work together in the evaluation of every ethical matter?

Practicing Ethical Decision-Making

5. Practice using the ethical method you've learned in this chapter by evaluating whether Christians should consume movies full of gratuitous and explicit objectional elements.
6. Practice using the ethical method you've learned in this chapter by explaining the appropriate response to classmates bullying or deriding another classmate for speaking up for what's right.

Analyzing and Evaluating Ethical Claims

7. How would you respond to someone who persists in the deontological approach, denying the need to consider ends, virtues, and context? In other words, this person only cares about absolute, universal principles (what a person does)—not goals and results or personal character and motives (why and how a person acts) or careful consideration of specific circumstances.
8. How would you respond to someone who persists in the teleological approach, denying the need to consider moral rules and virtues?
9. How would you respond to someone who practices virtue ethics while denying the need to consider moral rules, ends, and context?

Creating My Own Position Statements on Ethics

10. Defend the ethical method presented in the chapter.

The Ethics of Life and Death

09

What is a human life worth?

EXODUS 20:13;
MATTHEW 5:21–22

Ultimately, our chief end must be to glorify God. And we do that when we value His image-bearers.

9.1 Murder, Manslaughter, and Self-Defense

The ethics of life and death includes many issues. In this section we will consider murder, manslaughter, and self-defense. Are you ready to use the four basic questions for ethical decision-making?

context ① What is the situation requiring an ethical decision?

acts ② What does the Bible say about this issue?

ends ③ What sorts of outcomes might various decisions in this situation lead to?

agents ④ What motivations are involved—what virtues exhibited; what vices avoided?

YOU BE THE JURY context

The context you're in includes a basic understanding of the laws in the jurisdiction where you live. Context also includes the details of what was done by whom as well as why and how it took place.

Consider some basic definitions. According to the *United States Code,* "**Murder** is the unlawful killing of a human being with malice aforethought."[1] More specifically, a charge of **first-degree murder** is usually reserved for premeditated murder or murder committed alongside another serious crime. First-degree murder is punished by the death penalty or life imprisonment. **Second-degree murder** covers any murder that doesn't fit the definition of first-degree murder and may be punished by temporary imprisonment or life imprisonment.[2] "**Manslaughter** is the unlawful killing of a human being without malice."[3] It is considered **voluntary manslaughter** when it takes place impulsively in response to a heated exchange or serious provocation, and a person would be subject to a fine and up to fifteen years in prison. It is considered **involuntary manslaughter** when a death results from carelessness or occurs in conjunction with the commission of a minor crime, and a person would be subject to a fine and up to eight years in prison.[4]

Self-defense has been described this way: "The right to prevent suffering force or violence through the use of a sufficient level of counteracting force or violence."[5] Sometimes the use of deadly force and the killing of an attacker may be justifiable self-defense (generally when the attacker is using deadly force against the defender). Different US states have different philosophies for self-defense, such as a duty to retreat, the right to stand your ground, or the castle doctrine. If the circumstances of an event are deemed to fit the state's definition and philosophy of self-defense, then a person will not be criminally charged, even if the attacker is killed.[6]

Let's consider several fictional scenarios, imagining that you're on the jury. First, you need to gather the facts. Only then can the law be rightly applied.

SCENARIO 1:

A young woman returns to her rural home late at night. As she fumbles with her keys to enter her house, a man sneaks up behind her and points a gun at her. He starts to drag her off the porch toward his car. In the process, she begins to fight back. In the scuffle, the man pistol-whips her in the face; she falls backward off the porch and hits her head on the corner of the cement step, leading to her eventual death.

SCENARIO 2:

A high-rise building collapses, killing dozens of people. Soon, the public finds out there was considerable neglect in structural safety. Although inspectors raised questions and identified specific problems, these things were ignored by the owner of the building for many years.

SCENARIO 3:

A young man thinks he sees someone snooping around the back alley of a store. He suspects that the person might be the one involved in stealing merchandise since recent news reports had said the store was having problems. He calls out to the person, who bolts. He decides to run after him. When he catches up to the man, they get into a tussle. During the course of the tussle, the young man who chased down the suspected prowler pulls a gun and shoots the man dead.

How would you judge those who caused death in each scenario if you were on the jury? What other facts do you need? What would factor into your decision-making? What principles guide your understanding of each person's guilt or innocence, the significance of his or her actions or inaction? What consequences resulted from the actions or inaction in question—consequences for each person involved, for their families, and for society? What consequences would result from both the jury's verdict and the judge's sentence? What virtues and vices were involved that you would want to promote or punish? Although the perpetrator's intent certainly factors into the level of his or her sentencing, how would you respond to explanations for the criminal activity? What kinds of things, if any, would you consider as lessening his or her responsibility? Is there a difference between criminal guilt and moral responsibility (wisdom) in one or more of these cases?

EVALUATING
CONTEMPORARY EVENTS

Find a recent news story that recounts a murder, manslaughter, or self-defense case that created controversy. Evaluate the ethical reasoning in these discussions. Evaluate the approach of the news media. Evaluate the difference between popular opinions and the formal evaluation of all the evidence in a court case by an informed jury that must uphold definite laws.

God puts His image in every person He creates. Murder and manslaughter are failing to value another person who bears God's image.

Is it ever right to take a human life?

OUR RESPONSIBILITY TO VALUE HUMAN LIFE

What universal principles does the Bible provide regarding murder, manslaughter, and self-defense?

The General Principle

The Bible clearly teaches that all humans are made in God's image (Gen. 1:26–27). So we have a responsibility to value the lives of all image-bearers (Gen. 9:6). God demands an accounting for the unauthorized killing of any image-bearer (Exod. 21:12; Lev. 24:17; Num. 35:33). God alone gives life and God alone takes away life (Gen. 2:7; 3:19; Job 1:21; 33:4; Ps. 104:29–30; Acts 17:28).

What the Bible reveals about the sanctity of life for all image-bearers has also been written on the consciences of all humans (Rom. 2:14–15). The created order testifies to the special, intrinsic value of all human beings. Anyone who seeks to downgrade the status of a human being to justify taking a life suppresses the truth (Rom. 1:18) and is bound to commit or condone atrocities.

> *What the sixth commandment basically says is that life and death are God's business. He is Lord of life and death, and we may not take life without his authorization.* JOHN FRAME[7]

Specific Precepts Regarding Murder and Manslaughter

The sixth commandment forbids murder and voluntary manslaughter (Exod. 20:13; see also Deut. 5:17). The Hebrew verb used in this commandment is more specific than the English word *kill*. The sixth commandment does not disallow *all* killing, for the Bible itself allows for the killing of plants and animals (Gen. 9:3) and demands capital punishment for a murderer (Gen. 9:6; Num. 35:31). On the other hand, this Hebrew word is also broader than the English usage of the word *murder*. The Bible demands just retribution not only for murder but also for what US law calls *voluntary manslaughter*; the Bible does not necessarily distinguish voluntary manslaughter from murder (Exod. 21:12, 18–19, 22–25). The death penalty may be appropriate in both cases as long as sufficient evidence corroborates what took place (Deut. 17:6).

The Bible does make a distinction between murder and involuntary manslaughter (Exod. 21:13–14). In these cases, the killing is certainly an accident rather than motivated by hatred (Deut. 19:5). But the person is still guilty for failing to take sufficient care to protect the other person's life (Deut. 22:8). The cities of refuge provided a means to escape the death penalty as long as a person remained within that refuge until the death of the high priest (Num. 35:6, 9–34; Deut. 19:1–13). So it was still a crime that demanded the death of another.

The New Testament repeats the intention of the sixth commandment, condemning murder (Rom. 1:29; 1 Tim. 1:9; James 2:11; 4:2; Rev. 21:8). The New Testament clarifies that hatred is murder in its seed form; murder stems from a lack of love (Matt. 5:21–26; see also Gen. 27:41, 45; 49:6). The command not to murder is also a command to love (Rom. 13:9; 1 John 3:14–16). The sixth commandment includes more than a prohibition against unlawfully taking another person's life; it demands that we seek the well-being of others' lives as well. God's people should do all that they reasonably can to preserve life. God's people have an obligation to show great care and concern for the well-being of all image-bearers. And they are to seek reconciliation by settling matters rather than allowing hatred to grow.

Specific Precepts Regarding Self-Defense

The Bible forbids taking revenge; vengeance belongs to God (Rom. 12:14, 17–21) and to His governing authorities (Rom. 13:1–7). God's people must love their enemies when they experience persecution for their faith or when they encounter personal affronts. Christians are not to respond to insults in kind. They may have to submit to being taken advantage of in some court cases. They are to suffer and to respond by doing good (Matt. 5:38–44; 1 Pet. 3:9). The overall point is that the individual is subject to the rulings of court (even when they are unfair and unjust) and is not allowed to take justice into his or her own hands. This does not mean that you cannot seek justice in the courts (Acts 4:5–22; 5:27–42; 16:37; 25:10–12). It is a prohibition against taking vengeance.

However, if a person faces life endangerment, that person has a stewardship responsibility to preserve his or her own life and the life of other innocent people from the threats of evildoers; Scripture permits the defense of oneself and others (Exod. 22:2–3; Deut. 22:26–27; Prov. 24:11–12). Matthew 5:38–44 prohibits taking revenge. It does not prohibit self-defense. When a person does resort to self-defense, the response must be proportional to the threat. For example, the principle in Exodus 22:2–3 is that if there is a reasonable alternative (an ability to get help during the day) or a clear recognition that the crime is nothing more than thievery, then lethal force is not appropriate. But at night a person has a harder time getting help[8] or discerning thievery versus murderous intentions. In the latter case, a person has a right to self-defense with lethal force out of fear for his or her life.

 ## SOCIAL CONSEQUENCES WHEN LIFE IS DEVALUED

What are some common unbiblical views of murder, manslaughter, and self-defense? How do these unbiblical views affect society?

Certainly, there are evil people who believe they can get away with murder. They do not value the lives of other image-bearers (Ps. 10:8–11; Prov. 1:11, 18). The more people that are like this in a society (or neighborhood), the more dangerous that place becomes. The Bible requires that those who murder another should face the death penalty. Those who would harbor a fugitive (Prov. 28:17) or pity the murderer, in the sense of failing to give him his due penalty (Deut. 19:13), are acting contrary to Scripture. One purpose of consistently enforcing due retribution is to put fear into others to deter them from committing the same types of crimes (Deut. 19:19–20; Rom. 13:4).

On the other hand, a society may put to death innocent people. Either the death penalty is imposed when insufficient evidence is provided (Deut. 19:15), or the death penalty is used against political and religious enemies (Jer. 26:11, 15). A society that is governed in this unjust way also puts fear into people but for the wrong reasons.

The opposite kind of injustice occurs when a society is too lenient in punishing murder. A society may judge and sentence murder as if it were manslaughter. A society may accept pleas of self-defense in tenuous circumstances. To save time and expense, a society may allow for questionable plea deals in place of achieving true justice. These miscarriages of justice produce angry and discouraged citizens—some of whom may be tempted to take vengeance into their own hands rather than wait on God to set things right in the end.

Other less obvious influences in society may be at play in conforming to or working against biblical principles. Laws and social expectations can influence or incentivize a social order toward courageously protecting and defending the innocent from criminal threats. On the other hand, laws and social expectations can lower demands on people to avoid violence, use prudence, and take safety precautions. Both aspects of valuing life (thwarting criminal violence but also trying to prevent needless death) need to be rightly balanced. But societies tend to err in one direction or the other. How would you be able to tell whether a society places a high or low value on the life of God's image-bearers? Be careful in your evaluation. Both hindering self-defense and making it very easy to claim self-defense could work against protecting the high value of an image-bearer.

Do you live in a country that has carefully constructed laws and penalties for murder and manslaughter? Do you live in a country that has carefully crafted laws allowing for appropriate self-defense? How well are those laws enforced, and how are such acts judged in a court of law? Do your country's laws match up well with the biblical principles? Do the populace and its leaders embrace or reject good laws and proper enforcement? If a society embraces good laws and proper enforcement, it will flourish; if not, it will devolve into tyranny and anarchy. If the latter is the kind of culture in which you live, the unrest will make for a volatile atmosphere in your country.

Ultimately, our chief end must be to glorify God. And we do so when we value His image-bearers. Societies that place a low value on people's lives dishonor the God who made those people in His image.

agents> NECESSARY VIRTUES FOR UPHOLDING THE VALUE OF LIFE

What virtues are most relevant to the issues discussed in this section? How do these virtues affect a person's motives? Why does character matter?

An ethical person will be diligent about safety, courageous about defending others, prudent about when to use deadly force, self-controlled in tense situations, and willing to suffer wrong in order to preserve life (meek). Many other virtues may come to mind. But let's focus on three: courage, prudence, and meekness.

Courage is the boldness to stand up to protect something of value, even at personal risk. The courageous person overcomes fear and pain to rise to the occasion. If a terrorist is about to murder someone, we praise the self-sacrifice of courageous people who intervene to stop that murderous intent, even if lethal force is required.

Memorial at the crash site of United Flight 93. Courageous passengers prevented hijackers from reaching their intended target of Washington D.C. during the terrorist attacks of 9/11. The plane went down in a field near Shanksville, PA. All on board were killed.

Prudence is wisdom applied to careful decision-making (Prov. 8:12). This would include the diligence and foresight to ensure the safety of others. A prudent person will seek to avoid volatile situations rather than walking into them and afterward pleading self-defense. A prudent person will seek alternatives to deadly force, like escape (see 1 Sam. 19:10; Luke 4:29–30; 2 Cor. 11:32–33). A prudent person will check equipment (rather than cutting corners) to make sure workers are safe and won't be seriously injured because equipment was not maintained.

Meekness is a humble and calm disposition in situations that can lead to pride or anger. Murder stems from anger and hatred. But the meek person has the self-control and humility to resist flying off the handle when provoked to take revenge.

Virtues motivate.[9] In other words, a person will tend to respond to a situation a certain way based on the virtues that have been instilled within him or her. He or she will be trained to respond according to those virtues in the heat of the moment. The heat of the moment reveals that person for who he or she truly is—courageous, prudent, meek, and so forth.

Character matters. Many people do not commit crimes like murder or even manslaughter. Does that make them good people? Not necessarily. Someone might avoid doing wrong because he or she does not want to face the consequences. But a person with a righteous motive will do right not just to avoid bad consequences for him- or herself. A person of character truly values the lives of others and desires to glorify God.

RIGHTLY RESPONDING IN THE AFTERMATH OF A TRAGEDY

We live in a fallen world, in which unethical behavior takes place all the time. And those unethical behaviors are not always justly judged or rightly sentenced. What advice would you give to someone who has been affected by murder, manslaughter, or a questionable self-defense ruling? How would you be the right kind of friend, giving biblical advice? How would you counsel someone about appropriately offering forgiveness and appropriately seeking justice? What if you found *yourself* in a situation in which a relative was murdered or killed due to someone's criminal negligence (like drunk driving)?

Grappling with injustice in this world is hard. You may become disillusioned if you learn from the Bible the way things ought to be. If you assume that life will work out for you when you try hard to operate rightly, your world can be turned upside down by evil seemingly triumphing over good (Ps. 73; Isa. 5:20). Christians find comfort in knowing there is an ultimate Judge who will settle all things righteously in the final judgment (Isa. 26:21). The Christian must rest in the faithful Creator to sustain him or her in the meantime (1 Pet. 4:19). The Christian may desire immediate justice but need not be hopeless and despairing when justice is delayed. True justice will be done. Christians need not be bitter or vengeful in the meantime (Rom. 12:12–21).

On the flip side, if you were to end up being the one who had committed involuntary manslaughter through your own negligence (such as careless driving from texting, goofing off with friends, or driving way too fast), you would not be beyond the hope of God's forgiveness (Ps. 51:14). God's forgiveness would not remove all the consequences in this life. In fact, a person with a godly sorrow (2 Cor. 7:9–10) would willingly accept deserved consequences as appropriate (in contrast to an ungodly sorrow that simply wished to be free from consequences). But God's forgiveness could free you from the weight of eternal guilt. And you could seek to make restitution in the best way possible in order to reconcile broken relationships with others in this life.

NEWS

EVALUATING CONTEMPORARY EVENTS

Find a real-life news story that focuses on the response of the victim's family to a wrongful killing. Find a real-life news story that focuses on society's response to a justified self-defense killing. Evaluate the responses according to a biblical ethic.

1. Differentiate murder, manslaughter, and self-defense.

2. What general principle is written on everyone's conscience and clearly enunciated in the Bible as our responsibility regarding life?

3. How does the sixth commandment (and further biblical explanations of that command) slightly differ from US code on the matters of murder and manslaughter? How do the Bible and these laws agree?

4. What does the New Testament identify as murder in its seed form?

5. The command not to murder is also a command to do what?

6. True or False: A society may subtly undermine the value of life by either making it nearly impossible for someone to exercise self-defense or by making it far too easy for someone to claim self-defense. Explain your answer.

7. Identify one of the three virtues highlighted in this section that are necessary for upholding the value of life. Explain why the virtue is important.

8. If you found yourself the victim of a tragedy involving a wrongful death or if you found yourself the victimizer of someone else by murder, manslaughter, or accidental killing, how would a biblical view of justice and forgiveness be rightly applied to such a situation?

9.2 Suicide and Euthanasia

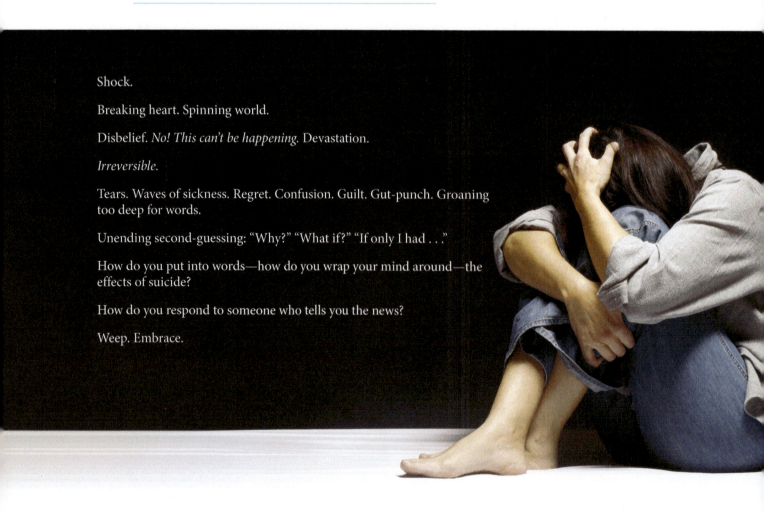

Shock.

Breaking heart. Spinning world.

Disbelief. *No! This can't be happening.* Devastation.

Irreversible.

Tears. Waves of sickness. Regret. Confusion. Guilt. Gut-punch. Groaning too deep for words.

Unending second-guessing: "Why?" "What if?" "If only I had . . ."

How do you put into words—how do you wrap your mind around—the effects of suicide?

How do you respond to someone who tells you the news?

Weep. Embrace.

JUSTIFICATIONS AND MOTIVATIONS FOR SUICIDE AND EUTHANASIA

Suicide, the intentional and voluntary taking of one's own life, is tragic, and yet it happens far too often. The Centers for Disease Control and Prevention found that in 2019, 6,488 people between the ages of ten and twenty-four took their lives by suicide, and it was the second leading cause of death for this age range.[10] What motivates people to commit or attempt to commit suicide?

The specific circumstances can vary widely, but the common thread tends to be despair and hopelessness due to some kind of suffering, emptiness, or guilt and shame. When someone is unable to cope with pressures, that person seeks a way out. Convincing themselves that there is no other way to find relief, many people overcome (or seek to overcome) the self-preservation instinct God built into each and every one of us.

Common causes of suicide include the following:

the overwhelming pains and pressures of life that can be (or seem to be) devastating, long-term, and irreversible

wrapping up one's own value, meaning, and purpose in life in what others think or in what life has to offer

saturation in a culture of bullying with little to no relief (especially in a social media age)

piling up poor habits of behavior with undesirable consequences, such as substance abuse, sexual promiscuity, morbid introspection, and dabbling in the occult

unrealistic expectations cultivated by a media-saturated culture of extravagance, materialism, and idealized images of other people's seemingly perfect lives

unrealistic expectations cultivated by a society driven by saving face and by extraordinarily high demands for achievement

neglecting to seek help from others who can advise how to cope with difficult circumstances

anger that seeks vengeance against others through the pain and guilt suicide inflicts on people in the deceased person's family and social circles

Euthanasia closely relates to the topic of suicide. This term refers to "the act of intentionally ending the life of a person who is elderly, terminally ill, or suffering from some incurable injury or disease."[11] It can be voluntary: at the request of a patient, a physician takes lethal action. (It is often called physician-assisted suicide when the patient is in control of a lethal act and the doctor simply facilitates.) It can be nonvoluntary: unwanted people who are severely debilitated are put to death without their consent.

How does a person get to the point that he or she desires a physician's help to end his or her own life? Usually, the person is suffering from a terminal disease. And the person does not want to endure the suffering or the degradation, or the cost and burden on others, that comes from the loss of independence and need for ongoing care.

The most common justifications for voluntary euthanasia include the following:

- the obligation to show mercy to people who are going to die anyway and who are currently suffering so terribly that they themselves greatly desire an end to their lives

- the desire to die with dignity—without having to go through the process of dying slowly while losing independence and quality of life (losses which lead to embarrassment and to becoming a burden on others)

- autonomy: the claim to a right to control one's own destiny, including "the right to die"

Some will even try to justify involuntary euthanasia by pointing to the following:

- the cost and burden of a person on society

- the lack of a person's contribution to society

- the poor quality of life for a severely mentally or physically disabled individual, sometimes accompanied by an appeal to what the person "would want" if able to express himself or herself

If you were in a situation involving excruciating pain leading to a certain death, wouldn't you want someone to help you end your life? If it were in the best interests of you and others, wouldn't that be the moral thing to do? These are powerful-sounding arguments to many people, as demonstrated by the fact that 81 percent of young adults supported physician-assisted suicide in a 2015 poll.[12] If you have a right to live, don't you also have the right to die on your own terms—to die with dignity? Who has any right to interfere with such a personal decision?

GOD'S AUTHORITY OVER LIFE AND DEATH

Humans cannot claim autonomy (complete independence) to do with themselves whatever they wish. They are created beings dependent on and obligated to their Creator. Their Creator made them with intrinsic value, whether they or anyone else recognizes it or not. That value forever remains because its basis is in a God-given status: the image of God (Gen. 1:26; 9:6). Who a person is can never be overturned or taken away as long as that person exists.

People who support euthanasia or who succumb to suicide have fundamentally misunderstood or rejected the true basis of human value. They tend to locate value in a person's contribution to society, in achieved desires, in status in the eyes of themselves or others, or in some kind of positive impact on others. While these are often good and desirable outcomes, none of these things determine the fundamental value of a human being.

The sixth commandment forbids murder (Exod. 20:13; Rom. 13:9). The commandment is not limited—as in, you are merely not to murder *others*. No, the command is not to murder, period. The command applies to self-murder, which is what suicide is (whether helped by a physician or not). Since no human owns himself or herself (Ps. 100:3; see also 1 Cor. 6:19–20), a person must care for the body, and a person who takes his or her own life is taking God's prerogative (Ps. 90). This is an affront to God's lordship and a denial of God-granted value (Job 14:5).

Taking your own life is a direct challenge to the One who created it and reflects the actions of someone who does not value God's authority over the number of our days. JULIE LOWE[13]

If you exist, you have extraordinary value, particularly in the eyes of the one who matters most: your Creator (Ps. 139:17–18; Matt. 10:31). As long as you are fooled into believing that your value comes from something other than your status as an image-bearer, you are in danger of devaluing what God has made and declared to be of immeasurable value. One of the most dangerous messages of our day is that you can be anything you dream to be—that your life is all about fulfilling self-made dreams, following your heart, and being true to yourself. Is it any wonder that suicide has skyrocketed? People find out that they are not in control of their lives, and then what happens to them? They run into futility and failure. They can't make life work the way they dreamed. This false message (that through self-determination you can do anything) backfires, resulting in a massive amount of suicide when life doesn't seem to be working out for so many.

Although suicide is not the unpardonable sin (1 Cor. 10:13), it is a fruit of a person's life that gives rise to questions about that person's spiritual condition (1 John 5:16–18). It is never appropriate to take this route to get to eternity faster. God can provide another way; God can sustain you through all the shame, pain, and difficulties in this life (Ps. 42; Rom. 8:25–39; 1 Cor. 10:13). The Bible does approve of self-sacrifice in the sense of laying down one's life for another (John 15:13). But nearly every biblical narrative that describes suicide describes it in a negative light (1 Sam. 31:3–5; 2 Sam. 17:23; 1 Kings 16:18–19; Matt. 27:3–5; Acts 16:28).

THE SOCIAL CONSEQUENCES OF SUICIDE AND EUTHANASIA

Many of the motives for suicide relate to wrong ends: wrapping up one's own meaning and purpose in oneself and in what one can get out of life in this world. This is not to downplay the real suffering many have endured. But living for a correct end will provide the strength and hope one needs to endure and to overcome suffering in this life. When your meaning and purpose in life are found in God's glory (1 Cor. 10:31; Col. 3:17; 1 Pet. 4:11) and in God's purposes for the suffering in your life (Gen. 50:20; Rom. 8:28; 2 Thess. 1:5–6), then His grace will be sufficient (2 Cor. 4:16–18; 12:9).

Many of the justifications for euthanasia relate to freeing someone from having to endure serious pain. But such reasoning ignores the alternatives that can successfully relieve pain and the value that can come from enduring pain. Many of the other justifications relate to wrong views of one's relationship to society: contribution, not draining resources, not being a burden to others. But what if society (and especially family) is supposed to set aside some of its resources, planning to care for people once they are in great need? What if society was designed to take care of people out of a great love for who those people are, regardless of their perceived contribution? Maybe a person's contribution is to humble us, to make us less selfish, to grow our compassion, to engender gratitude (so we won't take for granted our own abilities), and to inspire us with their endurance against all odds.

Wrong ends (whether in relation to suicide or euthanasia) have consequences on the operation of the social order, mainly expressed in a culture's expectations and laws. A society that excuses or even glamorizes suicide and euthanasia undermines the sanctity of life for all people and thus endangers individual lives—by pressuring people to end their own lives, opening up that option as acceptable, or even determining when others no longer deserve to live.

Another tragic effect on society (especially on friends and families) takes place when a person decides to take his or her own life. What happens in a church or school community when someone takes his or her own life? Excruciating sadness sweeps over the whole community. Sometimes this effect is the final vengeance desired by the person who takes his or her own life. This in itself is sad—that a person could be driven by such hurt and hate rather than seeking reconciliation. Yet, such an event is indeed a wake-up call for all of us to reexamine how we treat others and how we can better listen to, love, and encourage those who are facing overwhelming circumstances (which is not to say those things haven't happened in some cases where a person still decides to commit suicide). These tragedies remind us to go beyond superficial friendliness to truly befriend people and to speak the truth of the gospel into their lives.

agents ▶ VIRTUES NECESSARY TO OVERCOME DESIRES FOR SUICIDE AND EUTHANASIA

What does a person need in order to overcome his or her desires for suicide? Hope. Gratitude. What does a society need in order to overcome its desires to get rid of people deemed undesirable? Compassion. People and societies filled with hope, gratitude, and compassion will flourish in upholding the sanctity of life and in sustaining people who have given up on life.

Have you seen any shows or read accounts about extreme rescues? Someone falls into an icy crevice while skiing or gets caught in a sinking ship but survives in an air pocket until a rescuer comes. Would you rather live in a society that all too quickly just lets people die or one that against all odds makes extraordinary efforts to rescue people? We should support a society that is bent on extreme rescues for those who lose heart and want to give up on life.

How can I help a friend who is struggling with thoughts of self-harm?

People contemplating suicide or euthanasia need hope. They need a confident expectation, not that their circumstances will change for the better, but that Christ and His unfailing promises will sustain them through suffering and complete a perfect work in them (Rom. 5:1–5; James 1:2–4).

People contemplating suicide or euthanasia need gratitude. Instead of focusing on all that has gone wrong, a person needs to focus on all that has been granted. In the climax of his passage on suffering, James points us to the unchanging God who gives us every good and perfect gift, best exemplified by the Word of God that brings us eternal salvation (James 1:16–18 in the context of James 1:2–15). Sadly, many people treasure the things of this world and worry themselves to death over those passing things. Instead, we can rest in the care of the Father while we seek first His kingdom (Matt. 6:19–34). Living with gratitude for the basic necessities of life will sustain us and keep us from anxiety.

People contemplating suicide or euthanasia need compassion. A compassionate society plans to spend its time and resources to care for others. Only a selfish society spends all its time and resources prioritizing entertainment and pleasure in place of caring for others. A compassionate society seeks to make a suffering person as comfortable as possible through pain management. Very few cases cannot be managed in this way. A compassionate society seeks to encourage and to help those who go through the process of deterioration and experience shame from losing independence. A compassionate society communicates how much it respects those who are suffering and persevering through it.

COPING WITH SOMEONE'S DECISION TO END THEIR OWN LIFE

In a fallen world, we are sure to face circumstances in which a person decides to take his or her own life. How should we respond in the face of suicide or euthanasia?

There are many practical things you can do to show compassion and to offer help. But the most important thing you can do is to point yourself and others to the Lord and His gospel for grace and hope. Know that God cares (Ps. 34:17–18) even when you may not see or feel that He does. Look for meaning and fulfillment in eternal things. Encourage yourself and others to persevere, to continue in hope. Find your identity in Christ. And be grateful for all that God has given you, particularly life.

Thinking It Through 9.2

1. Explain at least three common justifications for suicide.

2. How does euthanasia relate to physician-assisted suicide?

3. Explain at least three common justifications for euthanasia.

4. Does the Bible give a person the right to take his or her own life? Explain your answer using Bible passages used in the chapter.

5. What are some reasons (wrong ends) that lead a person to contemplate suicide or that lead a society to promote euthanasia?

6. What are some of the consequences of these wrong ends?

7. List and explain three virtues that would head off the desire for suicide and euthanasia.

8. What is the most important response after experiencing the devastation of someone committing suicide?

9.3 Abortion

Abortion can be defined as "any action that intentionally causes the death and removal from the womb of an unborn child."[14] Is your heart tender enough to grieve over what has been done for decades to innocent babies? Do you know the magnitude of the death count? Are you aware of the horrific and callous processes that are involved in disposing of so many helpless little ones? Few atrocities could give you more cause to weep.

> *Rivers of waters run down mine eyes, because they keep not thy law.* PSALM 119:136

> *Horror hath taken hold upon me because of the wicked that forsake thy law.* PSALM 119:53

God's law is clear: we must not murder (Exod. 20:13). We must protect the most innocent and vulnerable among us (Pss. 72:12–14; 82:3–4). Why would the psalmist weep and become righteously angry toward lawbreakers? He had such a love for God and the goodness of His law that he was heartbroken and dismayed by those who would act so wickedly. God is a God of life; it is Satan who seeks to destroy it (John 8:44).

And yet, there are many in our society who would balk at the charge that abortion is murder. Society has conditioned people for decades to redefine this sin.

Abortion is described as medical care, a woman's choice to do with her own body what she will. Many do not regard the fetus in the womb as a person, so they do not consider the removal of the fetus by abortion to be murder. Many women who have believed the lie that abortion is not murder get pressured into making a sinful decision to abort. Nevertheless, a God-given conscience causes many of these women to suffer from guilt, especially if they realize later that they have taken the life of an unborn baby. Further complicating the situation, many women (for example, those caught in sex slavery) are victims of the wickedness of others who pressure or force them to undergo abortions.

What should be the Christian assessment of and response to a culture that promotes abortion? Rather than soften the reality of what abortion is and of one's personal responsibility for choosing it (with the recognition that people may have varying levels of complicity and guilt based on the situation), Christians magnify the gospel hope of God's great grace and forgiveness. God's great love shines brighter in the darkness; thus, we do not uphold the greatness of God's love by downplaying the wickedness or by excusing it (Luke 7:47).

Do you have a heart that reflects the character of God—full of righteous indignation against wickedness while at the same time extending grace, mercy, and love toward those who would repent and be transformed?

context▶ APPEALS TO DIFFICULT CIRCUMSTANCES

Doing the right thing seems so easy until you find yourself in a situation of great pressure and fear. Suddenly, you find yourself justifying the unimaginable.

Abortion is commonly justified for the following reasons:

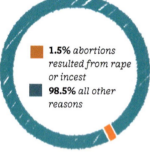

1.5% *abortions resulted from rape or incest*

98.5% *all other reasons*

rape or incest
The child conceived would always remind the victim of the crime against her.

the life of the mother
Due to pregnancy complications, there may be situations where there's no other way to save the mother than to end the life of the baby.

birth defects
A child with serious birth defects would be deemed less than normal and would likely have a poor quality of life.

youth or unmarried status of the mother
She is not ready for the responsibility of motherhood. She may be under pressure to hide the shame of immorality; she may fear the social or familial consequences if she is found to be pregnant.

poverty or other financial considerations
Many single mothers will struggle to make ends meet financially, especially if they lack support from the child's father or their families; in such cases the child's quality of life is in question. Some parents simply wish to avoid the expense and responsibility that would come with having a child.

privacy and autonomy
Some women simply don't want the child; regardless of the reason, that is a personal decision they have a right to make ("My body, my choice").

career pursuits and feminism
Women, like men, should be able to enjoy sex without consequences or responsibility; they should be able to advance their careers without the obligations of motherhood, if they so choose. Requiring a woman to give birth and take on the responsibility of motherhood is a way men dominate women.

ADVOCATING AND OPPOSING ABORTION

If you search online on the topic of abortion, you will find numerous articles advocating for or opposing abortion. Look for the reasons given to support abortion, and look for other articles that oppose abortion and the reasons they give. Are there reasons in addition to the ones listed here in your text-book? What are the most common reasons in support of abortion?

What reasons do you think would be the most persuasive? Saving the life of the mother (even for most pro-lifers) and rape or incest (for some pro-lifers) are the most persuasive arguments for many people. How often do the most persuasive reasons motivate the abortions that actually take place in our society? Magnuson, citing research, concludes, "One percent claimed to be a victim of rape, less than 0.5 percent became pregnant as a result of incest, and statistics did not register anyone who claimed to have an abortion to save their life."[16] (This statement is not suggesting abortions are never done to save the life of a mother, but these are so rare that they are not even reflected in the statistics.)

In other words, the most compelling reasons for abortion are those that motivate abortions *least* frequently. It's safe to say that most abortions do not take place in the context of a moral dilemma.[17] Many pro-lifers will allow for abortions for these reasons in an effort to ban all other abortions, though in principle many recognize it's wrong to kill an innocent human being regardless of the circumstances. But the majority of abortions are sought to make life easier for the mother—to avoid financial pressures, to maintain respectability, to avoid inconvenience. Abortion, though it takes the life of an innocent person, relieves such pressures. But for believers, God provides a path forward without having to resort to sin (1 Cor. 10:13).

acts ▶ THE FUNDAMENTAL PRINCIPLE: THE SANCTITY OF LIFE

In the debate on abortion, one crucial question must be answered:

Does abortion take the life of a person?

First, understand the key arguments on both sides of the debate. The pro-choice side will argue that a woman has the fundamental freedom to pursue her own self-interest and the rights to privacy and to control over her own body. Thus, she must be allowed to end a pregnancy deemed to be detrimental to her own well-being and health (broadly defined to include both physical and psychological factors).[18] The 1973 *Roe v. Wade* case guaranteed legal abortion in the United States through the first two trimesters of pregnancy. Over the years, various modifications and clarifications have been made, usually in response to state or federal attempts to regulate abortion.[19] One key point of contention is the question of fetal viability[20]—the time during a pregnancy after which a baby can survive outside the womb. Roe seems to define viability as the point at which a fetus "has the capability of meaningful life outside the mother's womb."[21] The timing of viability changes with advances in medical technology.

In 2021, the *Dobbs v. Jackson* case rose to the Supreme Court, in part because of arguments over viability.[22] As a result of the Supreme Court's review of the alleged constitutional right to an abortion, the court overturned *Roe v. Wade* in 2022. And now the determination of abortion rights is in the hands of the states.[23]

• other priorities

A child would interfere with plans (travel, lifestyle, career, education, or finance) for some people, including some married couples. Abortion can be used for family planning if contraception fails.

• body image

Some women want to avoid the permanent changes to their bodies and appearances that will come from pregnancy and delivery.

• population control and eugenics*

The world is headed for an overpopulation crisis, and abortion is a means of avoiding that. Or abortion should be used to eliminate from the gene pool characteristics deemed undesirable for a society. (These justifications are less common today than they once were.)

eugenics: the quest to bolster human genetics by preventing people with traits deemed undesirable from reproducing, while encouraging people with traits deemed desirable to procreate; often associated with the idea that some races are superior to others.

Pro-life supporters will argue that there is no fundamental right to end the life of another person (since the fetus's life is distinct from the mother's body, having its own unique DNA from the time of fertilization) and that there *is* a fundamental obligation to sustain the life of another human being. The disagreement is over the sanctity of life versus the freedom of a woman to maintain her own pursuits without the burden of an unwanted pregnancy. The pro-lifer is not dismissive of the difficult circumstances many women face. Crisis pregnancy centers alleviate some of these burdens and counsel alternative options for dealing with troubling circumstances. But they cannot concede that killing a human being is appropriate for relieving a burden or freeing someone to pursue other priorities in life.

Pro-lifers appeal to a variety of principles:

- The Bible reinforces the personhood of all those in the womb (Gen. 25:22–23; Exod. 21:22–25; Judg. 13:5; Job 31:15–18; Pss. 51:5; 139:13–18; Jer. 1:5; Luke 1:41, 44). The creational order testifies that life begins at conception (in other words, at fertilization). That life may develop and mature, but it is the same unique individual from the time of fertilization onward. Advancements in science support this reality[24] so that few abortionists today can argue that what's in the womb is only a blob of tissue or a part of the mother's own body. Many honest abortion advocates have had to admit that abortion takes a human life.[25] Yet, supporters of abortion still try to justify it as appropriate based on whether that life is viable. They favor the rights of the mother by allowing her to decide how *her* life will be affected.
- The taking of any innocent human life cannot be justified, even if that life is dependent on another for viability (Gen. 1:26–27). Dependency only increases the responsibility to care for life (Pss. 72:12–14; 82:3–4). If dependency were a legitimate reason to end someone's life, scores of human beings outside the womb could lose their lives, and "the sanctity of life" would be meaningless.
- God is the giver of life from conception (Gen. 4:1; Ps. 113:9). He alone has authority over life and death (Gen. 9:6).
- Children are a blessing, not a burden (although the Fall makes childrearing challenging, to be sure). The blessing of children (Pss. 127:3–5; 128:3–4) far outweighs the struggles involved in rearing them, even if a parent's circumstances may be difficult.
- Personal responsibility requires us to consider and accept the consequences of our actions. If someone consents to sexual relations (i.e., in all circumstances other than rape or sex slavery), then that person must be willing to take responsibility for caring for any children that may result (1 Thess. 4:3–5; 1 Tim. 5:8; 2 Tim. 2:22). If the parents cannot care for a child, adoption is an alternative, even in a case of sexual assault. God is able to bring about a positive outcome from any circumstances that produce human life (Gen. 50:20).

Although the debate may seem complex at times (particularly in legal arguments), the fundamental issue should be clear for the Bible-believing Christian. God holds everyone morally responsible to make every effort to preserve the life of an innocent person. If a situation arises in which a doctor has no choice but to remove a baby who would die anyway, to save the life of a mother (as in an ectopic pregnancy*), then that surgical removal should not be construed as murder. The doctor is unable to save both, so he or she concentrates on saving the mother. The doctor's intent is not to end a life that could otherwise be saved; even if he or she put all his or her efforts into saving the baby, those efforts would be futile.

THE IMPACT OF ABORTION ON SOCIETY

What does the loss of over sixty million lives in a few decades mean to American society? What does a culture of abortion—a culture of death—mean for people living in that culture? Guilt. Desensitization. Polarization.

Many women who undergo an abortion admit to overwhelming feelings of guilt

From the moment of conception, God crafts an individual human being in His image.

ectopic pregnancy: a pregnancy in which the fetus never implants in the uterus but begins to develop elsewhere, usually in a fallopian tube; the baby cannot survive, and the mother will likely also die without intervention.[26]

and remorse, even to the point that they contemplate suicide.[27] Abortion hurts not just the unborn baby but also the mother, the father, the family unit, and the community. There are those, however, who boast in their callousness. They're proud that they chose to do away with an unwanted life, shameless that it was indeed a life they had the power to nurture or dispose of. They're desensitized to the evil they boast of. And the social order has been locked into a polarizing battle for decades now. Not only have lines been drawn between the pro-choice and pro-life positions, but differing strategies set pro-lifers at odds with each other.

A culture of abortion normalizes medical procedures like embryonic stem cell research, in vitro fertilization (see Chapters 12 and 13), and the use of abortifacients* for birth control. Although the number of surgical abortions has been dropping according to statistics, those statistics are based on what is known and reported. Although surgical abortions are decreasing, chemical abortions (by means of pills) are increasing. Whatever the means of ending a pregnancy, life begun at fertilization is being snuffed out.

How can pro-lifers impact the society they live in? They must reckon with the pressures many women face and offer alternatives to abortion: adoption, financial assistance during and after pregnancy, counseling that encourages right priorities and upholds children as a blessing, and support systems such as crisis pregnancy centers. Underlying all the resources should be an effort to inculcate respect for innocent children as image-bearers of inestimable value, regardless of whether they are intentional additions to a family or the result of sexual assault. It's important to educate people about how certain kinds of birth control work (those that prevent fertilization versus abortifacients that terminate life after fertilization) and to point people to the gospel for forgiveness and transformation.

 ## THE NEED FOR A CHANGE OF HEART

Ultimately, any change in a society's stance on abortion must come from a change of heart. The proper virtues must be cultivated. Only a virtuous people will uphold virtuous laws and practices. Certainly, the transforming work of the gospel is the fundamental need. But by God's common grace, some cultures, though filled with unconverted people, tend to be more virtuous than other cultures. Three virtues stand out above the rest in these cultures: love, courage, and gratitude.

Every kind of murder is rooted in a lack of love for God and others. True love will never consider taking innocent life. By God's common grace, people should recognize that compassionate love for the unborn would be the most natural response of a mother toward her own child. But our culture has moved away from God's creational order, which protects and values the lives of those made in His image. We are left with a society that does not uphold and value the God-given instincts of a woman to nurture and protect her child. Life-affirming virtues have been replaced by self-love—demanding autonomy, privacy, freedom, and "the right to choose," even at the expense of the most helpless among us.

Tough situations like unwanted or unexpected pregnancies will always be present in a fallen world. And when people get desperate in those situations, they are naturally tempted to take what has been falsely advertised as the easy way out (abortion). It takes courage to do the right thing—to bring a new life to birth. What if a culture supported an ethical view of enduring hardship and of steadfastness in the face of temptation? Christians should be there to help instill this courage and point women to its source: Christ, who alone forgives sin, frees from guilt, and empowers His children to lead godly lives.

Gratitude engenders satisfaction with the basic blessings of life, God's provision of "our daily bread" (Matt. 6:11). The result of gratitude is selflessness and contentment. Ironically, the most prosperous societies, which have the greatest reasons for gratitude, tend to justify abortion based on supposed financial needs. God's people should model contentment for their cultures and give generously to support those in need.

abortifacients: drugs that cause an abortion

UNCOMPROMISED COMPASSIONATE COUNSEL

How would you respond to women who admit they're considering an abortion or have had an abortion? You should respond wisely with truth in love. Truth and love should not be pitted against one another. The truth should be conveyed in love, and real love must be truthful. What does a wise response look like?

First, no one should go away from your counsel thinking it would be okay to opt for an abortion and rely on a gracious God for forgiveness later. That would be a complete misunderstanding of God's grace (Titus 2:11–12) and would reveal a careless attitude toward sin (Rom. 6:1–2; Jude 1:4).

Second, you should communicate clearly to any repentant person who is suffering from the guilt of having had an abortion that she should rest in God's mercy and grace for forgiveness; abortion should never be seen as an unpardonable sin. Although some consequences are irreversible in this life, God can use these kinds of circumstances to draw people to Himself, and God's mercy and grace can sustain people through any difficulty. Despite regret for the loss of relationship in this life, a woman who has had an abortion may find comfort in the knowledge that the baby enjoys eternal life in heaven with the Lord.

Thinking It Through 9.3

1. Summarize three of the common justifications for abortion.

2. Identify and explain the key arguments for the pro-choice position in the abortion debate.

3. Identify and explain the key arguments for the pro-life position in the abortion debate.

4. What are two of the principles pro-lifers appeal to in opposition to abortion? How would you use these principles when talking to a person who is unsure about the morality of abortion?

5. What's at least one personal or social consequence of abortion?

6. What is one key virtue that orients a person away from getting an abortion and a culture away from advocating abortion? Explain why.

7. What would be an inappropriate response to someone who is contemplating having an abortion or who confesses to having had an abortion? What would be a better alternative response?

Review

09

Terms to Remember

- murder
- first-degree murder
- second-degree murder
- manslaughter
- voluntary manslaughter
- involuntary manslaughter
- self-defense
- suicide
- euthanasia
- abortion

Scripture Memory

Exodus 20:13; Matthew 5:21–22

Understanding Ethics

1. What does the Bible teach about the source of a person's value?
2. What does the Bible teach about who has the authority over life and death?
3. What does the Bible teach about the sanctity of life from conception?

Practicing Ethical Decision-Making

4. How should you respond when you learn that a classmate is contemplating self-harm?
5. What are some practical ways you can involve yourself in the fight against abortion?

Analyzing and Evaluating Ethical Claims

6. How would you respond to someone claiming that a husband and father ought not use lethal force to protect his wife and children from an armed home invader?
7. How would you respond to someone claiming that suicide might not always be sinful? Conversely, how would you respond to someone claiming that suicide is an unforgivable sin that guarantees someone who committed it is in hell?
8. How would you respond to someone claiming that withholding food and water from a dependent is the same as removing artificial life support and allowing someone to pass naturally?
9. How would you biblically respond to the pro-choice slogan "My body, my choice"?

Creating My Own Position Statements on Ethics

10. Write a one- to two-page paper that summarizes your understanding of a biblical position on the sanctity of life as it applies to the issues in this chapter. Or write a pro-life pamphlet that you could share with friends, co-workers, and family members.

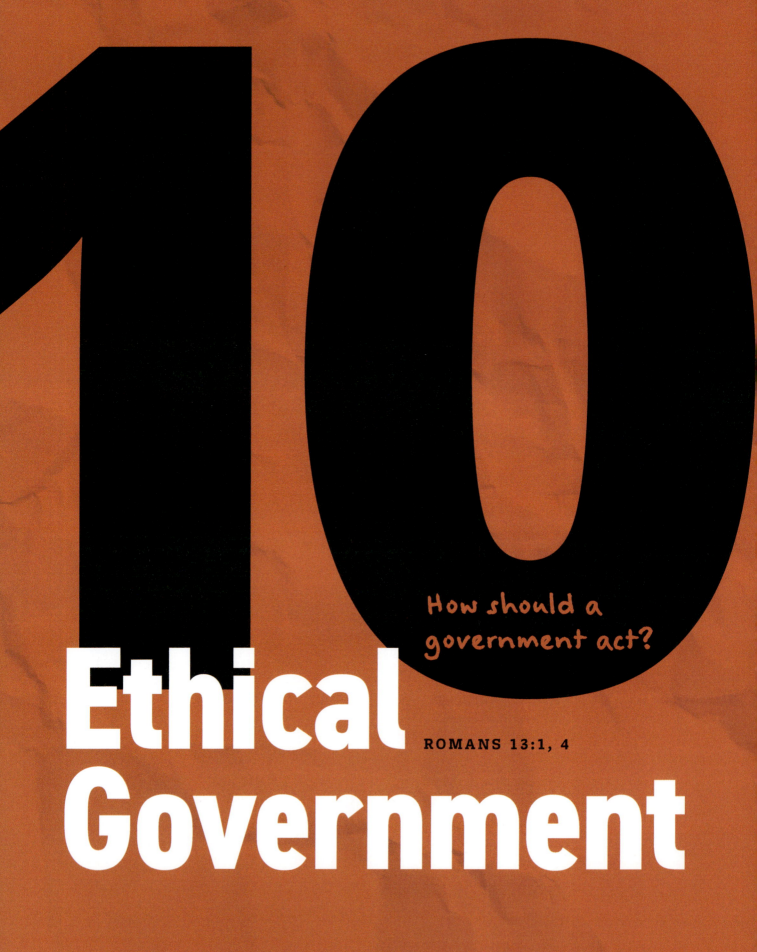

10

Ethical Government

How should a government act?

ROMANS 13:1, 4

10.1 Capital Punishment

The government is people. Have you ever thought about the government this way? You might think of buildings, courtrooms, laws, or politicians when you hear the word *government*, but those in charge of running a country are people. They will either pursue justice and righteousness (thus meeting God's approval and blessing the citizens) or they will deal out injustice and unrighteousness (earning God's disapproval and leading to the citizens' loss and frustration).

This chapter addresses four government-related issues (capital punishment, just war, immigration, and Christian disobedience to authority) that impact believers. In our fallen world, there will be unethical aspects in any government, but that reality doesn't make room for believers to respond unethically. Even in the area of government, Christians must live ethically, as unto the Lord, no matter how complicated or costly it might be to do so.

VIEWS ON CAPITAL PUNISHMENT

The previous chapter covered the ethics of life and death. Capital punishment is certainly an issue of life and death. But we are covering this topic in this chapter because **capital punishment** is a government's use of execution as a criminal penalty. Capital punishment is not becoming any less controversial. People on both sides of the issue argue passionately for their position. So, what are some different views on capital punishment?

Oppose—Abolish Entirely

Those who advocate for the abolishment of capital punishment do so for a variety of reasons. Below is a brief description of these arguments.[1]

Secular advocates ignore the Bible's teaching on capital punishment. Christians who hold this view interpret biblical texts to fit with secular thinking about capital punishment.

> Capital punishment is revenge approved of and carried out by the state.

> Capital punishment doesn't deter heinous crimes any more than other punishments.

> Capital punishment is inhumane and tramples people's dignity and rights.

> Capital punishment cannot be carried out in a just manner.

> Capital punishment is at odds with the Bible's ethic of life, love, and forgiveness.

Support—For Significant Crimes

Those who advocate for this position appeal to biblical evidence of God's approval of capital punishment (Gen. 9:5-6; Exod. 21:12; Rom. 13:4). The Mosaic law prescribed capital punishment for approximately twenty different sins.[2] Advocates also point to the God-appointed role the government plays in carrying out punishments like capital punishment (Rom. 13:1-7; 1 Pet. 2:13-14).

Support—Only for Murder

This third view is similar to the second one, but it is slightly more nuanced and specific. It also builds a strong biblical case and highlights God's disapproval of and due consequence for murderers (Gen. 9:5-6). The main difference is that advocates of this view are most comfortable limiting capital punishment to those who commit exceptionally violent murders.[3]

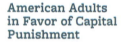

SCRIPTURE'S VERDICT ON CAPITAL PUNISHMENT

We have already briefly mentioned a few passages that support or command the use of capital punishment. Now we want to dig a little deeper into those and other passages that will help believers get a handle on what the Bible teaches on this topic. Public opinion, which is always fluctuating, is not the authority for determining the ethics of capital punishment, but it does help us to understand a culture's character. In 2022, 55 percent of American adults were in favor of capital punishment. This is down from the 71 percent who viewed the death penalty as morally acceptable in 2006. Interestingly, but not surprisingly, there was lower support for the death penalty among liberals (40 percent) than support from conservatives (67 percent).[4]

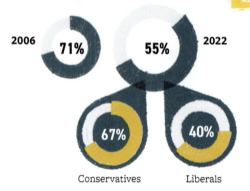

American Adults in Favor of Capital Punishment

2006 — 71%
2022 — 55%
Conservatives — 67%
Liberals — 40%

How seriously does God view murder?

Respect for the Image of God in Man—Genesis 9:6

The first and main reason murder is a grievous sin is because the unjustified taking of someone's life is highly offensive to God. God made man and woman in His image, to bear His likeness (Gen. 1:26-27). So every human being intrinsically has value because of whose image he or she bears. To murder someone is to destroy one who reflects God Himself. That is a capital offense by any measure! But it is God's measure that matters, and He has determined that the just penalty for murder is capital punishment (Gen. 9:5-6). After the global Flood, God told Noah a remarkable three times that He would "require" (demand retribution for) the lifeblood of slain humans (Gen. 9:5). This is just, reciprocal retribution foreshadowing the future "eye for eye" principle in the law of Moses (Exod. 21:24). God's message to us is essentially, "If you dare take a life when you shouldn't, you must forfeit your own life for this highly offensive sin."

Life is so valuable to God that He even provided protection for those who killed someone unintentionally (Num. 35:9-34). But the only condition that freed the one who accidentally took a life was the (eventual) death of another, the high priest (Num. 35:25). Even in this situation involving manslaughter, the death of another (in this case, a substitute) was the price to pay for the death of the innocent—only a loss of life covers another loss of life (Num. 35:33).

Enforcing the Sixth Commandment—Exodus 20:13

Believers today are part of the New Covenant announced by the prophets and inaugurated by Christ (Jer. 31:33; Ezek. 36:26-37; Luke 22:19-20). The Mosaic Covenant isn't binding on Christians since they are part of the New Covenant. But just as two different states can have the same law, some of the laws in the Mosaic Covenant are the same under the New Covenant. This is the case with the sixth of the Ten Commandments. Exodus 20:13 says, "Thou shalt not kill." This Hebrew word for *kill* refers to murder or to an unintentional killing (the same term is used for both a manslayer and a murderer in Numbers 35). This verb never refers to killing when done in warfare. This detail is important, especially considering the next section on just war. So, the sixth commandment isn't a universal prohibition against taking someone's life, but a prohibition against taking innocent life.

Part of the instruction God gave Moses included the repeated command to sentence murderers to death (Exod. 21:12, 14; Lev. 24:17, 21; Num. 35:16–21, 30–31). The sixth commandment codified a principle that already existed, and so it endures till today. The command of a life for a life and blood for blood was first given to Noah, the father of all nations after the Flood, way before the time of Moses. This means it was intended for all people in all places for all time. A violation of the sixth commandment was, is, and will always be serious to God.

Responsibility of the Government—Romans 13:4; 1 Peter 2:13–14

In the New Testament, Scripture teaches that the government is in charge of punishing those who do wrong and rewarding those who do right (Rom. 13:1–7; 1 Pet. 2:13–14). Romans 13:4 is very similar in principle to the passage in Numbers 35 discussed above. But rather than a family member of the slain doing the avenging, the government is God's servant, "a revenger to execute wrath upon him that doeth evil." This verse teaches the government's responsibility to use "the sword" in punishing wrongdoing, an image which surely suggests the death penalty (Rom. 13:4). Along these lines, Paul himself said he was ready to suffer the death penalty if he deserved it (Acts 25:11). He was guilty of no crime, so his eventual execution was actually an injustice. But Paul never questioned his government's authority to use the death penalty. In a fallen world, governments can and sometimes do misuse their authority and rule unjustly, but that is not an argument against the *legitimate* authority God has given them.

Punishing crimes other than murder with the death penalty is an ethically challenging proposition. There is precedent in the biblical text, as seen above, for this approach. Historically, the United States did apply the death penalty more broadly. An example is that of the Rosenbergs, sentenced to death during the Cold War after being convicted of espionage.[5] But only people convicted of murder have been executed since 1976.[6] Examination and prudence are needed to apply capital punishment for crimes that aren't directly related to murder, but Scripture seems to support its broader use.

> *Christians may therefore affirm government's authority to use the death penalty in response to murder, but must also hold the government accountable to justice in its administration.* KEN MAGNUSON[7]

CONSEQUENCES OF WRONG
APPROACHES TO CAPITAL PUNISHMENT

For almost every situation or concept, there are two extreme positions. The number is commonly two because on a linear graph there is a line that forms a spectrum having two ends that are opposite one another; these ends represent the extremes. Consider the use of a turn signal while driving. You could never use it. That's one extreme. Or you could overuse the turn signal by using it for every bend in the road and by turning it on two blocks too early before each turn. Both are wrong approaches. Both could cause an accident.

What would happen if society took one extreme or the other regarding capital punishment? Are there consequences for a society that takes a wrong approach to this important issue? Consider the complete abolishment of capital punishment for any crime. If the death penalty is not a legal resource, how do you punish the worst and the most dangerous criminals? (There is considerable disagreement on the advantages and disadvantages of our current prison system, including sentences of life in prison.)

Look at the example of a Norwegian political extremist turned mass murderer, Anders Breivik. He killed seventy-seven fellow Norwegians in Oslo in one day back in 2011 before surrendering to the police. He was given the maximum sentence Norwegian law allowed for his murderous terrorism—twenty-one years behind bars. And in early 2022, he made an appeal for parole claiming that he would no longer be violent. His petition was denied, and he will likely finish out the remaining years of his sentence. Norwegian law *does* allow for the possible extension of imprisonment for those still deemed dangerous.[8] But where is the justice for the seventy-seven victims killed by Breivik? Prohibiting capital punishment in Norway is a tragic injustice. It is unjust for murderers like Breivik not to receive a swift carrying out of the death penalty. In addition to the lack of justice, another consequence is a lack of deterrence. What prevents another terrorist like Breivik from committing similar or worse mass killings? Twenty-one years in prison might seem quite tolerable for someone who truly believes in his or her cause. It might be difficult to discern whether the death penalty acts as a deterrent to heinous crimes,[9] but it cannot function as a deterrent if the law doesn't provide for it.

2011 Oslo bombing

On the other end of the spectrum is the immediate application of capital punishment for any and all heinous crimes upon conviction. The implications of this position might sound fair enough, considering the biblical evidence for the validity of capital punishment for murder and other crimes. But a swift carrying out of capital punishment assumes a just conviction. It also assumes that capital punishment is a just sentence for the crime a person has been convicted of. If there is confidence in the evidence, eye-witness testimonies, and any confessions, then it *is* unethical to have a criminal guilty of such a crime sit on death row for decades. However, delay in carrying out justice may benefit those who are truly innocent if the judicial system wrongly convicted them. An example is the case of Donald Gates, who was wrongly convicted of rape and murder before being exonerated twenty-eight years later.[10] But what is the truly just solution to such wrongful convictions? Is it decades on death row while years of appeals wind their way through the court system? No (although there should be a reasonable time window to appeal). Is it abolition of the death penalty since someone might be wrongly convicted? No. The solution (in any society) is criminal justice reform, such that (1) the standard for conviction is high; (2) the death penalty applies only for crimes worthy of it; and (3) those who give false evidence, coerce confessions, and fabricate evidence are punished with the punishment they would have brought on the innocent (see Deut. 19:15–21). Hard, irrefutable evidence needs to be obtained prior to sentencing someone to death. If that case can be made justly, then the lethal punishment is also just.

As seen in the Scripture passages treated earlier, capital punishment (for murder, at the very least) is a biblical and just mandate. Abolishing capital punishment provides no justice for the victim or relief for the victim's family. Abolishing capital punishment removes a possible deterrent from those considering committing heinous crimes. But failing to obtain accurate and just convictions damages the just purpose of capital punishment. Society needs a legal system it can count on to enforce just laws justly. And the government needs laws with just consequences for crimes—laws that also help keep potential criminals in check.

That severe punishment underscores the severity of murderous violence and of God's wrath against evil, which will ultimately be carried out in the final judgment by God directly, but which for now is administered by governing authorities as God's servants.   KEN MAGNUSON[11]

MOTIVES FOR CAPITAL PUNISHMENT

How do love and forgiveness and justice go together? Some proponents of abolishing capital punishment will appeal to their understanding of the Bible's ethic of life, love, and forgiveness. But the Bible's ethic on these topics isn't without sacrifice and loss of life. Just think of the whole sacrificial system God gave to the Israelites so they could live in fellowship with Him (Lev. 1–7); death for sin was central to that system. Most Christians and many non-Christians are familiar with one of the most popular verses in the Bible, John 3:16: "For God so loved the world, that he gave his only begotten Son, that whosoever believeth in him should not perish, but have everlasting life." This verse combines (eternal) life, love, and forgiveness in one sentence. But Christ, being innocent, had to give up His life so those guilty and deserving of death could live! This is a beautiful picture of God—His mercy and justice simultaneously on display.

LOVE + FORGIVENESS ≠ JUSTICE

But isn't the death of a murder victim enough violence already? What could motivate someone to add death upon death? These questions assume that executing a murderer is another unjust homicide. But the opposite is true; what is at stake is whether the person who committed the actual unjust homicide will be brought to justice. Those who oppose capital punishment purportedly believe the highest goal is the preservation of life. John Frame discusses the realities and effects of capital punishment this way:

> Objectors often assume, furthermore, that death is the absolute end of human existence, whereas Scripture teaches that there is a life to come. Murderers who repent of their sins and embrace Christ will spend an eternity in glory. Capital punishment is not an absolute deprivation of existence. It is rather a means of turning a person over to God for final judgment.[12]

Those who oppose capital punishment have an idea of justice that doesn't match with God's determination of the value of human life and the (corresponding) consequences for murder. Christians need to follow God's declaration of what justice looks like and let God's ways motivate them to support a just carrying out of capital punishment.

Many would like to substitute capital punishment with reformation and rehabilitation. Instead of a life-for-a-life biblical framework, they want to see the murderer be reformed and possibly rehabilitated back into society. But this idea is motivated by a wrong understanding of the morality of human nature. For some crimes, like theft or vandalism, restitution can be made where the guilty party pays for what he or she stole, broke, or damaged. In the case of murder, however, the murderer cannot restore the life taken; the person who committed the murder must forfeit his or her own life. Restitution cannot be done in the case of murder. Murder demands retribution since each crime must be punished in proportion (Lev. 24:17–23). Restitution and rehabilitation for certain crimes have their place. Capital punishment should be motivated by just retribution. Those guilty of murder must face the consequences of their actions—only another life can pay for the sin of murder.

CAPITAL PUNISHMENT FOR MURDER = JUSTICE

If we desire to value what God values and treat sin like God treats it, capital punishment won't sound immoral or unfair to us. Sin is tragic, and so are its consequences. Believers are motivated by faith in God and His ways and by the understanding that implementing capital punishment responsibly and justly is what is best for society.

 MURDER HITTING HOME

> *Capital punishment is not perfect justice, but it is part of the process by which God brings his judgments to bear on a sinful world.* JOHN FRAME[13]

To be affected by murder, a miscarriage of justice, or the execution of a loved one on death row is extremely difficult. Even in these tragic scenarios, God is sovereign and gives His grace to those where murder hits home. Probably the most difficult of those three scenarios is to see justice being trampled on and twisted. This could be where someone you know is wrongly convicted or where someone who murdered your loved one doesn't receive the death penalty. How do you respond when you are helpless to effect any change, being at the mercy of what the state or federal government decides?

Pray

When you pray for local, state, and federal leaders, pray specifically that they would make just laws and decisions and fix the wrong decisions brought to their attention (1 Tim. 2:1–3). If faced with injustice, pray that God would give you grace and the boldness to have a faith-filled testimony during such a difficult time (1 Thess. 1:3, 6).

Advocate

Reach out to your elected representatives and use processes for legal appeals. You might have limited power to appeal to the judge or authorities that were involved in the miscarrying of justice, but there is usually a process for appeal and review by higher authorities. Find out how you can appeal and keep pursuing justice.

Trust

Trust in the Lord and in His will for you and your family, even when you don't understand His purposes. This sin-laden world is hard and frustrating. Turn to the Lord, keeping your faith and trusting Him to work in and through this terrible situation. Even when murder hits home, the Shepherd is with His people to comfort and guide them (Ps. 23:4).

Thinking It Through 10.1

1. Define *capital punishment*.

2. List and briefly explain the three views presented above regarding capital punishment.

3. Summarize the biblical teaching on capital punishment.

4. What are some societal consequences of unbiblical views regarding capital punishment?

5. What motives should undergird supporting capital punishment?

6. How would you help a friend who suffered injustice related to capital punishment?

10.2 Just War

Courage, strength, determination—these three words can describe the popular image of a soldier. Soldiers protect our freedoms. But soldiers can also be used as pawns in the hands of tyrannical leaders. Have you ever considered becoming a soldier or joining the military? For many, the thought of defending their homeland trumps the thought of the pain and suffering they might experience fighting a war.

Is it permissible for Christians to engage in warfare? Governments declare war and use their citizens to fight those wars. Before we can discuss the virtues a believer needs if called upon to fight in a war, we must consider the various views on war, what the Bible has to say about engaging in warfare, and both the goals and consequences of war.

 PERSPECTIVES ON WAR

One end of the spectrum views war through **militarism**. This perspective sees war as the means to fulfilling the desires of a country or its leaders. Think about the empires of the distant past (e.g., Greek and Roman) that expanded their territories to display their military prowess and to prosper financially. For more modern times, think of Hitler's Germany around the mid-twentieth century. The mentality of militarism is "I want it, and I will go to war to get it."

On the other side of the spectrum is pacifism. **Pacifism** in its most extreme form opposes all forms of violent action, even those which would avoid great harm or promote a great good. For the first three hundred years of the church's existence, Christians weren't keen on fighting even in just wars because that would have meant joining forces with a pagan government who persecuted them.[14] When Christianity became the official religion of the Roman Empire, the hesitancy of Christians to serve in the military lost most of its influence.[15] At the time of the Reformation in Europe, the Anabaptist movement emerged and was well-known for including pacifism as one of their tenets.[16] Groups like the Plymouth Brethren and the Mennonites have perpetuated pacifism in the United States.[17] The mentality of the most extreme pacifism is "Avoid war, and especially killing someone in war, at all costs."

Christian pacifists support their beliefs by appealing to various teachings in Scripture. From the Old Testament they interpret the sixth commandment, "Thou shalt not kill" (Exod. 20:13), as prohibiting taking a life even in war. From the New Testament they appeal to Jesus' teaching about believers as peacemakers (Matt. 5:9), to a believer's responsibility to turn the other cheek when slapped (Matt. 5:39), and to

pacifism ▶

just war doctrine ▶

realism ▶

militarism ▶

the commandment for believers to love their neighbors as themselves (Matt. 22:39). Also, Matthew 5:43–44 is combined with what Romans 12:14 says to support loving and blessing the enemy instead of engaging him in battle.

There are two perspectives on war toward the middle of the spectrum. The first is realism. **Realism** is utilitarian and pragmatic, viewing wars as necessary evils, where any moral considerations either don't exist or are very flexible. The mentality of realism is "All is fair in love and war."

The final view on war is the teaching of just war doctrine. **Just war doctrine** sets ethical parameters on when war is ethically viable and how to conduct oneself in war because war is a moral matter—human life is at stake.[18] A just war is used by a government to ensure justice for its own country or close allies.[19] Just war doctrine has a biblical basis, not just a philosophical one. Each tenet of just war doctrine can be supported from various scriptural principles. Human government is entrusted with the power of the sword to punish those who do wrong (Rom. 13:4). The mentality of just war is: "War should be fought ethically and only when necessary to defend one's country and seek justice for one's own people and close allies."

THE TENETS OF JUST WAR DOCTRINE[20]

Over time, the just war ethic has developed a common set of criteria that can be used to decide if going to war in a specific situation is right. These include the following:

(1) **just cause**
is the reason for going to war a morally right cause, such as defense of a nation? . . . [cf. 2 Kings 19:32–35];

(2) **competent authority**
has the war been declared not simply by a renegade band within a nation but by a recognized, competent authority within the nation? cf. Rom. 13:1;

(3) **comparative justice**
it should be clear that the actions of the enemy are morally wrong, and the motives and actions of one's own nation in going to war are, in comparison, morally right; cf. Rom. 13:3;

(4) **right intention**
is the purpose of going to war to protect justice and righteousness rather than simply to rob and pillage and destroy another nation? cf. Prov. 21:2;

(5) **last resort**
have all other reasonable means of resolving the conflict been exhausted? cf. Matt. 5:9; Rom. 12:18;

(6) **probability of success**
is there a reasonable expectation that the war can be won? . . . [human life is valuable and shouldn't be needlessly spent; cf. Gen. 9:6];

(7) **proportionality of projected results**
will the good results that come from a victory in a war be significantly greater than the harm and loss that will inevitably come with pursuing the war? cf. Rom. 12:21 with 13:4;

(8) **right spirit**
is the war undertaken with great reluctance and sorrow at the harm that will come rather than simply with a "delight in war," as in Ps. 68:30?

In addition to these criteria for deciding whether a specific war is "just," advocates of just war theory have also developed some moral restrictions on how a just war should be fought. These include the following:

(1) **proportionality in the use of force**
no greater destruction should be caused than is needed to win the war; cf. Deut. 20:10–12;

(2) **discrimination between combatants and noncombatants**
insofar as it is feasible in the successful pursuit of a war, is adequate care being taken to prevent harm to noncombatants? cf. Deut. 20:13–14, 19–20;

(3) **avoidance of evil means**
will captured or defeated enemies be treated with justice and compassion, and are one's own soldiers being treated justly in captivity? cf. Ps. 34:14;

(4) **good faith**
is there a genuine desire for restoration of peace and eventually living in harmony with the attacking nation? cf. Matt. 5:43–44; Rom. 12:18.

PACIFISM AND REALISM UNDER BIBLICAL SCRUTINY

What does the Bible teach about Christians participating in war? We want to elaborate on a few passages that pacifists use to support their position. We will also look at the arguments that realism offers. (Realism is much more common in our day than straightforward militarism. The empires of centuries and millennia past that were won and maintained through military might are no longer the way of our modern times. Militarism is essentially an extreme version of realism in that it actively and unashamedly uses military force when the powers at be deem it appropriate.)

Pacifism

Some who hold the pacifist position believe that killing someone in war or self-defense is off the table. Others would make allowances for lethal force in limited circumstances.[21] Some pacifists might simply look for non-lethal ways to defend themselves and others. Christian pacifists support their beliefs by appealing to certain Scripture passages. Their interpretations of these passages tend to ignore the surrounding context, and little effort is made to synthesize these passages with other teachings in Scripture. For example, Exodus 20:13 isn't a universal prohibition against all taking of life. The sixth commandment prohibits individuals from taking the life of a person through murder, voluntary manslaughter, or negligence. It also prohibits taking justice into one's own hands. Individuals, therefore, are not on their own terms to hate, attack, kill, or threaten the life of even a legitimate personal enemy. In just war, however, a government responds to an invasion or an attack and righteously defends its people and their livelihood. Pacifists would oppose even preemptive attacks,* which may save much loss of life by avoiding a full-out conflict altogether. But preemptive attacks which hinder injustice from happening can be accommodated in just war doctrine. A government that refuses to defend and protect its people by engaging in a just war renounces its responsibility to rule over God's world.

Love for one's neighbor does not nullify the requirement to carry out God's justice on wrongdoers. WAYNE GRUDEM[22]

Realism

War is a part of life. Someone will be the victor. The victor gets the spoils. And all people want spoils. This, in part, is the mindset of those who see war as a real part of life. But realists are very utilitarian in that any war that gives the greatest amount of good to the greatest number of people is justified. Realists also use this mindset to justify how they fight a war. A lack of morality affects how pragmatic realists are in doing what it takes to win a war. Why does this viewpoint violate a biblical worldview on what constitutes a just war?

Even if a nation has a just reason for entering a war, that doesn't mean those fighting the war are allowed to do anything and everything that ensures victory. Humane conduct during warfare has been codified by international agreements, beginning in 1864 at the initial Geneva Convention and continuing through the Rome Statute in 1998, which created the International Criminal Court.[23] Even secular states realize that war crimes and atrocities of war are immoral and should be prevented and prosecuted where possible. Morality is found in God and in His revelation (Exod. 34:5–7; Matt. 22:37–40). All humans, including soldiers and civilians involved in war, should pursue that morality, not a morality of their own creation. A soldier fighting for the side who started the war can still fight in a way that qualifies as just.

Just war doctrine gives peace its proper place as preferable to bloodshed and loss of life on both sides. But even when pulled into war, believers can be confident that just war doctrine provides superior guidance to that of either pacifism or realism. Knowing that God has given governments authority to punish evil and provide justice for their citizens (Rom. 13:3–4; 1 Pet. 2:13–14) should be a great comfort. Yet punishing evil doesn't make room for immoral and unethical behavior in how one makes war against an aggressor nation or its civilians.

Sound familiar? With what ethical approach is realism most closely associated?

preemptive attack: a military attack intended to avoid a full-out war or to protect from an imminent attack from the enemy

When is it
right to go
to war?

 ends ▶ ### THE EFFECTS OF WAR ON SOCIETY

We need to look more closely at war and its effects on society when viewed from pacifist and realist perspectives. When a war is over, the hardship and challenges for many are just beginning. The leaders of nations might sign a peace treaty and go back to their homes, but the devastated soldiers, their families, and the communities directly affected by the war must begin the process of healing and restoration. Michael Walzer addresses the ethical obligations of the victor of a just war:

> Once we have acted in ways that have significant negative consequences for other people (even if there are also positive consequences), we cannot just walk away. Imagine a humanitarian intervention that ends with the massacres stopped and the murderous regime overthrown; but the country is devastated, the economy in ruins, the people hungry and afraid; there is neither law nor order nor any effective authority. The forces that intervened did well, but they are not finished.[24]

Since every war leads to devastation that must be addressed, the reasons for going to war must be just and worthy of the immense sacrifice.

For pacifism, warfare is never justified. Since many nations go to war for unjust reasons, commit genocide, and disrupt a country's infrastructure, who would make sure that the spread of oppression and injustice by a nation making unjust war didn't go unchecked? These are thorny questions for pacifism. It is unfortunate that wars have to be fought to end wars and avoid future wars. But they are necessary and can and should be fought justly. The Cold War between the United States and the Soviet Union (1947–91) shows how pacifism would have been disastrous for the world. At the end of World War II, communism began to slowly spread into various regions across the world. Even if the Soviet Union didn't fight many wars directly, it supported the furtherance of its ideologies in each nation where it maintained a foothold. The United States was directly involved in fighting against or supporting resistance to the Soviet Union in these countries, with mixed levels of success:

Greece, China, Korea, Vietnam, Cuba, and Afghanistan.[25] Pacifism would have meant little to no participation in these conflicts, and the spread of communism would have been much greater and much stronger as a result.

For realism, the pragmatic benefits or advantages of war mean that war may be waged whenever a nation deems it wise and beneficial for them. A nation would count the cost, but this calculation doesn't invoke the principles of just war doctrine. A more pragmatic, and ultimately self-serving, approach to war is taken. This results in more powerful nations increasing their power and influence while weaker nations struggle to survive and do what they can to avoid being attacked by a powerful opponent in war. Without the right reasons for going to war and the right goals, realism can't achieve righteous ends. Realism produces an unstable world order where the playground bully is justified in pushing everyone around.

 ## FIGHTING A WAR JUSTLY

So how can a Christian engage in a war in a just manner? What virtues do Christian combatants need as they participate in a just war? Love, courage, and prudence are needed to fight a just war. Even though love seems antithetical to war, some Christian thinkers as far back as Augustine have associated just war with love for neighbor.[26] Love, because those who fight a just war do so out of love for the people and values they are defending. Love, because loving God and others means that believers value what God values. Governments will need to go to war to defend their citizens' well-being and freedoms. But while at war, love governs how Christians treat non-combatants, enemies who surrender, and the natural resources of the enemy. It would be unloving to cause unnecessary short-term and long-term harm to non-combatants and their communities.

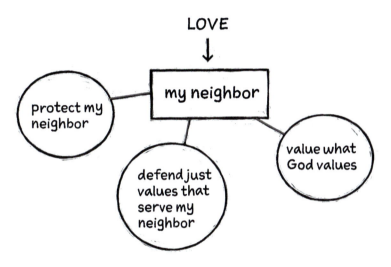

If a Christian must fight in a war, then he or she will need courage. Courage for the right causes is virtuous. The Scriptures use various warfare analogies to charge believers to live for the Lord (for example, see Eph. 6:10–17; 2 Tim. 2:3–4; 2 Cor. 10:1–6). Opposing sin, temptation, and all sorts of evil takes real spiritual courage. Thankfully, believers trust in an almighty God who fights for them (Ps. 24:8). The same truth applies to a physical battle. God gives the courage Christian combatants need to fight a just war even in the face of defeat and death.

And Christians need prudence to help them determine if a war their government is entering is just for them to participate in. This prudence could lead to hardship if those required to fight decide to oppose their government by refusing to take up arms in an unjust conflict. Prudence guides the believer to determine what aspect of a war effort (perhaps behind the front lines in a supporting, non-combat position) he or she can participate in. Prudence also guides the soldier in making good decisions, though potentially at great cost, while fighting on the front lines.

 ## JUST WAR HITTING HOME

How would you respond if your government drafted you into the military to fight a war? Could you apply a biblical worldview to everything surrounding the war? Would you be able to demonstrate the virtues of love, courage, and prudence as you waded into the situation? Always remember God's purpose for government. And always remember your responsibilities as a citizen of heaven and as a citizen on earth.

1. Define the four perspectives on war.

2. Evaluate pacifism and realism according to Scripture.

3. What consequences does society face if pacifism or realism are practiced?

4. Why are the virtues of love, courage, and prudence required for believers to act ethically regarding warfare?

5. How would you respond to being called to go to war? Defend your answer biblically.

10.3 Immigration

"Home is where the heart is" goes the popular saying. But what happens when your heart yearns for a place where you no longer live? Uprooting oneself or one's family to move to a new country is no small undertaking. Chances are someone in your family's not-too-distant history immigrated to the country where you live. And you may know an immigrant or the child of an immigrant. An **immigrant** is someone who relocates to a country other than his or her own. Assessing the ethicality of a nation's immigration policy is not easy. But it is a relevant issue for Christians to consider.

 ### WHY IS IMMIGRATION A HOT TOPIC?

Immigration is a hot topic, and not only in the United States. Why do so many people feel so passionately about immigration and immigration policy? Countries that offer consistent employment, good wages, political freedom, law and order, a comfortable standard of living, and educational opportunities are desirable for millions of people who live in countries that don't offer these things. Many are willing to leave their homelands for countries with greater opportunities. But even countries that receive only a few immigrants still struggle to treat them ethically when they do arrive. Ethnic, cultural, and religious differences; stereotypes; language barriers; and socioeconomic disparities make it difficult for immigrants to adapt quickly or easily. When the host nation rejects immigrants or when immigrants refuse to respect the ways of the host nation, these difficulties are compounded.

So what policies should govern our borders? What are we to do with the unauthorized immigrants* who are currently living in our country? What should the enforcement of our borders and immigration laws look like? Since immigration is such a hot topic that raises challenging questions with complicated answers, what light can the Bible shed on this issue?

 ### THE BIBLE ON IMMIGRATION

We will examine three main approaches to immigration. The Bible, however, doesn't contain a handbook on how the United States should issue visas to foreigners or secure its borders. Before mentioning the three philosophical frameworks that may describe a society's general approach to the topic of immigration, let's examine the biblical teaching on the two main disputed topics.

Borders—Laws

The Bible demonstrates that since the beginning of civilization, there have been borders that separate groups of people from each other (Gen. 4:16–17; 15:18–21). God created nations, and as such they can regulate their borders (Gen. 10:31–32; Judg. 11:16–20). Edom is an example of a nation wrongly governing its borders in

unauthorized immigrants: those who have entered a foreign country without proper permission or who remain in a foreign country after their official documentation has expired dealing with foreigners (Num. 20:14–21). This episode shows the legitimacy of borders (the need to ask permission to enter a foreign land) as well as the need for a compassionate ethic in dealing with people who come inside one's borders or request permission to enter one's territory.

Immigrants—People

God commands His people to care for and love individuals who have crossed borders and are now living among them. All people, regardless of their immigration status, are made in the image of God and thus worthy of dignified and compassionate treatment (Gen. 1:27). When commanding the just treatment of immigrants in Israel, God appeals to the fact that Israel had been a nation of immigrants in Egypt (Lev. 19:34; Deut. 10:19). Other passages address the justice that Israel should give to foreigners in their midst, as opposed to oppression, which was a common sinful treatment of immigrants (Deut. 27:19; Zech. 7:9–10). The New Testament records Christ's teaching on the loving treatment of others, which would include loving treatment of immigrants (Luke 10:25–37). Certain passages in the Epistles also emphasize the importance of showing hospitality (Rom. 12:13; Heb. 13:2).

Three Frameworks

In the previous section on just war, we learned about *realism*. In the debate over immigration, the same pragmatic approach, devoid of a governing moral ethic, can be found. **Realism** acknowledges the current makeup of countries and their governments and recognizes that each state will act in accordance with its own best interests.[27] In this model, a country's immigration policy is crafted to serve the needs of the country, as determined by its leaders. This framework generally emphasizes the importance of borders and laws.

A second framework is called *cosmopolitanism*. This view focuses on the needs and well-being of the individual. In contrast to realism, **cosmopolitanism** looks past borders and governments and makes the treatment of each individual person, irrespective of citizenship, its primary concern.[28] This view stands in opposition to laws that limit immigration and, therefore, would generally emphasize the importance of treating immigrants as people.

But cosmopolitans overlook a government's primary obligation to care for its own people and the good and necessary role borders play. How to treat individuals ethically is part of the immigration discussion, but the challenge for cosmopolitans is to justify overlooking the interests of their fellow citizens (also individuals) in favor of the interests of individuals who enter their country for any number of reasons.

And finally, *communitarianism* falls in between the two previous views. Like realism, it recognizes the primary obligations that nations have to their own people. But **communitarianism** operates with a moral ethic that governs its treatment of immigrants as individuals.[29] Mark Amstutz contrasts certain aspects of the cosmopolitan and communitarian positions:

> Since cosmopolitans view the nation-state as an impediment to global justice and the promotion of human rights, they favor an open-borders approach to migration. . . . Communitarians, by contrast, believe that sovereign states can only maintain social solidarity by regulating borders. For them, the state must give priority to the needs of its own people before it addresses the needs of peoples in foreign societies.[30]

Communitarianism defends the prerogative of each nation to govern its borders while simultaneously keeping in mind the challenges immigrants and refugees* face that the host nation can help meet.

Realism

Communitarianism

Cosmopolitanism

refugees: those displaced from their home country due to natural disaster or social unrest

Takeaways for Christians from the Three Frameworks

Without necessarily subscribing to everything communitarianism believes, we can say that this perspective seems closest to balancing the biblical concerns of justice on this issue. A biblical assessment of immigration policy must balance the two concerns highlighted earlier. On the one hand, laws and borders are important, and nations have the responsibility to construct their immigration laws in a way that prioritizes the needs of their own citizens. On the other hand, love and compassion for those fleeing poverty and instability should also motivate immigration policy. Offering opportunities for uncomplicated *legal* immigration to those willing to start over, work hard, and integrate into their new homeland is consistent with *both* biblical concerns—laws and people. When a country has a strong economy with a healthy infrastructure, it can be generous with its resources and benefit from immigration.[31] A government that provides well for its own citizens is also able to provide in good measure for immigrants that it welcomes into its country.

A great example in Scripture of how all these concerns can work together is that of Abraham securing a burial site for his wife Sarah (Gen. 23). Abraham was a foreigner in the land of the Hittites. He followed all the proper legal proceedings to purchase the land and cave for the burial site. Abraham was the outsider, and he willingly followed all the customs and laws of the land he was living in, insisting on paying the full price for the field rather than accepting a handout from the Hittites (Gen. 23:9, 11, 13, 15–18). The Hittites, for their part, did not attempt to take advantage of the foreigner among them. Instead, in Abraham's time of grief, they even offered to give him a tomb in their land free of charge; eventually, far from fearing the influence of a foreigner, they gave Abraham the dignity of purchasing and the legal status of owning property in their own land.

Christians should make much of the Bible's teaching that God cares for those who are at risk of being mistreated, including immigrants, and the fact that God doesn't show partiality to or favoritism for one group of people over another (Deut. 19:17–18; Ps. 146:9; Acts 10:34). Christians should also recognize a country's right to control its borders and the responsibility of immigrants to respect the laws and appropriately adapt to the customs of the land in which they are trying to live.

 ## IMMIGRATION DONE WRONGLY IN SOCIETY

A government's policies on immigration can have positive or negative effects on society. But a greater concern, one more fundamental, is whether a government's immigration policies are biblically just. Realism isn't a plausible option for believers because this view picks and chooses which morality serves its purposes best rather than seeking to follow God's prescribed morality. But someone calls the shots and affects the policies that are implemented in society. Who is running the show? For the realist the answer is whoever is in charge at a given moment. And those in charge might want any version of open or closed borders. For a time, either option might be advantageous. The political parties in charge of the White House, the Senate, and the House of Representatives favor immigration policies that further their agendas. This is acceptable to a good number of people in the nation. But if certain immigration policies are supported out of mere loyalty to one's party or to sway voters, then morality is not the goal. Realism has no objective ethical guidelines to shape immigration policies into something biblical and beneficial to a nation and those who immigrate to it.

But cosmopolitanism also comes up short in terms of ethical immigration policies. Advocates would say that immigrants are people, and we should love all people. But governments that adopt this view can end up making decisions that are unloving to their own people! Consider the impact on a country's limited resources if they must be shared with millions of immigrants,

We have so much to offer!

But we can't let in EVERYONE.

many of whom are in the country illegally. The allocation of taxpayers' dollars (health services, education, food and housing assistance, etc.) could be stretched thinner than necessary, which might mean citizens with legitimate needs would struggle to see those needs met. The negative effects of this view aren't limited to economic issues.

Another important end to consider is the effect of immigrants on a society's cultural identity. Every nation has its own cultural identity built by its history, traditions, and values. The fabric of many societies' cultures was woven by many generations of heavy immigration as well as by certain core principles—the United States of America is a prime example. The question for any nation is how much immigrants should be allowed to contribute to and change that culture.

Answering that question with one extreme or another is bound to be detrimental to a culture. This is because most cultures have aspects that are positive, biblically defensible, and in line with God's creational design. Conversely, all cultures also have aspects that are negative, unbiblical, and opposed to God's creational design. A society that is too proud and ultranationalist might embrace a closed border, no immigration. But that isolation would limit good influences from other cultures that might make a society stronger. It is arguable that immigrants from cultures with strong family ties could possibly help the current American society, where the family is in decay. On the other hand, a society that dismisses its traditions and distinct national identity might embrace an open border policy. But that society would soon lose its own identity and open itself uncritically to bad influences from other cultures that might destroy human flourishing. In the process, it could lose the positive distinctives that made it attractive to immigrants in the first place.

There are other concerns regarding the societal consequences of unbiblical views of immigration. Is there any correlation between lax border enforcement and an increase in crime? The data say no,[32] but not being able to track down a terrorist group or individual as he or she enters and exits the country is a problem. Would very restrictive immigration policy turn a blind eye to oppressed and persecuted foreigners in need of asylum or refugee status in a safe country? What criteria should be used to screen those applying for a visa, and how many visas should be issued per year? Adopting a strict position for open or closed borders can bring on serious negative societal consequences.

EVALUATING CONTEMPORARY EVENTS

[NEW]

And what about the challenge of illegal immigration? In the United States, this is a serious and divisive issue. What are the best ways to secure the country's borders against unlawful crossings? How can the government ensure that those who come in via visas renew them appropriately or return to their countries when their authorized stay expires? What is the just and compassionate way to handle the millions of unauthorized immigrants who are living and working in the country now, especially immigrant children who have grown up in the United States? Does the cheap labor that comes from unauthorized immigrants benefit American businesses so much that serious change is hindered? Does encouraging illegal immigration enable the exploitation of unauthorized immigrants? Is it possible both major political parties use the controversial issues of illegal immigration and border security to their own advantage instead of providing real, helpful solutions?

Christians need to pay attention to all of these issues so they can be citizens who contribute to ethical solutions while caring for the real needs of immigrants they encounter.

ATTEMPTING TO GET IMMIGRATION RIGHT

Believers need to pursue and be motivated by various virtues as they encounter ethical difficulties (2 Pet. 1:5–8). Immigration has to do with people, and many times immigrants are trying to provide themselves and their families with a better life, new opportunities, or a fresh start. Compassion, righteousness, and prudence are three virtues that should motivate the humane treatment of immigrants and the development of ethical immigration policy.

How should I treat foreigners in my community?

Compassionately

Those who hold to cosmopolitanism are likely to be accused of being too compassionate. They care so much about immigrants that they can't think of a good reason to turn any away. To them, that would be missing the mark of showing compassion. However, this way of thinking can be misdirected sentimentalism rather than true compassion. On the other hand, a realist could go to the extreme of limiting immigration so much that even legitimate refugees are turned away—this would be a gross display of indifference.

How can a believer show compassion in a fair but loving way? First, as you come across any immigrants in your neighborhood, workplace, school, or church, you can treat them with loving compassion without jumping to conclusions about their legal status (Matt. 7:12). The immediate response of a believer to foreigners should be to welcome them (see Gen. 18:2–8; 24:18–20, 31–33; Exod. 2:20; Ruth 2:8–10; 1 Kings 17:9–15; Job 31:32; Matt. 25:34–39; Heb. 13:2), not to judge them (Matt. 7:1–2; John 7:24). They are fellow image-bearers of God! Second, you can support legislation that resolves some of the current immigration problems. It is not compassionate to allow people to break the law without consequences or to ignore a scenario in which millions of immigrants are vulnerable to exploitation. Third, you can appeal to your elected representatives for the humane and fair treatment of immigrants. Fourth, you could give to trustworthy agencies that can facilitate the distribution of financial aid to refugees who haven't been given asylum in the United States yet. Fifth, you can show compassion by praying for and helping immigrants you come into contact with who have been displaced and have acute needs.

Righteously

Even though the topic of immigration is complicated, believers should apply the virtue of righteousness to this topic. The laws that govern who is allowed to immigrate, the visa process, the treatment of immigrants, and the expectations for immigrants should all be governed by God's righteousness. For example, this could include streamlining the approval process for family-sponsored visas by giving priority to immediate family members over extended family members.[33] God's righteousness (as seen in both justice and mercy) should also be applied to the steps unauthorized immigrants are legally required to take to correct their undocumented status.

We know that God deals justly with humanity in every way (Rev. 15:3). Believers need to pursue justice and equity with those who come looking to live in their country. There should be accountability for those who fail to obtain authorized permission to enter a country. But it would be ungodly, the opposite of righteous, to demean, ridicule, or discriminate against immigrants. There is no room for hatred or mockery of people who are of a different ethnicity, who have foreign cultural customs, or who have an unstable financial footing. Believers should seek to align their sentiments toward immigrants with God's righteous care and concern for those facing the challenges of immigration (Exod. 22:21; Lev. 23:22).

Prudently

Just as it is true that the fairer the skin, the more sunblock is necessary, more prudence is required for more complicated issues (like immigration). This is not just because most politicians and lawmakers hold to various forms of realism, cosmopolitanism, or communitarianism. Immigration requires prudence because the public and national opinion is divided on what the best approach to immigration is. This problem is compounded by the fact that the government has allowed illegal immigration by not taking steps to prevent or deter it effectively. The government sends a mixed message by communicating one thing to immigrants through laws but in practice essentially allowing for the opposite by ineffective and inconsistent enforcement. Prudence is required to know how to effectively enforce current policies, how to develop future policies, and who to prioritize when implementing immigration policies.

One way to implement prudence on a local, personal level is how you vote once you turn eighteen. Voting for local, state, and federal officials impacts the development of your country's policies on immigration. You need prudence to vote for the candidates who best reflect biblical principles on immigration. You cannot fail to consider that every political candidate also holds other positions of varying ethical merit. You also need prudence to decide whether, or to what extent, you might involve yourself in meeting the needs of legitimately needy immigrants. Is there a need you can fill, or do community programs sufficiently help immigrants get on their feet and see that their basic needs are met? Serving immigrants could provide great gospel opportunities as well as clear chances to show love to your neighbors.

Christians can never go wrong showing wise compassion for the needy, engaging in righteous interpersonal conduct, and constructing prudent priorities. This is true for interacting with unauthorized immigrants just as much as with legal immigrants. You might not be called to develop immigration policy, but you are called to relate to others virtuously, including immigrants in your community.

EVALUATING CURRENT IMMIGRATION POLICY

What reform, if any, should the government of the United States submit its immigration policies to? That is a big question for a high school student! You cannot assume that the current policies regarding immigration or the security of your nation's borders are ethical. Most presidents make changes to their predecessor's immigration policies. You need to consider some current statistics on immigration in the United States. Refer to the infographic in this section to see some of those numbers.

Nations typically place annual limits on the number of visas they may issue and the number of refugees they may accept. What matters more than the limits is the number of immigrants actually allowed entrance into the country on any given year. Nations also regulate who gets approved: family members of current residents or citizens, specialized

Rate that non-US citizens are becoming lawful permanent residents

Lawful permanent residency means a person is allowed to live, study, work, and do business in the United States as well as be protected by and be held responsible for the laws of the land.[34]

= 38,000 people

1,063,000 immigrants per year gained permanent residency.[35]

(2010–19)

those approved for permanent residency based on family ties to people already lawfully in the United States[36]

(2018–20)

2/3

Immigrants becoming US citizens
(2017–20)

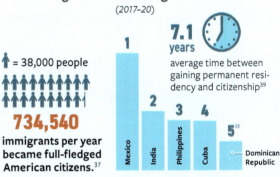

= 38,000 people

734,540 immigrants per year became full-fledged American citizens.[37]

1. Mexico
2. India
3. Philippines
4. Cuba
5. Dominican Republic [38]

7.1 years average time between gaining permanent residency and citizenship[39]

Unauthorized immigrants residing in the United States
(as of January 1, 2018)[40]

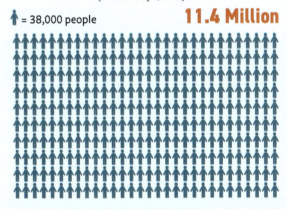

= 38,000 people

11.4 Million

People admitted as refugees or granted asylum
(2019)

29,916 people admitted as refugees

46,508 people granted asylum

Asylum-seekers are in the United States or coming into a US port of entry, whereas those seeking refugee status do so from outside the United States.[41]

workers, public figures, and so on. Depending on your view of how a nation should regulate immigration, you might decide that there shouldn't be caps on visas at all, that they should be lowered considerably, or that the distribution between visa categories should be altered. But what should be considered when evaluating the current immigration policy of your country?

Christians thinking through the ethical difficulties of immigration policy can come at the task from various angles. Since governments will always have to deal with immigration, the subject is always relevant. Believers should keep the following points in mind:

> *Immigration is social engineering. . . . You're building the population of the future.* JUSTIN GEST[42]

- ▸ The second Great Commandment, "Thou shalt love thy neighbour as thyself" (Matt. 22:39), summarizes all the Old Testament laws relating to how we should treat people, including the laws on the treatment of immigrants (see Matt. 22:36–40; Lev. 19:18, 33–34). It is hard to love people you don't come into contact with. The neighbors that believers are called to love are those they encounter who need help (for example, see Luke 10:29–37). Men are called to provide for those under their immediate care (1 Tim. 5:8), and all believers are called to "do good unto all men, especially unto them who are of the household of faith" (Gal. 6:10). In sum, the priority is to care well for those closest to you, but you should expand the reach of your compassion and generosity as you have the ability and opportunity. Providing well for those closest to us prepares us to help our immigrant neighbors in need. Remember that immigration policy involves current immigrants (our present neighbors) as well as future immigrants (our future neighbors).

- ▸ A country is healthy when its economy is stable and growing. Thousands of jobs require specialized workers that authorized immigrants willingly and capably fill. This setup is ideal because the immigrants, the companies, and the nation's economy all benefit from this arrangement. But stable and growing economies often benefit from cheap, unskilled labor. One question is whether unauthorized immigrants are taking jobs from citizens; a government needs to prioritize opportunities for its own citizens. However, if unauthorized immigrants are filling jobs citizens don't want and businesses are willing to employ them because that saves them money, then our society has to ask itself whether we're really just content to benefit

from the status quo. If the market needs inexpensive unskilled labor, a more ethical solution would be to meet that need with current citizens or legally permit more such laborers to enter the country, but to pay them reasonable wages. On the other hand, it is helpful to train authorized immigrants in our institutions of higher education since the host nation benefits from the contributions of excellent students and future workers. An immigrant shouldn't be considered for citizenship based solely on the value of his or her contribution to society. But new citizens should be encouraged to be valuable contributors to the society they are joining.

- ▸ There should be compassion and sympathy for the immediate family members of immigrants (both legal and unauthorized) who are here or are desiring to come to the United States. Children should be raised by both of their parents whenever possible. Immigration policy that seeks to unite extended family members seems ethically defensible since family members need one another for care and support.

- ▸ There should be consequences for lawbreaking. The penalties unauthorized immigrants receive when apprehended upon illegal entry into the country or when they commit certain crimes should be carefully considered and just. Deportation should be an option, especially once unauthorized immigrants get on the radar of government officials by committing some other offense. But the situation should still be considered. What penalty applies best to this specific individual? Would an immediate deportation separate a parent from a dependent child, for example? Nevertheless, since the unauthorized immigrant entered the country illegally, a case can often be made for eventual deportation of one who commits a serious crime.

The fact that the United States offers a more comfortable life than many other countries doesn't mean the US government must accommodate every visa applicant. But immigration is real, and immigrants are people. Compassion, righteousness, and prudence are needed in great quantities for believers, their fellow citizens, and lawmakers alike. On the subject of immigration, pray for wisdom and pray for gospel opportunities.

1. What are a few of the important questions regarding immigration?

2. Compare and contrast the biblical teaching on the national and individual treatment of immigrants with the three frameworks discussed in this chapter.

3. Analyze possible societal consequences of unbiblical views regarding immigration.

4. Explain how the three virtues discussed above are important for a biblical position regarding immigrants and ethical immigration policy.

5. What is your biblical response to current immigration policy?

10.4 Christian Disobedience to Authority

Many people avoid disobedience, some at any cost. Christians usually lead the way opposing disobedience. But disobedience can't always be sidestepped, nor should it always be. Disobedience, though not entered into lightly, is a very real option when a citizen is confronted by a government that requires immorality or forbids morality.

But what should a citizen's normal and expected disposition to government be? Citizens should respect, honor, obey, and submit to the God-given authorities in their land (Acts 23:5; Rom. 13:1; Titus 3:1–2; 1 Pet. 2:13–14, 17). Christians should also pray for their leaders (2 Tim. 2:1–2). Even though citizens should expect the government to fulfill its roles of punishing evil and protecting its citizens, Scripture teaches the obligations of citizens to their governments.

But governments don't always govern well—even when they have good intentions. Since this is true, a category of careful yet convictional disobedience to authority becomes viable for believers. Governments don't have absolute authority and shouldn't command blind allegiance from their people. The rest of this section will explain the ins and outs of affirming that at times citizens can and must disobey their government or other authorities.

CHRISTIAN DISOBEDIENCE TO AUTHORITY VERSUS REBELLION

What is the difference between a protest and a riot? A riot involves violence and damage to property. But a protest is a non-violent gathering of people to call attention to a specific issue. What is the difference between a reformation and a revolution? A revolution topples the current government and builds another one from the ground up. A reformation takes what exists and pushes for change, improving it.

Now, think of the difference between Christian disobedience to authority and rebellion in a similar way. A protest and a reformation correspond somewhat to Christian disobedience to authority, while a riot and a revolution correspond to rebellion. **Christian disobedience to authority** is a refusal to obey a legitimate authority's laws or commands that contradict the commands of God. Christians engage in disobedience to governmental authorities out of moral obligation and not simply to see an immoral law changed, though that is a valid outcome. A **rebellion** rejects the current government's authority and, through violence, asserts its own opposing agenda.

An example of Christian disobedience to authority is Chinese Christians disobeying the mandate that all churches must be registered with the government. Every time unregistered churches meet, they run the risk of seeing their services interrupted and their properties raided because they are operating outside the law. It is not uncommon for the authorities to shut down churches and arrest members and pastors. But the Christian church in China is growing by leaps and bounds, and this is in part due to the consistent practice of Christian disobedience to authority by many Christians.[43]

An example of rebellion is what happened in Russia in 1917. There were two revolutions, one in March and one in November. The Russian monarchy, in power for over three hundred years, was overthrown by revolutionaries (industrial workers on strike, hungry peasants, and fed-up soldiers) in Petrograd in March. The monarchy was replaced by a provisional government. In November of that same year, Vladimir Lenin's revolutionary Bolshevik Party replaced the provisional government, with hardly any bloodshed, with his communist government and its long-reaching influence.[44]

In both examples, people are taking matters into their own hands. Chinese Christians are in the right because the government mandates are immoral and restrict what God has commanded. The Russian Revolution of 1917 was a rebellion in which the people, having been mistreated by their government, used force to see that their demands were met.

It should be clear which option is valid for Christians to engage in, when necessary. Christian disobedience to authority shouldn't be entered into lightly. Mario Morelli offers a helpful insight that applies to Christian disobedience to government authority. (What Morelli says about "the civil disobedient" would also apply to a Christian forced to disobey the government.)

> Unlike the ordinary criminal, motivated by self-interest or malice, the civil disobedient is often moved by moral or conscientious motivation, in the sense that a moral belief prompts the illegal act. The revolutionary aims, at least ultimately, at overturning the existing political or legal order.[45]

An arrogant attitude is the wrong approach to any type of Christian disobedience to authority. A mere dislike for certain officials in the government doesn't justify breaking any law you disagree with. That would be rebellion. And Christian disobedience to authority isn't limited to governments. Other authorities are also in view and can include employers, teachers, and even parents.

 ## A BIBLICAL DEFENSE FOR CHRISTIAN DISOBEDIENCE TO AUTHORITY AND AGAINST REBELLION

Christian disobedience to authority isn't the norm for believers today. Neither was it the norm for God's people in the Old and New Testaments. But there were still many times when those in positions of authority were evil or demanded their subjects to sin. We'll look at some of those examples below. There is only one absolute authority in the world—God (Rev. 4:11; 5:12–13). Only God can be fully trusted. And rebelling against God, directly or indirectly, is consistent with the lives of unbelievers, not believers (Rom. 1:21, 25, 32). So even in the face of governmental pressure to sin against God or others, rebellion isn't an option for believers (Matt. 5:3–12, 43–48). God demands that His people do justice and that they let Him repay evil as He sees fit (Deut. 16:20; Rom. 12:17–19). That sounds nothing like rebellion. What passages in Scripture teach on this topic, and what are some examples of Christian disobedience to authority from Scripture?

> *Romans 13:1–7 and 1 Peter 2:13–17 are decidedly antirevolutionary in their emphasis.*
>
> JOHN FRAME[46]

Foundational Passages

Romans 13:1–7 and 1 Peter 2:13–17 are foundational passages for civil *obedience* and make a case against rebellion. That's what also makes them foundational for our current topic! Romans 13 describes obeying the governing authorities as equal to obeying God who appointed them. 1 Peter 2 essentially says the same thing while referencing the reality of higher (national) authorities and lower (local) authorities that both require our submission. These two passages guide Christians how to live as good citizens of the nations where they reside (see also 1 Tim. 2:2). Christians shouldn't develop an unruly or haughty attitude toward their government because they think they are above the laws of their land. That kind of attitude fuels rebellions. Christians should consistently pray for their local and national government authorities (1 Tim. 2:1-2, 8). Paul also gave instruction for all believers to submit to the established authorities in a respectful and ethical manner (Titus 3:1-2).

The beginning of the book of Acts provides two foundational passages for the exception to the rule—Christian *dis*obedience to authority. In Acts 3, Peter healed a lame beggar. The religious leaders became upset because Peter and John were preaching in the name of Jesus after this miraculous healing. Their solution was to command Peter and John to stop preaching and teaching about Jesus (Acts 4:18). Peter and John were Jews and, like the rest of the Jewish people, had a certain obligation to follow their leadership's instruction. The two apostles responded by stating, "Whether it be right in the sight of God to hearken unto you more than unto God, judge ye. For we cannot but speak the things which we have seen and heard" (Acts 4:19-20). The second passage is even clearer. With a memorable declaration, the apostles committed to do God's work by obeying God's commands rather than those of human authorities: "We ought to obey God rather than men" (Acts 5:29).

The apostles were not bluffing or bucking the established system for the fun of it. They were committed to truth and righteousness; they were obligated to fulfill their God-given mission. They preached and performed miracles and served the Lord faithfully even to the point of death or imprisonment (Acts 12:1-4). They willingly accepted the consequences of their faithfulness to God. They didn't take matters into their own hands and overthrow Rome's appointed leaders. Since God has absolute authority over all spheres of life, His commands supersede any human commands (Matt. 28:18-20; Acts 1:8). But when human commands align with government laws and God's revelation, those human commands must be obeyed in order for us to be faithful to the commands of God. In the case of the apostles in the book of Acts, Christian disobedience to authority meant showing their worship of and devotion to Christ instead of obeying human commands that were opposed to Christianity. Christ is above the state. Christ is over all (Col. 1:16-17).

Primary Examples

Are there other examples in Scripture where God's people had to disobey man in order to obey God? Yes, there are. And none of these cases turned into a rebellion or hinted at the need for one. The Pharaoh of Moses' infancy commanded the Hebrew midwives to kill the baby boys that were born to the Hebrew women. But the midwives feared God; their disobedience to Pharaoh's command proved their obedience to God (Exod. 1:15-17). Esther disobeyed the laws of the land where she lived, risking her own life. She went before the king without an invitation to plead for the lives of her people (Esther 4:16). Daniel disobeyed the king's commands and didn't even adjust his already-established custom of prayer (Dan. 6:7-10). And Daniel's three friends violated the clear command to worship the idol of the king and in their integrity were willing to suffer the consequences of obeying God rather than man (Dan. 3:10-12, 16-20).

Because of the stark contrast between good and evil in these examples, the Christian disobedience to authority practiced on an individual level almost seems obvious or even easy. But that didn't make it easy for these saints to disobey their governing authorities, especially because they could have lost their lives (and many did) for their courageous stances! Rebellion wasn't even on the table. In our day opposing unrighteous laws seems much more complicated. Rebellion is tempting since so many anti-God policies are being made into laws (e.g., abortion, gender and sexuality issues, teaching evolution in public schools). Refraining from rebellion in favor of Christian disobedience to authority (when warranted) is an act of faith!

But Christian disobedience to authority is not the only solution. For example, during the Divided Kingdom, Ahab was Israel's most wicked king, and his extended family followed his example. His daughter Athaliah tried to murder all the rightful royal heirs in order to take the throne in Jerusalem for herself (2 Chron. 22:10).

Is it ever right to disobey the government?

Rather than rebelling through a military operation, one of former king Ahaziah's sisters saved young Joash so he could one day rightly replace Athaliah and her unjust rule (2 Chron. 22:11–23:15). Another example is Paul, who experienced an unjust imprisonment at the hand of the Jews and Romans (Acts 24:27; 25:7–10). Paul didn't rally a band of friends and supporters to overthrow the local Jewish or Roman authorities. Paul used the available legal channels to make and defend his case (Acts 25:11). Straightforward godly disobedience to authority (other than hiding Joash) was avoided in both of these examples. But rebellion was purposefully avoided as well. Ahaziah's sister and Paul prudently chose the best ethical and legal options available to them. Christian disobedience to authority is valid when necessary, but at times other legal options, still in opposition to and in disagreement with a government mandate or action, are more prudent.

ANARCHY VERSUS TYRANNY

Have you ever had to care for a houseplant? If so, you might have learned that too much of a good thing (water or sunlight) can be a bad thing. And then maybe the next time you cared for a houseplant, you provided it with too little of a good thing, with similar consequences. Let's face it, not everyone has a green thumb!

What are the societal consequences of unbiblical views of Christian disobedience to authority and rebellion? We are making the case that Christian disobedience to authority can be good and necessary, when done properly, with the right motives, and for the right goals. We are also making the case that rebellion is not an alternative Christians should turn to. How do Christians discern when disobedience to authority is the appropriate response? Christian disobedience to authority *can* get out of hand and be harmful to society. When too much focus is placed on the *disobedience to authority* part and not enough focus is placed on the *Christian* part, rebellious behavior can raise its ugly head. And if that happens, an actual rebellion could break out, which could lead to anarchy. Anarchy throws the baby (an organized government) out with the bath water (the abuses and shortcomings of the government), leaving chaos and disorder to rule. If every citizen took it upon himself or herself to determine which laws he or she deemed constitutional and unconstitutional (and thus non-binding for him or her), we would find ourselves in the days of the judges when "every man did that which was right in his own eyes" (Judg. 17:6; 21:25). If you know anything about the book of Judges, you probably know this: no king in Israel meant unprecedented levels of sinful behavior and societal decay.

Christian disobedience to authority should not be the Christian's first recourse when thinking that the government has overstepped its proper biblical bounds. There are many other avenues that should be attempted before Christian disobedience to authority. In addition to prayer, Christians living under republican forms of government should first challenge unconstitutional laws in court or seek to overturn such laws legislatively. There are some laws that would overstep a biblical understanding of the rightful authority government has been given by God and yet are not causes for Christian disobedience to authority. The governments that Daniel, Ezra, Peter, and Paul lived under used their God-given authority for evil. Indeed, these governments were foreign rulers of the Jews. Yet they were the existing governmental power of their day, and God's people were expected to submit to them.

Believers need to proceed with care when considering whether Christian disobedience to authority is justified and necessary and suffering persecution is the godly and ethical option to choose. Tyranny and anarchy are not situations which believers should be comfortable with. But it's important to remember that good citizenship will use the proper governmental channels and representatives to push back against an immoral government.

In a wisely framed government, citizens have recourse against tyranny. The reformer John Calvin observed that, in many governments, there are government officials who have the responsibility for resisting the tyranny of other governmental officials when it occurs. When these other governmental officials, or magistrates, are

Hananiah, Mishael, and Azariah resisted the command to bow down before an idol of a pagan king, choosing to obey God instead (Dan. 3:10–12, 16–20).

in place, it is their solemn responsibility, within the legal scope granted to them, to resist unjust laws and protect citizens from them.[47]

These officials, also known as lesser magistrates, are a legitimate and helpful resource for believers to oppose unjust government mandates. Bradford Littlejohn clarifies that "there is a crucial difference between an *unjust law* and a law that *requires us to do injustice*."[48] He also reminds us that we can appeal to the lesser magistrates even concerning laws that may seem unjust:

> For Christians convinced that certain government actions represent an overreach of the government's own laws, the proper course of action is to appeal to the courts—the "lesser magistrates"—for protection. (To be sure, sometimes the most straightforward way to do so is to disobey in a pointed fashion so as to force the legal issue, but this should be done with great care and humility.)[49]

For example, Paul wasn't afraid to take advantage of his rights under the Roman rule of his day in demanding justice and fairness (Acts 16:35–39; 22:25–29). But Paul's employment of his rights wasn't a personal, subjective, or violent resistance to laws he deemed unrighteous. He rightfully and publicly pushed back against the illegal injustices he was receiving.

 THE VIRTUES REQUIRED FOR CHRISTIAN DISOBEDIENCE TO AUTHORITY

To be involved in Christian disobedience to authority is no small matter. But if your government does require you to engage in behavior God has forbidden or to refrain from doing what God has commanded, then Christian disobedience to authority is your duty. There are several virtues that need to guide and influence the Christian who finds himself in this situation: faith, patience, courage, and prudence.

Faith is needed because you must trust in God's designed purpose for government (Rom. 13:3–4, 6; 1 Pet. 2:14). And you need faith to rest in God's timetable for punishing evildoers. This is exactly what Jesus did through suffering an unjust trial and crucifixion (1 Pet. 2:23). Christians must tolerate the uncomfortable consequences of having wicked people in government who revel in opposing God and His standards. It takes faith to rest in God's plan for the world and in His protection of His people.

Patience is needed because if you engage in Christian disobedience to authority hoping for change, the desired change might not happen when you would like to see it happen or might not happen at all. You need patience as a citizen because the candidates you vote for might not get elected, and if they are elected, they might not be able to do as much good as you hoped. The virtue of patience helps believers battle the urge to rebel or start a revolution when things aren't going their way politically. It also takes patience to endure pressure and persecution from the wicked. God keeps an account of all the wicked's deeds, and believers are called to live for the Lord and patiently wait for Him to accomplish His will (Ps. 37:34).

Courage is needed because it is difficult to defend and live by godly convictions. It takes courage to live by a biblical ethic and do your part to hold accountable those who make and enforce policy. Even though a government might not force its citizens to offer sacrifices to any idols, it takes godly courage to denounce ungodliness in society (e.g., abortion, LGBTQ+ agenda). The psalmist encourages believers by saying, "Be of good courage, and he shall strengthen your heart" (Ps. 31:24). Much courage and strength from the Lord will be required to do what is right if your freedom to live according to biblical convictions is threatened.

And prudence is needed to determine when Christian disobedience to authority may be necessary and to discern the wisest way to proceed. It takes prudence to understand what is at stake and then pursue the appropriate, God-honoring strategy to exercise Christian disobedience to authority (or pursue a legal alternative).

Knowledge of laws and legislation isn't sufficient for believers to make ethical decisions. The virtues of faith, patience, courage, and prudence all interact with one another as believers wrestle with challenging issues that might require Christian disobedience to authority. Do you have patience to suffer and an enduring faith in God's ways that would help you courageously and prudently confront government-sanctioned evil?

RIGHTEOUS CHRISTIAN DISOBEDIENCE TO AUTHORITY

How would you respond to a government mandate that required you to put your children in the public school system? If that happened, private Christian schools and homeschooling would be illegal. Since the Bible doesn't give us commands to only homeschool our children or only put them in Christian or public schools, the best way to answer this question is to use the Scriptures to discover if the state or the parents are responsible for educating children. If a husband and wife know that it is their God-given right and responsibility to guide their children's education (Deut. 6:4–9; Eph. 6:4), then opposing such a mandate could be a prudent course of action that doesn't necessarily have to turn into Christian disobedience to authority. Even if a government decided to mandate obligatory schooling in solid, conservative Christian schools, it would still interfere in a sphere of society that doesn't belong to it. Local and state governments, along with community-based advocacy groups, should be able to legally question and oppose unethical and manipulative mandates. Christians can use the lesser magistrates to push back against inappropriate government mandates.

But how would you handle a government mandate that criminalized the biblical teaching on gender and sexuality? This would mean that any teaching that opposed the LGBTQ+ agenda and sensibilities would be outside the scope of what is lawful. Based on your knowledge of the Bible's teaching on this topic, you know that your church could not comply with such a mandate. The process of Christian disobedience to authority would need to start right away. Certainly, churches should appeal to all the appropriate lesser magistrates, including fighting the mandate in the courts. But also, you and your church should be prepared for any consequences of not complying with this mandate. Your church shouldn't even consider agreeing to the demands of such a mandate, nor should your church remain silent about certain sins—because "we ought to obey God rather than men" (Acts 5:29).

In any instance of potential Christian disobedience to authority, pray that your faith would be strong, that your patience would endure, that your courage wouldn't falter, and that your prudence would be sharp. As a rule, submit to the government. But never disobey God's commands in your pursuit of obedience to human government. Be vigilant about where your government is headed and how it seeks to impact its citizens, believers especially, with its laws and regulations.

Thinking It Through 10.4

1. Compare and contrast Christian disobedience to authority and rebellion.

2. What is the biblical teaching on Christian disobedience to authority and rebellion?

3. What are some of the societal consequences of unbiblical views regarding Christian disobedience to authority and rebellion?

4. Assess the virtues necessary to act ethically regarding Christian disobedience to authority.

5. What would your biblical response be to situations where Christian disobedience to authority would be ethical and necessary?

10 ETHICAL GOVERNMENT Review

Terms to Remember

- capital punishment
- militarism
- pacifism
- realism (on war)
- just war doctrine
- immigrant
- realism (on immigration)
- cosmopolitanism
- communitarianism
- Christian disobedience to authority
- rebellion

Scripture Memory

Romans 13:1, 4

Understanding Ethics

1. How seriously does God view murder?
2. When is it right to go to war?
3. How should I treat foreigners in my community?
4. Is it ever right to disobey the government?

Practicing Ethical Decision-Making

5. Two friends ask your opinion of their job choices. One will be a prison guard, overseeing lethal injections when capital punishment is administered. The other is joining the military. He will have a frontline battle position if your country goes to war. What do you tell them?
6. You have a classmate or friend on your street who came to the United States with his parents illegally as a baby. His father was recently deported, and his mother is struggling to make ends meet at home. How do you respond when he asks to carpool with you and asks for other favors that would help meet real needs that he is currently experiencing? How does his legal status affect your treatment of him?

Analyzing and Evaluating Ethical Claims

7. How would you counter the following claim? "Capital punishment only adds violence to violence. Christians should seek to break the cycle of violence, not commit more of it."
8. Based on the tenets of just war, do you think it's possible to defend any war from the past or present? Do you think a Christian can participate in a war with a clean conscience? Explain.
9. How would you respond to a friend who says, "Entering the United States illegally is breaking the law, so all illegal immigrants should be imprisoned or deported immediately"?
10. How would you respond to a friend or church member who says, "I answer to God alone, so I choose which federal and local laws I obey"?

Creating My Own Position Statements on Ethics

11. How should a government act? Write a brief statement answering this question as it applies to the four topics in this chapter.
12. How should you relate to your government's laws and policies regarding the four topics of this chapter?

Ethical Society

MATTHEW 7:12

How does a Christian ethic form a good society?

The ripple effects of our choices extend further than we realize. Our immediate circle of family and friends are obviously impacted by the choices we make, but the larger society is also affected, even if it is less obvious. Every choice has ethical implications for society.

Framing our choices in terms of their impact on society can be a bit overwhelming. The point, however, isn't to overwhelm but to debunk the myth that what people do in private is of no consequence to society. Popular sentiment says, "I can do whatever I want as long as I'm not hurting anyone." The assumption is that it's possible to seal off the impact of one's choices, as if foolish decisions only hurt the one making them. Take, for instance, drug abuse. While clearly hurting the individual abuser, drug abuse also hurts society.

Given the fallen human condition, we understand that not everyone in society will embrace the Christian ethic (John 3:19–20). But if the book of Acts and church history teach us anything, it is that corruption in society is no match for the power of the gospel (for example, see Acts 1:8; 13:47; 17:6). With God's blessings, the gospel can spread like leaven throughout society, giving people a new appetite for true justice and deeds of love (Acts 2:37–47). As more hearts in society are changed, the ethical character of society is also changed. A society shaped by Christianity is a society where people generally treat others as they want to be treated (Matt. 7:12).

One way to think of Christian ethics as it relates to society is to think of it in terms of Christians pressing the claims of Christ's lordship over all reality. Our study in this chapter is concerned with what that might look like with respect to some of the social problems of our day. What does Christian ethics have to say about racial discrimination and inequality? Does Christian ethics have an answer to the problem of substance abuse? Is Christian ethics capable of restoring decency to our communication and media use? And how can Christian ethics improve business practices? Even if Christians cannot bring cultural change in these areas, they still live within culture and need to think about how a Christian should address these issues.

11.1 Racial Discrimination and Inequality

A society consistently shaped by a Christian ethic would not discriminate against people because of their race or ethnicity. Race-based slavery, as seen in American history, is a clear example that the Christian ethic has sadly not been consistently applied. Although many white Americans misused the Bible to justify discrimination against black Americans, there were other courageous voices who appealed to Scripture in order to end racial discrimination. Therefore, we maintain that a consistent application of a Christian ethic produces real justice and real equality for all people.

 ## DEFINING RACE, RACISM, AND INEQUALITY

To get a handle on this subject, we need clear definitions. Unfortunately, there's disagreement on how to define terms such as *race*, *racism*, and *inequality*. If we had common definitions in society, it would make it easier for people to have a conversation about race.

Race and Ethnicity

The term *race* has commonly been defined in terms of skin color and other features such as kind of hair or the shape of various facial characteristics. However, there is no biblical or creational basis for this definition of race. The selection of which characteristics define a "race" is arbitrary, and a different selection would result in different racial groupings. As one author notes,

> All racial taxonomies—whether popular or scientific—are the product not of nature but of the imagination combined with inherited cultural stereotyping as well—to be fair—as the empirical observation of genuine (though superficial, trivial and inconsequential) biological differences.[1]

Sometimes it's unavoidable to speak of *race* in this manner since this is how many people still understand the term, but this definition cannot be supported by an examination of creation through the lenses of Scripture. Apart from God's revelation regarding the human race, people groups have historically made their "racial" differences an occasion for prideful division.[2] Being a believer does not guarantee racial harmony with others. The history of racism in the United States among professing evangelical Christians is proof of that. But Christian acts of unbelief in the area of race do not change the truth that racial harmony is impossible apart from God's revelation about the human race.

There are two other definitions of **race** that do conform to biblical teaching and creational norms. *Race* can be used to refer to the one human race—the Bible speaks of all humanity in its unity as descended from Adam (Acts 17:26). By starting with what unites all people as *one* race, we set the stage for a constructive conversation about ethnic diversity as part of God's good design.

On the other hand, *race* in the sense of ethnicity is also a biblical concept. Paul said that God made the nations, meaning ethnic groups (Acts 17:26). The diversity of nations is a creational norm worked out over time. While the origin of diverse human languages traces back to the Tower of Babel, the origin of ethnic diversity does not. If it did, ethnic diversity would be a result of the Fall instead of God's creational intention.

Nations or ethnic groups will continue to exist in the eternal state (Rev. 7:9; 21:24–26). We should celebrate God's amazing creativity manifested in the ethnic diversity of the human race. We should also recognize that ethnicity is broader than the term *race* as commonly used to refer to skin color and other features. People of different biological ancestry can be incorporated into a different ethnic group, as in the case of biblical figures like Rahab, Ruth, and Uriah. Though not biologically Jewish, they became part of ethnic Israel. Thus, nations are not static; they include people from different and mixed biological backgrounds who come together to form nations or ethnic groups.

Racism and Inequality

Proper definitions for *racism* and *inequality* help provide clearer conversation and therefore a higher probability of successful communication. The *Oxford English Dictionary* defines **racism** as

> prejudice, antagonism, or discrimination by an individual, institution, or society, against a person or people on the basis of their nationality or (now usually) their membership of a particular racial or ethnic group, typically one that is a minority or marginalized. Also: beliefs that members of a particular racial or ethnic group possess innate characteristics or qualities, or that some racial or ethnic groups are superior to others; an ideology based on such beliefs.[3]

Since an attitude of racial superiority can reside in anyone's heart, anyone may be guilty of racism. Honesty requires us to acknowledge that historically when a majority ethnic group views itself as superior to a minority ethnic group within a culture, the minority ethnic group has suffered the brunt of racist behavior. This has often resulted in laws and customs that deprive minority groups of equal treatment. **Inequality** before the law and within society occurs when certain groups are treated as less worthy of respect and dignity than other groups.

UNDERSTANDING RACIAL PREJUDICE, DISCRIMINATION, AND ANTAGONISM

Racial prejudice is a dehumanizing attitude toward a group of people based on their physical features. Racial prejudice may then produce discrimination in the laws or customs of a society. People who are the objects of racial prejudice may be denied certain rights and privileges that the more powerful ethnic group enjoys in that society. This denial of rights and privileges is what constitutes discrimination. On the other hand, a society might afford everyone the same legal protections and thereby outlaw discrimination. But even in this situation, racial prejudice and antagonism (personal hostility) could still exist in a society because there may be some who view those of a different ethnicity as inferior to them. A just society should ensure that its citizens are not, on the basis of physical characteristics, denied the rights and privileges that other law-abiding citizens enjoy. A just society should also discourage racial antagonism—because all people have equal value as bearers of God's image.

Top left, clockwise: segregated gas station restrooms, South Carolina, 1965; Japanese Americans arriving at an internment camp during World War II; *The Indian campaign- prisoners captured by General Custer* by Theodore R. Davis; political cartoon during the Chinese Exclusion Act, 1882.

context RACISM AND INEQUALITY IN AMERICAN HISTORY

Americans are today wrestling with controversies over race because racism and inequality have been part of the legal and social structure of America. For example, at various times, laws protected the slave trade (contrary to Exod. 21:16), required the return of runaway slaves (contrary to Deut. 23:15–16), and treated black Americans as second-class citizens (contrary to Lev. 24:22). Laws were used to prevent black Americans from voting. Under the guise of "separate but equal," black children were forced into schools with facilities and educational materials that were not equal to those of white schools. There was a time when the Federal Housing Administration would not grant loans to black citizens that it was granting to white citizens. Such laws and policies were supported by and gave cover to racist customs such as businesses that would not serve black Americans. These examples have focused on the plight of black Americans, but additional examples of racism in America include the removal of American Indians from their lands, the Chinese Exclusion Act, or the internment of Japanese Americans during World War II.

Most Americans would now condemn these aspects of our history. However, controversy exists regarding whether there are enduring effects from past racism that need to be addressed, whether racism remains a significant problem in current American culture, and what the best ways are to achieve racial reconciliation in the present.

UNBIBLICAL SOLUTIONS TO RACISM

Secular solutions to racism tend to exacerbate racial problems because they misidentify something that is creational as evil and live contrary to the way God made His world to work. They also look to something in God's creation for "racial salvation," rather than looking to God. As Christians evaluate secular approaches, they should not expect them to be wrong on every point. These approaches have often correctly grasped one or more creational norms. Nevertheless, Christians cannot simply adopt the view of one or another secular approach to racism because all secular approaches have been warped by the Fall and are rival worldviews to a biblical one.

Thus, in evaluating false systems of thought, we will (1) look at the creational structure that is identified as part of the problem, (2) look at the creational structure that is idolized as the means of salvation, (3) look at the aspects of the Fall that a view has neglected, and (4) acknowledge the creational norms that a given view has recognized, at least in part. We will survey two popular secular approaches to addressing racism. One approach could be called the *white responsibility* model, though today the term *antiracism* is often used. Another approach could be called *majority conformity*. Both descriptions below are brief generalizations of viewpoints held by many people with many different variations. While space requires us to be brief, we have sought to be fair and accurate in our summaries.

White Responsibility

This approach sees racism as structural (that is, it is embedded in the structures, laws, and customs of a society) and places the responsibility for solving racism on the white majority group. Racism is defined as "the effort by the majority to maintain economic and emotional advantages over the minority."[4] By this definition, minorities can be prejudiced, but they cannot be racist.[5] According to this view, racism in America continues for two reasons. One, the historic impact of slavery and discrimination is still with us. Two, though white individuals may not personally be racist, their participation in a social system that benefits them and hurts minorities is ongoing racism.

White people, therefore, need to change the social systems so that they no longer have economic and emotional advantages over minorities. To be antiracist, whites need to dismantle their privilege and the social structures that sustain it. There are numerous proposals for how this is to be done. One controversial approach is through payment of reparations.* These could take various forms: financial investments in more conscious efforts to promote equity (e.g., in government, business, and various industries), trust funds to support minority community improvement, or investment targeted toward minority business development.

This view identifies "whiteness" as the problem at the root of racial conflict. *Whiteness* is used to describe the ways in which whites maintain their dominance. We should acknowledge that there have been social systems created by whites to maintain social dominance and that the effects of these systems are still present in society. But the charge to dismantle "white social systems" is so broad that too often it includes systems that are creationally normative such as the family, diligence in education, or hard work. It is also wrong and counterproductive to use *whiteness* as a tag for what is racially wrong in the world because white ethnic groups are also part of God's created order. "Whites" are not monolithic; to negatively stereotype a group of people on the basis of physical characteristics is itself racism. In addition, while it is undoubtedly true that some people are born more privileged than others, the Bible does not permit this to be a point of prejudice or resentment (Lev. 19:15; Eph. 4:31) even while it requires those who have been blessed to help those in need (Gal. 6:10; 1 Tim. 6:17–19; James 2:16; 1 John 3:17). Many white abolitionists (before and during the Civil War) and integrationists (during the civil rights movement) leveraged their privilege to promote justice.

reparations: "monetary or other compensation payable by a country to an individual for a historical wrong"[6]

White
Responsibility
Approach

This view also elevates minority groups, seeing their attainment of social power as the means of salvation from racial conflict. This, however, neglects the truth that all humans are sinners. It neglects the fact that some of the problems ethnic minorities face are due to their own sins. This approach also relies on giving ethnic minorities a great deal of power without acknowledging that any sinner with unchecked power is liable to abuse it. In fact, this view often exacerbates racial conflict because white citizens feel that this power is already being misused and that the charges against whites are so sweeping as to be unfair.

While this approach is unbiblical, Christians should not dismiss the idea that sin can be institutionalized and systematized, as it was with slavery and segregation. Likewise, the idea that sins committed by nations or families, or leaders who represent them, have corporate consequences is well attested in Scripture (1 Kings 11:31–35; 14:9–14; 2 Kings 24:3; Zech. 8:14; Neh. 9:2). Finally, though the reparations schemes promoted by advocates of this view tend to be unbiblical and unjust, Christians should recognize that restitution for past wrongs is part of the biblical pattern (Exod. 21:23–27, 33–36; 22:1–17; Luke 19:8–10). If an institution or family can track down descendants of people they wronged, it would be in keeping with the spirit of Scripture to attempt some kind of restitution for the wrong done.

Majority Conformity and Colorblindness

The majority conformity approach operates from an individualistic definition of racism, though with acknowledgement of past structural injustices. The responsibility for solving unequal outcomes for various ethnicities lies primarily with the minority groups. This approach holds that racism is no longer a significant problem in the United States and that racial discrimination no longer holds ethnic minorities back from achievement. The problem as it now exists is a class problem, not a race problem. If people would stop talking about race and if minority groups would conform to majority norms, they would become upwardly mobile.

Colorblind
Approach

The colorblind approach thinks the whole idea of seeing multiple ethnic groups instead of one humanity is the fundamental problem. On the one hand, this view is correct in seeing all humans as part of a unified human race; on the other hand, the Bible sees ethnic diversity as part of God's good creational design. To view oneness as salvation from our racial conflicts is to idolize that aspect of God's creational design.

The problem with these approaches is they tend to deny the ongoing effects of long-term national sins. This can lead to an unwillingness to even consider historical and contemporary accounts of such injustice on the grounds that we must move past such things. In advocating conformity to majority norms, the first approach ignores or downplays the effects of sin on all cultures, including majority cultures. Because the Fall has corrupted cultures, there is no aspect of any culture untouched by the Fall. All cultures, majority and minority, must be measured by the standard of Scripture rather than serving as the measurement for other cultures. Thus, while it would be good for Americans of all ethnicities to forge a unified, shared culture, this project is likely to fail if minority cultures are required to abandon what is positive in their own cultures.

While these approaches are unbiblical, Christians should be careful not to dismiss what they get right. They rightly recognize the unity of the human race and the ideal of treating all people fairly regardless of their ethnicity. They also recognize the danger (and the dehumanizing effect) of treating minority people primarily as victims.

acts ⟩ A BIBLICAL VIEW OF RACE AND RACISM

The various secular models have all failed to bring about racial reconciliation, and Christians, insofar as they have adopted secular viewpoints, have also failed in this project. However, the Bible is sufficient for providing us with the wisdom needed to address the issues of racial controversy (2 Tim. 3:16–17). The biblical doctrine of creation makes Christian ethics uniquely qualified to speak to racial discrimination. All people are descendants of the historical Adam and Eve and are therefore physically united in one human race, and all the ethnic groups that have emerged since Adam and Eve were "made" by God (Acts 17:26). The biblical doctrine of creation accounts for both human unity and human diversity.

Racism is a form of sinful partiality, which the Bible forbids (Lev. 19:15; James 2:1–4). It is a fundamental denial of our shared equality as God's image-bearers (Gen. 1:26; 5:3; 9:6; James 3:9). A biblical approach to racism recognizes that all people bear God's image and that all people are sinners. Thus, a biblical approach would recognize that both majority and minority groups have incentives to slant conversations on race to their own advantage. A biblical approach would encourage people from all groups to build respectful, enduring, cooperative, and equal relationships across ethnic lines. It would encourage those groups who have historically faced oppression, and who continue to face racism, to speak constructively about injustices but to avoid a life focused on grievances.

Christians should not be surprised if much of the racial conflict in the United States today is the direct result of the nation's sins regarding racial discrimination and segregation. Churches, institutions, and organizations that have contributed to racism could follow a biblical model of corporate repentance by making statements that their past actions were wrong and by demonstrating change (Ezra 9; Neh. 1:6–7; Dan. 9:3–19), with the offended extending forgiveness according to the pattern of God's forgiveness.

The biblical model of reformation (not revolution) is the best way to promote true racial justice. Instead of tearing down existing societal structures and thereby leading to greater injustice, we should seek to align societal structures with the creational norms of a just society (for example, see Ps. 37:30; Prov. 31:8–9). A biblical approach would not accept the idea that all racial disparities are a sign of racism. However, it would recognize that some racial disparities may point to problems that need addressing. It would be open to appropriate reforms to policies and laws. It would also seek to promote creationally and biblically sound social norms among all groups (e.g., the importance of intact families).

A biblical approach would involve gratitude for the progress that has been made in repudiating racism, while also recognizing that sin problems like racism will stubbornly persist in a fallen world. Christians can work on addressing racial problems on the national level, but they should also advance solutions on the personal, organizational, and local levels—arenas in which they may have more influence and responsibility (for instance, see Acts 20:28). Finally, Christians should not depend on their own efforts for success. Dependance on God through prayer will be essential to progress in this matter.

The goal for the nation should be to unify all ethnic groups around core values (biblically understood) while allowing all groups to continue to value and practice the creationally normative traditions of their own ethnic heritage.

Within the church, Scripture's teaching on the unity of believers is essential in overcoming racial animosity. It's impossible to overcome racial divisions in the church in any meaningful fashion without the concept of the body of Christ. John 17 calls for unity in the body, implying that ethnic divisions that disrupt that unity are a contradiction of our shared union in Christ. Ephesians 2:11–3:10 indicates that the bringing together of people from different ethnic backgrounds into a unified Christian body is something that brings glory to God because it bears witness to the world that we are the one people of God.

Wayne Grudem summarizes the ultimate expression of ethnic diversity, found among the worshipers of God in heaven. "If we skip to the end of the Bible, we see the same emphasis on racial and ethnic unity, because the innumerable multitude of people worshiping before God's throne in heaven includes people from every tribe and nation of the earth:"[7]

> After this I beheld, and, lo, a great multitude, which no man could number, *of all nations, and kindreds, and people, and tongues*, stood before the throne, and before the Lamb, clothed with white robes, and palms in their hands; and cried with a loud voice, saying, Salvation to our God which sitteth upon the throne, and unto the Lamb. (Rev. 7:9–10, emphasis added)

 ## THE EFFECTS OF RACISM ON SOCIETY

There is an inevitable breakdown in a society where racism exists. For example, we can look back to the days of Jim Crow laws in America and recognize this period as one characterized by enormous social upheaval. Treating a minority group as second-class citizens is not only immoral, but also bad social policy. It is only natural for that minority group to rise up in defense of their dignity and demand from the larger society equal treatment and equal opportunities. The long struggle for civil rights in America challenged the white majority to acknowledge the racial injustice enshrined in the law and to admit how poisonous this was for the entire body politic.

Many voices of the civil rights movement appealed to the conscience of the nation, calling the country to live up to the ideals of America's founding documents, which were influenced by a biblical worldview. If America is described as a nation of people "endowed by their Creator with" the "unalienable Rights" of "Life, Liberty, and the pursuit of Happiness,"[8] then this principle must equally apply to black Americans. The efforts of the civil rights movement led to crucial legislative changes and court decisions. In following years, making good on the promises of the US Constitution has struck a chord with many white Americans, and the tide has turned toward a more just society.

How should I foster racial reconciliation?

 ## VIRTUES THAT PROMOTE RACIAL RECONCILIATION

Discussing race relations can be difficult because emotions run high on this issue, but Christians should be eager to enter the conversation with humility and hope (see Acts 10–11). Our humility and hope stem from several biblical realities, not least of which is the unifying power of the gospel of grace that reconciles a repentant and believing humanity both to God and to one another. Focusing on biblical solutions to the problem of racial discrimination neither minimizes the complexity of the issue nor surrenders to the status quo. Those seeking racial reconciliation need *humility* as they address a complex problem (Phil. 2:3–4); *prudence* to find better solutions (Ps.

37:30; Prov. 14:15); *love* for those impacted by racism (Phil. 2:1–2); and *hope* that racism can be effectively addressed (Rom. 15:13).

Humility is necessary in dealing with racial problems because it will enable us to consider arguments that challenge our preconceived ideas about race. This doesn't mean we will always agree with opposing arguments, but it does mean we will give them a fair hearing before deciding. In some cases, we may recognize an element of truth in another person's critique of our own attitudes about race. The key is to sift all arguments about race—our own arguments as well as those of others—through a biblical lens of Creation, Fall, Redemption.

Prudence enables us to develop constructive ways of pursuing racial reconciliation where it is genuinely needed. This is in contrast to the destructive path of revolution, which is typically the impatient person's way of dealing with social problems. Prudence should not be mistaken for apathy toward racism, because prudence does not stand alone from the virtues of love and hope.

Love for those impacted by racism should lead us to vigorously pursue righteous solutions, knowing that such solutions may require long-term effort. As we nurture the hope that the Christian ethic can prevail in producing a more just society for all people, we not only guard against the temptation to adopt secular solutions, but we also promote the kind of racial reconciliation rooted in the reconciling power of the gospel of Jesus Christ.

To have a truly integrated church (reflecting the demographic profile of the neighborhood in which it is found) takes hard work, very substantial forbearance, self-sacrificing winsomeness, patience—in a word, love. D. A. CARSON[9]

Thinking It Through 11.1

1. How should we define race and ethnicity from a biblical perspective?
2. How does the *Oxford English Dictionary* define racism?
3. What is wrong with the white responsibility view of race?
4. What is wrong with the majority conformity and colorblind views of race?
5. How does a biblical model of reformation promote racial justice?
6. How do the virtues of humility, prudence, love, and hope promote racial reconciliation?

11.2 Addictions

One of the signs of Christianity's waning influence upon Western societies is the removal of restraints on addictive behaviors. Though alcoholism and drug abuse are still regarded as social problems to be solved, there's been a moral shift in our society's attitude toward harmful, intoxicating substances. The legalization of marijuana is evidence of this. Societies whose governments profit from the taxation of recreational drugs and addictive behaviors (like gambling) reveal an ethical and social erosion. Individuals are not served well when their government risks their well-being for the sake of monetary gain.

For our society to recover from this ethical erosion, we will need to recover certain Christian virtues. Honesty, hope, and self-control would be a good place to start.

We need to be honest about the personal and social devastation caused by addictive vices. At the same time, we need to offer hope to those trapped in various forms of addictions. And finally, instead of mocking the virtue of self-control, we need to elevate self-control as an essential part of our human dignity. Indulging oneself in intoxicating substances may seem cool to some people, but when it costs them their dignity and even their lives, it doesn't look cool at all.

What is controlling me?

`context` ## THE NATURE OF ADDICTION

Addiction is by definition enslaving; it exercises paralyzing control over the addict. Once enslaved to a particular addiction, many live in denial about the seriousness of their problem. While addicts bear personal responsibility for their behavior, they delude themselves by thinking they can quit anytime they choose. Genuine recovery begins by admitting one has a problem and by asking for help.

Alcohol abuse is by far the most common addiction. The pressure on young people to conform to their worldly peers is part of the problem. At the average secular university, excessive drinking at raucous parties is virtually a rite of passage for young people. Our culture sends mixed signals with regard to drunkenness. On the one hand, it glorifies debauchery and unrestrained freedom. On the other hand, it spends millions of dollars on alcohol rehab.

Given the biblical prohibitions against drunkenness, you might think that all Christians would agree on a biblical response toward alcohol. However, there are at least two common positions among Christians. The **abstinence** position emphasizes both the necessity of avoiding drunkenness and the wisdom of abstaining from that which gets someone drunk. Other Christians who are equally opposed to drunkenness argue that the problem is not alcohol *per se* but the abuse of alcohol. Responsible, moderate drinking, they argue, is biblically permissible.

The Moderation Position

One advocate for moderate drinking offers the following considerations. First, while wine in the ancient world was often diluted with water, the fact that drunkenness was a problem as far back as Noah and Lot indicates that alcohol was not always diluted (Gen. 9:21; 19:30–36). Therefore, Scripture's allowance for wine, coupled with its prohibition of drunkenness, assumes a moderation position (Ps. 104:14–15; Eph. 5:18). Second, while abstinence certainly guarantees that drunkenness will be avoided, it is also true that many Christians practice moderation without becoming drunk. Third, given the biblical celebration of wine, it seems the abstinence position requires a stricter position than does Scripture (Prov. 3:9–10; Eccles. 9:7; John 2:9–10).[10]

The Abstinence Position

One advocate of abstinence provides four considerations. First, the ancient world lacked the technology that we possess today to prevent the fermentation of grape juice. Second, the ancient practice of diluting wine with water means that wine in biblical days doesn't compare to the high alcohol content of modern alcoholic beverages; the "wine" of today is not the same as the wine the Bible refers to. In other words, we should avoid modern alcohol because of its significantly higher alcohol content. Third, Scripture's warnings against the dangers of alcohol (coupled with the serious danger of addiction) mean that abstinence would be the most appropriate biblical application today (for example, see Prov. 20:1; 23:29–35; Isa. 5:22; 28:7–8). Fourth, even if drinking alcohol could be construed as a matter of Christian liberty, believers should avoid it because it (a) is especially prone to enslaving people, (b) offers nothing in terms of edification, and (c) poses a stumbling block to others (1 Cor. 6:12; 8:9, 13; Rom. 14:17, 21).[11]

Proponents of abstinence respond to the first moderation argument by pointing out that, in the ancient world, those who wanted to become intoxicated would seek out the wine before it was mixed. In response to the second moderation argument, when people drink modern alcoholic beverages, the alcoholic content is significantly higher than the alcoholic content of the beverages drunk by those in Scripture. In response to the third moderation argument, in biblical times wine was a staple, like bread. The rejoicing associated with it was not tied to its alcoholic content but to the fact that God was supplying the basic needs of His people. Proponents of this form of abstinence reject the claim that their position is stricter than Scripture.

Everything the Bible says about drunkenness can be applied to drug addiction. Scripture has nothing positive to say about **recreational drugs**.* Recreational drugs like marijuana have proven to have harmful consequences even in low doses. Claims of marijuana's medicinal value are not an argument for recreational use but rather an argument for continued scientific research to create new medicines that do not have the addictive or intoxicating effects of marijuana use.[12]

Gambling

Gambling is included in this discussion because it, too, can have a controlling influence on people, with devastating social consequences. Gamblers talk about the rush of winning; this rush has effects on the human brain similar to those of illicit drugs. And like a drug that requires higher doses to get the same effect over time, gambling requires more bets to maintain the rush. As the losses continue to mount, the gambler is under compulsion to gamble more.[13] How else is he supposed to recover his losses except from a huge win? That's how a gambling addict reasons.

A BIBLICAL RESPONSE TO ADDICTION

Being under the control of alcohol, drugs, or a vice like gambling is incompatible with the Christian life, where the controlling influence is supposed to be the Holy Spirit (Eph. 5:18). Whereas self-control is the fruit of the Spirit (Gal. 5:22–23), lack of control is the fruit of addiction. God created man to rule over creation, but at present the fallen creation often rules over man. Addiction is an example of creation ruling over man.

Numerous biblical texts condemn drunkenness and by extension the intoxication from other drugs (for example, see Prov. 23:20–21; 1 Cor. 6:10; 1 Pet. 4:3). Additionally, the biblical view of wise stewardship argues against any form of gambling (Luke 16:11).

Responding to Substance Abuse

Because secular notions of bodily autonomy pervade our society, many people justify substance abuse on the grounds that they can do with their bodies as they please. The biblical doctrines of creation and redemption provide a correction to this outlook. When we remember that our bodies are a gift from our Creator and that they ultimately belong to Him, we come to understand that there are some good and necessary limits to what we should do with our bodies. Scripture amplifies this point when speaking of Christian redemption (1 Cor. 6:19–20). Christians are to glorify God in their bodies because they've been bought with the price of Christ's own blood (Eph. 1:7; 1 Pet. 1:18–19). As Christians weigh what they do with their bodies, they should always consider whether their choices will glorify the Savior who bought them.

We could apply this principle to the practice of vaping. Nicotine (present in many vape products) is extremely addictive, and the withdrawal symptoms are so difficult that many people struggle to stop once they begin. Many young people mistakenly

recreational drugs: drugs "that some people take occasionally for enjoyment, especially when they are spending time socially with other people."[4]

believe that vaping is a safer option than smoking. Research is still underway about possible heart and lung damage, but one thing is certain: nicotine addiction from vaping is still a destructive addiction. Glorifying God with our bodies precludes such an addiction.

Responding to Gambling

The idea of gaining money without work is contrary to the Creation Mandate (Gen. 1:28). Yet that's exactly what gambling falsely promises: the ability to reap financially without contributing to the improvement of society. Comparing gambling with investing in the stock market is a red herring that proponents of gambling often use. Scripture encourages wise investing because it provides opportunities to produce something that benefits society (Deut. 28:12; Eccles. 11:2; Matt. 25:14–30). Gambling, on the other hand, is strictly a game of risk, one that heavily favors the house.* It's a poor stewardship of one's resources (Prov. 21:5; 28:20). Unlike investments, where people on both sides have the potential of winning, gambling requires some people to lose in order for others to win.

Christians can debate the wisdom of a school raffle. (Most people recognize it as a benefit to the school. Basically it's a donation.)[15] But the gambling industry has no redeeming qualities. Gambling is based on the love of money, is accompanied by an array of immoral and criminal behavior, and is proven to be addictive (1 Tim. 6:9–10; James 1:15–17). Our concern for gambling addicts is heightened when we realize that the gambling industry preys on the poorest and most vulnerable among us. The false promise of striking it rich is like setting a trap for the poor. Therefore, Scripture's warning about taking advantage of the poor applies to the gambling industry (Prov. 22:22–23; Phil. 2:4).

THE SOCIAL CONSEQUENCES OF ADDICTION

An ethical society depends, among other things, on its members exercising their God-given abilities for the well-being of the larger society. But addictions incapacitate individuals, robbing them of the dignity of work and of serving others. The societal benefit that might have accrued from the individual's contribution is lost to the addiction. This is the negative cost of addiction, the good it *removes* from society.

 ends

The Social Cost of Substance Abuse

Addictions also cause positive social harm; they *add* problems for families, governments, economies, health care systems, employers, and more. Alcohol abuse has been particularly devastating, often leading to physical abuse in the home, causing thousands of deaths each year from drunk driving, and resulting in various physical problems, as well as being associated with mental illness.[16] Drug addictions take a similar toll on families and society. Marijuana deprives people of sound judgment, motivation, and mental alertness. It, too, has led to traffic accidents and fatalities. It is also known as a gateway drug.[17] Many cocaine and heroin addicts started with marijuana.

We can add to these social costs the criminal activity often associated with substance abuse and addiction. Some addicts engage in illegal behavior to fund their addiction. And some people profit from the addictions of others through drug trafficking. Drug cartels are notoriously violent, frequently at war with each other and with government authorities. This dark underbelly of the drug world is both a cause and a consequence of addiction.

The Social Cost of Gambling

Money wasted on gambling is money that could have been spent on food and rent, a reality many families experience firsthand from having a gambling addict in the family. Having a gambler for a parent deprives many children of daily necessities as well as a better financial future. In some cases, gambling tragically deprives children of the life of a parent. Suicide is not uncommon for gambling addicts. The

the house: the casino running the gambling operation

self-inflicted humiliation and despair that stems from squandering everything on a roll of the dice leads many people to end their lives.[18]

Studies indicate that, wherever gambling is legalized, crime goes up. Governments that profit from this corrupt enterprise are complicit in gambling's destructive effects upon individuals and society. This includes state-sponsored lotteries, which use deceptive advertising regarding the odds of a big win.[19] Raising funds for public education with a lottery is like raising funds for health care by taxing marijuana. It is self-contradictory and self-defeating.

 ## VIRTUES THAT COUNTERACT ADDICTION

Honesty, hope, and self-control are three Christian virtues well-suited to counteract addiction. Honesty is necessary to counteract the lies that people tell themselves about their addictions. Hope is necessary to counteract the despair that addicts experience. And self-control is necessary to counteract the out-of-control nature of addiction itself.

Getting Honest about Addiction

Admitting that one has a problem with addiction is difficult for a couple of reasons. First, it's a blow to one's pride. You have to be honest about having made poor choices and about needing help. Second, it means giving up something you love, namely the pleasure that comes from whatever you're addicted to. An honest addict will not fool himself or herself; withdrawals will be painful, and victory over the addiction will be costly.

Honesty is a virtue that grows in the soil of the gospel. In other words, the offer of forgiveness in the gospel means the addict does not have to hide in shame. He or she can bring his or her sin to Christ with honest confession and repentance to receive a complete pardon from God. Although this first step does not impart immediate victory over the addiction, it's a necessary step on the long road of recovery.

Gaining Hope over Addiction

Relapse among addicts is extremely high. Drug and alcohol rehab centers will attest that many of their patients will graduate from their program only to return again. This can increase the sense of despair and hopelessness an addict may experience. Believers struggling with addiction need constant reassurance that no matter how strong their addiction is, the power of Christ is even stronger.

Some addicts have heard the gospel message many times and have grown numb to it. Others, however, have found real hope in the gospel, especially as they were surrounded by loving and patient Christians who shouldered their burden with them. This gave the addicts hope that, as they relied on Christ for help, He would not abandon them to their addictions.

When you call addiction a sin issue of the heart rather than... a disease, then you have biblical words, biblical language, to offer them ... the hope of the gospel for the heart of addiction. MARK SHAW[20]

Growing in Self-Control and out of Addiction

Addiction robs a person of control over himself or herself. Reversing this situation is stressful but not impossible. Exercising self-control is like exercising a muscle; the more one exercises self-control, the more one grows in self-control. The virtue of self-control arises from the Holy Spirit's work in a believer's life. Nevertheless, self-control must be exercised for a believer to become proficient in it.

What does it look like to exercise self-control with regard to addiction? It looks like the daily habit of putting "off the old man" (Col. 3:9) and putting "on the new man" (Col. 3:10) as described in Colossians 3:1–14. Given that a believer has been raised with Christ to "walk in newness of life" (Rom. 6:4; see Col. 1:1–3), that person is no longer enslaved to his or her former addiction (Rom. 6:16–23). The flesh may still crave the addiction, but a believer is able to resist these cravings in the power of the Spirit. Putting off the old man means accepting the pain of addiction withdrawals. Putting on the new man means finding one's pleasure in being a child of God, chosen and loved by Him, and adding new virtues and habits to one's life (Col. 3:12–17).

Thinking It Through 11.2

1. What is the nature of addiction?

2. What is the biblical response to substance abuse?

3. Do a search for "Is it okay to gamble?" How would you biblically respond to an article defending gambling?

4. How does the virtue of honesty help a person to resist or defeat these vices?

5. How does the virtue of hope help a person to resist or defeat these vices?

6. How does the virtue of self-control help a person to resist or defeat these vices?

11.3 Communication and Media Use

Everything about our social interaction with one another is of ethical significance, including our communication. What we say, how we say it, and even what we refuse to say reveals much about ourselves individually and culturally. The verbal as well as the non-verbal messages that people exchange every day are value laden, though most of us are unaware that our values rest on the surface of everything we say.

The forms of communication that our society finds acceptable and unacceptable can be difficult to evaluate. As we've done in previous lessons with other topics, we need to apply some biblical worldview thinking to the subject at hand. Our model (Creation, Fall, Redemption) has real advantages for evaluating communication and media use; it gives us wisdom to distinguish that which is consistent with creational norms and that which is fallen.

In addition, we need to look at certain Christian virtues that directly relate to this subject. If we want to please God in our communication and media use, we will need to grow in the virtues of honesty, gentleness, and righteousness. Each of these virtues is a necessary correction to the vices that characterize so much of our society.

COMMUNICATION AND MEDIA: WHAT ARE THE ETHICAL ISSUES?

What ethical issues come to mind when you think of communication and media use? Social media bullying? Virtue signaling? Trolling? Forcing politically correct speech? These are common problems in our current media environment. In addition, there are ethical problems that have been with us for much longer—profanity,* crude joking, gratuitous violence in entertainment, and a loss of modesty.

Such things have always been part of our fallen culture. There was a time, however, when debased forms of communication caused the general public to blush. As our society continues its moral decline, we're witnessing an increase in vulgarity* and a decrease in blushing. There seems to be a race to the bottom when it comes to communication and media use.

While communication is creational, the worldviews embedded in the current social media platforms assume that humans are basically good and that giving every human a voice will have beneficial consequences. But in actuality, social media tends toward pride, narcissism, and the idea that we can construct our own realities. It has also loosened certain restraints. Many people who express themselves inappropriately on social media might think twice if they were face-to-face with a person. Bullying has become rampant on social media. The pressure to present a picture-perfect life leads some to embellish their lives on social media. And regret from posting explicit images or video of oneself on social media has become such a huge problem that companies now exist to do reputation repair. Many Christians speak and share falsehoods online because they don't take the time to check whether what they read is true or not.

Although the medium by which we communicate is important, the nature of our communication is more important. Where social media and entertainment are being used effectively to communicate messages consistent with a biblical ethic, we should be thankful and follow those examples.

COMMUNICATION AND MEDIA: HOW SHOULD WE THINK?

What proceeds from our mouths (and our keyboards) reveals the moral condition of our hearts (Matt. 12:34). Corrupt communication flows from fallen hearts, and clean communication flows from redeemed hearts. This is true whether our communication is spoken or written, whether our interactions are face-to-face or on Instagram. What we post on social media is just as revealing and consequential as the words we speak.

The Origins of Communication

Human communication is a gift from God, and we have a responsibility before Him to steward this gift well. It was originally designed as a reflection of God's nature and God's character. A biblical understanding of communication must begin here. To think of communication as a mere social convention rather than a reflection of the Creator deprives society of the richness and fullness of communication. We'll never be able to elevate our communication in society until we understand its elevated origins.

God is a speaking God. There once was a time when no one existed but God. No angels. No humans. No created speaker. Yet communication has always existed. It existed by virtue of the fact that God is a triune God. The communication between Father, Son, and Holy Spirit is eternal and perfect. There never was a time when they were not speaking to one another, and there never was a time when their speech was inappropriate. Divine communication, therefore, is synonymous with fellowship in the Godhead.

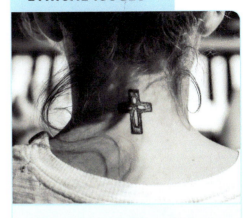

GRAPPLING WITH ETHICAL ISSUES

Ink and Communication

Tattoos are another form of communication worthy of ethical consideration. The Bible addresses tattoos in Leviticus 19:28: "Ye shall not make any cuttings in your flesh for the dead, nor print any marks upon you: I am the LORD." These instructions come as part of a series of instructions for the Israelites to not follow the pagan practice of disfiguring the body in various ways. Since humans are made in God's image, disfiguring the body dishonors God. Some Christians defend tattoos on the grounds that they no longer have pagan associations. Other Christians observe that the pagan connotations of tattoos have persisted across cultures for thousands of years. These connotations will not easily be lost—especially in an increasingly paganized Western culture. The existence of tattoos reflecting devotion to God does not negate the numerous non-Christian tattoos that don't communicate devotion to God. In addition, the more fundamental principle behind Leviticus 19's prohibition of tattoos is a refusal to deface the body since humans bear the image of God. The fundamental question for the Christian to ask is: What does inking the body communicate about the Creator of the body?

profanity: "a type of language that includes dirty words and ideas"[21]

vulgarity: "the quality of being crude and lacking refinement. Many people consider swearing to be a form of vulgarity."[22]

FATHER

GOD

SON   SPIRIT

It was by divine communication that God created the world. When God turned His attention to human beings, He designed our communication to facilitate fellowship with Him and with other people. Fellowship occurs when our speech is truthful, righteous, honorable, gracious, and peaceable. Speech that reflects God's character also promotes human flourishing. Society functions more efficiently and effectively when communication is ethical.

The Fall and Restoration of Communication

Ever wonder why people misunderstand one another, why they twist the meaning of each other's words, and why they sometimes cease to communicate with certain people? The answer lies in the fact that we live in a world marred by sin. Although communication still facilitates human fellowship and human flourishing, it is at best a frustratingly poor reflection of what it once was. At its worst, communication is misused to dishonor God, to deceive other people, and to destroy relationships.

James warns that the tongue (and we can extend this to online speech) "is a fire" (James 3:6) and "an unruly evil" (James 3:8). He also warns against bitter envy, strife, and boasting deceit—and says such things are demonic (James 3:13–18). Galatians 5:15 warns about speech that devours others. Proverbs 6:19 says that God hates those who sow discord. Exodus 20:16 prohibits bearing false witness.

Redemption is God's answer to broken communication. The righteous judgment that fell upon human communication at the Tower of Babel has its redemptive parallel at the Day of Pentecost. Whereas the former incident resulted in confused human languages to frustrate man's sinful goal, the later incident overcame those barriers to advance God's redemptive goal. Redemption enables believers to encourage others with wise and helpful words instead of destroying them with foolish and hurtful words.

 ## COMMUNICATION AND MEDIA: WHAT HAS HAPPENED TO US?

Living in this present evil age is difficult for the redeemed because the world treats unethical communication as normal and ethical communication as prudish. Corrupt uses of media are more common than noble uses. Christian communication and media consumption, however, should further a life of purity and righteousness. This means Christians will have to go against the tide of culture in their communication and media use.

Profanity, crude joking, lying, gossiping, and the general promotion of messages that dishonor God and debase human beings have not served our society well. Words are powerful, and when they're misused, they do not cease to be powerful. Their power is merely directed to destructive ends rather than constructive ones. Individual families suffer from harsh words spoken in the home, from the undiscerning use of media, and from the absence of reassuring words of love. Multiply this situation in families throughout society, and the culture becomes desensitized to the coarsening of communication.

Unethical communication and media use not only reveals the character of our society, but it also plunges society into an unsustainable situation. Just as ethical communication is essential to building trust in society, so unethical communication guarantees the erosion of trust. Gossip and slander erode the trust necessary for hurting people to confide in others, pushing them into the shadows of society. The hopeless ones often resort to self-harm or harming others in part because of bullying. The normalization of profanity and vulgarity produces a society of cynics who no longer trust that the sacred is real and worthy of respect. Deception in news media and misinformation on social media create an environment of distrust. The loss of trust spells the loss of social cohesion. This is the price that a society pays for tolerating unethical communication.

When the overuse of technology is mixed into the equation, the result is a society of people unable to properly interact with one another. Human beings in such a society become hollow, a shell of what they were meant to be. Just think of a family sitting around the table at a restaurant—dad, mom, brother, and sister all looking at their smartphones and unable to enjoy the company of their family. The negative social impact of all these behaviors may take time to notice, but eventually people realize their relationships are deficient.

COMMUNICATION AND MEDIA: WHERE DO WE GO FROM HERE?

The biblical reality of our world is this: we currently live in the overlap of two ages. The age of redemption has invaded this present evil age, and that should give every Christian hope. The devastating cultural effects of unethical communication and media use should not be minimized, but neither should they be given the last word.

For all the destructive words on social media and in our personal lives, God's final word to us in Christ will prevail in the end. The triumph of righteous communication was initiated when the eternal Word became flesh, communicated words of grace and truth throughout His life on earth, and then nailed to the cross every sinful word from our hearts and lips.

Union with Christ transforms our communication. It replaces dishonesty with honesty, harshness with gentleness, and vulgarity with righteousness. Our honesty should proceed from a love for the truth and a willingness to speak the truth, even when it is unpopular. Our gentleness should arise from a consciousness of the power of our words and the obligation to use that power for the good of our listeners. Our righteous speech should spring from a desire to reflect our righteous God, knowing that it pleases Him and blesses others.

Believers should take care that their speech influences society for the better and that their media use influences themselves for the better. As our communication and media use is suffused with the virtues of honesty, gentleness, and righteousness, we can promote God's intention for human fellowship and human flourishing. A society that values these virtues is a society whose members can trust one another.

How can I please God in my communication and media use?

You represent Christ in a real way even if it is in the virtual world.

KEVIN DEYOUNG[23]

1. What are the ethical issues related to communication and media use?

2. How does a biblical view of God and creation shape our understanding of communication and media use?

3. How do the biblical concepts of the Fall and redemption shape our understanding of communication and media use?

4. What are the personal and social consequences of unethical communication and media use?

5. How can the virtues of honesty, gentleness, and righteousness improve our communication and media use?

11.4 Business Ethics

Perhaps you've had your own lawn-mowing service or babysitting service. If so, you understand the value of hard work and the mutual benefit of serving others. Exchanging a product or a service for money is a blessing because it improves the quality of life for everyone involved. A farmer feeds the community, a teacher educates the children in the community, and a police officer protects the community. Each receives compensation for their skill and their labor, thereby enabling them to secure the products and services of others.

Christian ethics is qualified to give meaning and purpose to the business enterprise because it honors the dignity of people and the dignity of work. It also equips society with principles for addressing corruption in business (such as greed, theft, and laziness). In addition, Christian ethics promotes the virtues necessary for conducting business in an ethical society (such as love, diligence, and righteousness).

ETHICAL PROBLEMS RELATED TO BUSINESS

Money is not the root of all evil. The love of money is (1 Tim. 6:10). This distinction is important to keep in mind when thinking about the ethics of business. Currency is an efficient and effective way of making economic transactions. It's impossible for the car mechanic to trade his services for everything he needs and wants. With currency, however, he can earn money and trade it for goods and services.

Problems with money arise because of misplaced priorities and misdirected trust. Jesus said, "No man can serve two masters: for either he will hate the one, and love the other; or else he will hold to the one, and despise the other. Ye cannot serve God and mammon" (Matt. 6:24). Mammon (or money) is a suitable servant. But as a master it corrupts the workplace and the marketplace through the vices of greed, theft, and laziness.

Corruption in the Workplace

While the employer-employee relationship should be honored as a creational norm, we should also identify and correct instances of corruption that may arise in the workplace. Greed corrupts this business relationship when employers overwork their employees, demanding that they prioritize the company over their families. Theft and laziness corrupt this business relationship when employees neglect their work and receive compensation for work not done. More egregious forms of theft occur when employees steal money, supplies, or products from their company.

Bribery* and **extortion*** are also forms of corruption. A company paying a government official to secure a contract is an example of bribery. An employee blackmailing an employer guilty of something illegal or embarrassing is an example of extortion. In each case, the love of money is the driving motivation behind these corrupt practices.

bribery: "an attempt to make someone do something for you by giving the person money, presents, or something else that he or she wants"[24]

extortion: "the act of getting something, especially money, by force or threats"[25]

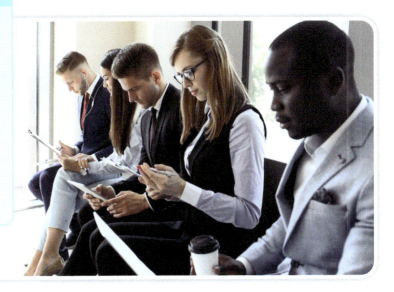

Corruption in the Marketplace

The marketplace consists of various players (producers, distributors, advertisers, consumers, etc.). In short, there are those who have something to sell and those who wish to purchase what's being sold. Greed and theft corrupt this otherwise beneficial economic arrangement too.

For instance, producers who use unsafe materials to save money risk their customers' health and safety. Advertisers who misrepresent a product deceive the buying public. Businesses that engage in price gouging during times of emergency take advantage of the helpless and needy (e.g., during natural disasters when water, gasoline, and other supplies are in high demand).

Consumers also corrupt the marketplace when they steal from business establishments. Some thefts are blatant smash-and-grab larcenies. Others are more subtle. Switching the price tag of an item with a lower price tag is theft. Purchasing an item of clothing with the full intention of returning it for a refund after wearing it once is also theft. These thefts eat into business profits, and the cost is then passed on to honest customers in the form of higher prices.

 ## BIBLICAL PRINCIPLES REGARDING BUSINESS

The purpose of business is for human beings to fulfill the Creation Mandate in the most efficient and effective way for the glory of God and for the flourishing of human society. To achieve this goal, societies must conduct business according to the ethical principles set forth in Scripture. Christian ethicist Wayne Grudem identifies six core principles.

First, since God is the God of truth and requires truthfulness from us, our business practices should be conducted in all truthfulness (Eph. 4:25). This means companies should honestly advertise their product or service, not claiming more for them than is accurate. It also means candidates for a job should be truthful on their resumes, not embellishing their accomplishments.

Second, private property is a key creational norm that underlies business ethics. Scripture's prohibition against stealing is predicated on the notion that God has entrusted individuals with the right of ownership (Exod. 20:15). Therefore, for example, "you should never put personal (nonbusiness-related) items on a business receipt and claim more reimbursement than is due to you."[28] Taking what belongs to another person (or company) is wrong.

Third, since God requires faithfulness in marriage, companies should establish reasonable boundaries for their male and female employees. For example, sending two employees of the opposite sex on a business trip without safeguards is inviting temptation. To mitigate temptation, the employees should never be alone together during the business trip.

Fourth, love of neighbor extends to the people with whom we conduct business. "In bargaining for a price, love for neighbor means understanding a 'good deal' is one that is not only good for you but also allows the other person to make some money and to have some benefit from the transaction."[29] A simple way to apply this principle is to treat others the way you want to be treated (Matt. 7:12).

Fifth, since God provides wisdom and direction for His people, we can be confident that a righteous solution is available when facing difficult business decisions. This principle refutes the notion that some business situations present us with nothing but sinful options. This is never the case because, no matter how difficult the decision, God promises to provide a way of escape from sin and invites us to ask for the wisdom to see it (1 Cor. 10:13; James 1:5–6).

Sixth, every business decision should be made in dependence upon God, seeking to please Him in every transaction and trusting Him to "supply all [our] need according to his riches" (Phil. 4:19). This means that it is better to make less money on an honest deal than it is to make more money on a dishonest deal (Prov. 16:8). Practicing biblical principles in business is not an automatic guarantee of financial success, but it does guarantee personal integrity, which is far more valuable in the eyes of God.[30]

CONSEQUENCES OF ABUSING BUSINESS

ends — *Is a business practice right just because it is legal?*

In general, businesses cannot survive without advertising, making a profit, and competing against other businesses. Instead of abandoning what is morally good about these business practices,[31] we should ensure that the above-mentioned biblical principles guide our practice. Otherwise, society becomes locked in an economic battle where unethical means are justified by sheer profit. The consequences of abusing legitimate business practices are that people are dehumanized and society is destabilized. Consider the following abuses.

Abuse of Advertising

The purpose of advertising should be to inform the public about the benefits of a company's product. However, certain kinds of advertising dehumanize people. For example, the use of sensual images to attract attention to a product is crass **exploitation*** of people. A company may justify the practice on the grounds that they couldn't compete otherwise. Though this form of advertising is legal, it's not right. It debases the people being exploited, and it desensitizes society to the exploitation of others, as well as causing many who view it to fall into sexual sin (Matt. 5:27–28; Mark 9:42).

Unbridled pragmatism in advertising has a destabilizing effect on the moral foundation of society. If advertisers concern themselves only with increasing sales without also concerning themselves with righteousness, they reinforce a consequentialist ethic for their audience. They contribute to an atmosphere of moral compromise, making it more difficult for society to define and defend moral norms. Dishonesty in advertising is one way marketers frequently manifest this pragmatism.

Abuse of Profit

Commercialism is the abuse of profit-making that dehumanizes people by reducing them to cogs in an economic machine. Making reasonable profits and making wise purchases are both morally good. The problem arises when businesses intentionally appeal to the covetousness of potential customers. One result is a society of affluent yet ungrateful individuals who are not content with what they have.

exploitation: "the use of something in order to get an advantage from it"[32]

Abusing the practice of profit-making also destabilizes society by obscuring the deeper and more fundamental priorities of human existence (e.g., raising children within stable families). Because our society places economic pressure on both parents to work outside the home, many children are raised by someone other than a parent. Even more tragic is how abortion advocates insist that a woman's success in her career depends on her ability to be free from the responsibility of children. The negative social consequences of sacrificing children on the altar of economic prosperity are a sad and present reality in Western society.

Abuse of Competition

In an ethical society, competition motivates companies to innovate and avoid stagnation. Earning a customer's business should be about honestly providing the best product at the lowest cost. However, unrestrained competition dehumanizes people because it allows businesses to treat competitors as mere rivals to be crushed. Businesses that lie about their competitors violate their dignity. Businesses that steal their competitors' ideas or designs violate their property rights.

These things have a destabilizing effect on society. First, they weaken consumer confidence in the marketplace. Consumers are not quite sure which businesses they can trust. Second, honest people are discouraged from starting their own businesses. Starting a business is risky even in the best of ethical environments. But if a society tolerates a company breaking the rules of fair play, honest people face a disincentive for taking a business risk.

 ## VIRTUES FOR ACTING ETHICALLY IN BUSINESS

Despite the challenges of doing business in a fallen world, people still have a responsibility to utilize their talents and skills, often either as an employee of a reputable company or as an owner and operator of one. God still rules over creation, and He is able to protect and to prosper those in business. Every legitimate business enterprise that advances the Creation Mandate has the stamp of God's approval. If God is calling you to serve Him in business, then that is also your mission field as a Christian.

To faithfully represent God in all of our business activities, we must be growing in certain virtues. Ethical Christians should be motivated by *love* for others, be *diligent* in all their work, and be *righteous* in all their dealings. These virtues are relevant for employers and employees, for business owners and for customers.

Business is an essential sphere in the unfolding work of God in Christ.

WILLIAM MESSENGER[33]

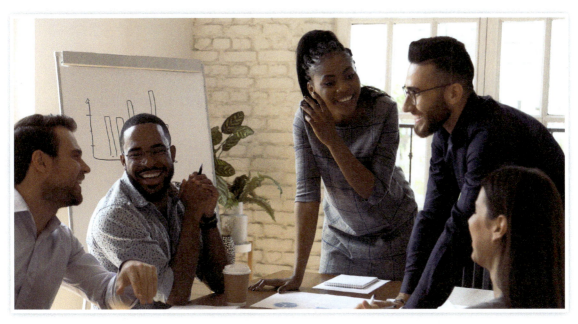

Love Promotes Ethical Business Practices

It would be incorrect to view love and profit as competing motives in business, as though an ethical person should be disinterested in personal profit. Instead, we should think of love for others as the virtue that properly directs our profit motive. Love ensures that we profit by doing good to others and that we avoid profiting from the harm of others.

For instance, a business owner who loves his employees will share his company's profits with them by paying them a fair wage as opposed to paying them meager wages to enrich himself. Conversely, an employee who loves his employer will work diligently to help grow the company's profits as opposed to doing the bare minimum with no other concern than getting a weekly paycheck.

Love is also essential in promoting an ethical relationship between business owners and customers. For example, a restaurant owner motivated by love will serve his customers the kind of food that has been advertised, not deceptively serve an inferior substitute. Similarly, a customer motivated by love for a restaurant owner will not dishonestly complain about a good meal in order to manipulate the owner into canceling his bill, because that would be stealing.

Diligence Promotes Ethical Business Practices

Diligence is the virtue that undergirds excellence in business. Employers recognize diligence in those employees who strive to perform their duties to the best of their abilities. Customers recognize diligence in a business that goes the extra mile to provide friendly customer service.

On the other hand, slothfulness is a vice that leads to poverty (Prov. 10:4; 13:4; 20:4). For those who are capable of working but refuse to do so, Scripture has this to say: "If any would not work, neither should he eat" (2 Thess. 3:10). Fallen people often look for ways to satisfy their desires for daily necessities without expending much effort.

Although the creational norm of labor has been frustrated by the Fall, Christians understand the importance of diligence in overcoming certain frustrations. For example, builders face frustration with their building projects (e.g., getting permits, returning defective material, facing delays). Nevertheless, a diligent builder overcomes these frustrations. The builder's work ethic produces a building that is structurally sound and within budget as much as possible.

Righteousness Promotes Ethical Business Practices

Righteousness is the virtue that guards against unethical compromises in our business dealings. Doing what is right must always take precedence over earning money, achieving success, and the thrill of competition. A Christian takes seriously the words of Jesus: "What shall it profit a man, if he shall gain the whole world, and lose his own soul?" (Mark 8:36). Being righteous in business is about learning how to succeed without losing your soul.

There will always be some wins and some losses for everyone in business. Righteousness is a virtue that enables Christians to accurately weigh the wins and losses. It evaluates each business decision by what matters for eternity. Sometimes an employee loses a job because of a righteous stand. Sometimes a business loses a customer because of a moral position on a cultural issue. But these are minor losses compared to the eternal losses some businesspeople will experience.

Of course, acting ethically in business can lead to success in this world. This is a good thing, and Christians should be thankful when God prospers them. Some of the most successful businesses have also been the most ethical. The world needs more businesspeople who are motived by love for others, diligent in all their work, and righteous in all their dealings. Having an ethical society depends upon it.

Thinking It Through 11.4

1. What are some common ethical problems in the workplace?

2. What are some common ethical problems in the marketplace?

3. What are the six core biblical principles for ethical business practices?

4. How does sensuality in advertising dehumanize people and destabilize society?

5. How does commercialism dehumanize people and destabilize society?

6. How do the virtues of love, diligence, and righteousness promote ethical business practices?

Terms to Remember

- race
- racism
- inequality
- abstinence
- recreational drugs
- bribery
- extortion
- exploitation
- commercialism

Scripture Memory

- Matthew 7:12

Understanding Ethics

1. What does the Bible teach about the origin of communication?
2. What does the Bible teach about substance abuse?
3. What does the Bible teach about truthfulness with respect to business practices?

Practicing Ethical Decision-Making

4. How should you respond when you hear a friend make a racist comment?
5. What are some responsible ways you can use social media?

Analyzing and Evaluating Ethical Claims

6. How would you respond to someone claiming that white responsibility is the solution to racial discrimination?
7. How would you respond to someone claiming that profanity and vulgarity are ethically neutral forms of communication?
8. How would you respond to someone claiming that gambling is a harmless activity?
9. How would you respond to the claim that love and profit are incompatible motives for Christians engaged in business?

Creating My Own Position Statements on Ethics

10. Write a one- to two-page paper that summarizes your understanding of a biblical position on racial discrimination. Explain why a biblical solution is more just than secular solutions.

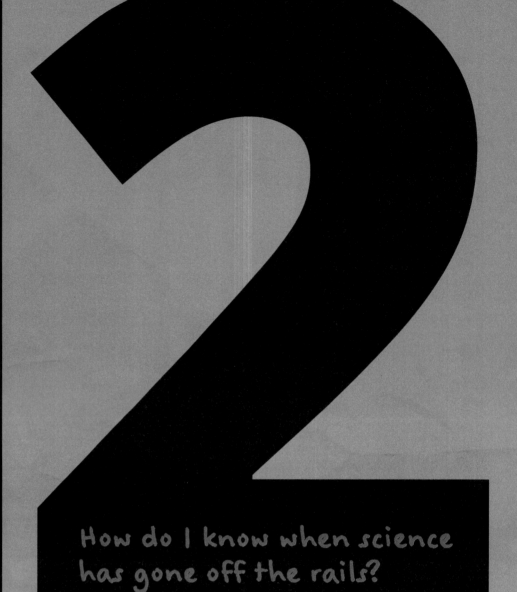

12

How do I know when science has gone off the rails?

Ethical Science

GENESIS 1:28–30

12.1 Stem Cell Research, Cloning, and Gene Editing

Have you noticed that sci-fi movies give technology a dominant role in the future? Technology—and its related field of science—features heavily in the undoing of society in end-of-the-world-type scenarios. Typically, it is a zombie apocalypse or computers or robots (artificial intelligence achieving a life of its own) taking over and oppressing humans. Futuristic sci-fi scenarios aside, technology is pressing forward at breakneck speed and in areas that directly impact human flourishing. What are Christians supposed to make of advances in medical science?

 ## INNOVATIONS IN MEDICAL SCIENCE

The study of the human body, on the cellular level specifically, is a field that has exploded in the past few decades. According to the Mayo Clinic, "Stem cell therapy, also known as regenerative medicine, promotes the repair response of diseased, dysfunctional or injured tissue using stem cells or their derivatives. It is the next chapter in organ transplantation and uses cells instead of donor organs, which are limited in supply."[1]

Stem cells were identified in the 1960s in mice,[2] and by 1981, embryonic stem cells were identified for the first time, also in mice.[3] One article explains,

> The human body contains more than 200 types of cells. Most of the cells are of a particular type and have a specific function. . . . **Stem cells** are different, though, in that they are relatively undifferentiated and unspecialized, meaning they have not yet obtained a special structure and function."[4]

Embryonic stem cells, available in embryos in their first few days of development, are the most versatile and valuable for medical scientific research because they can develop into any type of cell in the body.[5] But these gold mines of medical science research usually originate from mere days-old human embryos. The potential benefits of using embryonic stems cells seem to be tremendous. They may have great potential for treatment of serious diseases, injuries, and conditions. But the cost of those benefits is horrendous. Embryonic stem cells are normally derived from a destroyed human embryo.

Cloning is a related method of medical science research and itself is an area of ethical difficulty. **Cloning** is a form of reproduction, but instead of the natural method of using a sperm and an egg, genetic material from a single person is used to manufacture a new, almost identical, but separate, individual.[6] Joe Carter provides a helpful explanation of how cloning takes place:

> Human cloning is achieved by a technique referred to as somatic cell nuclear transfer (SCNT). The process involves introducing material from the nucleus of a human somatic cell (any biological cell forming the body of an organism, though for the purposes of SCNT, usually a skin cell) into an oocyte (a female egg cell that has not yet gone through the process to become an ovum) whose own nucleus has been removed or inactivated. The oocyte becomes an ovum that now no longer needs to be fertilized, because it contains the correct amount of genetic material. This new entity begins dividing and growing, yielding a cloned human embryo.[7]

There are three types of cloning: gene, reproductive, and therapeutic. Gene cloning is the least ethically problematic since it involves only copying certain genes or parts of DNA rather than producing a whole animal or person. This type is used for researching diseases and treating diseases in the laboratory. We will focus on the other two types of cloning. Reproductive cloning involves taking a cloned embryo and implanting it in a surrogate womb to produce a live offspring. This is how the famous groundbreaking animal clone, Dolly the sheep, was produced. And therapeutic cloning involves the creation of embryos from a donor's DNA with the intention of using embryonic stem cells to develop treatments for the donor or another person.[8]

Reproductive cloning of humans is riddled with ethical challenges and red flags. God's design for and blessing on human procreation is through a man and a woman within the covenant of marriage. Cloning eliminates the need for two parents and requires so much trial and error—the deaths of many human embryos—that trying to justify it biblically or ethically is impossible.

Therapeutic cloning has been envisioned to create "spare parts"[9] for individuals who need certain treatments. There appear to be significant obstacles to successful cloning and to using embryonic stem cells to treat disease in humans.[10] Additionally, the National Human Genome Research Institute says, "Despite several highly publicized claims, human cloning still appears to be fiction."[11] But just like embryonic stem cell research, therapeutic cloning would create life to extinguish it within days. That would be barbaric because it would be the sinful murdering of days-old people in the name of the advance of medical science. Cloning's sense of mystery, its reputation as a technological advancement, and its potential benefits don't remove its scientific, medical, legal, and ethical difficulties and ramifications. Christians must be aware of how a medical treatment was developed before being able to accept or support its use.

A final ethical difficulty in the field of medical science is gene editing. This innovative approach is just one more medical breakthrough that allows humans to manipulate the genetic makeup of a person's DNA. Joe Carter defines **gene editing** as "a form of genome engineering in which DNA is inserted, replaced, or removed from the genetic material of a cell using artificially engineered enzymes, or 'molecular scissors.'"[12] According to Gabriella Beer, "A genome is an organism's complete set of DNA." She continues by comparing it to a paper's structure by saying the following: "If the DNA code is a set of instructions that's carefully organised into paragraphs (genes) and chapters (chromosomes), then the entire manual from start to finish would be the genome."[13]

Dolly the sheep, the world's first cloned adult animal

DNA, made of genes, is stored in chromosomes in the cell nucleus.

All the DNA together makes up the genome.

Another important term in this field is **germline**. Once again Joe Carter offers a definition:

> Our genes, the basic physical and functional unit of heredity, are passed on from generation to generation through our sex cells (i.e., ovum [egg] and sperm). These sex cells are part of the germline. The term germline can refer to these cells in an individual or to the lineage of cells spanning generations of individuals. The other cells in the body that are not part of the germ line (and hence do not pass on traits to other generations of people) are called somatic cells.[14]

To date, the most profitable and efficient process to perform gene editing is the use of CRISPR. This acronym stands for clustered regularly interspaced short palindromic repeats. With this method, scientists insert engineered strands of DNA into the nucleus of a cell and use the protein Cas9 to cut the cell's DNA. The process ensures that the new DNA binds with the cell's DNA, essentially editing the cell's DNA sequence and creating a modified blueprint for producing future DNA.[15] The potential for gene editing is far reaching and includes gene therapy, where defective or diseased genes can be swapped out for healthy versions of the same gene. Even cancer is a target for treatment through developments of gene editing.

The key questions with gene editing (especially as its uses expand) are (1) why a modification is being made and (2) whether a modification will have enduring effects on future generations. Are genetic modifications being made to treat a real disease or condition that resulted from the Fall, or are they being made to boost characteristics we consider desirable? An alteration of a person's *somatic* cells to treat a disease in that person seems ethically acceptable. On the other hand, editing a person's *sex* cells (changing his or her germline) to permanently alter characteristics for following generations of offspring seems more questionable. Does God expect us to permanently reengineer certain aspects of the way He made us? Do we know all the consequences of such fundamental changes to our programming, especially if we pass those changes on to our posterity? Curing injuries and diseases is one thing. But to alter DNA God sovereignly gave us when we were just a single cell, merely for our own preferences, is to oppose the wisdom of His creative purposes.[16]

Each of these innovations in medical science raises multiple ethical concerns. Is it ethical to pursue long-term benefits for millions of people with harmful or life-threatening diseases by killing unborn babies? Is it ethical to create a life in a laboratory in a way that diverges from God's established norm of a husband and wife conceiving within the covenant of marriage? Is it ethical to permanently alter someone's genetic makeup for any reason (either a pragmatic enhancement or to correct hereditary diseases)?

BIBLICAL GUIDANCE FOR MEDICAL SCIENCE

Christians can't allow themselves to blindly follow technology wherever it takes them. People are made in God's image and therefore can achieve remarkable feats. Reading up on records people hold in all areas of athletics, art, and engineering proves this. Browse scientific and medical journals to learn of the most recent achievements in those fields. But the fact that people are *capable* of building supersonic jets, landing men on the moon, putting robots on Mars, exploring the deepest trenches in the ocean, creating babies in test tubes, and permanently altering someone's DNA doesn't automatically make each endeavor ethically valid. What teachings in Scripture provide foundations for our beliefs regarding advancements in medical technology and science?

God Is Sovereign over Life and Death

The first chapters in Genesis give us a look at who the Creator is, how He made man, and what expectations He gave to mankind. At the end of God's creation of all things, He capped it off with the creation of man and woman (Gen. 1:26–27; 2:7, 21–22). He also determined that all future generations of humans were designed

At what point in development is it no longer acceptable to experiment with human embryonic cells?

1 cell zygote
(fertilized egg)

2-cell zygote
24–36 hours

8-cell zygote
3 days old

to come through procreation by the joining together in marriage of one man with one woman (Gen. 1:28; 2:24; 4:1). We see in Scripture that God alone gives life and grants authority to take it away (Job 1:21; 12:10). God is sovereign over the life span of every human (Ps. 90:3; James 4:14–15). Because of the Fall, all people must die (Rom. 5:12; Heb. 9:27), yet God detests murder (Exod. 20:13). Even killing a newly formed, unborn baby in the womb or in a laboratory extinguishes the life of a person made in God's image (Gen. 9:6).

It is sinful and unethical to nurture the formation of a new life to serve a purpose (embryonic stem cell research or therapeutic cloning) that results in the guaranteed death of a human embryo. Francis Beckwith presents a case comparing the protection of a ten-year-old's life to protecting a fetal clone:

> If it is wrong to kill a 10-year-old as a result of taking his kidneys and giving them to people the government thinks will benefit society (e.g., scientific geniuses on the verge of curing cancer or AIDS), it is wrong to kill a 20-week-old fetal-clone as a result of taking his kidneys and giving them to his genetic progenitor, a scientific genius, who needs them to survive so that he may continue his work on cures for cancer and AIDS.[17]

Since life begins at conception, "farming" human embryos for research, stem cell collection, or even therapeutic use is appalling to the Christian ethic and devoid of any alignment with God's standards. This loss of life is the primary objection to these methods of medical science research. A righteous dominion over creation does not include the heartless formation and destruction of human embryos for the purpose of research or treatment. In response to sin's destructive effect on all creation, believers should seek the restoration of fallen creation rather than contribute to the worsening of its broken condition.

Humanity Rightly Pushes Back against the Effects of the Fall

There is good news for stem cell research: not all treatments derived from stem cells have to be from embryonic stem cells. There have been developments in stem cell research where certain types of valuable stem cells are collected from placentas[18] or developed from adult skin cells.[19] The Fall and the Curse corrupted every aspect of creation, including the cells and genes in the human body, and man still has to fulfill the God-given mandate to subdue and have dominion over the earth and everything in it (Gen. 1:28). Gene cloning is being used to this end. Stem cell research is revealing many insights and treatments that in effect help reverse the decay and disease brought on by the Fall. Scientists are hoping to use stem cells to research disease, treat a variety of conditions, and test drugs.[20]

God is in the business of restoring His creation by pushing back against the evil and damaging effects of the Fall. Prophets of the Old Testament, apostles of the New Testament, and Christ Himself engaged in many miracles of healing sickness, removing disease, and reversing death. These were real reversals of the effects of the Fall but only happened occasionally and on a very small scale. One day in the future, God will permanently restore all that the Fall has tarnished and twisted (Rom. 8:18–23; Rev. 21:1). But for now, what is the standard for knowing when humanity has gone beyond the bounds of what pushing back against the effects of the Fall is supposed to look like? What limits does developing therapeutic treatments have? Is there an

Blastocyte
5 days old

2 weeks old

4 weeks old

6 weeks old

ethical line that is crossed when we go from medical therapy to elective enhancement?

What limit does the Bible's teaching place on this type of medical science research? When the death of human embryos (immediately or after a few days or weeks) is the expected or unavoidable result, we have passed the limit. We can't accept a utilitarian approach where the focus is the advancement of technology for the betterment of future people at the cost of killing unborn people in the form of countless human embryos. That is unacceptable from a biblical worldview; it is a position that cannot be compromised.

Gene editing involves using technology and detailed knowledge of the human genome to attempt to treat diseases in people or prevent their children from inheriting certain diseases. Treating someone's current condition has fewer

ethical question marks than preventing diseases in someone's descendants would. Neither therapy is free from serious potential side effects, including death.[21] But gene editing has other possible uses. Are cosmetic changes—enhancements rather than therapies[22]—pushing back against the effects of the Fall, or are they merely serving someone's conception of beauty? Restoring the creation order is noble. But trying to improve on the creational order by permanently altering what humans look like and can physically do is a problematic idea that carries with it unforeseen consequences. God did design man to create, develop, and cultivate technologies to be used for taking dominion over and subduing creation. But God's rule and power and design of all things, including human appearances and abilities, remain God's prerogative and right (Job 40:6–42:4).

How should science improve my quality of life?

What about Elective Cosmetic Surgery?

Plastic surgeons can alter virtually any part of the human body. Elective cosmetic surgery is the non-therapeutic enhancement or alteration of a body part. This can include things like a facelift or a nose job. The purpose of elective cosmetic surgeries is often to satisfy the person's sense of beauty or worth. But not all plastic surgeries are of this nature. For example, those who suffer the loss of a limb or severe scarring due to an accident require plastic surgery to regain (as close as possible) the function and appearance their bodies had prior to their traumatic accident.

But what about physically changing the way one looks, in a surgical and essentially permanent fashion, based on feelings or perception rather than health? Regularly visiting the dentist to ensure good tooth and gum health is different than going for sessions of teeth whitening. Similarly. wearing contact lenses to correct one's poor vision is different from getting colored contact lenses to change one's eye color. These cosmetic changes aren't automatically unethical or sinful. But you should evaluate your priorities, motivations, and goals when considering whether to change your appearance, no matter how minor or major the change.

Gene editing might be able to produce a tall, green-eyed, slender-nosed, muscular boy. Even if that were realistically possible, how ethical would it be for parents to choose how their offspring look when God alone has had that prerogative since Eden? From the beginning, God has formed and fashioned humans, and that includes governing the way each gene and chromosome shapes the unborn

baby (Ps. 139:13–16). Shortness, brown eyes, big noses, and slender frames don't fall outside God's sovereignty and wisdom in how He creates each human being.

When one's physical appearance becomes an idol, Christians struggle to discern ethical choices from unethical ones. There is room to want to be attractive and to appreciate the inherent beauty in each image-bearer of God. But attractiveness keeps getting redefined by our culture, and it commonly becomes an end in itself. God is the ultimate standard for beauty and, therefore, what He does bears the marks of the beauty that He determines (Pss. 19:1; 27:4; 96:6). Our physical appearance isn't unimportant. But we need to stop to consider our underlying motivations and the long-term effects when considering elective cosmetic surgery.

THE PATH OF MEDICAL SCIENCE

Medical scientists today must feel like kids in a candy shop. Compared to just a few decades ago, the possibilities for treating diseases with stem cells, cloning, and gene editing are mind-boggling. From a Christian perspective, this reality increases the need for believers (as patients, doctors, or scientists) to use discernment as they engage with these aspects of medical science. Believers can only find wisdom and discernment by submitting to God's ways and by seeking His help to make hard decisions (Prov. 9:10; James 1:5). It is wise to recognize the limitations humans have. We aren't God, and even though we can't truly usurp His role, we should beware of trying to. In contrast to those who want to live as if their actions have no consequences and they are responsible to no one (Rom. 1:18–23), believers should recognize and honor God's power and authority.

Prudence works side-by-side with discernment and wisdom to not only assess a challenging situation correctly and intelligently but also carefully choose the best righteous alternative and seek a just outcome to the ethical difficulty. Discernment about the topics of this section will lead to confidence in your acceptance or rejection of treatments that are derived from stem cells, cloning, or gene therapy. Knowledge of the ins and outs of each of these subjects is extremely important in learning to discern their morality or immorality. It is worth repeating, especially with this topic, that the ends don't justify the means.

If medical scientific research can make leaps and bounds going forward without harvesting human embryos, the outlook will be much more positive. Altering the creational order through editing the germline is where gene editing technology may be heading. The Bible is full of instances of physical suffering and all the challenges of living in a fallen world in imperfect, dying bodies. And the teaching is that believers are to trust God and care for one another as they make their pilgrim journey to God's eternal kingdom (Rom. 8:23; 2 Cor. 5:2; James 5:13–14). The elimination of disease and sickness is promised for all believers in the new heaven and earth (Rev. 21:4)—not in the here and now. This truth must stay in the forefront of our minds when considering the trajectory of gene editing and the frontiers of medical science.

agents **GODLY ENGAGEMENT WITH MEDICAL SCIENCE**

Many of us might not pursue a career in the medical sciences. But it will still help us to consider which virtues should guide medical research that involves stem cells, cloning, and gene editing. We are impacted by the research that lies behind various treatments available to us—vaccinations, fertility treatments, autoimmune disease treatments, and more. Medical science today needs the influence of the Christian virtues of kindness, humility, and righteousness.

Ethical science requires showing kindness to others, especially kindness to the most vulnerable. David exemplified this type of kindness when he lavished it on Mephibosheth, who couldn't contribute to David's reign because of his physical disability (2 Sam. 9:3–9). Medical scientists do care about the physical well-being of children and adults who suffer from various diseases and conditions. But kindness to one group of people, the chronically sick, doesn't justify cruelty to another group of people, the unborn. We must recognize our limitations in providing ideal and comprehensive care to all people. All life is valuable, so kindness must be shown to the human embryos who are sometimes used as the building blocks of scientific advancement in this field. Kindness in medical science research involves looking for alternate ways to show kindness to those who have already been born—ways that don't involve killing those who have yet to be born.

Ethical science also requires humility on the part of the scientists. There is only one omnipotent Creator of every molecule in the universe—God. Scientists might feel like they can "play God," but in the end, man is man and God is God (Ps. 90:2). Psalm 8 wonderfully weaves together God's majesty, man's lowliness, and man's responsibility to properly steward the resources God has given him. Beware of the proud attitude captured in an interview with in vitro fertilization pioneer Robert Edwards:

> "I wanted to find out exactly who was in charge, whether it was God Himself or whether it was scientists in the laboratory."
>
> And what did he conclude? "It was us."[23]

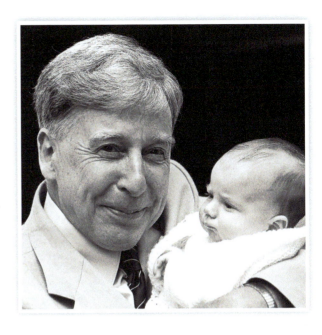

Since God is the giver and taker of life, we must approach these issues with great humility.

Ethical science also requires one to pursue righteousness. Researching and producing life in a laboratory still needs to meet God's standard of righteousness. Death is unnatural to God's original creation and is the enemy of mankind. However, that doesn't give man a free license to do everything and anything possible to slow down the process of death or lengthen the human life span (Ps. 90:10; 1 Cor. 15:26). Preserving life is generally good, as is improving one's quality of life. But both must be held in check by righteousness. Prudence plays the role of assisting the scientist, patient, citizen, or lawmaker to choose the righteous decision rather than the utilitarian one.

context THE NEXT STEP FOR INNOVATIVE SCIENTIFIC RESEARCH METHODS

Everyone would like to see Alzheimer's disease, Parkinson's disease, and cancer eradicated. To see these diseases go the way of smallpox and rinderpest,* total eradication,[24] would provide relief to millions of people and their families. Medical researchers must ask whether human embryos are being sacrificed to reach this goal and whether the creational order established by God is being disturbed. Believers need to ask these two questions as they watch society take the next steps in innovative medical science.

Thinking It Through 12.1

1. What scientific research methods raise ethical questions? Why do they?

2. What is the Bible's teaching on repairing the effects of the Fall through medical science?

3. Why do we need discernment regarding the consequences of scientific research and applications?

4. Which virtues are necessary to pursue advances in medical science ethically? Why these specific virtues?

12.2 Organ Donation and Transplantation

You have likely heard praise for athletes who suffer physical harm while exerting themselves to score a point or win the game. "No pain, no gain" is a popular motto. Athletes suffer bruises, scrapes, cuts, concussions, sprained joints, dislocated joints, pulled muscles, and broken bones, all for the sake of beating their opponents. But what is the ultimate sacrifice a person could give *for another person*? Their life. Images of soldiers dying in battle might come to your mind. Maybe your thoughts go to a parent saving his or her children from an attack and dying in the process. Christ's death for sinful humanity is the best example of ultimate sacrifice (Rom. 5:7–8).

rinderpest: a deadly disease affecting cattle in the 18th through 20th centuries[25]

Are there other contexts in which people would sacrifice their bodies for the good of others? Choosing to die for someone when there are non-lethal options available would be ethically wrong and is a form of suicide. Organ donation for transplantation is a great example of someone sacrificing his or her body, while alive or upon death, for the good of others. **Organ donation** is when a person willingly makes available certain organs or tissues to replace someone's defective or damaged organs or tissues. **Organ transplantation** is the replacement of a defective or damaged organ or tissue in one person with a healthy organ or tissue taken from another person. How should Christians view organ donation and transplantation?

 ## THE REALITY OF ORGAN DONATION AND TRANSPLANTATION

How should Christians view organ donation?

Organ transplantation is a relatively new medical wonder. In 1954 the first organ transplantation occurred—a kidney from a living donor.[26] Kidneys and lungs are paired organs, and as such living patients can donate one of their kidneys or all or part of one of their lungs. Other organs, parts of organs, and tissues such as the liver, pancreas, intestines, skin, bone, bone marrow, and blood can also be donated by living patients.[27] But for most organ transplants (e.g., heart transplants), a donation from a deceased donor is required. In a world of such advanced medical research and technology, why are organ transplantations even necessary?

Organ transplantations are necessary for people who have organs that have ceased to operate normally. Organ failure can be brought on by a hereditary condition. Sometimes lifestyle issues (e.g., habitual smoking, excessive drinking, poor diet) hasten the deterioration of certain organs. Injuries, diseases, or birth defects can also cause organ failure.[28]

This fallen world is an environment where brokenness and pain flourish like wildfire in a dry field (Gen. 3:16–18). Medical science pushes back against the unrelenting destructive effects of the Fall. Organ donation is a tool used by thoughtful and loving people to attempt to give someone the gifts of health and life. Organ donation is truly a matter of life or death. Over 106,000 people were on the national transplant waiting list in early 2022. At that time, every nine minutes a new individual was added to that waiting list. But sadly, around seventeen people waiting for a transplant die each day.[29]

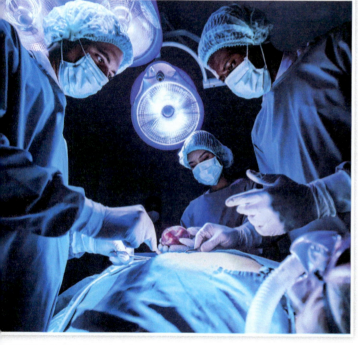

Doctors performing a heart transplant procedure

 ## THE BIBLICAL TEACHING ON ORGAN DONATION AND TRANSPLANTATION

What are the ethical red flags raised when discussing organ donation and transplantation? Does the teaching of the Bible oppose or support organ donation and transplantation?

The Personhood of Man

Some might equate the issues surrounding organ donation to the issues surrounding cremation.* The belief is that the body is disrespected if it is disturbed (reduced to ash or has organs removed) after death. The belief is that the personhood of man is affronted and the image of God in man is defaced if cremation or organ donation takes place. The Bible shines some light on the practices of burial and cremation—believers in both testaments exclusively practiced burial. But Scripture doesn't directly address the topic of organ donation and transplantation.

cremation: reducing a corpse to ashes by fire

Surely, God has made man in His image (Gen. 1:26–27). And man is body and soul. His personhood isn't wrapped up in either just the body or just the soul. It is the unity of these two parts of man, one material and one spiritual, that makes man the person he is. The body isn't a prison house for the soul, nor is the body an object of worship. People who undergo serious, life-altering surgeries (including amputations and the removal of injured or diseased organs) don't become any less of a person, nor is their personhood disrespected. Organ donation and transplantation are like other lifesaving surgeries. There must be a realistic understanding of what respect looks like when dealing with the body that the soul of a person has left behind at death. This realistic understanding must be rooted in the Bible. And a biblical understanding of man's personhood is critical in evaluating organ donation from a biblical worldview.

The biblical doctrine of bodily resurrection also impacts our understanding of the personhood of man. At Christ's return, all people will be resurrected either to life or to death (John 5:28–29; Rev. 20:6, 12–15). The bodies of all people, regardless of where or how they died, will be restored and reunited with their souls to spend eternity in the new creation or in the lake of fire (Rev. 21:1–3, 8). The effects of organ donation and transplantation are no obstacle to the power of God to reconstitute the bodies of all human beings. The same omnipotent God who created each atom in the universe out of nothing will reunite each person's soul with his or her resurrected body.

The Care of the Body

The overall tenor of Scripture regarding how we should use our bodies is responsible, faithful work, not sloth or entertainment (Eccles. 9:10; Matt. 24:45–46; 2 Thess. 3:10). Caring for or respecting our bodies doesn't mean isolation from anything that might endanger them. Believers are called to endure the hardships and physical sufferings that accompany a life in service of Christ (Luke 9:23; Rom. 12:1).

Is there a verse that teaches us to care for the bodies of others? What about Matthew 22:39, "Thou shalt love thy neighbour as thyself"? This verse doesn't teach believers to actively love and care for and pamper themselves. It teaches believers to go to the same extremes to which we love ourselves in loving others. We are already highly interested in our own well-being, including the well-being of our bodies. While we shouldn't be self-consumed, we should care for the well-being of others (including the well-being of their bodies) to the same extent we care for our own. Ethical organ donation is a selfless act of love for someone with a dire physical need.

Caring for our own bodies or for the bodies of others requires prioritizing the well-being and life of each person made in God's image. The following points express the biblical priority of life as well as the dignity of everyone in life or death:

- It is wrong for someone to donate an organ if he or she knows that the donation would lead to his or her own death.
- It is wrong to take an organ from a terminally ill but living person if taking that organ would result in that person's death.
- It might be unwise for a living donor with health risks to donate an organ, because that donation could result in serious harm to the donor. But as a rule, organ donations from living donors aren't wrong.
- It is wrong to disrespect the body of the deceased when legally procuring the donor's organs.

An ethical approach to organ donation and transplantation provides people with the opportunity to show loving care for the body of the organ donor and for the body of the organ recipient.

Jehovah's Witnesses and Blood Transfusions

Jehovah's Witnesses, an unorthodox religion with a global following, believe that any introduction of blood into their bodies violates Scripture. They abstain from blood, including blood transfusions, based on their interpretation and application of texts like Genesis 9:4, Leviticus 17:14, and Acts 15:20. They say, "God commands that we abstain from blood because what it represents is sacred to him."[30] Though the organization did oppose organ transplants in the 1960s–70s,[31] Jehovah's Witnesses aren't entirely opposed to organ transplants now, provided all the blood is drained from the organ. But in their attempt to respect the sanctity of life, they elevate blood to a position that is not based in faithful exegesis of Scripture. And in doing so, they deprive themselves or others of life when a necessary blood transfusion is rejected.[32] Bible-believing Christians can submit to God's teaching in the three passages mentioned by abstaining from eating or drinking blood. Blood transfusions and organ transplantations are distinct practices from making a meal out of animal blood.

THE ETHICAL LIMITS OF ORGAN DONATION

What happens when you push a good thing too far? The saying "Too much of a good thing is a bad thing" is usually true. An occasional bowl of ice cream before bed (or any time of day for that matter) is a good thing. But multiple bowls of ice cream every day would be bad for anyone's health. Working a job you enjoy to make an income you need is a good thing. But to put in forty-plus hours per week on top of finishing high school would be a bad thing. You would begin to give up other obligations and activities that are good and necessary (personal, educational, familial, religious, social).

Organ donation and transplantation are good, in that people who would otherwise die or live in chronically poor health can benefit from the organs donated to them. But if these life-saving medical practices are pushed too far, then ethical lines are crossed. This can result from a consequentialist approach in which the end seems so beneficial that the way one accomplishes that goal is nearly irrelevant. How could this go wrong with organ transplantation? Consider the following scenarios:

- Organs are taken from individuals who said no to organ donation.
- Organs are taken from individuals who were silent on the question of organ donation, but consent isn't sought from family members.
- Organs and tissues are harvested from aborted unborn babies.
- Organs and tissues are harvested from laboratory-created human embryos or fetuses.
- Organs and tissues are harvested from cloned human embryos or fetuses.
- Organs are taken from those who have chosen physician-assisted suicide to end their suffering.
- Organs are taken from elderly or disabled people who are euthanized.

Organ donation veers into questionable territory when consent isn't given or can't be given by the individual whose organs or tissues are taken. Organ donation is abused when an unethical practice is encouraged directly or indirectly for the sake of obtaining useful organs and tissues. Taking organs should be off the table if a person would be brought into existence for the purpose of harvesting their stem cells, tissues, or organs. Abortion, suicide, and euthanasia are all murder and are entirely unethical, regardless of any possible benefit of taking and transplanting healthy organs.

When death becomes simply an obstacle on the way to organ procurement, we permit our desire to mitigate the organ shortage to undermine our attempts to keep company with the dying. GILBERT MEILAENDER[33]

The scarcity of viable organs from deceased individuals adds pressure to the temptation to push the ethical limits of organ donation. Only three people out of one thousand die in a way where their organs are salvageable for organ donation.[34] Typically, those who suffer an accident involving serious head trauma die in a way that their heart and lungs can be artificially supported, even though they are dead, to preserve the organs until they arrive at a hospital where they are removed.[35]

Having no ethical limits or boundaries for those who desire more widespread organ donation and transplantation would quickly turn into a futuristic science-fiction horror film. Similar to the serious ethical violations involved in embryonic stem cell research, cloning, and germline gene editing, harvesting organs from the most vulnerable in society is extremely problematic. Believers are called to demonstrate virtuous character while following a careful decision-making process regarding organ donation and transplantation.

Animal Organ Transplantation?

How ethical is using organs or tissues from animals to supplement the limited availability of human organs for transplantation? Medical scientists and doctors collaborated and successfully transplanted a heart from a genetically-modified pig into a man with terminal heart disease in early 2022. He died two months later,[36] but the science behind animal organ transplantation is continuing to develop.

It is one thing to use animal tissues or organs to replace defective or damaged human tissues or organs. Since as far back as 1838, pig skin has been used to graft on humans who had serious burns.[37] However, it is an entirely different thing, having serious ethical ramifications, to alter a human or animal embryo in such a way that a hybrid is created. To produce an embryo that has animal and human genes, DNA, organs, and features is to cross the line of human and animal differentiation. God established this division when He created all things (Gen. 1:20–30). Although both man and beast are described as having "the breath of life" (Gen. 2:7; 7:15), only man is created in the image of God (Gen. 1:26–27). Blurring or erasing this distinction is a direct affront to God's wise and purposeful creational order.

AN ETHICAL APPROACH TO ORGAN DONATION

Christians need to have reasons for their convictions for or against organ donation. They need to ground their beliefs in Scripture and, when confronted with challenging ethical situations, be ready to make the right decisions. You might think one way about organ donation when looking at it from afar, considering it theoretically. But you might change your mind when you or someone close to you requires an organ transplant to continue living. Virtues serve as guardrails to keep believers on the right ethical and moral path when navigating this challenging topic.

Compassion, prudence, and righteousness are necessary for discerning when organ donation is appropriate. A common scenario is when a live donor is required to provide one of his or her kidneys to someone experiencing kidney failure. Compassion plays the role of seeing a legitimate need; a donor who is a perfect match could offer his or her kidney, out of loving compassion, to meet that need. But prudence also plays a role in determining whether the donor can assume the risks of the surgery and of living the rest of life with only one kidney. Life situations, health issues, and other factors all demand prudence to help determine whether this is a good choice for the donor. And righteousness is also necessary in this situation because the motive, means, and ends all have to be righteous by God's standards for Christians to participate in organ donation. It would be ungodly for a person to knowingly put his or her life at great risk by donating a kidney. Changing which person is seriously ill is not the purpose of organ donation, nor does it really solve the problem. Offering payment for an organ to a living donor clouds judgment and opens the door for abuse and pressure. This would be a total lack of prudence as well as being unrighteous.

What if a person who expressed a desire to donate his or her body or organs passes away without any written record of personal wishes, but the closest family members don't want to go through with it? Prudence is required to discern whether the deceased person's wishes were well-informed and definitely expressed. But if the person's wish to donate is confirmed, wouldn't it be righteous for the family to respect the wishes of the deceased and allow the organ donation to take place? Compassion for their loved one and for all who would benefit from the donation should also make the right decision clear. Prudence may also be required by medical professionals to navigate the wishes of the deceased and the wishes of the family. Righteousness plays the role of making sure that the motives, means, and outcomes in such scenarios conform to God's righteous standards.

On the other hand, prudence is also involved in making sure a loved one who wishes to donate isn't pressured or neglected in receiving care before he or she dies. It would be unrighteous for the doctors to prematurely and purposefully reduce the number of the loved one's final days or adjust his or her care simply to hasten an organ donation.

CONCLUSION

Take care not to force organ donation and transplantation. Done ethically, organ donation and transplantation are great benefits of modern medical science. Even an ethical use of animal-derived organs or tissues holds some promise to contribute to preserving human life. The need for donated organs is overwhelming, but that doesn't eliminate the ethical approach required for this endeavor. Remember the virtues of compassion, prudence, and righteousness as you engage with this challenging topic.

Thinking It Through 12.2

1. List various scenarios that require the donation and transplantation of organs.

2. What is the biblical teaching regarding the nature of personhood and the care of the body?

3. List various societal consequences of exploitative organ harvesting.

4. In what ways are compassion, prudence, and righteousness necessary to discern when organ donation is appropriate?

12.3 Conservation, Environmentalism, and Animal Rights

Why do homeowners post No Trespassing and Private Property signs at the edges of their property? Is it simply because they like their privacy? Most do, but the main reason homeowners post these kinds of signs is because they don't want trespassers stealing, vandalizing, or messing with their stuff. Most people enjoy a clean, organized, and attractive home and yard. However, unless measures are taken to protect and maintain the place we live, chaos and ruin tend to follow.

Christians point to Adam and Eve's fall into sin as the reason for everything bad and wrong in the world (Gen. 3:6, 16–19; Rom. 5:12; 8:20–22). Unbelievers point to the second law of thermodynamics that states entropy is inevitable, that energy is being spent and therefore the material world is running down, not getting better. But beyond natural decay, many believe that, if the earth is the Titanic, then mankind has already rammed into the iceberg and the ship is sinking. Describing a 2019 United Nations General Assembly meeting, an article from the UN's website carried this title: "Only 11 Years Left to Prevent Irreversible Damage from Climate Change, Speakers Warn during General Assembly High-Level Meeting."[38] According to this position, by 2030 we will have compromised the earth in such a way that catastrophe and global harm will be the unavoidable reality.

Society has come up with three main approaches to deal with the current and future state of our planet. Conservation, environmentalism, and animal rights are offered as solutions to the damage man has inflicted, and is inflicting, upon the earth and its non-human inhabitants. **Conservation** is the effort to preserve or improve certain resources so that they remain available for use in the future. This applies to natural resources such as water, trees, plants, and animals; to air quality; and to the climate overall. **Environmentalism** seeks to protect the environment from human destruction and improve the conditions of the environment through social and political action. **Animal rights** is the idea that animals are entitled to the same rights and privileges that humans are entitled to—no exploitation and no abuse—and generally includes the notion that any killing or prolonged caging of animals to benefit humans is unethical.

ETHICAL ISSUES IN CREATION

Is the human race on the verge of extinction? We're not talking about extinction from an asteroid or nuclear holocaust but from humans overpopulating the earth, polluting it, and depleting its resources beyond repair. Organizations like the World Economic Forum take the data they have and make projections and predictions about the next ten, twenty, or one hundred years. Their presentation is apocalyptic when describing the floods, fires, droughts, and destruction they say await the earth if major changes are not made.[39] Ken Magnuson summarizes the worries by saying the following:

> Many concerns are raised about the environment and its future. The most prominent concern, and one that relates to many of the others, is global warming or climate change. . . . Related concerns include rise in sea level, overpopulation and the earth's "carrying capacity," biodiversity loss and species extinction, deforestation, air and water pollution, human consumption and waste, and sustainable farming, to name a few.[40]

So, should Christians join the ranks of those predicting the earth's impending demise? Is humankind really set on a path to ruin our planet unless drastic measures are taken?

One organization called The Partnership Project partners with several environmental groups "addressing the climate crisis, accelerating the transition to clean energy, reducing the use of fossil fuels, and amplifying the work of environmental justice."[41] In this organization's own words: "We are the Partnership Project, your partner to save the planet."[42] Notice how they end their list with climate.

Why has The Partnership Project gotten behind the specific issues it has outlined? The environmental and climate research done by scientists includes gathering data from the atmosphere, water, and ice caps and comparing that information to data from previous decades. It is true that no one benefits from nor enjoys a damaged climate or polluted environment. But one's understanding of the source and purpose of creation also directs one's use and stewardship of that creation. Those who don't have Christ only have this world. Many of the ethical issues on conservationism's and environmentalism's agendas are hot-button issues for unbelievers for this very reason. At the same time, Christians can put forth helpful questions and endeavor to answer them:

- Is the earth warming?
- Are humans contributing to the warming of the earth?
- Are the consequences of a warming earth good, bad, or mixed?
- What are the proposed solutions?
- What is the impact of those solutions?

Christians can't ignore accurate data and statistics gathered from the environment. Even so, believers must carefully distinguish a secular and worldly interpretation of the data from a biblically informed interpretation, one that incorporates God's design for the earth and man's responsibility to use and protect the earth and its resources. The significant environmental issues brought about by man's irresponsibility must be dealt with biblically and ethically. A proper biblical worldview is necessary for this endeavor.

Another ethical issue in creation is that of animal rights. According to PETA (People for the Ethical Treatment of Animals), one of the most outspoken and proactive defenders of animal rights, people are animals, and all animals are beings and should thus be afforded the same treatment as human beings.[43] Make sure you notice that their use of the term "ethical" by no means implies a biblical ethic. The founder of PETA, Ingrid Newkirk, made this statement that clearly explains this organization's view on human and animal life: "When it comes to pain, love, joy, loneliness, and fear, a rat is a pig is a dog is a boy. Each one values his or her life and fights the knife."[44]

Is a vegan lifestyle the only option for people who care about animals? Has humanity been abusing and exploiting animals, either out of ignorance or purposefully, for millennia? The question of animal rights affects farming, food production, medical research, scientific research, pharmaceutical research, clothing, accessories, entertainment, pets, and even how one treats unwelcome animals in one's home. The issues raised touch on how we live every day of our lives! There must be a biblical response to how we can properly and ethically treat animals and care for creation.

> "The earth is the habitat not only for human beings but for other creatures as well, and human beings have the responsibility to manage it well for our own sake, for our descendants, and for other creatures."
>
> KEN MAGNUSON[45]

BIBLICAL CARE FOR CREATION

Do you step on ants that cross your path? Do you swat flies in your kitchen in the summer? Do you kill or trap pests on your property? If so, that would imply a certain dominance or advantage that humans have over animals. Animals do attack and sometimes kill people. Many insects, reptiles, and fish bite or sting in self-defense or as a reflex, and many of these animals are venomous or are otherwise capable of lethal attacks. The Bible explains why humanity's relationship to animals went from peaceful coexistence to fearful dread—sin (Gen. 2:19–20; 9:2). Even man's relationship to plants and the natural world in general changed as a result of the Fall and the Curse (Gen. 2:8, 15; 3:17–19).

We need biblical guidance to know how to relate to creation in general and to animals in particular. We can't just do what has always been done if there isn't a biblical basis for those habits. Psalm 104 describes God's greatness and how that is shown in His governing all of creation. God is praised for His unfathomable wisdom in creating everything (104:24). This psalm serves as a guide for how man, made in God's image, should care and provide for and govern over creation. And man needs wisdom—wisdom God provides—to care for creation well.

In the United States, states have specific hunting seasons and game laws to control animal populations. How might this be good dominion over animals?

Responsible Stewardship of Resources

God created everything for His own glory (John 1:3; Col. 1:16). But God delegated to man the responsibility of stewarding all the resources that He made (Gen. 1:26–31). This was a very good creation, all of it, and man had the privilege to work and tend the garden where God placed him (Gen. 2:15). Dutch theologian Abraham Kuyper reinforces this by noting some biblical reasoning which explains why we should apply good stewardship of creation to animals specifically:

> Only because God gives the animals to us and further grants us permission to slaughter and eat them do we human beings have the right to use animals in this way. . . . The commonly accepted view that people may do with an animal just as they please "because it is only an animal" must for that reason be resisted by all Christians, because the animals are not ours but God's. We do not have the least right to them, because we did not create them. . . . Without God's permission we have no right to haul even one fish out of the water and kill it, to shoot down and pluck a single bird, or hunt and slay any game.[46]

No part of creation was off-limits from man's subduing and having dominion over it (Ps. 8:4–8). Only man was made in God's image, which made him the only being capable of having a relationship with God and governing creation.

Man was designed to use the earth and its natural resources to flourish, resulting in praise to God for His gift of creation (Deut. 8:7–10). Nevertheless, God instructed the people of Israel to be responsible and wise when besieging an enemy city. He told them not to cut down the fruit trees (Deut. 20:19–20). It wasn't a ban on cutting down any tree, because some could be used for their wood, but they were not to cut down the trees that would continue to produce fruit after the battle was over.

John 6:12 contains an interesting short phrase that impacts our current discussion: "that nothing be lost." Jesus had just fed more than five thousand people with five loaves of bread and two fish. But Jesus didn't want to see the extra twelve baskets full of leftovers go to waste—even though He was able to miraculously produce more food. We can't know for sure what the disciples did with the extra food. It was likely given to the poor or maybe even consumed by them as they continued their journey. The point is, God expects us to be good stewards of the resources (e.g., food, water, energy, clothes) He has provided for us, so we should not be wasteful.

Animals for Food

Are vegetarians* or vegans* more ethical in not using animals for food? Where do Christians turn to justify mass-producing animals and animal products for food? On this side of the Fall, in God's reiteration of the Creation Mandate to Noah, we find God's pronouncement that all animals are available to humans as food (Gen. 9:1–3). This passage is in essence a repetition of the Creation Mandate originally given to Adam in Genesis 1:26–28 (see also 1:29–30). But Genesis 1 was prior to the Fall, when humans didn't use animals for food. On this side of the Fall, after God inaugurated the use of animals for humans by fashioning animal skin coverings for Adam and Eve (Gen. 3:21), animals serve the purpose of feeding humans and providing for their needs. Mankind is free to enjoy scrambled eggs, milkshakes, and hamburgers.

The New Testament contains a few mentions of the good use of animals for food (Acts 10:10–16; Rom. 14:14; 1 Tim. 4:3–4). These examples already assume that man has been eating meat, at least certain kinds, all along. God didn't change His position on giving us animals for food (although He did regulate clean and unclean foods for Israel for a season). What He revealed to us in His Word, in both testaments, remains true.

The humane use of animals for human well-being and flourishing isn't pragmatic or consequentialist. It is obedience to God's command to do so.

Treatment of Animals

The fact that God has given humans animals to use for food doesn't mean that we may mistreat, abuse, or torture animals. Since man is made in the image of God, man is still to accurately reflect the image of his kind Creator as best as he can. To mistreat an animal for fun or sport is cruel and evil. A proverb teaches us on this topic: "A righteous man regardeth the life of his beast: but the tender mercies of the wicked are cruel" (Prov. 12:10). In the fourth commandment on keeping the Sabbath day, God made provision for work animals to rest (Exod. 20:10; Deut. 5:14). Other laws in the Old Testament also take into account the considerate and good treatment of animals (Deut. 22:4, 6; 25:4). God even allowed Balaam's donkey to call out Balaam for beating her unjustly (Num. 22:23–32)!

Despite today's advancements in scientific research and technology, the use of animals for experimentation remains critical. The fact that an animal subject might suffer some pain during the experimentation doesn't invalidate the use of an animal for that trial. The alternative would be to use a human subject or to release a product for consumption that could be harmful if not lethal to the customer or patient. This is an unfortunate reality due to the fallen world we live in. How we treat other people and how we treat animals tells a lot about us, for good and for bad. God cares for the creatures He created (Ps. 147:9; Matt. 10:29, 31). His people should show them equally humane treatment in all normal circumstances.

The humane treatment of animals used to contribute to human well-being and flourishing is ethical because God placed animals under human stewardship.

vegetarian: does not eat any type of meat

vegan: does not eat any meat or animal-based product of any kind

Caring, Not Worshiping

In prioritizing the worth of humans, animals, and creation in general, humans come out on top every time. Christ reaffirmed this truth in His parable about doing good on the Sabbath—man is better than a sheep (Matt. 12:12). Although man is the pinnacle of God's creation, he is still a created being, and we shouldn't worship anyone except God (Exod. 20:3). God alone is deserving of our worship (Exod. 20:4–6). In discussing the extent to which man rebels against God and sins against Him, Paul pointed out the idols man makes out of creation instead of worshiping his Creator (Rom. 1:22–25). We must take great care not to elevate any part of God's creation, be it animals or stars, higher than God Himself. Believers are obedient stewards of God's creation when they care for it well and use it for the purposes God has intended.

The support of human life through fishing, farming, mining, and processing in factories is according to God's design. The ultimate goal of humanity isn't to have as many untouched and undeveloped natural landscapes as possible. The Bible gives humans the responsibility to steward creation, and believers should take seriously what wise stewardship of creation looks like. That might well include things like recycling, conserving energy and resources, and safely disposing of waste. There is a balance that must be struck. Future generations need to use this planet and its resources, but we don't get there by worshiping creation. We need to care for creation without elevating it above the Creator.

CONSEQUENCES OF MISUSING CREATION

ends

The fact that God entrusted man with the Creation Mandate at the outset of creation doesn't mean that man does a good job subduing and having dominion over creation. Because of the Fall, abuses and excesses in using creation became not only possibilities but realities. The media does a good job at presenting doom and gloom photos and videos of our broken planet. Skinny polar bears, turtles skewered by plastic straws, and seagulls floundering in oil slicks combine with aerial or satellite imagery of melting ice caps, retreating glaciers, dwindling rainforests, and growing deserts. These images might all be realities, but what is presented as causing all these tragedies and what responses are proposed reveal one's worldview concerning conservation, environmentalism, and animal rights.

Most agree on what qualifies as a blatant misuse of creation. Examples might include destroying magnificent natural rock formations, cutting down emblematic trees, pumping toxic waste straight into a body of water, or releasing harmful factory gases and smoke straight into the atmosphere. The two former examples are misuses of creation by someone raising a hand against God and His beautiful creative abilities. The latter two examples are misuses of creation because they affect millions of people and multiple generations of people. Air and water pollution are serious and growing problems in many parts of the world. You don't have to be a biblical scholar, tenured professor, or acclaimed scientist to know that we need clean air to breathe and clean water to drink to survive.

Is it the end of the world if you occasionally litter small pieces of trash? Water treatment plants can handle a few toxins in the ground water, right? Leaving lights on in your home and letting the water run a long time in the shower aren't that big a deal, are they? There is a principle that's also the title of a children's book: *If Everybody Did.*[47] You can imagine the consequences of certain actions if everybody (billions of people) did them repeatedly. On the flip side, if everyone planted a few trees to make up for all that are being cut down, you can imagine the positive benefits that might result. A concerted effort goes a long way in either direction! Loving one's neighbor and doing unto others as you would want them to do to you are biblical principles (Luke 6:31; 10:27). A biblical view of creation care results in positive outcomes for creation and our neighbors, not negative consequences.

There are negative consequences to misusing creation in two different ways that are on opposite ends of a spectrum. On one end of the spectrum is an unhindered, short-sighted, and careless use of energy sources, food sources, and other natural resources. This approach would not take into account the effects on the environment of obtaining and using energy sources and other natural resources. Neither would this approach consider the side effects of depleting a food source and the chain effect that would have on the rest of the food chain and ecosystem. On the other end of the spectrum would be eliminating or severely limiting the use of certain energy sources, to the extent that there would be an energy crisis resulting in no access to energy or extremely high prices for that energy. Outlawing or severely limiting certain food sources would have a similar effect—food shortages or extremely high prices for some foods.

Most environmentalists don't like the extraction, refining, and burning of fossil fuels (e.g., petroleum, natural gas, coal). They consider carbon emissions to be one of the lead factors in what they describe as climate change. Others propose the use of nuclear energy, but the potential for leaks in the plants (e.g., the Fukushima Daiichi accident, March 2011) and the disposal of radioactive waste are both problematic. But hydraulic, wind, and solar energies aren't sufficient for the current usage of the world population. There must be wisdom and balance in the pursuit of clean energy. Regarding animal species, Adam named land animals and birds as one of the ways he ruled over the creation God made and put him in charge of (Gen. 2:19–20). When an animal species disappears forever, that specific reflection of God's creative power and genius disappears as well. Even when plant species go extinct something is lost. To poach an animal to extinction or to wipe out an animal completely that is a perceived nuisance is a gross misuse of creation.

The western rhinoceros and the passenger pigeon are two examples of extinct species.

How involved should I be in caring for God's creation?

agents CHRISTIANS CARING FOR CREATION

When you stayed the night at a friend's house, did your parents ever tell you to leave the place better than you found it? This teaches a principle that we can apply to caring for creation. Improving what you use and replacing what you have consumed or broken expresses the virtue of gratitude. Being truly thankful for the creation God has entrusted us with should motivate us to take care of, even improve, the parts of creation we come into contact with. To mistreat or exploit aspects of creation, spoiling those aspects for anyone else now or in the future, shows ingratitude and selfishness.

Christians should also exhibit humility in caring for creation. God has entrusted us with a great task—to govern creation in a way that imitates God's governance of all things. Any comparison of yourself or your work to God and His work should cause you to be humble. And it takes humility to not think we are entitled to waste resources and pollute the environment irresponsibly and unnecessarily. It takes humility to see the other people who are affected by our actions when it comes to our use or abuse of God's creation. Humility also submits to God's power to sustain the earth and all He has created until He brings judgment and restoration—rather than believing humanity has power to either save the world or destroy it.

Lastly, Christians need to approach caring for creation with prudence. Issues concerning the environment and shared resources that every human needs and uses call for wisdom and discernment. Much of the decision-making is done by governments and community leaders, but individuals can have a say in certain local decisions as well. The virtue of prudence allows Christians to determine whether a certain choice is helpful in the long run as well as the short run. A certain course of action might have ramifications that must be studied and addressed. Prudence helps Christians apply their biblical worldview to guide their interpretation of the latest conservation effort or environmental concern. Whether to speak up regarding a restrictive or permissive measure calls for prudence.

RESPONDING TO EXTREME VIEWS OF CARING FOR CREATION context

How would you respond to individuals with extreme responses to the current state of our world's climate, energy production, and food consumption? Start thinking about the short- and long-term effects of those who abuse creation. Also consider the short- and long-term effects of those who idolize creation. Do you personally have a tendency either way? To what areas of your daily routine should you apply gratitude, humility, and prudence in order to care for creation better? When it comes to conservation, environmentalism, and animal rights, strive to be a responsible and obedient steward of what God has generously blessed you with.

Teen Climate Crisis activists in London, England, strike from school as part of the global movement started by Swedish teen Greta Thunberg, demanding climate action from political leaders.

Thinking It Through 12.3

1. List the main ethical issues regarding the environment and animals. Why did these make the list?

2. What is the biblical teaching regarding the Christian's relationship to the natural world?

3. What are some consequences of unbiblical views of creation stewardship?

4. How do the virtues of gratitude, humility, and prudence motivate appropriate care for the earth and animals?

5. How would you respond to someone who abuses creation?

6. How would you respond to someone who idolizes creation?

Terms to Remember

- stem cells
- embryonic stem cells
- cloning
- gene editing
- germline
- organ donation
- organ transplantation
- conservation
- environmentalism
- animal rights

Scripture Memory

Genesis 1:28–30

Understanding Ethics

1. How do you know when science has gone off the rails in the areas this chapter covers?
2. How should science improve your quality of life?
3. How should Christians view organ donation?
4. How involved should you be in caring for God's creation?

Practicing Ethical Decision-Making

5. How would you respond to a family member who asked whether becoming an organ donor (live or upon death) was an ethical thing to do? How would you respond to a family member who needed an organ to survive but wasn't sure whether receiving an organ transplant was right for a Christian?
6. Suppose an employee of the power company in your town visits your home and gives your family a box of energy-saving LED lightbulbs that he recommends you substitute for the incandescent bulbs you currently use. At the dinner table that evening, what suggestion do you offer if most in your home prefer the warmer feeling of incandescent light?

Analyzing and Evaluating Ethical Claims

7. How would you respond to someone who says that the Bible has nothing to say about science, much less ethical science and how it applies to a whole society?
8. How would you respond to someone who justifies using embryonic stem cells to save the lives of many people and improve the lives of many more?
9. Medical students and scientific researchers need to practice and study the human body in detail. The use of a cadaver is the best way to do this, as it gives the closest parallel to doing the same procedures and seeing the same anatomy on a live patient. Do you think Christians should be able to donate their bodies to science? Explain.
10. Does the assumption that those who recycle follow a liberal agenda and those who sacrifice the environment to benefit business follow a conservative agenda hold true? Explain your answer while discussing the value of recycling and the significance of industry's impact on the environment.

Creating My Own Position Statements on Ethics

11. Based on your understanding of the image of God in man and the personhood of all human beings, how would you respond to the ethical questions raised by stem cell research, cloning, and gene editing?
12. Apply the Creation Mandate and the virtues of gratitude, humility, and prudence to the ethics of a Christian's obligation to care for creation.

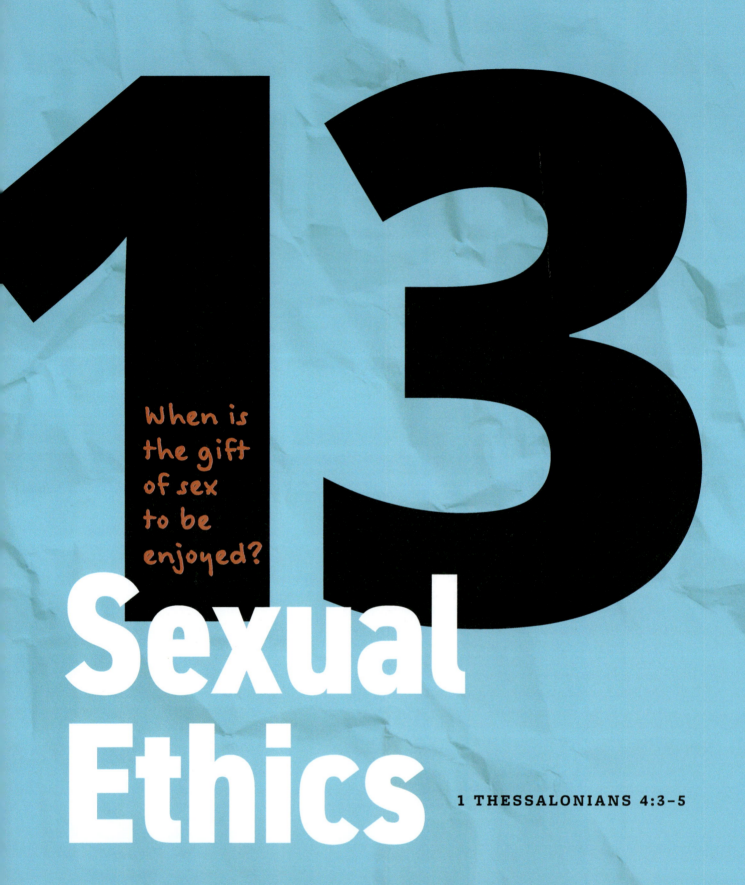

13

When is the gift of sex to be enjoyed?

Sexual Ethics

1 THESSALONIANS 4:3–5

13.1 Marriage and Divorce

How do you view marriage? What has shaped your view?

Maybe you've always dreamed of the perfect wedding and of getting married to the "one and only." You can just imagine what a satisfying life of enjoyment lies ahead of you as you fulfill all your dreams alongside your soulmate. Or maybe your experiences in real life have led you to be more cynical. You've mostly observed heartbreak, conflict, and betrayal. You think it's best to avoid taking the chance of getting hurt.

Or perhaps you want to avoid either idealism or cynicism regarding marriage. You know that marriage is a lifelong commitment and that there are many trials along the way. But you also know that a good marriage is worth fighting for because marriage was beautifully designed by God. And maybe you have been privileged to observe the faithful efforts, if not of your own parents, of godly men and women in your church.

COMMON ATTITUDES TOWARD MARRIAGE

Our world has normalized disregard for marriage. Marriage is still common—though less so than in the past. For the most part, it's viewed as optional and easily dissolved. Far from being seen as an essential institution, marriage seems to many to be an unnecessary formality. It's now hard for many young people to imagine a world in which marriage—the lifelong commitment of spouses until death parts them—was the norm for the majority of people.

How has our society been transformed with respect to marriage in recent decades? Although there may be many factors, one idea and one legal reality undergird what has become the "new normal" in recent generations. The one fundamental idea that seems so common-sense that most people couldn't fathom thinking otherwise is the idea of compatibility. The one legal reality that has made possible our current situation is the introduction of "no-fault divorce" laws.

The prevailing idea of **compatibility** is that couples must be able to get along well to remain together. To get along well requires couples to share similar interests, goals, temperaments, likes and dislikes, enjoyable intimacy, continuing attraction, and so on. To discern whether they are compatible, couples need to try each other out to find out how well they work together. This involves recreational dating (with generally low moral boundaries) and may include **cohabitation**: living together before marriage. Only after testing each other out (sometimes long-term) might a couple decide to get married. Of course, many couples don't see much point in getting married if they were able to cohabit for so long without marriage. Nonetheless, many couples end up getting married if that is deemed advantageous to both parties involved.

The legal reality of **no-fault divorce** allows for the dissolution of a marriage for as minor a cause as one person's claim of incompatibility. In other words, a divorce can happen at will for almost any subjective reason one person gives for desiring that divorce. Not much can stop it. This means that individuals remain viewed as individuals even in a marriage: self-interest can rip such a marriage apart at a whim. The marriage relationship is never legally viewed as a one-flesh relationship that should never be torn apart.

acts GOD'S CREATION OF THE MARRIAGE COVENANT

In contrast to what has been normalized in society, the Bible stands as a witness to God's original design for marriage. God created marriage to be a lifelong covenant of love between one man and one woman. God created woman to be a counterpart to man, to complement and complete what was lacking in him when he was alone (Gen. 1:27; 2:18, 21–23). God created man to lead, as God's representative (1 Cor. 11:3). God's design was to join a man and a woman together as one (Gen. 2:24), inseparably bound to each other until death (Matt. 19:4–6; Rom. 7:2; 1 Cor. 7:39).

According to this original design, the joining of a man and woman was formally recognized by a covenant: a solemn commitment to companionship that ought to be faithfully kept (Mal. 2:14). And this kind of unity and unbreakable commitment was designed by God to be a picture of Christ's relationship with the church (Eph. 5:31–32; see also 5:23). Furthermore, the institution of the family was the first and most fundamental unit in God's design of social order. For a society to grow and flourish, marriages must be protected.

Marriage Joins Together in Partnership

Should a Christian ever date or marry an unbeliever? The Bible is clear that believers should not join themselves to unbelievers in partnerships that would compromise their commitment to God. Believing widows who remarry are told to marry "in the Lord" (1 Cor. 7:39). The Old Testament is full of warnings not to intermarry with idolaters (Exod. 34:16; Deut. 7:3–4; Josh. 23:12–13; Ezra 9:14), and Solomon exemplifies what happens when such warnings are ignored (1 Kings 11:4). Too many people are deceived into thinking they have the power in themselves to change someone else, to convince the other person to live for the Lord. They end up in marriages where the spouses find themselves at odds in many areas. Nevertheless, if one spouse trusts Christ after marriage, the Bible encourages maintaining that marriage and striving to be a good witness to the unbelieving party (1 Cor. 7:12–14, 16; 1 Pet. 3:1–2).

God is grieved by divorce because divorce breaks apart God's good design. Marriage is one of His greatest blessings for men and women on this earth (Mal. 2:16). When Jesus was asked about divorce, His response was to reinforce God's original design: the permanence of marriage (Matt. 19:3–6). Jesus made clear the general rule that divorce followed by remarriage is no different than committing adultery (Matt. 19:9). That's a serious charge. This teaching was so shocking to Jesus' disciples that they could hardly fathom anyone's risking marriage in the first place without the option to divorce and remarry (Matt. 19:10). The commands against adultery and the consequences for adultery highlight the seriousness of this sin and are meant to protect the sacred covenant of marriage (Exod. 20:14, 17; see also Lev. 20:10; Prov. 6:29–32; Rom. 13:9; James 2:11). Christians are encouraged to seek reconciliation (1 Cor. 7:10–16; see also Hosea 3:1–5).

> *The fundamental question is not to ask when divorce is justified, but to ask what God's will is for marriage, and whether divorce is ever justified.*
>
> KEN MAGNUSON[1]

There are indeed two possible biblical exceptions to the general principle; these exceptions make an allowance for divorce (and likely remarriage) in two situations: the case of sexual immorality or the case of abandonment (Matt. 5:32; 19:9; 1 Cor. 7:15; see also Hosea 1:9; Jer. 3:8). However, the exceptions should not overshadow the general rule. The reason for these allowances has to do with God's mercy in the face of the hardness of sinful people's hearts (Matt. 19:8; see also Deut. 24:1–4). God cares for those who must cope with life in a broken world in which a spouse fundamentally breaks the marriage covenant and refuses to repent. When the innocent person is abandoned by or trapped with a perpetually fornicating, unrepentant spouse, God makes a way of escape.

 ## THE CONSEQUENCES OF BROKEN COVENANTS

While people generally divorce to escape a seemingly unbearable situation, statistically, second marriages rarely work out much better.[2] That's because most people's biggest problem is not the circumstances they find themselves in but their own responses to those circumstances. Sadly, too many people simply weigh the perceived positives and negatives of a divorce and convince themselves that the positives outweigh the negatives. Have they really reckoned with the negative outcomes of divorce?

As much as society would like to normalize divorce, it cannot escape divorce's negative consequences. Both adults and children suffer greatly from the resulting broken relationship.[3] Divorce has negative emotional effects on all involved, and these effects may lead to struggles with life's normal responsibilities. God's grace can help people better cope with challenges to their quality of life in the face of the instability caused by a divorce. Knowing the grief and hardship that follow, Christians should step in to lend their support to those going through divorce, particularly to innocent children affected by it.

Since the family unit formed by marriage is the building block of society, the breakdown of the family leads to the breakdown of society. To reverse this trend in society and repair the family unit, people need to reexamine their goals in marriage. The goal of any marriage according to a biblical model is loving, self-sacrificial service to one another for the glory of God. God provided the gift of marriage to enable people to be fruitful and multiply and to be stewards of this world together. God designed marriage so that a man and a woman could give to one another as they serve God and others together.

Marriage covenants are prone to break when marriage is entered into with the wrong ends in mind: self-fulfillment, self-serving romance and intimacy, and self-oriented life achievements (seeking a so-called soulmate who satisfies one's own selfish desires). In this approach, marriage is reduced to the means of fulfilling personal ambitions.

But marriage covenants will remain intact only through fidelity to the right ends: mutual love and permanent covenant companionship in service to God. By God's grace, spouses can fulfill their duties through self-sacrificial fidelity. In this approach, marriage is a means to serve God. That service is richer when performed by the two becoming one than if each person tried to do so individually.

 MAINTAINING THE MARRIAGE COVENANT

For people to maintain a godly marriage, they will need to be people of virtue. The most relevant virtues for a lifelong commitment include love, faithfulness, and patience. These virtues produce other virtues, like truthfulness and open communication. Maintaining the marriage covenant depends on the grace of God, which teaches us to turn away from ungodliness and to cultivate virtues (Titus 2:11–12).

What are the keys to staying married when it is difficult?

Love is one key to staying married when marriage is difficult. But love must be rightly defined, rightly directed, and rightly sourced. Marriage breaks apart when love is understood as nothing more than sentimentalism or emotionalism, when it is directed by one's feelings and the definitions of popular culture, and when it is sourced in one's own imagined ability to be loving. Marriage grows strong when love is understood as a heart of great affection for another person, manifested through fulfilling self-sacrificial duties. True love is directed by God's moral norms (John 14:15); God's commands describe what it means to love the other person in a marriage relationship. All this is made possible by God's love transforming our own hearts.

Faithfulness is another key to staying married when marriage is difficult. This shows itself in one's steadfast commitment to keep the covenant promises made at the commencement of the marriage. The waves can pound the rocks, but the rocks remain firm. Such faithfulness stems from the empowerment of the Holy Spirit that enables a person to respect the seriousness of the marriage commitment and the God-given design for marriage. This covenant should not be entered into flippantly, nor should it be easily forsaken. Faithfulness perseveres through great hardship rather than bailing when life gets tough. Instead of taking the easy route of escapism, faithfulness leads people to work through their difficulties and come out stronger, closer, and more loving.

Patience is a key to staying married when marriage is difficult. There's often no quick fix to major problems. As a tender plant must be cultivated over time to grow, so also marriages revive only after patient effort to nourish the marriage with the right inputs. Counseling, biblical teaching, and cultivating new selfless patterns in response to another's needs all take time. Demonstrating the fruits of true repentance may take time. Marriages cannot last without a willingness to wait on God to sanctify one's own heart and the heart of one's mate. Patience is key for living with one another in an understanding way, giving honor and respect to one another (1 Pet. 3:1–7).

GRAPPLING WITH HARDNESS OF HEART

Most likely, we all know someone who has been touched by divorce. You may know someone who is experiencing it or contemplating it right now. How should you respond to someone contemplating a divorce? How should you respond to someone who has already gotten a divorce, especially if that divorce did not fit within the parameters of the biblical exceptions and allowances?

The right response depends on your relationship with that person and your appropriate role in that person's life. You may not have the authority or the closeness to give advice, but you may be able to point him or her to a trusted friend or authority who can give biblical counsel.

If you have a friend who is being affected by the decisions of others, be compassionate. Point your friend to the guidance and comfort of the Scriptures. But in seeking to show compassion, avoid justifying wrongdoing. Truth about sin in God's Word cannot be set aside or overshadowed by our own desires to solve things in our own way or to avoid offending someone. The solution is not to avoid recognizing sin but to learn how to rightly respond to sin. God's Word provides counsel on how to respond to the unbiblical actions of others. It gives us the resources we need for encouragement and for perseverance in the face of the sinful decisions of others.

Those touched by divorce often feel shocked when it occurs. Divorce was not the plan. And it's hard to fathom how it could have happened, especially if those involved thought they were doing all the right things. Such circumstances demonstrate that we are not in control of life or the decisions others make. We are challenged to trust in God's good sovereignty to uphold us through the trials of life. Every tragedy He allows in our lives has as its purpose to test and refine us. In your own life and in the lives of those with whom you interact, the best advice is to look to Christ for wisdom and for comfort (James 1:1–18).

Thinking It Through 13.1

1. What common idea about marriage and what legal reality have led to marriage being viewed as optional and easily dissolved?

2. What did God create marriage to be? Explain God's design in marriage (Gen. 1:27; 2:18, 21–24; Matt. 19:4–6; Rom. 7:2; 1 Cor. 7:39).

3. According to God's design, the joining of a man and woman is to be formally recognized by what? Explain its significance (Mal. 2:14; Eph. 5:31–32; see also 5:23).

4. What should be our general attitude toward divorce, based on God's will for marriage (Matt. 19:3–6)?

5. What are two possible biblical exceptions to the general rule, which make an allowance for someone to divorce (and likely to remarry without being charged with adultery) (Matt. 5:32; 19:9; 1 Cor. 7:15; see also Hosea 1:9; Jer. 3:8)?

6. What are the wrong ends or goals for marriage that often lead to divorce? What should be the ultimate goals of any marriage?

7. What three virtues are keys to remaining married?

8. How should you respond to a friend whose parents have decided to divorce?

\boxed{\textbf{13.2}} Fornication, Adultery, and Marital Purity

Sex! Is that a dirty word?

Sex is good and wonderful! The Bible does not condemn *sex* as dirty or wrong (Prov. 5:18–19; see also Song of Solomon). The Bible condemns *immorality* (Prov. 5:15–17, 20; 1 Thess. 4:3–5). God created sex (Gen. 2:24–25); He blessed humans with this gift of companionship to be exercised within the lifelong covenant of marriage (Heb. 13:4).

The word *sex* and other words associated with it should not be thrown about carelessly or coarsely (see Section 11.3). The world often degrades what God made to be beautiful. Society shamelessly vulgarizes* things out in the open that should be treated with respect and sobriety in their proper contexts. (For example, talking about body parts in the privacy of a doctor's office due to a medical necessity—with safeguards of accountability in place even in that situation—is far different than yelling out those same words in public to get attention.) Demonstrate maturity, godliness, and purity as you think through, talk about, and respond to the content in this chapter (Titus 1:15; see also Eph. 5:4).

INAPPROPRIATE SEXUAL ACTIVITY

Perhaps you've been asked a series of questions such as: "Why won't your parents let you see the latest R-rated movie? Sure, there are some sex scenes, but do they really think it's all that bad?" "Why can't you join us for the party we've been planning? Your parents don't have to know." "Don't you keep up with the latest celebrities?"

Peer pressure—even in Christian schools and churches—can lead to feeling beat-up for trying to walk worthy of the Lord. Or it can lead to feeling like you need to break out and have a little freedom and fun. Which way are you inclined? There's one good answer to all that peer pressure: Proverbs 14:16. If you fear God, you won't fit in with the "norms" of the fleshly, indulgent society around you, and neither will you want to. If you routinely seek to fit in, that fruit reveals who you really are and what your end will be (Prov. 1:20–33).

Rampant sexual immorality in the surrounding culture is nothing new; it marks most cultures, ancient and modern (Gen. 6:5; Lev. 18:3; Eph. 4:17–21). Yes, the Christian ethic has influenced many societies, providing some restraint at times. Many societies may cover their wickedness in darkness and hypocrisy for a time (John 3:19–20; Eph. 5:11–13), but eventually they grow bolder, parading perversions out in the open for all to see (Rom. 1:24–32; 2 Tim. 3:13; 1 Pet. 4:3; see also Jer. 13:27). You live in a morally corrupt culture. But what you face is not unique. God has always called believers to live transformed lives, distinct from the depraved cultures surrounding them (1 Cor. 6:9–11). And God calls on you to do the same (Eph. 2:1–5). He can empower you by His Spirit and sanctify you so that you can put off the works of the flesh (Eph. 4:22–24).

context
What kinds of inappropriate sexual activity are discussed, excused, or even celebrated in our society?

acts
What does the Bible have to say about each of these activities?

vulgarize: to make lower or to debase

Defining Inappropriate Sexual Activity:
Context and Acts

sexual immorality
a phrase often used by modern Bible translations to express the Greek word *porneia*, which is a general word for any kind of sexual perversion (something that twists God's intended design)

immodesty: *drawing attention to one's sexuality or sexual parts through the cut of clothing, the fit of clothing, or a lack of clothing*

God designed the function of clothing to cover nakedness (Gen. 3:7, 10–11, 21; see also Gen. 2:25); it is not fitting to expose one's nakedness to others (Gen. 9:20–27; Lev. 18) or to dress and behave in a manner intended to evoke sexual desire outside the bounds of marriage (Prov. 7:10; 1 Tim. 2:9). Christians are responsible to refrain from lustful gazing (Job 21:1; Ps. 101:3; Matt. 5:27–30; see also 2 Sam. 11:2) and to not purposefully seek to attract lustful gazing (Prov. 6:25–26; 7:10 and context).

pornography: *pictures, videos, or graphic descriptions intended to stimulate sexual desire*

We live in a pornographic world; you don't have to go to a pornographic website—these kinds of images inundate mainstream advertising and entertainment and contribute to styles and fads embraced by the culture.

The principles that address immodesty apply even more emphatically to pornography. Feeding one's lust by pictures, videos, or descriptions of nudity and of people performing sexual acts is a blatant sin against God's holy design for sex. Pornography takes something beautiful and turns it into something dirty.

masturbation: *sexual self-stimulation*

The purpose for sex is not isolated personal enjoyment, but giving yourself to your spouse and receiving pleasure from your spouse. Sexual self-stimulation results from and leads to lust, physically harming oneself, sexually defrauding a spouse, and misusing the purpose of sex (1 Thess. 4:4). It can also burden you with guilt, negatively affecting your general spiritual walk.

Biblical principles regarding the purpose of sex within marriage (for procreation and the mutual giving of pleasure between spouses) as well as those forbidding lust (Col. 3:5) would seem to forbid this practice even without a specific text of Scripture on this matter.

sexual activity outside of marriage

This includes the stoking of sexual desires (lust) through sexting (texting sexual content), intimate touching, making out, dirty talk, and other types of sexual stimulation that don't involve intercourse but may lead to it.

Multiple passages in Scripture warn against this (Prov. 7:10–20; Matt.15:19; Acts 15:20, 29; 1 Cor. 7:2; 1 Thess. 4:3; Rev. 21:8) as well as the lust (the inward desire) and seduction that draw people into sexual activity forbidden in God's law (Matt. 5:27–28; Gal. 5:19; Eph. 5:3; Col. 3:5).

fornication: *sexual intercourse between two unmarried people*
(The KJV sometimes uses this word more broadly to indicate sexual immorality in general.)

Though it doesn't involve breaking marriage vows, sexual intercourse before marriage twists God's design (Gen. 2:24–25; Exod. 22:16–17; Deut. 22:20–21), and sexually joining oneself to another apart from a marriage covenant harms many.

prostitution: *providing sex acts for pay or in return for some benefit*

The Bible clearly forbids and warns against prostitution (Lev. 19:26; Prov. 23:27–28; 1 Cor. 6:13–18). Turning the most intimate act of unity into a commodity to be sold cheapens and defiles the Lord's gift.

incest: *sexual relations among family members*

People from the same general family unit (siblings and half-siblings, parents and children or stepchildren) are to be protected from turning a family relationship into a sexual relationship. Failing to provide a safeguard leads to twisted relationships, broken trust, trauma, and abuse.

Both the Old (Lev. 18:6–18) and New Testaments (Luke 3:19; 1 Cor. 5:1) clearly forbid incest. (Early on, before the Mosaic law, brothers and sisters would have married. But the lifespans of people were much longer, and marriage may have taken place later in life, so it is unlikely these brothers and sisters grew up in the same household at the same time.)

sexual immorality *(continued)*	
sexual abuse: *any criminal activity that forces any kind of sexual perversion on another person; includes rape and pedophilia*	
This is both a criminal and moral matter, so it must be addressed both as a crime by the appropriate governmental authorities and as sin by the appropriate authorities in the church. Many of the same arguments that have been used to persuade society to embrace homosexuality as a person's identity are being used to defend pedophilia.	Under the Mosaic law, rape was a serious offense (Deut. 22:25–29); the New Testament makes clear that someone who would harm a child deserves the harshest of punishments (Matt. 18:6).
homosexuality: *sexual desires and actions between people of the same God-given sex (males with males or females with females)*	
Both homosexual desires and behavior are clearly condemned (Gen. 19 with Jude 1:7; Lev. 18:22; Rom. 1:24–27) and must be turned away from in repentance (1 Cor. 6:9–11). The Bible does not condone treating	sinful desires as an unchangeable part of a person's identity. True, the sin nature is part of who we are after the Fall, but it must be repudiated and put to death (Rom. 8:13; Col. 3:5–10). This will be discussed in detail in Section 13.3.
bestiality: *sexual behavior with animals*	
This is a form of abuse toward an animal and is unfitting for a human being, who should be matched with his or her own kind.	This practice, though rare, is flatly condemned (Exod. 22:19; Lev. 18:23; see also Gen. 2:20).
adultery: *marital unfaithfulness; lust or sexual activity that violates the marriage covenant of one or both people involved*	
Such infidelity breaks trust and deeply damages what is supposed to be a special, unique, and valuable companionship.	The Bible strongly prohibits a married person from engaging in sexual activity with someone outside his or her marriage and condemns those who violate someone else's spouse (Exod. 20:14, 17; Lev. 20:10; Prov. 6:23–35; Matt. 5:27–30; 15:19; 19:9, 18; Rom. 2:22; 13:9; James 2:11). It upholds the importance of marital faithfulness (Mal. 2:14–15).
polygamy: *having multiple spouses at one time*	
Although this practice is currently less common in Western culture, discussions for allowing it have recently increased, and it has been portrayed on television.	God's original design was for an exclusive relationship between one man and one woman (Gen. 2:24). Many Old Testament narratives describe tensions and negative consequences that resulted from polygamous relationships. Elders in the church, who are exemplars of what all Christians ought to be, are not to be in polygamous relationships (1 Tim. 3:2). Nevertheless, this practice was tolerated but limited in the Old Testament (Exod. 21:10–11; Deut. 17:17), and it seems that if a practicing polygamist in our day is converted to Christ, he or she should fulfill familial obligations.

Inappropriate sexual activity is often fueled by carousing and revelry. Partying often includes drinking, drugs, suggestive clothing, certain types of music, and carnal dancing that all promote a sexually loose atmosphere that lowers inhibitions and fuels lust (Rom. 13:13; 1 Pet. 4:3). The world loves to party, arousing the lusts of the flesh and the eyes (1 John 2:15–17). Don't be deceived by the promises of freedom and fulfillment dangled before you by perversions of God's design for sex (Rom. 7:11). Listen to the instructions of the wise and godly people in your life, and be willing to submit to their attempts to protect you from yourself (Prov. 5:1, 20; 7:1; Heb. 3:13).

Marital purity can be defined as forsaking all forbidden sexual activity and partaking in the sexual activity God designed for a man and woman within the bounds of marriage (1 Cor. 7:2–5). Appropriate sexual activity has been limited by God to the marriage relations of one man and one woman for life (Gen. 2:24–25; Prov. 5:18–21; Song of Sol. 1–8; Heb. 13:4).

We should cultivate purity of heart in sexual matters, avoiding occasions of temptation.

JOHN FRAME[4]

Cultivating purity of heart gets to the root of the problem: lust (Rom. 6:12; Col. 3:5; 2 Tim. 2:22; James 1:14–15). The Bible teaches us to make no provision for the flesh—avoid things that will stoke your lust (Rom. 13:14; 1 Pet. 2:11). Instead, we must walk in the Spirit and by God's grace turn from worldly lusts (Gal. 5:16; Titus 2:11–12; 1 Pet. 4:2–3). This endeavor is diametrically opposed to the spirit of our age (Jude 1:18). Even false teachers within the church will downplay and excuse sexual sin (2 Pet. 2:18–22). Don't be deceived; sexual perversion cannot be excused or toyed with (Prov. 6:27–28; Gal. 6:7). And someone who has engaged in these sexual perversions while in pastoral ministry should never be quickly restored to such a position since he cannot be trusted as an exemplar to lead the church (1 Tim. 3:2). The fruits of true repentance must be demonstrated over a long period of time (2 Cor. 7:10).

THE DAMAGE OF PROMISCUITY

Why is sex only for marriage?

God's commands describe what it means to love both Him and others. God's commands also reflect the good design of the creation, which in turn reflects God's perfect character. Living according to that design promotes the flourishing of our lives (although we will still suffer in a fallen world). Therefore, we should not view God's restrictions as hampering our fun and freedom. Rather, God's commands are designed for our well-being and the well-being of others. That's why we can delight in God's commands (Pss. 1:2; 119:174; Rom. 7:12, 22; 1 Tim. 1:8). God's commands are not burdensome (Matt. 11:30; 1 John 5:3). They give us true freedom—freedom from the deceptive slavery of sin (Rom. 6:15–16; Gal. 5:13). God reserved sex for marriage to preserve its exquisiteness, creating a unique covenant bond of companionship. By promoting our flourishing, God's commands protect us and others from being used, abused, and thrown away. That's why sexual immorality often leaves people feeling broken, dirty, and traumatized.

The consequences of promiscuity can be greatly damaging in several ways: spiritually, physically, and societally. First, sexual promiscuity damages our relationship with God, who has called us to purity (Eph. 1:4; 4:1). A pattern of promiscuity characterizes those who have been separated from God and do not have a true saving relationship with Him (2 Pet. 2:18–22; Rev. 21:8), and it harms the souls of God's people (Ps. 51:3, 8). Second, sexual promiscuity often causes sexually transmitted diseases (STDs) and other medical problems for those who use and abuse their bodies contrary to God's cre-

ational design for sexuality. Third, sexual promiscuity has a ripple effect of disaster that extends from the promiscuous person (guilt and harmful addictions) to his or her family (distrust, shame, hurt, broken relationships), to his or her social circles (disruptions to work, removal from positions, shock and dismay or worse among friends and at church), and to society as a whole (destabilization of communities, negative effects on education, financial costs of broken homes).

In contrast, Christians must be driven by their chief end to glorify and enjoy God by living for God's kingdom and His righteousness (Matt. 6:33). Their pursuit of pleasure should be aligned with God's commands (Ps. 37:4). When pursuit of pleasure runs contrary to God's commands, that pursuit will eventually lead to ruin and judgment. Such deceitful pleasures will never truly satisfy. Considering all the guilt, shame, and ruin caused by sin, people need the hope of the gospel with the forgiveness it offers (1 Cor. 6:11). When a person has felt the full force of the destructiveness of sin, he or she may come to his or her senses and realize the value of serving a loving Father (Luke 15:11–32). But the opportunity for such repentance doesn't last indefinitely (Prov. 1:20–33; Heb. 3:12–15). The wise person learns from instruction rather than through personal destructive experience (Prov. 5:7–14; Eccles. 12:1, 13).

VIRTUES NECESSARY FOR SEXUAL PURITY

Sexual purity requires the cultivation of virtues from within. Three virtues stand out. *Love* is one. And true love is *self-controlled* and *faithful*. In fact, if someone claims to love but lacks these other virtues, that person is most likely being controlled by lust. And such so-called love will likely fizzle out (2 Sam. 13:15).

A person who has cultivated the virtue of true love will recognize the damage done to oneself and others by engaging in inappropriate sexual activity. Therefore, a person who truly loves another will refrain from sexual activity outside marriage. This is important to understand, because one of the main excuses for extramarital sex is how much two people supposedly love each other and just can't help expressing that love sexually. This is patently false and based on a false sense of love. True love is self-controlled and faithful.

Faithfulness binds a person to another person in a commitment that will be steadfastly maintained. Faithfulness rules out even a consideration of inappropriate sexual activity. Instead, faithful couples cultivate a deep love, focusing on remaining loyal to each other and to their unconditional commitment promised in the marriage ceremony before God and witnesses.

If the heart of the problem is lust (out-of-control sexual desire), then one of *the* key virtues to cultivate within yourself would be self-control. In clarifying what exactly lust is, John Frame makes these helpful comments:

> Lust is not sexual desire as such. That is something good, a God-given incentive to marriage, to intimacy within marriage, and to reproduction. . . . First Corinthians 7:9 does not condemn the desire itself, but only a desire that cannot be controlled.[5]

Self-control is not the only thing that will keep you sexually pure. But it is certainly one virtue that will keep you from being foolish. How many teens could have prevented their lives from being turned upside down if they had waited only a few more years for marriage? Exercise of self-control (and willingness to submit to the safeguards of accountability) could save much destructive living and heartache.

PLANNING TO LIVE WITH CONVICTION

How can you plan to maintain sexual purity before and during marriage? Read Proverbs 7:1–6, and then consider these guidelines drawn from the rest of Proverbs 7.

Don't be naive, thinking you're above sin and its consequences. Stay on guard (7:7).

Don't approve of or practice immodesty; both men and women can be culpable of enticing by what they wear and of lusting when enticed (7:10).

Don't approve of or practice double-entendre (veiled dirty talk) or brazen impure talk (7:10–11; 16–18, 21).

Don't put yourself in compromising situations (7:8–9, 12).

Don't be alone with someone of the opposite sex without accountability; welcome the oversight of others who will help protect you (7:19–20).

Don't play around with physical intimacy that draws you into more and more physical intimacy (7:13).

Don't be duped by flattery and enticements to sin (7:13–21).

Count the cost of immorality: it leads to ruin (7:22–27).

Thinking It Through 13.2

1. Define *fornication*.

2. Define *adultery*.

3. Define *marital purity*.

4. Identify and explain at least three types of inappropriate sexual activity. Provide biblical support.

5. Summarize three consequences of sexual promiscuity.

6. Identify and explain one virtue that would address the root problem of sexual promiscuity.

7. Provide at least three guidelines that would help you plan to avoid sexual impurity.

13.3 Homosexuality, Bisexuality, and Transgenderism

The discussion in this section demands a lot from you: maturity, humility, a commitment to truth and righteousness, and compassion. If you love God, then you will have an unwavering commitment to His righteous character, His created order, and His Word. If you love others, you will display compassion informed by God's view of what is good and right for people's well-being according to His wise design.

We all need to have compassion without compromise. That means that we will not accept, accommodate, or approve of *unethical desires and behavior*. We also will not deride or act in ungodly ways toward *a person made in God's image*. The difficulty in walking this fine line is that our culture is confused about what is ethical and what is creational (the essence, or objective reality, of who a person is, regardless of feelings). You may be accused of hating the person whose unethical desires and behaviors you oppose because those desires and behaviors are made out to be that person's identity.

For example, a baker has baked cakes for a customer who identifies as a homosexual, even cultivating a friendship over the years. (The baker has no problem treating the customer well as an image-bearer of God.) But that same baker refuses to bake a wedding cake for a homosexual wedding ceremony, due to religious and moral convictions. (He cannot participate in, promote, or help with what he considers to be sin.) That baker gets sued for discriminating *against those persons*. Our culture has blurred the lines between opposing a person and opposing what a person stands for and wants everyone else to support.

Before continuing our evaluation of our culture and the biblical teaching and virtues that drive an ethical response, we need to understand some basic terms. The term *homosexual* (which includes both lesbian and gay categories, the *L* and the *G* in the **LGBTQ+** abbreviation) refers to someone with sexual desires for a person of the same sex or who engages in sexual behavior with a person of the same sex (male with male or female with female). The term *bisexual* (the *B* in the LGBTQ+ abbreviation) refers to someone with sexual desires for or who engages in sexual behavior with both men and women. The term *transgender* (the *T* in the LGBTQ+ abbreviation) refers to someone who thinks of him or herself as having a gender different from his or her sex. This category is based on an assertion that people can choose gender for themselves rather than genders being determined by God-granted biology and genetics (males have XY chromosomes and females have XX chromosomes). The *Q* in the acronym can refer to *queer* or *questioning*. The + is shorthand for more letters that are sometimes included to represent the growing spectrum of invented gender identities.

LGBTQ+ TRENDS

Same-sex sin and gender confusion aren't anything new. The Bible dealt with these issues in ancient Israel (Gen. 1:27; 19:4–8 with Judg. 19:20–30 and Jude 1:7; Lev. 18:22; 20:13; Deut. 22:5) and in the first century (Rom. 1:26–27; 1 Cor. 6:9–11; 1 Tim. 1:10). Humans from every era and in every place have the same sinful heart (Ps. 51:5; Rom. 3:23).

However, cultures in different times and places can manifest different kinds of sinfulness to a greater or lesser degree (2 Tim. 3:13). In fact, when a culture spirals deeper into depravity, it blatantly manifests these kinds of sins (Rom. 1:24, 32). Through the restraining work of the Spirit, the influence of Christians and Christian ethics, and even the consciences of unsaved people, these kinds of sins may be uncommon or at least hidden—due to a cultural recognition that such behaviors should be viewed as depraved. Recognition of this kind of depravity used to be the common understanding of much of the Western world, highly influenced by a biblical ethic—until recently. Denny Burk and Heath Lambert summarize the staggering change that has taken place in America:

> Most Christians have been surprised by the velocity of cultural change on the issue of homosexuality. Just one measure of that change is the acceptance of homosexual marriage. In 2005, same-sex marriage was illegal in every state in America. In 2015, the Supreme Court of the United States has declared same-sex marriage to be a constitutional right nationwide. That is a tremendous amount of change for one decade.[6]

In addition to the changed perspective in society, the church has also grappled with challenges to the biblical ethic on this matter as never before. Wayne Grudem says,

> To my knowledge, no evangelical Christian pastors or Bible scholars in previous generations ever claimed that the Bible gives moral approval to any kind of homosexual conduct. The unanimous consensus of centuries of Christian teaching on such a major moral issue cannot be dismissed lightly.[7]

More recently, however, self-professed evangelicals have been trying to find ways to accommodate the Bible to homosexuality, bisexuality, and transgenderism. Bible-believing pastors, counselors, and scholars have had to write numerous, detailed defenses of the biblical ethic in response to challenges to its clarity.

What led to this hypersonic change in sexual ethics? The changed perspective in society didn't come out of nowhere. Ideas have consequences. And some key philosophical influences on our society have produced this changing ethic. Just one of those influences can be traced back to a philosopher you were introduced to in Chapter 2: the existentialist Jean-Paul Sartre. This philosopher is famous for teaching that existence precedes essence.[8] That means that you exist first as a person. Then you create for yourself the essence of who you want to be. You're in charge of the very essence of your being. In other words, you are in charge of who you want to be or become.

The complexities of philosophy get translated into the simplistic sayings of popular culture: "Follow your heart." "Be true to yourself." "You can become anything you want to be."[9] And by "anything," our culture means *anything*: a man can choose to become a woman, and a woman can choose to become a man. Society increasingly rejects the idea of a God-created, God-designed, and God-granted essence to one's existence that is objectively real, regardless of one's feelings.

THE CLARITY OF THE BIBLE ON GENDER AND SEXUALITY

Gender

We are not our own, and this reality should cause us to rejoice (Ps. 100:3)! Because God created us, we belong: we have purpose. We are not lost, left to figure out who we are and what we should be doing. We don't need to find ourselves. We find security and stability in our lives by joyfully submitting to our Creator and His perfect created order designed for human flourishing.

God's created order includes two distinct genders (male and female) in one human race, labeled *man* (Gen. 1:26–27; 5:1–2). Gender is not a psychological construct—with endless ideas about where one might fit on a spectrum between male and female. Gender corresponds with biological reality. The so-called gender spectrum is rooted in distorted thinking arising from fallen desires that must be repudiated as untrue and wrong. Regardless of what a person does cosmetically to hide or change appearances, genetic realities define one's essence as designed by God.

Scripture never distinguishes gender from biology; Scripture presumes that it is readily apparent who is a male or female based on biological observations. It addresses men as men and women as women with the assumption that nobody is truly confused over who is who. Scripture condemns men who portray themselves as women and women who portray themselves as men (Deut. 22:5). The Mosaic law includes commands like this that reflect an application of creational norms that transcend the Old Covenant. Thus, this command would, in principle, also apply to us today. Nature itself teaches appropriate gender distinctions (1 Cor. 11:14–15); our rebellious culture makes it difficult to distinguish between men and women. Our culture is also rebelling against gender roles. The Bible distinguishes the roles of men and women in society (Gen. 3:16; Isa. 3:12), the family (1 Cor. 11:3), and the church (1 Tim. 2:11–15).

Sexuality

The biblical pattern for appropriate sexual desires and behaviors is given in Genesis 2:22–24 and reinforced by Jesus Himself in Matthew 19:4–6: one man and one woman joined by covenant for life. God designed this sexual union for two distinct, complementary individuals who are joined together as one flesh, often resulting in procreation. Deviations from that pattern are flatly condemned in both the Old (Gen. 19:4–8; Lev. 18:22; 20:13) and New Testaments (Rom. 1:21–32; 1 Cor. 6:9–11; 1 Tim. 1:10; Jude 1:7).

Both the biblical pattern and Scripture's verdict on deviations from that pattern should be clear enough if you take the time to read each text. However, each text has been challenged by those who support homosexual desires or behavior while seeking to retain some adherence to the Bible. As weak as these arguments are, they have influenced many who have a superficial understanding of Scripture or a feeble commitment to its authority. You need to be equipped with answers to some of their most popular arguments.

Know Ye that THE **LORD** **HE IS GOD:** IT IS HE THAT HATH *made us* AND NOT WE OURSELVES. *We are His people and the* sheep of His pasture.

PSALM 100:3

> *Every person's sense of his or her own 'gender identity' should be the same as that person's biological sex.*
>
> WAYNE GRUDEM[10]

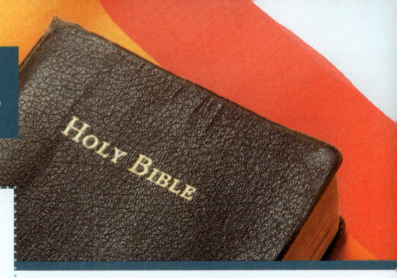

Are Christians wrong to use the Bible to condemn homosexuality?

Some professing Christians question whether the Bible condemns all homosexual behavior or desires. They use alternative interpretations of Scripture to challenge Christians who have traditionally interpreted and applied the Bible as wholly condemning such things. In addition, even Christians who believe homosexual behavior is wrong debate about how homosexual sin should be understood and how Christians who battle homosexual temptations should label themselves. What follows addresses these arguments and questions.

FALSE ARGUMENT #1

"The story of Sodom does not condemn loving, committed homosexual relationships."

One common argument is that Genesis 19 has nothing to do with identifying homosexuality as the sin of Sodom. The claim is that the men of Sodom were guilty only of wanting to participate in a homosexual rape—the homosexual desires and behavior in general are not condemned but only the intention to rape. But this ignores both the pattern for human sexuality in Genesis 2 as well as the straightforward condemnations of homosexuality in other passages of Scripture (for example, see Lev. 18:22; 20:13). The men of Sodom were guilty of wanting to participate in homosexual rape, but *both* the rape and the homosexual desires were wrong.

Another argument claims that the men of Sodom were guilty only for inhospitality, since Ezekiel 16:49 lists pride and lack of

hospitality (failing to care for the poor), not homosexual sin, as Sodom's offense. However, Ezekiel 16:50 identifies Sodom's sin as "abomination," which would have been understood to be homosexuality (see Lev. 18:22). In addition, Genesis 19 must be read in context. Sodom's sin was considered "very grievous" (Gen. 18:20) and pervasive. Not even ten righteous people existed in that city (Gen. 18:32). The sin at Lot's house was one expression of a thoroughgoing cultural depravity. Furthermore, the Bible is clear that the euphemism of wanting to "know" someone (Gen. 19:5) means sexual relations (Gen. 4:1, 17, 25; Judg. 19:22). Finally, Jude 1:7 makes abundantly clear that the sin of Sodom was sexual. Sodom's sin was multifaceted: arrogance and autonomy led to gross inhospitality (more precisely, an absence of practical love) and to twisted rebellion against God's design for sex.

FALSE ARGUMENT #2

"Opponents of homosexual relationships pick and choose which Old Testament laws to follow."

Yet another charge against the biblical view is that Christians are picking and choosing which Old Testament laws to follow and which ones not to follow. The claim is that Christians eat shellfish and wear mixed fabrics (both condemned in the Mosaic law), but they still hold onto the laws against homosexuality. The implication is that Christians are inconsistent and should throw out the whole Old Testament law. This charge reflects a poor understanding of the Mosaic law and the Christian's relationship to the law. The laws regarding fabric and shellfish are unique to the Mosaic law and served a teaching purpose for Israel. Laws regarding sexual morality transcend the Mosaic law and are true in all times and places. How do we know this? First, same-sex lust and relations were contrary to God's creational design (Gen. 1–2) long before Moses gave the law to the nation of Israel. Second, the law of Moses is an application of God's creational design to

His people in that nation. The underlying creational design has not changed. Third, Leviticus 18:24–25 says that God judged the Gentile nations in Canaan for these sins. Thus, these prohibitions are not unique to the Mosaic Covenant or the nation of Israel. Fourth, none of the moral principles of the law are ever overturned. While the Mosaic law contains some provisions that are in force only under that covenant, other provisions are in force in all times and places because they are rooted in God's character and the moral order built into creation. Fifth, the New Testament repeats laws from the Old Testament that believers in Christ must clearly still follow (for example, see Rom. 1:21–32; 1 Cor. 6:9–11; 1 Tim. 1:10; Jude 1:7). The laws in Leviticus 18 that condemn sexual perversions are still relevant—against adultery, incest, bestiality, and sexual relations between people of the same sex.

FALSE ARGUMENT #3

"The New Testament does not forbid committed homosexual relationships, only predatory ones."

In response to the New Testament condemnations (particularly Rom. 1:21–32 and 1 Tim. 1:10), some have tried to claim that Paul was not really condemning homosexuality but homosexual predation. Others have tried to claim that Paul was telling people with a *heterosexual* orientation not to practice homosexuality; they claim Paul never said those who had a homosexual orientation by nature couldn't practice it. Still others claim that Paul was conforming to his own day's cultural expectations; they say our cultural expectations have changed, allowing for the practice of homosexuality now. All these reinterpretations of New Testament teaching are simply dishonest treatments of the text.

First, Paul was not limiting his condemnation to predation or exploitation. Both partners in the act are equally condemned, indicating that Paul was not condemning a more powerful predator while recognizing an innocent victim (by contrast, see the differentiation made in Deut. 22:25–26). Nothing in the text itself even suggests this claim; homosexuality is wholly condemned.

Second, the Bible never recognizes a homosexual orientation as an unchanging, essential part of a person's being. Rather, that kind of orientation stems from an ethical problem: sinful desires that stem from original sin. We are sinners by nature who twist God's creational design. It may be true that a person feels that he or she was born with a tendency to same-sex attraction. That tendency could exist as a manifestation of someone's sin nature and yet still be "against nature" (Rom. 1:26), that is, contrary to God's creational design.

Third, Romans 1 is not simply condemning sexual exploitation, a lack of committed relationships, or rebellion against cultural expectations of the day; it is condemning people for turning away from God's design in nature (Rom. 1:26–27). "Against nature" means contrary to the biological complementary design of male and female, a design made clear by the natural outcome of procreation that is part of God's intent for sexual relations. The point is that even pagans should know from observing the natural world that this behavior is depraved and contrary to God's design. This natural law should be evident even apart from the Mosaic law.

FALSE ARGUMENT #4

"The Bible does not talk much about same-sex relations and neither should the church today."

Another popular claim is that the Bible doesn't really say much about this sin. Instead of defending same-sex relations, those who speak this way often wish the church to be silent on this matter, a first step toward compromise on this issue.

It's simply untrue that the Bible does not talk much about this sin. Plenty of biblical texts have been surveyed here in this section. In addition, whenever the Bible upholds the pattern established in Genesis 1–2, and whenever the Bible condemns sexual immorality in general, the Bible is condemning homosexuality.

Why are Christians speaking against homosexual sins so often right now? Society is currently challenging the biblical ethic on this issue especially. Society at large sees opposition to homosexuality as an outrage, and its opposition to Christianity on this point is hindering some Christians' ability to practice their faith in the public square. The prominence of this issue in today's culture has forced Christians to respond with more focused attention than ever before.

FALSE ARGUMENT #5

"Homosexual sins are no worse than other sins."

It was once common to hear claims that homosexual sins were the worst possible kind of sin. It has now become popular to claim that homosexual sins are no worse than any other sin. The Bible teaches that all sin is sin—from showing partiality to unlawfully taking someone's life. A violation of God's law in a single point results in a guilty verdict before God. Nonetheless, the Bible itself teaches that some sins are greater than others (Ezek. 8:6; John 19:11). And some sins can reflect hearts that have gone from bad to worse (Rom. 1:21–32; 2 Tim. 3:13). The Bible even categorizes some sins as especially repulsive to God, calling them abominations (see Lev. 18:22, 26–27). Homosexuality is worse than many other sexual sins because it goes against the fundamental nature of God's created order[11] as expressed in the Creation Mandate. Nonetheless there are arguably worse sins than homosexuality—blasphemy of the Holy Spirit and unbelief, for example (Matt. 11:21–24; 12:31).

Are Christians wrong to use the Bible to condemn homosexuality?

FALSE ARGUMENT #6

"Same-sex attraction is not sinful."

Another challenge faces Bible-believing churches. How should people with same-sex attraction be counseled? There has been a lot of confusion over whether desires to sin are themselves sinful or simply temptations that fall short of being sin.

The Bible specifies that the root of sinful behavior is in the heart with its desires (James 1:13–14). The Bible warns against sinful desires: lust as well as the act of adultery is sinful (Exod. 20:14, 17 with Matt. 5:28), and covetousness as well as theft is sinful (Exod. 20:15, 17). If by *same-sex attraction* one means sexually desiring someone of the same sex, then same-sex attraction is a forbidden lust. The Bible teaches that God's goal is the transformation of the heart, not just external compliance (1 Sam. 16:7).

This is confusing to many who argue that temptations to sin are not themselves sinful. This was a matter of debate between the Protestant Reformers and Roman Catholics. The Reformers agreed with the Catholic Church that the "first stage" of temptation, an outward occasion or suggestion of sin, is not itself sin, because it is external to the person. The Reformers and Catholic Church also agreed that the "third stage" of temptation, in which a person gives in to the temptation, is sin. But they disagreed on the "second stage," in which a person desires the sin but has not yet decided to follow it. The Reformers asserted that desires to sin are themselves sinful.[12] Thus, temptations are not necessarily sin if the temptations are externally provoking us to sin, but temptations arising from our own degrading passions (Rom. 1:26) or "lust" (Rom. 1:27) entails sin because desiring to commit sinful acts is itself sinful. This is true whether those desires are heterosexual or homosexual. Everyone is born with a propensity toward sin, and that propensity is itself sinful. It is called *original sin*.

The whole point of the gospel is that, while we are unable to transform ourselves, *Christ can* transform us (Phil. 2:13). The sanctification process takes time, but Christians can put sinful desires to death (Rom. 6:12–14) through a pattern of putting off vices and putting on virtues and renewing the mind (2 Cor. 5:17; Col. 3:5–14; Ps. 51:10). Sinful desires may not be entirely eradicated in this life, but they can be more and more consistently turned away from (1 John 3:1–10) by the power of God, who transforms us through a process that includes our active submission to Him.

GAY CHRISTIANS?

Finally, there is a debate about whether Christians who battle same-sex temptations should be identified by the label *gay Christian*. Some Christians argue that the label *gay* simply refers to their temptations. However, it is unwise for Christians to identify themselves in terms of their sins. A Christian shouldn't identify as a gay Christian any more than someone should identify as an adulterous Christian or a lying Christian. First Corinthians 6:11 puts these sinful identifications in the past: "Such *were* some of you" (emphasis added). To be sure, Christians still struggle with temptation and with their flesh. But their identity is now in Christ, rather than in their sin.

CONCLUSION

The traditional biblical position has not been overturned by any of the arguments that seek to harmonize the Bible and homosexual practice. These arguments attempt to explain away what is clearly understood from a straightforward reading of the Scripture text in context. Bible-believing Christians should not be intimidated or moved from the biblical position by those who try to reinterpret or read into the Scriptures what has never been recognized by orthodox Christianity for thousands of years. Likewise, precision about the nature of homosexual sin and how to think about temptations in this area are important for the health of the church.

THE CONSEQUENCES OF REJECTING GOD'S DESIGN

Both personal and societal consequences can occur from living contrary to God's design. On the personal level, there is loss as transient relationships replace lifelong commitments. There is pain as relationships that are entered into without lifelong commitments break apart. And though not everybody who is sexually immoral contracts a sexually transmitted disease, STDs are a consequence for some. Most significant, an unrepentant immoral person is under God's judgment (Rom. 1:26–32).

Societal consequences also follow as more people stray from God's design for marriage. One consequence is that fewer people are having children. While at one time some (wrongly) worried about over-population, now the worry is that a shrinking population will disrupt economic prosperity to the point at which significant social unrest becomes more likely.[13]

As homosexual relationships are mainstreamed, it becomes more difficult for same-sex friendships to be deep without having to combat the perception that they are or should be sexualized. The same tensions present in friendships between men and women may affect friendships between men and men or women and women. Hesitance to build close friendships furthers the alienation that many in society are already feeling.

Debates over transgenderism have increased societal conflicts. As transgender advocates insist that men who identify as women be allowed in women-only spaces, such as bathrooms and women's shelters, many women argue that the intrusion of men into these spaces makes them less safe. Furthermore, with the slogan "Trans women are women," transgender advocates also insist that men who identify as women be allowed to participate in women's sports. But this slogan does not capture the biological differences between men and women that give men an advantage in these sports. More significant, many children who claim to be transgender have been given puberty-blocking drugs and have undergone irreversible surgeries. They will have to live with the effects of these procedures, and as some of them grow up and realize the gravity and permanence of what has been done to them, society will have to reckon with what it has promoted. At present, those who reject transgenderism are under pressure to speak and act in ways that they believe are truly harmful to those who identify as transgender. Failing to do so—for instance, failing to use a person's preferred pronouns—can result in job loss.

One thing is clear: sexual ethics is not merely a matter for consenting adults in the privacy of their homes. Sexual ethics invariably has significant society-wide consequences. How could it be otherwise, since God created a man and a woman and gave as His first command to them, "Be fruitful, and multiply" (Gen. 1:28)?

What Does It Mean to Love My Neighbor If My Neighbor Rejects God's Design for Sex?

Is the Bible's sexual ethic unloving?

The most common accusation against those who clearly enunciate the biblical ethic is that they are unloving. That accusation seems so powerful that some Bible-believing Christians are silent or accommodating on this issue. No doubt, some speak about homosexual sin in an unloving manner and with motives other than the salvation of the sinner. But there can also be clear statements of biblical teaching regarding homosexual sin that are motivated by true, biblically defined love (2 Tim. 4:2; see also Eph. 4:15).

Most of the time, the accusation that Christians are unloving is based on a wrong definition and description of love. Love is not merely sentimental affirmation of others. Calling people to live in conformity to God's commands is loving in that God's commands are designed for our flourishing. As Psalm 1 teaches, the blessed man is the one who delights in God's law; he is like a flourishing tree. God calls on all people to delight in His law because it is good and for their good. Sin is destructive: "the way of the ungodly shall perish" (Ps. 1:6). Ultimately that destruction will occur in the final judgment, but it can also manifest itself in the present. Indeed, Paul teaches that turning a people over to homosexual lusts is itself part of God's judgment (Rom. 1:26–27). Accommodating this culture's desire for so-called sexual freedom furthers its self-destruction and accelerates its judgment, which is hardly loving. The most loving thing to do is to call upon people to repent, submit to the God who created them, and begin functioning according to His good design.

But the heart behind the call to repentance must be love for the sinner. We have all seen or heard about those who spew diatribes like "God hates fags!", implying that God wants certain people to burn in hell. That's not the gospel or biblical Christianity! Biblical Christianity recognizes that we have all been under the judgment of God, deserving of hell (Rom. 3:23; 6:23). And biblical Christianity seeks to reach people, rescuing them from such a plight (Jude 1:18–23). Those who stubbornly harden their hearts will indeed face only condemnation. But those who still have an opportunity to repent should be offered the grace that teaches them to deny ungodliness (Titus 2:11–12).

Read "An Interview with Rosaria Butterfield—A Friend of Sinners" on AnswersinGenesis.org or in *Answers Magazine*. How did the pastor and his family show her compassion without compromise as they witnessed to her when she was a lesbian activist?

THE RIGHT MOTIVES AND CHARACTER NECESSARY FOR A RIGHT STAND

What marks the character of Christians who embrace God's design for sexuality and gender? Key virtues include faithfulness, righteousness, self-control, and steadfastness. Faithfulness to God's design for sexuality requires commitment to righteousness, Spirit-empowered self-control in the face of temptation, and steadfastness in the face of cultural pressure.

Christians need to be marked by faithfulness to God and His Word. In the face of intimidation, false accusations, threats, and even legal persecution, Christians must be unwaveringly brave and confidently loyal, determined to hold fast to what is right. Such faithfulness is cultivated by a commitment to God and His Word and revealed when there's pressure to compromise. You can develop these virtues through the influences of an uncompromising church and Christians who are not embarrassed by biblical stances. You can grow in faithfulness by growing closer to God, so that His opinion (His truth) is the touchstone for your responses (rather than prevailing popular opinion and fallen human reasoning).

What is right? God's own righteousness sets the standard. While the world tries to convince people that right is wrong and wrong is right, Christians must conform themselves to what God has revealed about Himself and His expectations in His inerrant and authoritative Word. Such conformity to God's righteousness is cultivated by actively getting to know your righteous God in a relational way through His Word and prayer. Develop this virtue by committing to a deeper daily study of God's Word and specific, Scripture-filled prayers that require time and attention (rather than shallow formulas repeated once a day to check "prayer" off your list).

But the battle we face is not simply external—pressures from the world around us. The battle is also internal—pressures from our own sinful nature. Christians must rely on the Spirit to help them actively put to death the desires of the flesh. Mortifying the flesh requires the fruit of the Spirit, self-control. Only God can help us to grow more consistently in saying

no to desires that seem to come naturally to us. You can develop this virtue by seeking accountability from mature believers and perhaps even formal biblical counseling to assist you in your battle against sin. You can read sound doctrinal and devotional books that help you effectively and actively combat sin.

The Christian has made a fundamental change from living for the flesh to living for Christ. But the Christian needs to remain steadfast in his or her profession of new life in Christ. The pressures from within and without mean that the Christian should not grow weary in well-doing. Don't give up in the face of lost battles. Keep waging war against the flesh, the world, and the devil. Wait patiently for the day when the Lord restores our broken world. You can develop this virtue by remaining in close fellowship with other believers who will encourage you, help you, counsel you, and keep you accountable (1 Thess. 5:14).

As unlikely as it seems that the biblical sexual ethic will triumph over the perverted ethic of our day, Christians should not grow weary in the face of growing oppression and persecution for their beliefs. Believers live for a goal that Scripture tells us will be our reward only through the path of great persecution (Matt. 5:10–12; 6:33; Acts 14:22; 2 Thess. 1:4–10). Our job is to remain steadfast (1 Cor. 15:58) as ambassadors for Christ (2 Cor. 5:20) while we sojourn in a foreign land (Heb. 11:13; 1 Pet. 2:11). We should not be surprised that we are persecuted in this foreign land (John 15:18–20; 1 Pet. 4:12–15). We are to be the purifying influence of salt and the bright, shining witness of light (Matt. 5:13–16; John 3:19–20; Eph. 5:8, 11).

RESPONDING BIBLICALLY TO A FRIEND

No doubt you will have conversations with friends who have adopted transgender, bisexual, or homosexual identities and relationships. Our society tries to normalize these unbiblical sexual choices, and it seeks to silence any opposition to them. You must have the character outlined in the previous section to discern how and when to address someone. There is no formula for how to do this without offending someone. But there are wise and unwise ways to approach the situation.

Helping a friend in this area requires dependence upon God's work in the heart and a loving commitment to speak the truth, which can set your friend free from slavery to sin. You must seek to demonstrate compassion without compromise. Compassion is demonstrated when Christians humbly recognize that we all need forgiveness and empowerment from God because we're all sinners. The question is whether we're repentant sinners actively engaged in putting sin to death by the enablement of the Spirit. Compassion is demonstrated when Christians refuse to join in belittling people made in God's image yet remain uncompromisingly opposed to that which is unethical. Christians cannot accept and enable unethical identities and behavior. But Christians can compassionately extend the grace of the gospel to those who heed the call to repent. Christians can be known for both their humble hospitality to sinful people *and* their honest and bold confrontation of sin. Both align with God's response to sin and sinners. The solutions for those trapped in sin are straightforward: salvation and sanctification—repentance and growth in Christ (1 Cor. 6:11).

As you seek to build redemptive relationships to speak the gospel into people's lives, you will have to make hard, careful decisions. For example, you may be able to go to dinner with an unsaved person who is living this kind of sinful lifestyle but not with a professing Christian in unrepentant sin (see 1 Cor. 5:9–13). Each person is made in the image of God; Christians don't reject a *person*. However, that does not mean that you can condone or support in any way that person's immoral choices. How is this put into practice? Though you might, as a Christian with a biblically informed conscience, eat a meal with an unbeliever living in open sin, should you feel free to attend a same-sex wedding? Your answer to this question will reveal your understanding of principles covered in this section.

Contemplating the possible situations you may face in your future should drive you to prayer for wisdom. It should motivate you to take the study of the Bible more seriously. It should encourage you to find joy in the fellowship of other believers in your local church, who will certainly need to uplift one another through harsh persecution in the coming days. Will you grow into the committed Christian, and perhaps leader, that the church needs?

Thinking It Through 13.3

1. Identify and explain the terms represented by the abbreviation *LGBTQ+*.

2. What are two major indicators of recent and rapid change for society and the church on ethical perspectives regarding LGBTQ+ issues?

3. Explain the biblical teaching on gender found in Genesis 1:26–27; 5:1–2.

4. Explain the biblical teaching on expressing one's gender found in Deuteronomy 22:5 and 1 Corinthians 11:14–15.

5. Identify two key passages that present the biblical pattern for sexual desires and behaviors.

6. Refute the arguments that Genesis 19 can't be used as proof that the Bible forbids homosexual desires and behavior.

7. Refute the arguments that Romans 1:21–32, 1 Corinthians 6:9–11, and 1 Timothy 1:10 can't be used as proof that the Bible forbids homosexual desires and behavior.

8. Is the Bible's sexual ethic unloving? Explain your answer.

9. What character will be needed in the life of a Christian to conform to the biblical ethic?

10. Contrast a biblical and an unbiblical response to a friend who is contemplating or has embraced homosexual or transgender behavior and identity.

13.4 Birth Control, Reproductive Technologies, and Eugenics

How many children do you plan to have? That might sound like a funny question to ask someone in high school. You probably have not given this topic serious consideration. But perhaps you and your friends have thrown out some numbers on how many children you think you would like to have. It's not such a far-out question for someone your age to consider. You're already projecting the kind of life you think you would most enjoy. And those desires and assumptions may affect your decisions just a few years from now regarding marriage and children. Maybe you've already formed an attitude that you would love to have lots of children, a few children, or no children. What factors into these different attitudes and desires?

Should all married couples have children?

context TO HAVE OR NOT TO HAVE CHILDREN—THAT IS THE QUESTION

As you consider your future, you must be very purposeful in determining to be God-centered and God-submitted. Otherwise, you can quickly resort to selfishness and unethical behavior. That goes for those who want lots of children, some children, or no children. Think about the possible motivations of a husband and wife in each case, and consider some fundamental ethical questions: Should married couples seek to have as many children as physically possible? Why should a married couple want to have children? Why wouldn't a married couple want to have children? What about couples who seem to be unable to have children? Should they use modern technology to overcome infertility?

The "No Children" Ideal

Why wouldn't a married couple want to have children? Could there be a legitimate reason? Are most reasons illegitimate? Although there may be some legitimate reasons to forego having children (such as severe physical problems), the majority of married couples who view being childless as an *ideal* tend to have wrong priorities rather than a biblical view of children: career pursuits, lifestyle preferences, greed, viewing children as a nuisance, or a simple fear of responsibility may be motivating factors. Such married couples can be tempted to resort to medical technologies used to take fetal life, such as what has become known as the morning-after pill or other abortifacients (this would include the **birth control*** method known as an intrauterine device [IUD]). Any method that ends unique human life begun at fertilization should be understood to be murder (see Section 9.3 on Abortion).

birth control: a general term that refers to preventing pregnancy; contraception; most often birth control takes place through the use of artificial methods (such as condoms, pills, barriers, or permanent sterilization) rather than natural methods (such as avoiding sex during a woman's fertile time of the month)[14]

The "Some Children" Ideal

Why should a married couple want to have some children? Are all reasons to limit the number legitimate? Married couples usually want to have some children. The desire to have children is both biblical and natural. Nevertheless, most couples want to limit the number of children they have. They have at their disposal both natural and artificial birth-control methods. The reasons some have for limiting the number of children they plan to have may be just as illegitimate as those given by couples who wish to remain childless. However, others advocate birth control for reasons that may be considered legitimate (assuming the contraceptive methods used *prevent* fertilization rather than end new life after fertilization). A legitimate argument for limiting the number of children will center on stewardship of responsibilities: recognizable human limitations to physical, emotional, and financial resources and abilities (Luke 14:28; Eph. 6:4; 1 Tim. 5:8).

All of life consists in deciding not to do some good things in order to be able to do some other good things.

WAYNE GRUDEM[15]

Perhaps the greatest struggle for those couples who would like to have some children is the inability to have any (or any more) children due to infertility. Such married couples can be tempted to resort to medical technologies that may bring about life at the cost of jeopardizing or even killing other life in the process. To make ethical decisions, infertile married couples need to become accurately informed about how various reproductive technologies work.

The "Many Children" Ideal

Should married couples seek to have as many children as physically possible? Is this a matter of preference, or is this a biblical requirement?

First, the Creation Mandate is a blessing and a stewardship responsibility. But it should not be understood to mean that a couple must literally multiply two or three times beyond the two people they start with. Rather, the blessing and responsibility are for the human race as a whole to accomplish, not for each individual couple to accomplish. Married couples should not purposefully live at odds with the Creation Mandate, but each couple is not responsible to fill the earth themselves.

Second, a couple can embrace the blessing of children without focusing on that one blessing alone and maximizing it to the fullest possible extent. For example, food is a blessing, but consuming it to an extreme is gluttony.

Rather, believers should steward and balance all their blessings with other priorities and good endeavors. What is prudent for one family may not be wise for another. There is no biblical requirement to have as many children as possible. Yet some couples may indeed be called and equipped to glorify God by raising large families. Other couples may be called to raise the children of others by fostering or adopting.

Third, God created sex for multiple purposes, not just for procreation. Procreation is one good result from sex. But the sexual relationship between husband and wife was also created for enjoyment and intimate companionship. It does not and need not always result in a child.

Finally, use of artificial birth control methods should not be understood as always usurping God's prerogatives. Artificial methods are no different from natural methods in this respect. Humans have been granted by God the responsibility of wise stewardship. Use of artificial methods (so long as they aren't ending human life) may be wise dominion—or they can be used unwisely. Each couple will have to assess its own situation and motives.

Some people will still be convinced that their family should avoid using birth control. On such matters, Christians should be able to honor the preferences of others and avoid judging each other for differing convictions (see Rom. 14:3–10).

THE BIBLICAL TEACHING ON PROCREATION

God's Word begins by helping us to understand our roles and responsibilities in God's creational order: having children is a normal part of God's plan for marriage (Gen. 1:26–28; 9:1; Mal. 2:15), though as we've noted already it is not the only purpose for sexual union within marriage. The Bible reinforces the Creation Mandate as a blessing by emphasizing that children are a blessing, a gift from God (Ps. 127:3–5; 128:3–4). They are not to be viewed as a nuisance (Matt. 19:13–15). In addition, the Bible recognizes both the great hardship of infertility (Gen.5:2–3; 1 Sam. 1:2–18; Luke 1:7) and the great joy that results when those who were barren are able to give birth (Gen. 21; 5:7; 1 Sam. 2:1–10; Ps. 113:9). Infertility is sad because it is a result of the Fall and not the way the world was originally designed to be for married couples. The desire for children is good, and sadness when this is not possible is appropriate. God has compassion, and we should have it too when we see the heartache of those who are childless.

We can use **assisted reproductive technology (ART)*** to overcome the effects of the Fall; in all areas of life, we exercise stewardship by pushing back against the effects of the Fall and the Curse (Gen. 1:28; 3:7, 10, 16–19, 21). However, while some technologies seem appropriate, others seem questionable, and others would certainly be inappropriate.

assisted reproductive technology (ART): a broad term referring to all types of medical technology used to promote reproduction to overcome infertility

Methods of Assisted Reproductive Technologies

ART that seem appropriate

Artificial insemination from a husband: collecting a husband's semen and injecting it into his wife's cervix or uterus.[16] This does not cause the death of any embryos. This mechanism also maintains the pattern of the marriage relationship by bringing together the reproductive elements of a husband and a wife rather than using a third party. This is a use of medical technology that simply helps someone overcome a physical problem.

Medical treatments that support bodily hormones or other bodily functions or surgically repair organs would also be completely appropriate.

ART that seem questionable

Artificial insemination from a donor: collecting semen from a man other than a woman's husband and injecting it into her cervix or uterus.

Although this does not cause the death of any embryos, it does not maintain the pattern of the marriage relationship by bringing together the reproductive elements of a husband and a wife. It brings in the reproductive element of a third party. While some Christians do not see this as problematic, other Christians rightly see this as troubling (see the discussion on surrogacy below).

In vitro fertilization (IVF): joining together a wife's egg and a husband's sperm to form an embryo in a laboratory. This usually involves the creation of many embryos in which one or a few embryos produce a baby or babies. This technique could be appropriate if the semen and egg come from a husband and a wife (maintaining the pattern of the marriage relationship) and if all the embryos are implanted in the wife's womb so that no embryos are destroyed. However, IVF often involves the reproductive elements of third parties and the creation of many other embryos that either are destroyed or left in a frozen state, likely to be destroyed in the future. Since an embryo is human life, destroying an embryo is destroying life, which is unbiblical. Nevertheless, recent advancements in IVF treatments where only one or two embryos are created have made it possible for Christians to consider these treatments.

Surrogacy: using the womb of a third party (a surrogate mother) for the gestation of a baby. The surrogate mother is impregnated either by artificial insemination or by implanting an embryo formed through IVF from the reproductive elements of both parents, one parent and a donor, or two donors.[17] Using donor reproductive elements and surrogacy leads to an extremely complicated lineage and relationships. The parties involved could include multiple combinations of the following: a mother, a father (or two men and two women in a same-sex relationship), a male donor, a female donor, and the surrogate mother who carries the baby.

Many Christian ethicists cite concerns with such a complex lineage and the emotions involved in these relationships. The pattern in the Bible reflecting God's intent is for conception to follow from the marital union of a man and a woman. Surrogacy does not fit this pattern, particularly when fertilization is accomplished from the sperm or egg of someone else other than the married partners. The question is whether surrogacy violates biblical morality. Certainly, one could not say definitively that surrogacy is equivalent to adultery (because there is no sexual activity occurring between two people in this situation). But we are still introducing a third party into the marriage relationship. Surrogacy also opens the way for people to have children outside the pattern of marriage. Nevertheless, children born as the result of surrogacy are to be treated with love and respect as image-bearers; there's no place for rejecting, deriding, or shunning innocent children who result from unions or methods that were not God's ideal.

ART that would be inappropriate

Artificial insemination or in vitro fertilization used to impregnate a woman who wanted to raise a child outside a biblically approved marriage relationship would be a means of bypassing a God-ordained marriage to have the blessing of children despite rebellion against God's design. This would also be true for the use of a surrogate to carry a child for a male same-sex couple. Such arrangements stand in opposition to God's design for marriage.

Eugenics is the quest to bolster human genetics by preventing people with traits deemed undesirable from reproducing, while encouraging people with traits deemed desirable to procreate. (Eugenics has often been associated with the idea that some races are superior to others.) Today, there are those who believe that only those who are desirable to a society should be allowed to live. This view may lead to killing embryos after genetic prescreening because of predicted disabilities or other characteristics considered undesirable. Such a practice violates the biblical prohibition against murder and is antithetical to the biblical view that all humans have value because they bear the image of God.

In conclusion, Christians should seek to preserve life. Christians should seek to procreate according to God's pattern and design for marriage. Any practice that undermines these principles should be questioned, if not rejected.

ends

AVOIDING IDOLATRY

Desiring to have children is a good thing; children are a blessing. But desiring to have children by any available means is not a good thing; it's idolatry. Christians who want to please the Lord above all will not resort to unethical means to produce children. They will rely on God to sustain them through heartache; they will wait on God to bless them with children, if it is His will, through ethical means. Though challenging to maintain, this attitude testifies of what it is to live for God's glory rather than live for something else.

Other forms of idolatry may be more obvious to us. Eugenics may lead to eliminating "undesirable" people due to idolizing certain traits or idolizing freedom from disease. There is a type of genetic prescreening that eliminates certain people from existing by screening them out, rather than by killing already-alive people. A couple considering having children may elect to be genetically screened to determine what might be passed on to the next generation. Prospective parents can thus determine the chances of their kids having various genetic disorders,[18] but in theory they could also be screened to determine their chances of having children with various other traits such as height, hair color, and the like. Parents might decide to forego having children if they don't like their chances of having their preferred kind of offspring. It's one thing to try to heal and prevent disease (an effect of the Fall). But it's another thing to try to prevent certain kinds of people from existing in the first place or to decide that certain aspects of God's good, diverse creation are undesirable.

agents

VIRTUES THAT COUNTERACT IDOLATRY

The key to avoiding such idolatry is to cultivate the virtues of faith, gratitude, and love. Those who are not able to have children need faith in God's purposes and gratitude for the blessings God has given. Like so many in Scripture, the childless must also believe that God is sovereign over the womb and is able to provide children if He wishes, even in seemingly impossible circumstances. Those who can have children need faith that God will provide for the needs of their family, and they must be grateful for the gift of children, even when the going gets tough. And rather than despising certain people as undesirable, we ought to cultivate love for all of God's image-bearers.

COUNSELING A STRUGGLING COUPLE

You never know what trials you may face in your future. The topics of this section may seem distant rather than relevant to your life. But what if someday you find yourself at a crossroads, needing to make decisions about birth control or ART? How would you counsel a married couple struggling over whether to have children or how to overcome infertility? Wisdom involves living in harmony with the created order, which means that most married couples should seek to have children. However, there are circumstances, such as health issues, that can affect this decision. Wisdom also involves a precise knowledge of birth control and ART options and the ethical questions involved.

Another option for Christian couples to consider would be the God-honoring decision to adopt or foster. Jesus Himself lived as Joseph's adopted son (Luke 2:41, 48). God is "a father of the fatherless" (Ps. 68:5); He shows tremendous care and concern for the orphan (Hosea 14:3; James 1:27). And He pictures one glorious aspect of our salvation in terms of spiritual adoption (Gal. 4:5). Many Christian parents can testify to the privilege and joy that come from rescuing, protecting, providing for, and nurturing a child in need of parents and a stable, loving home. That child becomes one of their own, a beautiful reflection of what Christ has done for us.

Thinking It Through 13.4

1a. In general, what do people resort to if they do not wish a pregnancy to result from sexual relations?

1b. In general, what do people resort to if they are trying to overcome infertility?

2. Summarize the pros and cons of each position on how many children to have.

3. Summarize the basic biblical teaching on procreation.

4. Describe one assisted reproductive technology (ART) that seems appropriate, one that seems questionable, and one that would be inappropriate.

5. Explain two forms of idolatry that relate to couples' views of procreation.

6. Identify three virtues highlighted in this section and explain how those virtues would help a person avoid idolatry related to procreation.

7. What is an alternative to the use of ART for infertile couples—an option that reflects what Christ has done for us in salvation?

Review

SEXUAL ETHICS

13

Terms to Remember

- compatibility
- cohabitation
- no-fault divorce
- immodesty
- pornography
- masturbation
- fornication
- prostitution

- incest
- sexual abuse
- bestiality
- adultery
- polygamy
- marital purity
- homosexual

- LGBTQ+
- bisexual
- transgender
- birth control
- assisted reproductive technology (ART)

- artificial insemination from a husband
- artificial insemination from a donor

- in vitro fertilization (IVF)
- surrogacy
- eugenics

Scripture Memory

1 Thessalonians 4:3–5

Understanding Ethics

1. Contrast the biblical view of marriage, divorce, and remarriage with common views found in the culture.
2. Explain the biblical teaching on inappropriate sexual activity.
3. Why is it not sufficient or appropriate to use conversion therapy to get a person to become heterosexual?
4. Should all married couples have children? Explain.

Practicing Ethical Decision-Making

5. How would you respond to a friend in the following situation? What virtues could have helped your friend avoid such a situation?

   Soon after graduating from high school, one of your friends moves out of his parents' house while they are gone over the weekend. Your friend moves in to cohabit with someone he met at work; both partners have had a string of previous sexual relationships. After several years of living in immorality (including having several children), your friend gets married to that same person. However, a year later your friend asks you to be a character witness in court since he is filing for divorce. He complains that his spouse is committing adultery, but he admits that he too has been unfaithful once or twice. Your friend also wants you to affirm that the divorce is biblically sanctioned.

6. How should you conduct yourself in the following situation to protect yourself (and show love for your Christian brother or sister), and what is one key virtue that you will need to live out?

   You are excited to attend your first junior-senior banquet (or prom). Although the event is chaperoned, many couples slip out of the event early and hang out afterward in groups. However, the other couple that was supposed to hang out with you afterward ditched you. You find yourself all alone with your date in a dark car. Barriers have been breaking down in the last half-hour. It's clear what's wanted.

7. How should you respond if you found yourself in the following situation?

   During high school you take up photography as a hobby. By the time you graduate from college, you've become quite skilled. You find wedding photography to be quite lucrative. However, you have nagging questions about your role in some situations. Some people dress extremely immodestly. And now you've been approached by a gay couple who wants you to photograph their wedding.

8. How should you respond if you found yourself in the following situation?

   You've just gotten married. You're both in grad school and both working full-time jobs. You have a lot of school debt. And you're trying to save up enough money to get an apartment or your first home and move out of your parents' basement. You want to use birth control, but your spouse isn't sure it's healthy or biblical.

Analyzing and Evaluating Ethical Claims

9. How would you respond to someone who claims divorce is the best decision they've ever made, who celebrates the benefits of divorce in general, and who scoffs at the negative consequences of divorce?
10. How would you respond to someone who claims Christianity teaches that sex is dirty?
11. How would you respond to someone who claims that committed homosexual relationships are never condemned in the Bible?
12. How would you respond to someone who claims that using the morning-after pill or an IUD is perfectly fine?

Creating My Own Position Statements on Ethics

13. Write a position statement on divorce and remarriage.
14. Write a position statement on homosexuality, bisexuality, and transgenderism.
15. Write a position statement on birth control and artificial reproductive technology.

conclusion

Do you seek to know God's will? Presumably, you'd answer "Yes, of course!"

Why do you seek to know it? Have you ever asked yourself "What am I trying to gain?" Can you identify your motivations for seeking that knowledge?

Perhaps we should get the magnifying glass off ourselves for a moment and be a little less personal. Let's ask, "Why do people in general seek to know God's will?"

People might want wisdom to make a decision that is very narrow. "Should I buy this car? Should I take this job?" Others might have broader concerns; they seek to know God's will because they want to create a Christian ethical system, like this textbook seeks to do. Other people might understand God's "will" as meaning God's good pleasure in general, not just for decision making. In that case, people might seek to gain knowledge simply to know Him.

Could it be that some individuals want knowledge of God's will to use as ammunition against others, or to gain leverage on people they want to control? The patriarch Jacob did that. He deceived his blind father into thinking that he was his brother Esau, and he lied when he passed off a slaughtered goat as wild game. Jacob's father Isaac noticed how soon the food had been prepared, and he knew hunting takes a long time, so he asked, "How is it that thou hast found it so quickly, my son?" Jacob told yet another lie, but this time he enlisted God in it: "The LORD thy God brought it to me" (Gen. 27:20). At this point in Jacob's life, God was just a tool to get what he wanted.

Why do *you* seek to know God's will? Can you identify a motive of yours? Let's compare our motives with Paul's words in Colossians.

Paul prays for Christians to be "filled with the knowledge of his will in all wisdom and spiritual understanding" (Col. 1:9). Paul wants this so "that ye might walk worthy of the Lord" (Col. 1:10). That is a statement of purpose. Paul is telling us what our purpose should be in seeking to know God.

To put it simply, we are to know God's will so that we will "walk worthy of" Him. Walking is a common biblical metaphor for living one's life. We are to know God's will to live in a way that is "worthy" of God, that is, in a way that treats God as He deserves to be treated and honors Him as He deserves to be honored. That implies something tremendous: *knowledge of God must radically change one's life into a God-honoring one.*

All our seeking God, all our gaining knowledge must funnel into this goal. When knowledge doesn't lead to our honoring the Triune God, it is futile, for it is disconnected from reality, and it is abortive, for it fails to achieve its purpose. God lets us know Him so that we will glorify Him.

It is natural to wonder what a worthy walk looks like. The rest of Colossians 1:9–14 explains that, and in doing so, it provides a well-rounded Christian ethic. It answers the questions "What makes a good deed truly good?" and "What makes a good deed worthy of God, or honoring to Him?"

A worthy walk is "unto all pleasing" (Col. 1:10). That is, a worthy walk fully pleases God. Other texts add specifics to that. "Without faith it is impossible to please him" (Heb. 11:6). So, pleasing God always involves faith in God, for there is no pleasing God without faith. In Romans 8:7–8 pleasing God is equivalent to being subject to God's law. That's talking about obedience to His commands. So, walking worthy of the Lord means trusting Him and obeying Him. These things are fundamental to a worthy walk. You don't honor Him as He deserves when you distrust Him and dismiss His commands.

A worthy walk is "fruitful in every good work" (Col. 1:10). "Fruitful" refers to producing works that please God. Fruitfulness "in every good work" may mean one of two things. Paul could mean something like this: "God wants you to bear fruit in every one of His commands." So, it could mean to obey everything God has said to do. Such an idea fits well with Paul's statements elsewhere, such as where he says that keeping God's commandments is what matters (1 Cor. 7:19). Jesus said with great simplicity: "If ye love me, keep my commandments" (John 14:15).

But fruitfulness in every good work may mean "God's norms are to be used in every conceivable activity." In other words, no endeavor should be thought of as secular, or removed from a religious worldview. If this is what Paul means, he is saying that a worthy walk makes Christ the Lord over every aspect of life. Whether Paul has this in mind here in Colossians or not, it is clearly a biblical point. Elsewhere, Paul tells Christians to glorify God in whatever they do (1 Cor. 10:31) and to take every thought captive to Christ (2 Cor. 10:5).

Paul may have only one of these meanings in mind here in Colossians, but a worthy walk surely includes both of the two options. We must obey all that God has commanded, and just as clearly, we must serve Him in all our endeavors to Him. Our norms come from God, and we must apply those norms to our situations. When we do so, we let Christ be our king.

A worthy walk means "increasing in the knowledge of God" (Col. 1:10). This means that a worthy walk is intellectual, God-centered, and relational. A worthy walk cannot involve mere activity without deep reflection on God. And that reflection must not be inactive in the soul but should be experiential. For how can a walk be worthy without the soul's soaring home to God in prayer? How can it be worthy without abasement before His majesty, joy in His mercy, worship of His Person? A worthy walk must include theological development and relationship with God in all its richness.

Let's sum up what Paul has said so far: we should seek to know God's will to walk worthy of Him. Walking worthy of God means pleasing Him by believing in Him, obeying Him, and gaining ever more knowledge of Him in relationship with Him.

But Paul's Christian ethic isn't complete yet.

A worthy walk means being "strengthened with all might, according to his glorious power" (Col. 1:11). A person might seek to please God but be self-reliant instead of relying on God's empowerment. That is called moralism. Being moral isn't necessarily Christian, and moral people who rely on themselves aren't walking worthy of Christ at all, because they presume that they have the ability in themselves to please God, when God says differently. This divine strengthening leads to "all patience and longsuffering with joyfulness" (Col. 1:11). This empowerment is truly wonderful, for it helps us endure doing right with patience and joy. Who among us doesn't feel his or her need for spiritual strength such as this?

We read more about this empowerment elsewhere in Scripture. In Acts 1:8 we're told that when the Holy Spirit came, the disciples would "receive power." In Ephesians 3:16, Paul prays that God would strengthen believers "with might by his Spirit in the inner man." The strengthening that we are to rely on is that which is given by the Holy Spirit.

Sometimes talk of the Holy Spirit can seem strange and mysterious to people. Someone might wonder, "How do you gain strength from the Spirit?" It comes down to two things: first, we must believe that the Spirit really is available to believers, which amounts to simply accepting by faith the biblical statements, such as those above. Second, we must pray for the Spirit's gracious filling. It may sound strange to ask God to fill you with the Spirit so that you can bear the fruit of His Spirit in your life, but that is exactly what the Bible says to do: "If ye then, being evil, know how to give good gifts unto your children: how much more shall your heavenly Father give the Holy Spirit to them that ask him?" (Luke 11:13). Paul's statement "be filled with the Spirit" (Eph. 5:18) amounts to a command to submit yourself to Spirit-filling constantly. Spirit-filling is part of the normal Christian life, and it is crucial to a truly Christian ethic.

Do you rely on God's power imparted through the Holy Spirit? Or do you think of the Christian life as primarily a matter of willpower and self-discipline? Paul is saying that relying on God's strength is how we become enabled to persist in obedience and joy. Without reliance on God, attempting to be moral goes astray. It becomes an arrogant ode to human ability, for it says, "I have the power to love and please God in myself." It becomes hypocritical, for it professes love for God but rejects His Word about our need for the Spirit. It becomes an impossible burden, for we cannot live up to God's ideals, and sin is ever with us. It sets up a false religion, for to seek to be godly in one's own strength and without reliance on God's specified help is the soul and substance of false religion. The world is full of Christless moralism. Christianity is moral, highly moral, but it is Christ- and Spirit-centered in its ethic. A Christian approach to living right never forgets that Christ gave the Holy Spirit to His followers, and if you want to walk worthy and please God, you must rely on that supply of grace. Paul put it very succinctly: "Walk in the Spirit, and ye shall not fulfil the lust of the flesh" (Gal 5:16).

But Paul's Christian ethic still isn't complete. A person could conceivably obey God's commands and do so seeking empowerment from God, but their obedience might still have little to do with God's redemption in Christ.

A worthy walk means "giving thanks unto the Father, which hath made us meet to be partakers of the inheritance" (Col. 1:12). How did God make us "meet" (or *fit*) to inherit? Paul says that God has "delivered us from the power of darkness" and transferred "us into the kingdom of his dear Son" (Col. 1:13). And he says that in Christ "we have redemption through his blood, even the forgiveness of sins" (Col. 1:14). He made us fit to inherit by Jesus Christ's saving work on the cross.

Look at all the activity in those verses: God made us fit; He delivered us from darkness, transferred us into Christ's kingdom, and redeemed us by Christ's blood. That is a lot of activity, and it is all God's. There is a tendency in the heart of fallen people to emphasize their own works for God and de-emphasize God's works for them. When this happens, religion becomes like a competitive sport, full of effort, panic, and self-comparison. That is not a worthy walk. It does not treat God as He deserves to be treated or honor Him as He deserves to be honored. To take one's eyes off God's works for you means all you have left is yourself and other people.

We must recognize that we were in the domain of darkness, not just a slave there, but a willing participant. We weren't poor captives in Mordor, to use a Tolkien illustration, we were orcs in Mordor. We were part of the darkness. We contributed to it. We aren't the heroes of any story. We're villains whom, for some reason beyond our capacity to understand, God had mercy on despite our crimes. And He not only had mercy on us and saved us, but He gave us an inheritance, placed us into Christ's kingdom, and greatest of all, He sent His Eternal Son to purchase our redemption with His own blood.

As long as these things are true, and they have been in God's plan since before He made the world, there is no such thing as a worthy walk that doesn't constantly rejoice in them. This is why Paul ends his discussion of the Christian life in Colossians 1 on the note of thanking the Father for His great mercy in Christ. Seeking to live a life of godliness without constant gratitude for God's salvation in Christ is not worthy of God; it is an affront to Him.

We have come to the end of Paul's discussion of Christian ethics, and we need to tie up all the strands of thought.

Here is Paul's teaching summed up, and this is a good lesson to end a book on Christian ethics. For a walk to be truly worthy, for a deed to be truly good and pleasing and honoring to God, it must be carried out by someone who has a certain state of mind and heart. Such a person must be informed by the knowledge of God's will, must carry out his works by the Spirit's power, and do them out of gratitude to the Father for His salvation in Christ. This is a consistent and fully formed Christian and Trinitarian ethic. Without these elements, good works aren't good.

Here is the teaching in the simplest terms: We must do what God wants, through God's Spirit, because of Christ, and for God's glory. Our norms, means, reasons, and purposes must be Trinitarian. Anything less is unworthy of God as He has revealed Himself to be; anything less does not treat God as He deserves to be treated and does not honor Him as He deserves to be honored.

This is how Paul conceived the broad outlines of the all the actions a Christian takes in this world. It is a comprehensive and universally applicable view of Christian ethics, and it is given in marvelous language that seems miraculously both full and concise. Paul could put an ocean of matter in a drop of language.

The final question before us is naturally applicational. "Do Paul's words describe how we live?" I would imagine that, if we've really digested what Paul says here, that we all feel quite lowly, insufficient, and wretched. We might even wonder if we've ever done a good work in our lives. What a wonderful way to finish an ethics book, make the students feel like complete wretches!

It is crucial to point out that Paul opens the paragraph by praying for this worthy walk (Col. 1:9), and he closes by referring to forgiveness of sins (Col. 1:14).

Paul seeks a worthy walk from God's gracious hand (Col. 1:9). He pursues God for it, and he relies on Him to give it. So, we see that a worthy walk takes divine power, just like any good we do. Without Christ we can do nothing, so we must seek Him for everything. If you feel convicted that you have fallen far short of Paul's view of the Christian life, follow Paul's lead and seek God for it, and for your friends and loved ones. God has promised to perform the good work He has begun in you (Phil. 1:6), but He wants you to seek Him for its progress. You must go forward on your knees all your life.

It is also crucial to point out that Paul ends this marvelous paragraph on a note of forgiveness in Christ. In Christ, "we have redemption through his blood, even the forgiveness of sins" (Col. 1:14). We see from this that if we are believers in Christ, we should not feel condemned and rejected for our many sub-Christian works. Every time the law of God comes and shows us our shortcomings, we should repent anew but also rejoice that there are no shortcomings in our High Priest who ever lives to intercede for us (Heb. 7:25). We are His, and He is ours. He bore the punishment for all our sins, and He gave us His righteousness when we believed (2 Cor. 5:21). We can look at all our failures, self-reliance, and self-glory, and we can denounce them all, knowing that we are not condemned by them. Though we have fallen far short of a worthy walk, Christ never has, and He obeyed perfectly not for Himself but for His people. A truly Christian ethic relies ultimately and joyously on the all-sufficient work of Christ that makes up for our innumerable deficiencies.

notes

Cover

The quotation that begins "It is never right" is from *The Chapel Sayings of Dr. Bob Jones Sr., founder of Bob Jones University* (Greenville, SC: Bob Jones University, 1976), 10.

Introduction to Ethics/Chapter 1: Creational Foundations for Ethics

1. Taken from pages 43–47 of *Invitation to Christian Ethics: Moral Reasoning and Contemporary Issues* © Copyright 2020 by Ken Magnuson, Invitation to Theological Studies Series. Published by Kregel Publications, Grand Rapids, MI. Used by permission of the publisher. All rights reserved.
2. Jonathan T. Pennington, *Jesus the Great Philosopher: Rediscovering the Wisdom Needed for the Good Life* (Grand Rapids, MI: Brazos, 2020), 22.
3. "The Shorter Catechism" in *Westminster Confession of Faith*, rev. ed. (Glasgow: Free Presbyterian Publications, 1994), 287.
4. Albert M. Wolters, *Creation Regained: Biblical Basics for a Reformational Worldview*, 2nd ed. (Grand Rapids, MI: Eerdmans, 2005), 34–35.
5. Taken from *Christian Ethics: An Introduction to Biblical Moral Reasoning* by Wayne Grudem, © 2018, p. 43. Used by permission of Crossway, a publishing ministry of Good News Publishers, Wheaton, IL 60187, www.crossway.org.
6. Subheadings below taken from Grudem, *Christian Ethics*, 57–61.
7. Football History, "The Development of Football Rules," accessed September 28, 2021, https://www.footballhistory.org/rules.html; Travis Yoesting, "22 Incredible Changes to Soccer Rules Since 1863," The 18, August 17, 2017, https://the18.com/en/soccer-entertainment /lists/timeline-soccer-rule-changes-evolution-laws; James Sweeney, "The Rise and Fall of the Golden Goal: How It Defined Tournaments and Created Legends," These Football Times, May 12, 2019, https:// thesefootballtimes.co/2019/12/05/the-rise-and-fall-of-the-golden -goal-how-it-defined-tournaments-and-created-legends/.
8. Magnuson, *Invitation to Christian Ethics*, 71.
9. "The Shorter Catechism" in *Westminster Confession of Faith*, rev. ed. (Glasgow: Free Presbyterian Publications, 1994), 287–88, 289.
10. Tom D. Crouch, Roger E. Bilstein, and Walter James Boyne, s.v. "history of flight," Encyclopedia Britannica online, last modified November 12, 2020, https://www.britannica.com/technology/history -of-flight/Construction-of-the-sustaining-wings-the-problem-of-lift.
11. Wolters, *Creation Regained*, 17; italics in the original.
12. Wolters, *Creation Regained*, 25; italics in the original.
13. Fleming James, *Personalities of the Old Testament*, The Hale Lectures (New York: Charles Scribner's Sons, 1939), 502.
14. Taken from page 34 of *The Defense of the Faith*, 4th ed., by Cornelius Van Til, ed. K. Scott Oliphint. Copyright 2008, P&R Publishing, Phillipsburg, NJ.
15. Excerpt from page 40 of *Reformed Ethics* by Herman Bavinck and John Bolt, ed., copyright © 2019. Used by permission of Baker Academic, a division of Baker Publishing Group.
16. Augustine, *City of God* 15.22, trans. Marcus Dods, with an introduction by Thomas Merton (New York: Modern Library, 1993), 511.

Chapter 2: The Fall's Effects on Ethics

1. Jobmaster Magnets, "What Exactly Is a 'Strong' Magnet?," July 8, 2015, https://www.jobmastermagnets.com/what-is-a-strong-magnet; Thomasnet.com, "Neodymium Magnet Applications," accessed on September 28, 2021, https://www.thomasnet.com/articles/electrical -power-generation/NIB-magnet-application/.
2. Bodie Hodge, "Should We Look to the Animal World for Answers?," *Answers Magazine*, January 1, 2007, https://answersingenesis.org /morality/should-we-look-to-the-animal-world-for-answers /; Pam Sheppard, "Of Penguins and People," Answers in Genesis,

October 1, 2005, https://answersingenesis.org/reviews/movies/of -penguins-and-people/.
3. Albert M. Wolters, *Creation Regained: Biblical Basics for a Reformational Worldview*, 2nd ed. (Grand Rapids, MI: Eerdmans, 2005), 59.
4. Excerpts taken from *The Doctrine of the Christian Life* by John M Frame. Used with permission from P&R Publishing, Phillipsburg, NJ.
5. Immanuel Kant, *Foundations of the Metaphysics of Morals*, trans. Lewis White Beck (New York: Bobbs-Merrill, 1959 [1785]), 39, quoted on page 25 of *Invitation to Christian Ethics: Moral Reasoning and Contemporary Issues* © Copyright 2020 by Ken Magnuson, Invitation to Theological Studies Series. Published by Kregel Publications, Grand Rapids, MI. Used by permission of the publisher. All rights reserved.
6. Frame, *Doctrine of the Christian Life*, 111.
7. Frame, *Doctrine of the Christian Life*, 112.
8. Frame, *Doctrine of the Christian Life*, 112.
9. Frame, *Doctrine of the Christian Life*, 114.
10. Magnuson, *Invitation to Christian Ethics*, 27.
11. Magnuson, *Invitation to Christian Ethics*, 27.
12. Magnuson, *Invitation to Christian Ethics*, 29.
13. Frame, *Doctrine of the Christian Life*, 116.
14. Aristotle, *Nichomachean Ethics* 4.3.1123b, trans. Terence Irwin, 2nd ed. (Indianapolis: Hackett, 1999), 56.
15. Taken from page 28 of "Greeks Bearing Gifts" in *Revolutions in Worldview: Understanding the Flow of Western Thought* by John Frame, ed. W. Andrew Hoffecker. Copyright 2007, P&R Publishing, Phillipsburg, NJ.
16. Magnuson, *Invitation to Christian Ethics*, 43–47.

Chapter 3: The Role of Redemption in Ethics

1. Albert M. Wolters, *Creation Regained: Biblical Basics for a Reformational Worldview*, 2nd ed. (Grand Rapids, MI: Eerdmans, 2005), 40.
2. Wolters, *Creation Regained*, 40–41.
3. John Owen, *Practical Exposition upon Psalm CXXX* (1835; n.p.: Wentworth Press, 2019), 85.
4. Sinclair Ferguson, "Union with Christ in Pastoral Ministry," conference session at Basics 2010 (May 11, 2010), audio, https://www.truth forlife.org/resources/sermon/union-christ-pastoral-ministry/.
5. Taken from pages 12–13 of *The Christ of Wisdom: A Redemptive-Historical Exploration of the Wisdom Books of the Old Testament* by O. Palmer Robertson. Copyright 2017, P&R Publishing, Phillipsburg, NJ.
6. See Francis Schaeffer, "08 - The Age of Fragmentation," episode 8 in *How Should We Then Live?*, 1977, Gospel Films, last updated July 17, 2017, https://www.youtube.com/watch?v=d0eYmFOQBs0&list =PLP0lSOp9RORx7W0REI8SVK2CNIrMjhS_T&index=8.
7. Tremper Longman III, *How to Read Proverbs* (Downers Grove, IL: InterVarsity, 2002), 16–17.
8. Robertson, *The Christ of Wisdom*, 13.
9. Craig G. Bartholomew and Ryan P. O'Dowd, Old Testament Wisdom Literature: A Theological Introduction (Downers Grove, IL: InterVarsity, 2011), 89.
10. Wolters, *Creation Regained*, 59.
11. Longman, *How to Read Proverbs*, 53–54.
12. "The Shorter Catechism" in *Westminster Confession of Faith*, rev. ed. (Glasgow: Free Presbyterian Publications, 1994), 287.
13. Augustine, *The Confessions of St. Augustine* 1.1, trans. E. B. Pusey and William Benham (New York: P. F. Collier, 1909), 5.
14. *Holman Illustrated Bible Dictionary* (Nashville, TN: Holman Bible Publishers, 2003), s.v. "meekness."
15. David Mathis, "We Will See His Face: What Is the Beatific Vision?" Desiring God, March 11, 2021, https://www.desiringgod.org/articles /we-will-see-his-face.

Chapter 4: Becoming Like Christ

1. For the understanding of virtue as excellence in moral character, see Kevin Timpe and Craig A. Boyd, eds., introduction to *Virtues and*

Their Vices (New York: Oxford University Press, 2014), 6.

2. See O. Bauernfeind, "ἀρετή," in *Theological Dictionary of the New Testament*, ed. Gerhard Kittel, trans. and ed. Geoffrey W. Bromiley (Grand Rapids, MI: Eerdmans, 1964), 1:457–61.

3. See Augustine, *City of God* 15.22, trans. Marcus Dods, with an introduction by Thomas Merton (New York: Modern Library, 1993), 511.

4. Taken from page 326 of *The Doctrine of the Christian Life* by John M. Frame. Copyright 2008, P&R Publishing, Phillipsburg, NJ.

5. Taken from page 37 of *Invitation to Christian Ethics: Moral Reasoning and Contemporary Issues* © Copyright 2020 by Ken Magnuson, Invitation to Theological Studies Series. Published by Kregel Publications, Grand Rapids, MI. Used by permission of the publisher. All rights reserved.

6. Frame, *Doctrine of the Christian Life*, 326.

7. Andrew M. Davis, *An Infinite Journey: Growing toward Christlikeness* (Greenville, SC: Ambassador International, 2014), 173.

Chapter 5: Three Central Virtues

1. Oliver O'Donovan, *Self, World, and Time*, vol. 1 of *Ethics as Theology* (Grand Rapids, MI: Eerdmans, 2013), 98–99.

2. O'Donovan, *Self, World, and Time*, 98–99.

3. John Calvin, *Institutes of the Christian Religion* 3.2.7, vol. 1, ed. John T. McNeill, trans. Ford Lewis Battles, The Library of Christian Classics, vol. 20 (Philadelphia: Westminster Press, 1960), 551.

4. Charles Spurgeon, "The Trial of Your Faith," no. 2055, sermon at the Metropolitan Tabernacle (December 2, 1888).

5. THE GREATEST LOVE OF ALL. Words by LINDA CREED. Music by MICHAEL MASSER. © 1977 (Renewed) EMI GOLD HORIZON MUSIC CORP. and EMI GOLDEN TORCH MUSIC CORP. Exclusive Print Rights Administered by ALFRED MUSIC.

6. Augustine, *On Christian Teaching* 3.10.16, in William Harmless, ed., *In His Own Words* (Washington, DC: CUA Press, 2010), 170.

7. Jonathan Edwards, *The End for Which God Created the World*, in *The Works of Jonathan Edwards*, rev. ed., ed. Edward Hickman (Edinburgh, UK: Banner of Truth Trust, 1974), 1.105; italics in the original.

8. J. C. Ryle, "Christian Love!," Monergism, https://www.monergism.com/christian-love.

9. John Webster, *Confessing God: Essays in Christian Dogmatics II*, T&T Clark Cornerstones (Bloomsbury T&T Clark: 2016), 196, 204–5.

10. Wilhelmus à Brakel, *The Law, Christian Graces, and the Lord's Prayer*, vol. 3 of *The Christian's Reasonable Service*, ed. Joel R. Beeke, trans. Bartel Elshout (Grand Rapids, MI: Reformation Heritage Books, 2015), 322.

11. James T. Dennison, Jr., comp., "Calvin's Catechism (1537)," in vol. 1, *Reformed Confessions of the 16th and 17th Centuries in English Translation* (Grand Rapids, MI: Reformation Heritage Books, 2008), 378.

12. Oliver O'Donovan, *Resurrection and Moral Order: An Outline for Evangelical Ethics*, 2nd ed. (Leicester, UK: APOLLOS / Grand Rapids, MI: Eerdmans, 1994), 253.

13. Webster, *Confessing God*, 205.

14. Charles Pinches, "On Hope," in *Virtues and Their Vices*, ed. Kevin Timpe and Craig A. Boyd (New York: Oxford University Press, 2014), 351.

15. À Brakel, *The Law, Christian Graces, and the Lord's Prayer*, 327.

16. D. W. Gill, "Hope," in *New Dictionary of Christian Ethics and Pastoral Theology*, ed. David J. Atkinson, David H. Field, Arthur F. Holmes, and Oliver O'Donovan (Downers Grove, IL: InterVarsity, 1995), 456–57.

17. Frank Thielman, *Ephesians*, BECNT (Grand Rapids, MI: Baker Academic, 2010), 356–57; *Biblical Worldview: Creation, Fall, Redemption* (Greenville, SC: BJU Press, 2016), 179.

18. Gill, *New Dictionary of Christian Ethics and Pastoral Theology*, 456–57.

Chapter 6: Virtues, Part 1

1. *Merriam-Webster.com Thesaurus*, s.v. "righteousness," accessed February 26, 2022, https://www.merriam-webster.com/thesaurus/righteousness.

2. "Deep Blue," IBM, Icons of Progress, accessed February 16, 2023, https://www.ibm.com/ibm/history/ibm100/us/en/icons/deepblue/; "Deep Blue," *Encyclopedia Britannica* online, last modified January 26, 2023, https://www.britannica.com/topic/Deep-Blue.

3. Clarke D. Forsythe, *Politics for the Greatest Good: The Case for Prudence in the Public Square* (Downers Grove, IL: InterVarsity, 2009), 24.

4. "The Fox and the Crow," *The Aesop for Children* (1919), adapted inter-

active book presented by Library of Congress, accessed November 11, 2021, http://read.gov/aesop/027.html.

5. W. Jay Wood, "Prudence," in *Virtues and Their Vices*, ed. Kevin Timpe and Craig A. Boyd (New York: Oxford University Press, 2014), 37.

6. Wood, "Prudence," 38.

7. Sir Walter Scott, s.v. "Sir Walter Scott on chivalry," *Encyclopedia Britannica* online, August 5, 2014, https://www.britannica.com/topic/Sir-Walter-Scott-on-chivalry-1987278.

8. Wilhelmus à Brakel, *The Law, Christian Graces, and the Lord's Prayer*, vol. 3 of *The Christian's Reasonable Service*, ed. Joel R. Beeke, trans. Bartel Elshout (Grand Rapids, MI: Reformation Heritage Books, 2015), 103–4; italics in the original.

9. Jim Berg, *Essential Virtues: Marks of the Christ-Centered Life* (Greenville, SC: JourneyForth, 2008), 173.

10. Berg, *Essential Virtues*, 173.

11. H. D. McDonald, "Courage," in *New Bible Dictionary*, 3rd ed., ed. D. R. W. Wood et al. (Downers Grove, IL: InterVarsity, 1996), 234.

12. À Brakel, *The Law, Christian Graces, and the Lord's Prayer*, 334.

13. Jerry Bridges, *The Practice of Godliness* (Colorado Springs: NavPress, 1983), 164; bold added; italics in the original.

14. Excerpt from the work by Robert C. Roberts entitled "Temperance" from the anthology book Virtues and Their Vices (by editors Kevin Timpe and Craig A. Boyd © 2014. ISBN: 9780199645541). Reproduced with permission of Oxford Publishing Limited through PLSclear.

Chapter 7: Virtues, Part 2

1. Jerry Bridges, *The Practice of Godliness* (Colorado Springs: NavPress, 1983), 91.

2. Bridges, *The Practice of Godliness*, 91.

3. Bridges, *The Practice of Godliness*, 220.

4. Taken from page 208 of *Known by God: A Biblical Theology of Personal Identity* by Brian S. Rosner. Italics in the original. Copyright © 2017 by Brian S. Rosner. Used by permission of Zondervan. www.zondervan.com.

5. Chromatius, "Tractate on Matthew 17.4.1–2" in *Matthew 1–13*, ed. Manlio Simonetti, vol. New Testament 1a of Ancient Christian Commentary on Scripture (Downers Grove, IL: IVP Academic, 2001), 82.

6. John MacArthur, *The Quest for Character* (Nashville, TN: Thomas Nelson, 2006), 25.

7. MacArthur, *The Quest for Character*, 72.

8. Jim Berg, *Essential Virtues: Marks of the Christ-Centered Life* (Greenville, SC: JourneyForth, 2008), 181. Berg seems to be building on William Barclay's description of *agapē* love in *New Testament Words* (Philadelphia: Westminster Press, 1964), 28.

9. Jonathan T. Pennington, "A Biblical Theology of Human Flourishing," Institute for Faith, Work, and Economics, March 4, 2015, https://tifwe.org/wp-content/uploads/2015/03/A-Biblical-Theology-of-Human-Flourishing-Pennington.pdf.

10. Bernadette Deron, "This Is How 15 Other Countries Around the World Celebrate Thanksgiving," All That's Interesting, updated November 9, 2021, https://allthatsinteresting.com/thanksgiving-in-other-countries.

11. Bridges, *The Practice of Godliness*, 127.

12. Bridges, *The Practice of Godliness*, 145.

13. Pennington, "A Biblical Theology of Human Flourishing."

14. Pennington, "A Biblical Theology of Human Flourishing."

15. John Webster, "The Fruit of the Spirit 4. Peace," Reformation21, August 26, 2015, Section IV, https://www.reformation21.org/articles/the-fruit-of-the-spirit-4-peace.php.

16. MacArthur, *The Quest for Character*, 86.

17. MacArthur, *The Quest for Character*, 40; italics in the original.

18. Taken from *Christian Ethics: An Introduction to Biblical Moral Reasoning* by Wayne Grudem, © 2018, p. 311. Used by permission of Crossway, a publishing ministry of Good News Publishers, Wheaton, IL 60187, www.crossway.org.

19. Adapted from Grudem, *Christian Ethics*, 311–12.

20. John Calvin, *Commentaries on the Four Last Books of Moses Arranged in the Form of a Harmony*, trans. Charles William Bingham (Bellingham, WA: Faithlife, 2010), 1:34–35.

Chapter 8: A Method for Handling Ethical Issues

1. Taken from page 43 of *Invitation to Christian Ethics: Moral Reasoning and Contemporary Issues* © Copyright 2020 by Ken Magnuson, Invitation to Theological Studies Series. Published by Kregel Publications,

Grand Rapids, MI. Used by permission of the publisher. All rights reserved.

2. "The Shorter Catechism" in *Westminster Confession of Faith*, rev. ed. (Glasgow: Free Presbyterian Publications, 1994), 287.

3. Magnuson, *Invitation to Christian Ethics*, 45.

4. The questions that follow and their later expansion owe most to Magnuson's ethical method as articulated in *Invitation to Christian Ethics*, 43–54. However, our method and questions have also been influenced by other writers, including pages 33–34, 49–51 of *The Doctrine of the Christian Life* by John M. Frame. Copyright 2008, P&R Publishing, Phillipsburg, NJ; and from *Christian Ethics: An Introduction to Biblical Moral Reasoning* by Wayne Grudem, © 2018, pages 107, 149–60. Used by permission of Crossway, a publishing ministry of Good News Publishers, Wheaton, IL 60187, www.crossway.org.

Chapter 9: The Ethics of Life and Death

1. 18 U.S.C. 1111(a), http://uscode.house.gov/view.xhtml?req=granuleid: USC-prelim-title18-section1111&num=0&edition=prelim; bold added.

2. See 18 U.S.C. 1111(a).

3. 18 U.S.C. 1112(a), http://uscode.house.gov/view.xhtml?req=granuleid: USC-prelim-title18-section1112&num=0&edition=prelim; bold added.

4. See 18 U.S.C. 1112(a).

5. "Self-Defense Law: Overview," FindLaw, last updated September 10, 2022, https://www.findlaw.com/criminal/criminal-law-basics/self -defense-overview.html.

6. "Self-Defense Law: Overview," FindLaw.

7. Taken from page 685 of *The Doctrine of the Christian Life* by John M. Frame. Copyright 2008, P&R Publishing, Phillipsburg, NJ.

8. Douglas K. Stuart, *Exodus*, New American Commentary (Nashville, TN: B&H, 2006), 503.

9. See Frame, *The Doctrine of the Christian Life*, 325.

10. Centers for Disease Control and Prevention, "Leading Causes of Death Report, 2019," WISQARS Injury Data, https://wisqars.cdc.gov /fatal-leading.

11. Taken from *Christian Ethics: An Introduction to Biblical Moral Reasoning* by Wayne Grudem, © 2018, p. 587. Used by permission of Crossway, a publishing ministry of Good News Publishers, Wheaton, IL 60187, www.crossway.org.

12. Andrew Dugan, "In U.S., Support Up for Doctor-Assisted Suicide," Gallup News, May 27, 2015, https://news.gallup.com/poll/183425/ support-doctor-assisted-suicide.aspx.

13. Julie Lowe, "Teens and Suicide: Recognizing the Signs and Sharing Hope," *Journal of Biblical Counseling* 35:1 (2021): 13.

14. Grudem, *Christian Ethics*, 566.

15. Melissa Webb, "Healing in Even the Darkest Places," *Answers Magazine*, January 1, 2019, https://answersingenesis.org/sanctity-of-life /healing-darkest-places/.

16. Taken from page 342 of *Invitation to Christian Ethics: Moral Reasoning and Contemporary Issues* © Copyright 2020 by Ken Magnuson, Invitation to Theological Studies Series. Published by Kregel Publications, Grand Rapids, MI. Used by permission of the publisher. All rights reserved. Magnuson cites Lawrence B. Finer et al., "Reasons U.S. Women Have Abortions: Quantitative and Qualitative Perspectives," *Perspectives on Sexual and Reproductive Health* 37, no. 3 (September 2005): 113 (Table 2), https://www.guttmacher.org/sites/default/files /article_files/3711005.pdf. Higher percentages of women (though still below fifteen percent) did cite health concerns for themselves as contributing factors, according to this table.

17. Magnuson, *Invitation to Christian Ethics*, 342.

18. Magnuson, *Invitation to Christian Ethics*, 339, who cites Doe v. Bolton, 410 U. S. 179, 192 (1973) and Francis J. Beckwith, *Defending Life: A Moral and Legal Case against Abortion Choice* (Cambridge: Cambridge University Press, 2007), 339.

19. Magnuson, *Invitation to Christian Ethics*, 340–41.

20. See Magnuson, *Invitation to Christian Ethics*, 339–40; Ariana Eunjung Cha and Rachel Roubein, "Fetal Viability Is at the Center of Mississippi Abortion Case. Here's Why." *Washington Post*, December 1, 2021, https://www.washingtonpost.com/health/2021/12/01/what-is-viability/.

21. Roe v. Wade, 410 U.S. 113 (1973) at 163.

22. See "Dobbs v. Jackson: A New Opportunity to Protect Life," The Heritage Foundation, December 2, 2021, https://www .heritage.org/citizens-guide-fight-america/2021-action-items/dobbs

-v-jackson-new-opportunity-protect-life; Leah Savas, "Abortion Battle Lines," World, January 29, 2022, https://wng.org/articles /abortion-battle-lines-1641864614.

23. Dobbs v. Jackson, No. 19–1392, 597 S. Ct. slip opinion (2022).

24. See Avery Foley, "When Does Life Begin?," *Answers Magazine*, December 1, 2021, https://answersingenesis.org/sanctity-of-life/abortion /when-does-life-begin/; David Menton, "Plan B: Over-the-Counter Abortion?," *Answers Magazine*, July 21, 2008, https://answersingenesis .org/sanctity-of-life/abortion/plan-b/.

25. Sarah Terzo, "Abortion Activists Admit: 'I Knew It Was a Baby,'" LifeNews.com, January 22, 2013, https://www.lifenews.com /2013/01/22/abortion-activists-admit-i-knew-it-was-a-baby/.

26. See "Ectopic Pregnancy," Mayo Clinic, accessed May 17, 2022, https://www.mayoclinic.org/diseases-conditions/ectopic-pregnancy /symptoms-causes/syc-20372088, and "Ectopic Pregnancy," Cleveland Clinic, last reviewed January 18, 2023, https://my.clevelandclinic .org/health/diseases/9687-ectopic-pregnancy.

27. See Abolghasem Pourreza and Aziz Batebi, "Psychological Consequences of Abortion among the Post Abortion Care Seeking Women in Tehran" *Iran Journal of Psychiatry* 6, no. 1 (2011): 31–36, https://www .ncbi.nlm.nih.gov/pmc/articles/PMC3395931/.

Chapter 10: Ethical Government

1. See summaries of and responses to these positions in pages 406–19 of *Invitation to Christian Ethics: Moral Reasoning and Contemporary Issues* © Copyright 2020 by Ken Magnuson, Invitation to Theological Studies Series. Published by Kregel Publications, Grand Rapids, MI. Used by permission of the publisher. All rights reserved.

2. Magnuson, *Invitation to Christian Ethics*, 395–96.

3. Magnuson, *Invitation to Christian Ethics*, 395–404, 412–20.

4. "Percentage of Americans Who View the Death Penalty as Morally Acceptable Remains Near Record Low," Death Penalty Information Center, June 16, 2022, https://deathpenaltyinfo.org/news/percentage -of-americans-who-view-the-death-penalty-as-morally-acceptable -remains-near-record-low, citing Megan Brenan, "Americans Say Birth Control, Divorce Most 'Morally Acceptable,'" Gallup News, June 9, 2022, https://news.gallup.com/poll/393515/americans -say-birth-control-divorce-morally-acceptable.aspx.

5. See "Atom Spy Case/Rosenbergs," Federal Bureau of Investigation, https://www.fbi.gov/history/famous-cases/atom-spy-caserosenbergs.

6. "Death Penalty for Offenses Other Than Murder," Death Penalty Information Center, https://deathpenaltyinfo.org/facts-and-research /crimes-punishable-by-death/death-penalty-for-offenses-other-than -murder.

7. Magnuson, *Invitation to Christian Ethics*, 404.

8. "Life Imprisonment in Norway," Wikipedia, accessed May 21, 2022, https://en.wikipedia.org/wiki/Life_imprisonment_in_Norway.

9. See discussion in Magnuson, *Invitation to Christian Ethics*, 409–10.

10. Maurice Possley, "Donald Eugene Gates," The National Registry of Exonerations, last updated November 20, 2015, https://www.law.umich .edu/special/exoneration/Pages/casedetail.aspx?caseid=3233.

11. Magnuson, *Invitation to Christian Ethics*, 404.

12. Taken from page 703 of *The Doctrine of the Christian Life* by John M. Frame. Copyright 2008, P&R Publishing, Phillipsburg, NJ.

13. Taken from page 704 of *The Doctrine of the Christian Life* by John M. Frame. Copyright 2008, P&R Publishing, Phillipsburg, NJ.

14. Oliver O'Donovan, *The Just War Revisited* (Cambridge: Cambridge University Press, 2003), 11; Charles Hodge, *Systematic Theology* (Peabody, MA: Hendrickson Academic, 1999), 3:367.

15. Hodge, *Systematic Theology*, 3:367.

16. O'Donovan, *The Just War Revisited*, 11.

17. Plymouth Brethren Christian Church, "Brethren Served in Both World Wars," What We Believe–Other, https://www.plymouthbrethren christianchurch.org/beliefs/other/; Mennonite Church USA, "Article 22. Peace, Justice, and Nonresistance," Confession of Faith in a Mennonite Perspective, https://www.mennoniteusa.org/who-are -mennonites/what-we-believe/confession-of-faith/peace-justice-and -nonresistance/.

18. Michael Walzer, *Arguing about War* (New Haven, CT: Yale University Press, 2004), 22.

19. O'Donovan, *The Just War Revisited*, 5.

20. The following box is taken from page 2555 of *The ESV® Study Bible*

(The Holy Bible, English Standard Version®), Copyright © 2008 by Crossway, a publishing ministry of Good News Publishers. Used by permission. All rights reserved. Some formatting has been altered; deleted material is indicated by ellipses; added material is in brackets.

21. Andrew Fiala, "Pacifism," under 2.1 Absolute vs. Contingent Pacifism, *The Stanford Encyclopedia of Philosophy* (Fall 2021 Edition), ed. Edward N. Zalta, https://plato.stanford.edu/archives/fall2021/entries/pacifism/.

22. Taken from *Christian Ethics: An Introduction to Biblical Moral Reasoning* by Wayne Grudem, © 2018, p. 514. Used by permission of Crossway, a publishing ministry of Good News Publishers, Wheaton, IL 60187, www.crossway.org.

23. Malcolm Shaw, "Geneva Conventions," *Encyclopedia Britannica* online, last modified October 20, 2022, https://www.britannica.com/event/Geneva-Conventions.

24. Walzer, *Arguing about War*, 20–21.

25. "Major Cold War Events," *Encyclopedia Britannica* online Student Center, accessed March 3, 2022, https://www.britannica.com/study/major-cold-war-events.

26. See O'Donovan, *The Just War Revisited*, 9, and Paul Ramsey, *The Just War: Force and Political Responsibility* (New York: Charles Scribner's Sons, 1968), 142.

27. Mark R. Amstutz, *Just Immigration: American Policy in Christian Perspective* (Grand Rapids: Eerdmans, 2017), in the introduction to Chapter 4, https://search.ebscohost.com/login.aspx?direct=true&AuthType=sso&db=e000xna&AN=1703973&site=ehost-live.

28. Amstutz, *Just Immigration*, in the introduction to Chapter 4.

29. Amstutz, *Just Immigration*, in the introduction to Chapter 4.

30. Amstutz, *Just Immigration*, in Chapter 1, under "Christian Ethics and Immigration."

31. Gretchen Frazee, "Four Myths about How Immigrants Affect the U.S. Economy," PBS News Hour, Making Sen$e, November 2, 2018, https://www.pbs.org/newshour/economy/making-sense/4-myths-about-how-immigrants-affect-the-u-s-economy; "How Does Immigration Affect the U.S. Economy?," The Science Behind It, National Academy of Sciences, accessed May 3, 2022, https://thesciencebehindit.org/how-does-immigration-affect-the-u-s-economy/.

32. Michael T. Light, Jongying He, and Jason P. Robey, "Comparing Crime Rates between Undocumented Immigrants, Legal Immigrants, and Native-Born US Citizens in Texas," *Proceedings of the National Academy of Sciences* 117, no. 51 (December 7, 2020), doi:10.1073/pnas.2014704117.

33. See Amstutz, *Just Immigration*, in Chapter 3, under "Shortcomings of the Current System," who mentions a similar policy as a recommendation of the Jordan Commission on Immigration Reform (among others) and cites William A. Kandel, "US Family-Based Immigration Policy," Congressional Research Service (November 19, 2014), 2.

34. "Rights and Responsibilities of a Green Card Holder (Permanent Resident)," U.S. Citizenship and Immigration Services, last updated July 15, 2015, https://www.uscis.gov/green-card/after-we-grant-your-green-card/rights-and-responsibilities-of-a-green-card-holder-permanent-resident.

35. Average number from 2010–19 from 2019 Yearbook of Immigration Statistics, Table 1, U.S. Department of Homeland Security, https://www.dhs.gov/immigration-statistics/yearbook/2019/table1.

36. 2020 Yearbook of Immigration Statistics, Table 6, U.S. Department of Homeland Security, https://www.dhs.gov/immigration-statistics/yearbook/2020/table6.

37. 2020 Yearbook of Immigration Statistics, Table 20, U.S. Department of Homeland Security, https://www.dhs.gov/sites/default/files/2022-07/2022_0308_plcy_yearbook_immigration_statistics_fy2020_v2.pdf.

38. "Naturalization Statistics," U.S. Citizenship and Immigration Services, last updated September 21, 2022, https://www.uscis.gov/citizenship-resource-center/naturalization-statistics.

39. "Naturalization Statistics," fiscal year 2020, U.S. Citizenship and Immigration Services, accessed March 16, 2022, https://www.uscis.gov/citizenship-resource-center/naturalization-statistics.

40. Bryan Baker, "Estimates of the Unauthorized Immigrant Population Residing in the United States: January 2015–January 2018," Population Estimates (DHS Office of Immigration Statistics, January 2021), Figure 1, https://www.dhs.gov/sites/default/files/publications/immigration-statistics/Pop_Estimate/UnauthImmigrant/unauthorized_immigrant_population_estimates_2015_-_2018.pdf.

41. Ryan Baugh, "Refugees and Asylees: 2019," Annual Flow Report (DHS Office of Immigration Statistics, September 2020), 1, https://www.dhs.gov/

42. Justin Gest, quoted in Quoctrung Bui and Caitlin Dickerson, "What Can the U.S. Learn from How Other Countries Handle Immigration?," *New York Times* online, February 16, 2018, https://www.nytimes.com/interactive/2018/02/16/upshot/comparing-immigration-policies-across-countries.html.

43. Lily Kuo, "In China, They're Closing Churches, Jailing Pastors - and Even Rewriting Scripture," *The Guardian* online, January 13, 2019, https://www.theguardian.com/world/2019/jan/13/china-christians-religious-persecution-translation-bible.

44. "Russian Revolution," History.com, last updated January 11, 2023, https://www.history.com/topics/european-history/russian-revolution#; "Nov 7, 1917 CE: October Revolution," *National Geographic* online education resource, accessed April 27, 2022, https://www.nationalgeographic.org/thisday/nov7/october-revolution/.

45. Mario F. Morelli, "Civil Disobedience," in *Civil Disobedience, Social Justice, Nationalism & Populism, Violent Demonstrations and Race Relations*, ed. Editors of Salem Press (Hackensack, NJ: Salem Press, 2017). https://online-salempress-com.eu1.proxy.openathens.net/articleDetails.do?articleName=GHCT17_0002.

46. Taken from page 618 of *The Doctrine of the Christian Life* by John M. Frame. Copyright 2008, P&R Publishing, Phillipsburg, NJ.

47. John Calvin, *Institutes of the Christian Religion* 4.20.31, vol. 1, ed. John T. McNeill, trans. Ford Lewis Battles, The Library of Christian Classics, vol. 20 (Philadelphia: Westminster Press, 1960), 1519.

48. Bradford Littlejohn, "Christian Citizenship and the Rule of Law," The Gospel Coalition (Canadian edition), December 9, 2020, https://ca.thegospelcoalition.org/article/christian-citizenship-and-the-rule-of-law/.

49. Littlejohn, "Christian Citizenship and the Rule of Law."

Chapter 11: Ethical Society

1. Colin Kidd, *The Forging of Races: Race and Scripture in the Protestant Atlantic World, 1600–2000*, (Cambridge University Press, 2006), 9.

2. Herman Bavinck, *Reformed Dogmatics: God and Creation*, vol. 2, ed. John Bolt, trans. John Vriend (Grand Rapids, MI: Baker Academic, 2004), 523.

3. *Oxford English Dictionary* online, s.v. "racism", last modified March 2022, https://www.oed.com/view/Entry/157097?redirectedFrom=racism#eid.

4. Noted in George Yancey, *Beyond Racial Gridlock: Embracing Mutual Responsibility* (Downers Grove, IL: IVP Books, 2006), 67.

5. Yancey, *Beyond Racial Gridlock*, 67.

6. Dictionary.com, s.v. "reparations", accessed July 21, 2022, https://www.dictionary.com/browse/reparations.

7. Taken from *Christian Ethics: An Introduction to Biblical Moral Reasoning* by Wayne Grudem, © 2018, p. 642. Used by permission of Crossway, a publishing ministry of Good News Publishers, Wheaton, IL 60187, www.crossway.org. Grudem quotes the same Scripture passage that follows and adds the same emphasis, but in a different English translation.

8. Declaration of Independence (1776), https://www.archives.gov/founding-docs/declaration-transcript.

9. Taken from *Love in Hard Places* by D. A. Carson, © 2002, p. 97. Used by permission of Crossway Books, a publishing ministry of Good News Publishers, Wheaton, Illinois 60187, www.crossway.com.

10. Grudem, *Christian Ethics*, 685–88.

11. Randy Jaeggli, *Christians and Alcohol: A Scriptural Case for Abstinence* (Greenville, SC: Bob Jones University Press, 2014), 11–36.

12. For more information, see Kevin J. Vanhoozer, "Should Followers of Christ Use Recreational Marijuana?," The Gospel Coalition, January 16, 2020, https://www.thegospelcoalition.org/article/followers-christ-use-recreational-marijuana/.

13. See John Rosengren, "How Casinos Enable Gambling Addicts," *The Atlantic*, December 2016, https://www.theatlantic.com/magazine/archive/2016/12/losing-it-all/505814/?utm_source=nl-atlantic-daily-112816.

14. *Collins COBUILD Advanced Learner's Dictionary* online, s.v. "recreational drug," accessed April 4, 2023, https://www.collinsdictionary.com/us/dictionary/english/recreational-drug.

15. Grudem, *Christian Ethics*, 1039.
16. Grudem, *Christian Ethics*, 676–77.
17. Grudem, *Christian Ethics*, 691–92.
18. Rosengren, "How Casinos Enable Gambling Addicts."
19. Grudem, *Christian Ethics*, 1040–41.
20. Mark E. Shaw, "What Does God Say to those Who Struggle with Addiction?," The Gospel Coalition Podcast, July 29, 2020, 8:02, https://www.thegospelcoalition.org/podcasts/q-a-podcast/what-does-god-say-to-those-who-struggle-with-addiction/.
21. Vocabulary.com, s.v. "profanity," accessed July 28, 2022, https://www.vocabulary.com/dictionary/profanity.
22. Vocabulary.com, s.v. "vulgarity," accessed July 28, 2022, https://www.vocabulary.com/dictionary/vulgarity.
23. Kevin DeYoung, "The One Indispensable Rule for Using Social Media," *DeYoung, Restless, and Reformed* (blog), The Gospel Coalition, June 13, 2012, https://www.thegospelcoalition.org/blogs/kevin-deyoung/the-one-indispensable-rule-for-using-social-media/.
24. *Cambridge Dictionary* online, s.v. "bribery," accessed July 29, 2022, https://dictionary.cambridge.org/us/dictionary/english/bribery.
25. *Cambridge Dictionary* online, s.v. "extortion," accessed July 29, 2022, https://dictionary.cambridge.org/us/dictionary/english/extortion.
26. Jeffrey Moriarty, "Business Ethics," under 6.1 "Hiring and Firing," Stanford Encyclopedia of Philosophy (Fall 2021 Edition), ed. Edward N. Zalta, https://plato.stanford.edu/archives/fall2021/entries/ethics-business/.
27. Summarized from Moriarty, "Business Ethics," under 6.1 "Hiring and Firing."
28. Grudem, *Christian Ethics*, 1060.
29. Grudem, *Christian Ethics*, 1062.
30. The preceding six principles have been adapted from Grudem, *Christian Ethics*, 1059–63.
31. See Grudem, *Christian Ethics*, 1066–72.
32. *Cambridge Dictionary* online, s.v. "exploitation," accessed July 30, 2022, https://dictionary.cambridge.org/us/dictionary/english/exploitation.
33. William G. Messenger, review of (and in this case, summarizing a theme of) *Why Business Matters to God (And What Still Needs to Be Fixed)*, by Jeff Van Duzer, *Themelios* 36, no. 2 (August 2011), https://www.thegospelcoalition.org/themelios/review/why-business-matters-to-god-and-what-still-needs-to-be-fixed/.

Chapter 12: Ethical Science

1. "Stem Cells: What They Are and What They Do," Mayo Clinic, accessed April 13, 2022, https://www.mayoclinic.org/tests-procedures/bone-marrow-transplant/in-depth/stem-cells/art-20048117.
2. Leonardo M. R. Ferreira, "Stem Cells: A Brief History and Outlook," Science in the News (Harvard University Graduate School of Arts and Sciences), January 2, 2014, https://sitn.hms.harvard.edu/flash/2014/stem-cells-a-brief-history-and-outlook-2/.
3. Andy Coghlan, "Stem Cell Timeline: The History of a Medical Sensation," NewScientist, January 30, 2014, https://www.newscientist.com/article/dn24970-stem-cell-timeline-the-history-of-a-medical-sensation/.
4. Joe Carter, "The FAQs: Chinese Scientists Create First Monkey-Human Embryos," The Gospel Coalition, April 19, 2021, https://www.thegospelcoalition.org/article/create-monkey-human-embryos/; bold added.
5. Carter, "The FAQs: Chinese Scientists Create First Monkey-Human Embryos."
6. Joe Carter, "9 Things You Should Know about Human Cloning," The Gospel Coalition, May 17, 2013, https://www.thegospelcoalition.org/article/9-things-you-should-know-about-human-cloning/.
7. Carter, "9 Things You Should Know about Human Cloning."
8. "Cloning Fact Sheet," National Human Genome Research Institute, last updated August 15, 2020, https://www.genome.gov/about-genomics/fact-sheets/Cloning-Fact-Sheet.
9. Carter's term (although he is focused more on cloning for research) in "9 Things You Should Know about Human Cloning."
10. See Carter, "9 Things You Should Know about Human Cloning"; "Cloning Fact Sheet," National Human Genome Research Institute.
11. "Cloning Fact Sheet," National Human Genome Research Institute.
12. Joe Carter, "The FAQs: What Christians Should Know about CRISPR Genetic Scissors," The Gospel Coalition, October 14, 2022, https://www.thegospelcoalition.org/article/the-faqs-what-christians-should-know-about-crispr-genetic-scissors/.
13. Gabriella Beer, "Science Surgery: 'What's the Difference between the Words Genome, Gene and Chromosome?,'" Cancer Research UK News, May 29, 2018, https://news.cancerresearchuk.org/2018/05/29/science-surgery-whats-the-difference-between-the-words-genome-gene-and-chromosome/.
14. Carter, "The FAQs: What Christians Should Know about CRISPR Genetic Scissors."
15. "How Does Genome Editing Work?," National Human Genome Research Institute, last updated August 3, 2017, https://www.genome.gov/about-genomics/policy-issues/Genome-Editing/How-genome-editing-works.
16. This evaluation generally follows and partially summarizes that of Carter, "The FAQs: What Christians Should Know about CRISPR Genetic Scissors."
17. Francis J. Beckwith, "The Human Being, a Person of Substance," in *Persons, Moral Worth, and Embryos: A Critical Analysis of Pro-Choice Arguments*, ed. Stephen Napier (New York: Springer, 2011), 67–68.
18. "Placental Tissue with CryoMaxx Processing," Americord, accessed April 8, 2022, https://www.americordblood.com/placental-tissue/.
19. Ferreira, "Stem Cells: A Brief History and Outlook."
20. Ferreira, "Stem Cells: A Brief History and Outlook."
21. Gilbert Meilaender, *Bioethics: A Primer for Christians*, 3rd ed. (Grand Rapids, MI: Eerdmans, 2013), 42.
22. Carter, "The FAQs: What Christians Should Know about CRISPR Genetic Scissors."
23. Anjana Ahuja, "'God Is Not in Charge, We Are'; Interview," *Times* [London, England], July 24, 2003, 6, https://link.gale.com/apps/doc/A105815467/STND?u=bju_main&sid=bookmark-STND&xid=d1445762.
24. Angel Corona, "Disease Eradication: What Does It Take to Wipe out a Disease?" American Society for Microbiology, March 6, 2020, https://asm.org/Articles/2020/March/Disease-Eradication-What-Does-It-Take-to-Wipe-out.
25. Corona, "Disease Eradication."
26. "History of Living Donation," United Network for Organ Sharing, Transplant Living, accessed April 19, 2022, https://transplantliving.org/living-donation/history/.
27. "Donate Organs While Alive," Health Resources & Services Administration, organdonor.gov, last reviewed April 2021, https://www.organdonor.gov/learn/process/living-donation.
28. "The Organ Transplant Process," Health Resources & Services Administration, organdonor.gov, last reviewed April 2021, https://www.organdonor.gov/learn/process/transplant-process.
29. "Organ Donation Statistics," Health Resources & Services Administration, organdonor.gov, accessed April 19, 2022, https://www.organdonor.gov/learn/organ-donation-statistics.
30. "What Does the Bible Say about Blood Transfusions?," JW.org, Bible Questions Answered, accessed April 20, 2022, https://www.jw.org/en/bible-teachings/questions/bible-about-blood-transfusion/.
31. Bodie Hodge and Roger Patterson, eds., *World Religions and Cults*, vol. 1 (Green Forest, AR: Master Books, 2015), 208.
32. Hodge and Patterson, *World Religions and Cults*, 207.
33. Meilaender, *Bioethics*, 104.
34. "Organ Donation Statistics," Health Resources & Services Administration.
35. Meilaender, *Bioethics*, 90.
36. "Man Given Genetically Modified Pig Heart Dies," BBC News, March 9, 2022, https://www.bbc.com/news/health-60681493.
37. Carter, "The FAQs: Chinese Scientists Create First Monkey-Human Embryos."
38. United Nations Meetings Coverage and Press Releases, March 28, 2019, https://www.un.org/press/en/2019/ga12131.doc.htm.
39. See video, "Here's What to Expect from Our Planet in the Next 100 Years If We Take No Action on Climate Change," World Economic Forum, July 2, 2021, https://www.weforum.org/videos/20257-2021-what-to-expect-from-our-planet-in-the-next-100-years-if-we-take-no-action-on-climate-change-uplinkmp4-a6c42fe4ce.
40. Taken from page 504 of *Invitation to Christian Ethics: Moral Reasoning and Contemporary Issues* © Copyright 2020 by Ken Magnuson, Invitation to Theological Studies Series. Published by Kregel Publications, Grand Rapids, MI. Used by permission of the publisher. All rights reserved.

41. "Our Partners," The Partnership Project, accessed April 3, 2023, https://partnershipproject.org/partners/.

42. "Who We Are," The Partnership Project, accessed April 3, 2023, https://partnershipproject.org/who-we-are/#our-story.

43. "What PETA REALLY Stands For," People for Ethical Treatment of Animals, accessed May 4, 2022, https://www.peta.org/features /what-peta-really-stands-for/.

44. Why Animal Rights?," People for Ethical Treatment of Animals, accessed May 4, 2022, https://www.peta.org/about-peta/why-peta /why-animal-rights/.

45. Magnuson, *Invitation to Christian Ethics*, 504.

46. Abraham Kuyper, *On Business & Economics*, ed. Peter S. Heslam, Collected Works in Public Theology (Bellingham, WA: Lexham, 2021), 78–79.

47. Jo Ann Stover, *If Everybody Did* (Greenville, SC: BJU Press, 1989).

Chapter 13: Sexual Ethics

1. Taken from page 202 of *Invitation to Christian Ethics: Moral Reasoning and Contemporary Issues* © Copyright 2020 by Ken Magnuson, Invitation to Theological Studies Series. Published by Kregel Publications, Grand Rapids, MI. Used by permission of the publisher. All rights reserved.

2. See *Christian Ethics: An Introduction to Biblical Moral Reasoning* by Wayne Grudem, © 2018, p. 802. Used by permission of Crossway, a publishing ministry of Good News Publishers, Wheaton, IL 60187, www.crossway.org. Grudem cites Judith Wallerstein and Sandra Blakeslee, *Second Chances: Men, Women, and Children a Decade after Divorce* (New York: Ticknor and Fields, 1989), 41.

3. W. Bradford Wilcox, "The Evolution of Divorce," *National Affairs* 1, Fall 2009: 81–94, https://www.nationalaffairs.com/publications/detail /the-evolution-of-divorce.

4. Taken from page 747 of *The Doctrine of the Christian Life* by John M. Frame. Copyright 2008, P&R Publishing, Phillipsburg, NJ.

5. Frame, *The Doctrine of the Christian Life*, 766–67.

6. Taken from page 14 of *Transforming Homosexuality: What the Bible Says about Sexual Orientation and Change* by Denny Burk and Heath Lambert. Copyright 2015, P&R Publishing, Phillipsburg, NJ.

7. Grudem, *Christian Ethics*, 843–44.

8. See *The Rise and Triumph of the Modern Self: Cultural Amnesia, Expressive Individualism, and the Road to Sexual Revolution* by Carl Trueman © 2020, p. 176. Used by permission of Crossway, a publishing ministry of Good News Publishers, Wheaton, IL 60187, www.crossway .org.

9. See Trueman, *The Rise and Triumph of the Modern Self*, 176.

10. Grudem, *Christian Ethics*, 874.

11. Rick Phillips, "Should We Equate Homosexual and Heterosexual Sin?," Reformation21, June 4, 2015, https://www.reformation21.org/blogs /should-we-equate-homosexual-an.php.

12. Godefridus Udemans, *The Practice of Faith, Hope, Love* (Reformation Heritage, 2012), Kindle edition, loc. 7235.

13. Jonathan V. Last, *What to Expect When No One's Expecting: America's Coming Demographic Disaster* (New York: Encounter Books, 2014).

14. "Current Contraceptive Status Among Women Aged 15–49: United States, 2015–2017," CDC National Center for Health Statistics, Data Brief 327 (December 2018), Figure 2, https://www.cdc.gov/nchs/data /databriefs/db327-H.pdf.

15. Grudem, *Christian Ethics*, 752.

16. Rachel Nall, "Everything You Need to Know about Artificial Insemination," last updated December 22, 2017, https://www.healthline.com /health/artificial-insemination#process.

17. Rebecca Buffum Taylor, "Using a Surrogate Mother: What You Need to Know," last updated November 04, 2021, https://www.webmd.com /infertility-and-reproduction/guide/using-surrogate-mother; "Surrogacy," Yale Medicine, Fact Sheets, accessed March 31, 2023, https:// www.yalemedicine.org/conditions/gestational-surrogacy.

18. "Carrier Screening FAQs," The American College of Obstetricians and Gynecologists, last updated December 2020, https://www.acog.org /womens-health/faqs/carrier-screening.

Glossary

1. Taken from *Christian Ethics: An Introduction to Biblical Moral Reasoning* by Wayne Grudem, © 2018, p. 566. Used by permission of Crossway, a publishing ministry of Good News Publishers, Wheaton, IL 60187, www.crossway.org.

2. David Mathis, "We Will See His Face: What Is the Beatific Vision?" Desiring God, March 11, 2021, https://www.desiringgod.org/articles/we -will-see-his-face.

3. *Cambridge Dictionary* online, s.v. "bribery," accessed July 29, 2022, https://dictionary.cambridge.org/us/dictionary/english/bribery.

4. Joe Carter, "9 Things You Should Know about Human Cloning," The Gospel Coalition, May 17, 2013, https://www.thegospelcoalition.org /article/9-things-you-should-know-about-human-cloning/.

5. Jim Berg, *Essential Virtues: Marks of the Christ-Centered Life* (Greenville, SC: JourneyForth, 2008), 164.

6. Wilhelmus à Brakel, *The Law, Christian Graces, and the Lord's Prayer*, vol. 3 of *The Christian's Reasonable Service*, ed. Joel R. Beeke, trans. Bartel Elshout (Grand Rapids, MI: Reformation Heritage Books, 2015), 103–4; italics in the original.

7. Grudem, *Christian Ethics*, 587.

8. *Cambridge Dictionary* online, s.v. "exploitation," accessed July 30, 2022, https://dictionary.cambridge.org/us/dictionary/english/exploitation.

9. *Cambridge Dictionary* online, s.v. "extortion," accessed July 29, 2022, https://dictionary.cambridge.org/us/dictionary/english/extortion.

10. John Calvin, *Institutes of the Christian Religion* 3.2.7, vol. 1, ed. John T. McNeill, trans. Ford Lewis Battles, The Library of Christian Classics, vol. 20 (Philadelphia: Westminster Press, 1960), 551.

11. Joe Carter, "The FAQs: What Christians Should Know about CRISPR Genetic Scissors," The Gospel Coalition, October 14, 2022, https:// www.thegospelcoalition.org/article/the-faqs-what-christians-should -know-about-crispr-genetic-scissors/.

12. Carter, "The FAQs: What Christians Should Know about CRISPR Genetic Scissors."

13. James T. Dennison, Jr., comp., "Calvin's Catechism (1537)," in vol. 1, *Reformed Confessions of the 16th and 17th Centuries in English Translation* (Grand Rapids, MI: Reformation Heritage Books, 2008), 378.

14. Jerry Bridges, *The Practice of Godliness* (Colorado Springs: NavPress, 1983), 91.

15. Taken from page 34 of *The Defense of the Faith*, 4th ed., by Cornelius Van Til, ed. K. Scott Oliphint. Copyright 2008, P&R Publishing, Phillipsburg, NJ.

16. Michael Walzer, *Arguing about War* (New Haven, CT: Yale University Press, 2004), 22.

17. Oliver O'Donovan, *The Just War Revisited* (Cambridge: Cambridge University Press, 2003), 5.

18. Augustine, *On Christian Teaching* 3.10.16, in William Harmless, ed., *In His Own Words* (Washington, DC: CUA Press, 2010), 170.

19. Grudem, *Christian Ethics*, 311.

20. 18 U.S.C. 1112(a), http://uscode.house.gov/view.xhtml?req=granuleid: USC-prelim-title18-section1112&num=0&edition=prelim.

21. See 18 U.S.C. 1112(a).

22. See 18 U.S.C. 1112(a).

23. 18 U.S.C. 1111(a), http://uscode.house.gov/view.xhtml?req=granuleid: USC-prelim-title18-section1111&num=0&edition=prelim.

24. See 18 U.S.C. 1111(a).

25. See 18 U.S.C. 1111(a).

26. *Oxford English Dictionary* online, s.v. "racism", last modified March 2022, https://www.oed.com/view/Entry/157097?redirectedFrom= racism#eid.

27. Collins COBUILD Advanced Learner's Dictionary online, s.v. "recreational drug," accessed April 4, 2023, https://www.collinsdictionary .com/us/dictionary/english/recreational-drug.

28. Bridges, *The Practice of Godliness*, 164.

29. "Self-Defense Law: Overview," FindLaw, updated September 10, 2022, https://www.findlaw.com/criminal/criminal-law-basics/self-defense -overview.html.

30. Joe Carter, "The FAQs: Chinese Scientists Create First Monkey-Human Embryos," The Gospel Coalition, April 19, 2021, https://www .thegospelcoalition.org/article/create-monkey-human-embryos/.

31. Carter, "The FAQs: Chinese Scientists Create First Monkey-Human Embryos."

32. See Augustine, *City of God* 15.22, trans. Marcus Dods, with an introduction by Thomas Merton (New York: Modern Library, 1993), 511.

glossary

A

abortion "Any action that intentionally causes the death and removal from the womb of an unborn child."[1]

abstinence With respect to alcohol use, the position that emphasizes both the necessity of avoiding drunkenness and the wisdom of abstaining from that which gets one drunk.

addiction Dependence on getting pleasure from a substance or behavior regardless of the negative consequences.

adultery Marital unfaithfulness; lust for someone or sexual activity that violates the marriage covenant of one or both people involved.

anger Intense displeasure arising from strong disagreement with a situation.

animal rights The idea that animals are entitled to the same rights and privileges that humans are entitled to—no exploitation and no abuse; generally includes the notion that any killing or prolonged caging of animals to benefit humans is unethical.

artificial insemination from a donor Collecting semen from a man other than a woman's husband and injecting it into her cervix or uterus.

artificial insemination from a husband Collecting a husband's semen and injecting it into his wife's cervix or uterus.

asceticism The severe denial of the normal physical needs of the body, usually for the purpose of gaining spiritual merit.

assisted reproductive technology (ART) All types of medical technology used to promote reproduction in order to overcome infertility.

authenticity Being true to oneself, being transparent, and following one's heart—most often leading to transparent sinfulness.

B

beatific vision "The sight that makes happy,"[2] specifically the direct sight of God Himself, which believers will experience in their glorified state.

bestiality Sexual behavior with animals.

birth control A general term that refers to preventing pregnancy; contraception through the use of artificial or natural methods.

bisexual According to LGBTQ+ advocates, someone with sexual desires for or who engages in sexual behavior with both men and women.

bribery "An attempt to make someone do something for you by giving the person money, presents, or something else that he or she wants."[3]

C

capital punishment A government's use of execution as a criminal penalty.

categorical imperative A maxim (or principle) that a person is convinced would guide all people to do the right thing if it were a universal law. This maxim is always true regardless of circumstances and is an obligation for all people at all times, according to Kant's formulation.

Christian disobedience to authority A refusal to obey a legitimate authority's laws or commands that contradict the commands of God.

Christian ethics The branch of theology that studies how man ought to live in light of Scriptural teaching, creational norms, and moral reasoning.

cloning A form of reproduction that does not use a sperm and an egg but takes genetic material from a single person to manufacture a new, almost identical, but separate, individual.[4]

cohabitation Living together before or apart from marriage.

commercialism The abuse of profit-making that dehumanizes people by reducing them to cogs in an economic machine, by appealing to their covetousness.

communitarianism (on immigration) A framework that when applied to immigration defends the prerogative of each nation to govern its borders with moral appropriateness, keeping in mind the challenges immigrants and refugees face that host nations can help overcome.

compassion An external manifestation of loving-kindness that sympathetically and indiscriminately meets a need.

compatibility The popular idea that, in order for a marriage to work, couples must have a lot in common.

consequentialist ethics Ethical choices are governed by the results or ends they will achieve. The proper end is that which achieves the greatest amount of good. The good is often happiness, as defined by the individual or by society.

conservation The effort to preserve or improve certain

natural resources so that they remain available for use in the future.

corruption Any harm done to God's good design and moral will for His creation.

cosmopolitanism A framework that when applied to immigration focuses on the needs and well-being of the individual regardless of a person's immigration status.

courage Spiritual strength to unashamedly do the right thing at the right time even at risk of one's own harm.[5]

covenantal identity Who a person is—based not on individual characteristics but based on his or her relationship to a representative head whom God established, either Adam or Christ.

cowardice Running away from danger; refusing to stand up to defend what is true and right when threatened.

creational norms Standards for how life in God's creation works, discerned by observing the design of the created order in light of Scripture's teaching.

cruelty The willful causation of distress or discomfort in others.

cunning Involves shrewdness as well as deception. Like prudence, cunning employs a thorough analysis of the situation, but it does so in order to obtain something through immoral means or to an unethical end.

deontological ethics Ethical choices are governed by objective, absolute, universal rules or principles and a selfless commitment to duty.

despair Hopelessness; describes giving up and being pessimistic about the outcome of a situation.

diligence *"The exertion of the spiritual and physical powers of a believer whereby he willingly, joyously, and earnestly executes that task which God assigns him, doing so because it is the will of God."*[6]

disloyalty Disregard (without a legitimate ethical reason) for any commitment to remain faithful and loyal to something or someone.

environmentalism A movement that seeks the protection of the environment from human destruction and the improvement of the conditions of the environment through social and political action.

ethical egoism A consequentialist approach in which pure, individual self-interest directed toward fulfillment of personal happiness is the governing goal.

ethics The branch of philosophy that studies how man ought to live.

eugenics The quest to bolster human genetics by preventing people with traits deemed undesirable from reproducing, while encouraging people with traits deemed desirable to procreate; has often been associated with the idea that some races are superior to others.

euthanasia "The act of intentionally ending the life of a person who is elderly, terminally ill, or suffering from some incurable injury or disease."[7]

existentialist ethics Ethical choices are determined by the freely choosing individual. In the absence of absolute truth or meaning, the individual creates his own meaning and essence by the choices he makes and must take full responsibility for the outcome of these choices.

exploitation "The use of something in order to get an advantage from it."[8]

external coherence The test of whether an ethical system aligns with real life.

extortion "The act of getting something, especially money, by force or threats."[9]

faith "A firm and certain knowledge of God's benevolence toward us, founded upon the truth of the freely given promise in Christ, both revealed to our minds and sealed upon our hearts through the Holy Spirit."[10]

faithfulness Steadfast loyalty to that which is morally acceptable and good, despite difficulty and conflict.

falsehood As a vice, describes the endorsement of untruths to harm someone else or for personal gain.

fornication Sexual immorality.

G

gene editing "A form of genome engineering in which DNA is inserted, replaced, or removed from the genetic material of a cell using artificially engineered enzymes, or 'molecular scissors.'"[11]

gentleness Tender care for others even when they are hard to deal with.

germline An individual's sex cells (ovum or sperm) or "the lineage of [sex] cells spanning generations of individuals."[12]

goodness Generously seeking others' happiness and well-being, as determined by God's righteous standards.

gratitude An attitude of thanksgiving to God for His provision and governance of all things.

H

harshness Unpleasantness, roughness, or meanness directed toward someone.

homosexual According to LGBTQ+ advocates, someone with sexual desires for a person of the same sex and/or who engages in sexual behavior with a person of the same sex.

honesty A devotion to truthfulness where one affirms and acts in accord with what is true and righteous.

hope "The expectation of the things that faith has believed to be truly promised by God."[13]

humility A lowly view of one's own importance, resulting from "a high view of God's person"[14] and a profound sense of one's own weakness and sinfulness.

image of God in man The essence of being human; a bestowed status whereby the whole person is made to be "like God in everything in which a creature can be like God."[15]

immigrant Someone who relocates to a country other than his or her own.

immodesty Dress, or undress, that draws sexual attention.

incest Sexual relations among family members aside from between a husband and wife.

indifference Apathy toward others and utter lack of concern for the ethical good of a situation.

inequality The treatment of certain groups as less worthy of respect and dignity than other groups.

ingratitude Taking things for granted, overlooking what is clearly worthy of thanks, and being unthankful for all the good one has.

internal consistency The test of whether an ethical system contradicts or undermines itself.

in vitro fertilization (IVF) Joining together a wife's egg and a husband's sperm to form an embryo in a laboratory.

joy A confident delight in God's sovereign work in all of life's circumstances.

just war doctrine A perspective on war that recognizes war as a moral matter[16] and also recognizes that war can be a legitimate way for governments to ensure justice[17]; sets ethical parameters on when war is ethically viable and how to conduct oneself in war.

kindness An internal sentiment, cultivated by the Holy Spirit, that motivates believers to indiscriminately do good to others.

kingdom of God The reign of the risen and enthroned Lord Jesus Christ; includes Christ bringing the saints to fulfill the Creation Mandate as well, so that they rule the creation as God intended.

legalism Trying to earn justification with God through works, or trying to earn a higher standing with God by the performance of works or rituals.

LGBTQ+ An abbreviation that stands for lesbian, gay, bisexual, transgender, queer (or questioning), and several other terms that are used to denote various types of gender identity confusion.

love "Any movement of the soul to enjoy God for God's own sake, and to enjoy one's self and one's neighbor for God's sake."[18]

lying Verbally declaring something that one knows to be false.[19]

manslaughter "The unlawful killing of a human being without malice."[20]

manslaughter (involuntary) Manslaughter that results from carelessness or occurs in conjunction with the commission of a minor crime.[21]

manslaughter (voluntary) Manslaughter that takes place impulsively in response to a heated exchange or serious provocation.[22]

marital purity Forsaking all forbidden sexual activity and partaking in the sexual activity God designed for a man and woman within the bounds of marriage.

masturbation Sexual self-stimulation.

meekness A humble and calm disposition in situations that can lead to pride or anger.

militarism A perspective that sees war as the means to fulfilling the desires of a country or its leaders.

moralism Trying to be a good, upstanding person through one's own good works; focused on social acceptability.

murder "The unlawful killing of a human being with malice aforethought."[23]

murder (first-degree) Premeditated murder or murder committed alongside another serious crime.[24]

murder (second-degree) Any murder that does not fit the definition of first-degree murder.[25]

naturalistic fallacy This fallacy assumes that what is natural is good. In other words, it assumes that if a behavior is found in nature, it must be morally acceptable.

no-fault divorce Divorce law that allows for divorce without the need for either party to demonstrate that the other has violated the marriage covenant.

 O

organ donation Voluntarily giving one's organs or tissues to replace someone else's defective or damaged organs or tissues.

organ transplantation The replacement of a defective or damaged organ or tissue in one person with a healthy organ or tissue taken from another person.

 P

pacifism A perspective on war that, in its most extreme form, opposes all forms of violent action, even those which would avoid great harm or promote a great good.

patience A believer's faith-filled and hopeful endurance under long-lasting difficult circumstances.

peace A harmonious wholeness produced when God's design of the world, including human relationships, is rightly ordered; as a virtue, describes the mindset and character of a believer, even during difficult and unpleasant circumstances.

polygamy Having multiple spouses at one time.

pornography Pictures, videos, or graphic descriptions intended to stimulate sexual desire.

pride An inflated estimation of oneself which attempts to rob God of His rightful place as sovereign Lord of all.

prostitution Providing sex acts for pay or in return for some benefit.

prudence The ability to choose the best course of action, having considered all the constraints of the situation, to obtain the most righteous and beneficial outcome.

R

race The single race of humans (all descended from Adam and distinct from animals) or a distinct cultural, ethnic, social, or people group within the human race.

racism "Prejudice, antagonism, or discrimination by an individual, institution, or society, against a person or people on the basis of their nationality or (now usually) their membership of a particular racial or ethnic group, typically one that is a minority or marginalized. Also: beliefs that members of a particular racial or ethnic group possess innate characteristics or qualities, or that some racial or ethnic groups are superior to others; an ideology based on such beliefs."[26]

rashness Acting in the moment with no regard for whether one's actions are the best way, or even a good way, to reach a desired end.

realism (on immigration) A framework that when applied to immigration recognizes that each government will act according to its best interests in relation to its own people. Borders and immigration laws feature positively in this framework.

realism (on war) A utilitarian and pragmatic perspective on war that views wars as necessary evils, where any moral considerations either don't exist or are very flexible.

rebellion The rejection of a current government's authority and the assertion of an opposing agenda through violence.

recklessness Throwing all caution to the wind and acting or reacting impulsively.

recreational drugs Drugs "that some people take occasionally for enjoyment, especially when they are spending time socially with other people."[27]

righteousness The conformity of an individual's life to God's standards of moral perfection.

 S

self-control "The exercise of inner strength under the direction of sound judgment that enables us to do, think, and say the things that are pleasing to God."[28]

self-defense "The right to prevent suffering force or violence through the use of a sufficient level of counteracting force or violence."[29]

self-indulgence Having no inhibitions, a total letting go of oneself to do as one pleases.

sexual abuse Any criminal activity that forces any kind of sexual perversion on another person; includes rape and pedophilia.

situation ethics A consequentialist ethical approach. A form of ethical relativism that holds that a person should always act in the way that is most loving in each situation. Love is not tied to any moral absolutes, and what love requires may be different in different situations for different people.

sloth Laziness; a lack of motivation to do necessary and productive work.

stem cells Cells that "have not yet obtained a special structure and function."[30]

stem cells (embryonic) A type of stem cell found in embryos in their first few days of development that can develop into any type of cell in the body.[31]

strife Adversarial contention that leads an individual to verbally disagree with, ideologically break away from, or physically engage the conflicting party.

suicide The intentional and voluntary taking of one's own life.

surrogacy Using the womb of a third party (a surrogate mother) for the gestation of a baby.

temperance Self-control and the avoidance of excessive behavior.

transgender According to LGBTQ+ advocates, someone who thinks of him- or herself as having a gender different from his or her sex.

ungodliness Anything that is contrary to God's nature or opposed to God's ways.

utilitarianism The most common consequentialist approach to ethics. Believes that the utility (usefulness) of an action to bring about an intended helpful end determines what is right or best. The end justifies the means, and the proper end (or goal) is to do the greatest good for the greatest number of people, usually understood as that which brings the most happiness and the least pain.

utopian Relating to an ideal society of perfect peace, justice, and prosperity; often intended as a description of an unrealistic hope.

vice A character trait or consistent behavior that is recognizably wicked or immoral; a deviation from God's upright standard. May be the exact opposite of a virtue or may be the twisting of a virtue into a counterfeit.

virtue Rightly ordered love,[32] which manifests itself in a person's character and behavior.

virtue ethics An approach to ethics that focuses on discerning what virtues lead to a flourishing life and on developing those virtues so they become habitual.

volunteerist perspective The belief that God's law is simply whatever He wills it to be and that right and wrong could have been opposite what they are, merely at God's whim.

W

wisdom The art of living well by observing creational norms through the lenses of Scripture, by listening to the counsel of the wise, and by being conscious that all of life is lived before the face of God.

workaholism Excessive engagement in work that leaves no room for and gives no attention to the other good and necessary parts of life that aren't work.

worry Emotional instability where someone rehearses all the what-ifs about a given situation and fails to trust God and His Word.

scripture memory

1. Creational Foundations for Ethics

ROMANS 1:18-20

For the wrath of God is revealed from heaven against all ungodliness and unrighteousness of men, who hold the truth in unrighteousness; Because that which may be known of God is manifest in them; for God hath shewed it unto them. For the invisible things of him from the creation of the world are clearly seen, being understood by the things that are made, even his eternal power and Godhead; so that they are without excuse.

2. The Fall's Effects on Ethics

ROMANS 3:10-12

As it is written, There is none righteous, no, not one: There is none that understandeth, there is none that seeketh after God. They are all gone out of the way, they are together become unprofitable; there is none that doeth good, no, not one.

3. The Role of Redemption in Ethics

COLOSSIANS 3:1-3, 12

If ye then be risen with Christ, seek those things which are above, where Christ sitteth on the right hand of God. Set your affection on things above, not on things on the earth. For ye are dead, and your life is hid with Christ in God. . . . Put on therefore, as the elect of God, holy and beloved, bowels of mercies, kindness, humbleness of mind, meekness, longsuffering.

4. Becoming Like Christ

2 PETER 1:3, 5-7

According as his divine power hath given unto us all things that pertain unto life and godliness, through the knowledge of him that hath called us to glory and virtue: . . . And beside this, giving all diligence, add to your faith virtue; and to virtue knowledge; And to knowledge temperance; and to temperance patience; and to patience godliness; And to godliness brotherly kindness; and to brotherly kindness charity.

5. Three Central Virtues

1 CORINTHIANS 13:13

And now abideth faith, hope, charity, these three; but the greatest of these is charity.

6. Virtues, Part 1

PHILIPPIANS 4:8

Finally, brethren, whatsoever things are true, whatsoever things are honest, whatsoever things are just, whatsoever things are pure, whatsoever things are lovely, whatsoever things are of good report; if there be any virtue, and if there be any praise, think on these things.

7. Virtues, Part 2

GALATIANS 5:22-23

But the fruit of the Spirit is love, joy, peace, longsuffering, gentleness, goodness, faith, Meekness, temperance: against such there is no law.

8. A Method for Handling Ethical Issues

PSALM 119:97, 101-4

O how love I thy law! it is my meditation all the day. . . . I have refrained my feet from every evil way, that I might keep thy word. I have not departed from thy judgments: for thou hast taught me. How sweet are thy words unto my taste! yea, sweeter than honey to my mouth! Through thy precepts I get understanding: therefore I hate every false way.

9. The Ethics of Life and Death

EXODUS 20:13

Thou shalt not kill.

MATTHEW 5:21-22

Ye have heard that it was said by them of old time, Thou shalt not kill; and whosoever shall kill shall be in danger of the judgment: But I say unto you, That whosoever is angry with his brother without a cause shall be in danger of the judgment: and whosoever shall say to his brother, Raca, shall be in danger of the council: but whosoever shall say, Thou fool, shall be in danger of hell fire.

10. Ethical Government

ROMANS 13:1, 4

Let every soul be subject unto the higher powers. For there is no power but of God: the powers that be are ordained of God. . . . For he is the minister of God to thee for good. But if thou do that which is evil, be afraid; for he beareth not the sword in vain: for he is the minister of God, a revenger to execute wrath upon him that doeth evil.

11. Ethical Society

MATTHEW 7:12

Therefore all things whatsoever ye would that men should do to you, do ye even so to them: for this is the law and the prophets.

12. Ethical Science

GENESIS 1:28–30

And God blessed them, and God said unto them, Be fruitful, and multiply, and replenish the earth, and subdue it: and have dominion over the fish of the sea, and over the fowl of the air, and over every living thing that moveth upon the earth. And God said, Behold, I have given you every herb bearing seed, which is upon the face of all the earth, and every tree, in the which is the fruit of a tree yielding seed; to you it shall be for meat. And to every beast of the earth, and to every fowl of the air, and to every thing that creepeth upon the earth, wherein there is life, I have given every green herb for meat: and it was so.

13. Sexual Ethics

1 THESSALONIANS 4:3–5

For this is the will of God, even your sanctification, that ye should abstain from fornication: That every one of you should know how to possess his vessel in sanctification and honour; Not in the lust of concupiscence, even as the Gentiles which know not God.

scripture index

1:24–32	18
1:33	18
2:6	2
2:6–9	95
2:14	31
2:20	92
3:5–6	19, 55, 140
3:5–7	16, 53
3:7	114
3:9–10	202
3:13–18	18
3:19	28
3:19–20	17
3:32	64
4:7	97
4:23	30, 67, 103
5:1	244
5:7–14	245
5:15–17	242
5:15–19	53
5:18–19	242
5:18–21	244
5:20	242, 244
6:9–11	104
6:16–17	114, 129
6:19	129, 208
6:23–35	244
6:25–26	243
6:27–28	245
6:27–29	53
6:29–32	239
7:1	244
7:1–6	246
7:7	246
7:8–9	246
7:10	243, 246
7:10–11	246
7:10–20	243
7:12	246
7:13	246
7:13–21	246
7:16–18	246
7:19–20	246
7:21	246
7:22–27	246
8:4	29
8:12	153
8:22–31	28
8:30	51

9:10	2, 18, 51, 97, 222
10:4	214
11:1	129
11:3	64
11:6	64
12:10	231
13:4	104, 214
13:10	97
14:5	129
14:6	138
14:15	201
14:16	105, 242
11:6	64
12:10	231
13:4	104, 214
13:10	97
14:5	129
14:6	138
14:15	201
14:16	105, 242
14:17	114
14:19	92
14:23	53
14:29	31, 114
15:8	64
15:16	79
15:22	97
16:8	212
16:18	114
18:9	104
18:13	98, 141
19:11	104
19:15	104
20:1	202
20:4	104, 214
20:9	30
20:11	64
21:2	174
21:5	204
21:8	64
21:25	104
22:22–23	204
23:6–8	67
23:20–21	203
23:27–28	243
23:29–35	202
23:33–35	107
24:4–5	53
24:11–12	151

26:4–5	39
26:13–16	104
26:27	140
27:6	138
28:17	151
28:20	204
29:23	114
30:5	128
31:8–9	199

ECCLESIASTES

7:20	30, 92
9:2	92
9:7	202
9:10	101, 225
11:2	204
12:1	245
12:13	19, 245

SONG OF SOLOMON

1–8	242, 244
2:15	105

ISAIAH

1:10–18	67
1:11–18	142
3:12	249
5:16	92
5:20	93, 153
5:22	202
6:3	15
9:6	123
9:7	123
11:2	97
11:4	113
12:2	15
26:21	153
28:7–8	202
28:24–29	18
31:1	77
32:15–18	123
37:16	14
40:10–11	115
40:28	14
46:10	104
52:7	123
52:7–9	124
53:6	30
55:8–9	79
64:6	30

7:12–14	238	10:1	112, 115	2:1–7	122
7:15	239, 241	10:1–6	177	2:2	64
7:16	238	10:5	39	2:2–3	128
7:32–35	107	11:13–15	128	2:4–5	117
7:39	238, 241	11:32–33	153	2:8–9	113
8:1	8	12:9	157	2:10	64, 68
8:9	202	12:20	107	2:11–3:10	199
8:13	202	13:11	125	2:13–19	122
9:21	48			3:12–13	102

GALATIANS

9:25	107–8			4:1	67, 245
9:25–27	106	2:20	49, 63, 68, 94	4:2	113, 115
10:12–13	31	3:21–22	68	4:13	64
10:13	157, 161, 212	3:22	30	4:15	6, 100, 253
10:31	5, 55, 67, 157	3:29	57	4:16–24	69
11:3	238, 249	4:4	48	4:17	125
11:14–15	138, 249, 255	4:5	260	4:17–19	30
12:4	69	4:6	69	4:17–21	242
12:13	68	4:7	57	4:20	64
13:3	81	5:5	85	4:22–24	105, 242
13:4	84	5:13	245	4:25	129, 211
13:6	82	5:14	95	4:25–5:16	138
13:7	108	5:15	208	4:28	144
13:13	79	5:16	95, 109, 245	4:29	129
15:26	223	5:16–17	69	4:29–32	118
15:54	85	5:19	243	4:31	129, 197
15:58	254	5:19–23	63	4:32	117

2 CORINTHIANS

		5:20	107, 114	5:1	69
		5:22	80, 95, 117, 124	5:1–2	69
1:20	49	5:22–23	24, 69, 115, 203	5:3	243
3:18	24, 56, 58, 66, 67	5:23	106, 114	5:4	242
4:4	6, 30	5:25	69, 95	5:8	254
4:5–6	56	6:1	64, 104, 113, 119	5:9	95
4:7–18	139	6:2	69	5:10	69, 138
4:16–18	157	6:7	140, 245	5:11	254
4:17–18	109	6:9	87	5:11–13	242
4:18	78	6:10	83, 184, 197	5:15	69

EPHESIANS

5:2	222			5:15–17	95, 100, 107
5:7	78	1:3	123	5:16	88
5:10	14	1:3–4	55	5:18	69, 202, 203
5:11	65	1:3–5	79	5:22–33	93
5:17	68, 69, 117, 128, 252	1:3–8	122	5:23	238, 241
5:18–20	126	1:4	140, 245	5:31–32	238, 241
5:20	254	1:7	203	6:1–4	83
5:21	92	1:14	85	6:4	190, 257
7:1	69	1:16–17	100	6:10	101
7:9–10	153	1:17	30	6:10–17	177
7:10	245	2:1–3	30, 93	6:10–20	101
8:1	83	2:1–5	242	6:11	102
8:2	82			6:13–14	102

topical index

Page numbers followed by "i" indicate an image on that page.

A

abortion
    counsel on, 164
    definition of, 159–60
    justifications for, perceived, 160–61, 160–61i
    and patience, 108–9
    and sanctity of life, 161–62
    societal impact of, 162–63
    virtues for taking a stand on, 163–64
abstinence, and addiction, 202–3
acts, in decision making, 138–39, 140i, 143i
addiction, 107, 107i, 201–6
adultery, 242–46
agents, in decision making, 140–41, 140i, 143i
alcohol abuse. *See* addiction
anarchy, 188–89
anger, 114, 114i
animal organ transplantation, 227
animal rights, definition of, 228. *See also* conservation, environmentalism, animal rights
animals, for food, 231
antagonism, racial, 195
approaches to ethics. *See* ethical approaches
artificial insemination, 258
asceticism, 107, 107i
assent, 76
assisted reproductive technology (ART), 257–58
authenticity, 71
authority, Christian disobedience to, 185–90
authority, of God
    about, 4, 15
    absence of, 29, 36
    over life and death, 156–57, 219–20

B

beatific vision, 58
beatitudes, 57
Bible
    authority of, 21, 23, 39 (*see also* authority, of God)
    creational norms in, 18, 23, 52–53
    use of in ethical approaches, 35–36, 39–43
    on wisdom, 52–53
birth control, definition of, 256
birth control, reproductive technologies, eugenics, 256–60
bisexuality, definition of, 247. *See also* homosexuality/LGBTQ+

blessedness, 54, 57–58
blood transfusions, 225
bodies, Christian care of, 203–4, 207, 225
bribery, 210
business ethics, 210–14

C

capital punishment, 150, 167–72, 167i, 168i
categorical imperative, 34–35, 39–40
character of mankind, virtuous, 36–37, 42, 69
cheating, 125
children, decision to have or not, 256–57
choices, the Fall and, 31–32
Christian disobedience to authority, 185–90
Christian ethics, definition of, 2
Christian love, 81–82
Christlikeness, 54, 56, 66–69, 67i. *See also* Jesus Christ; virtues
climate change, 228–29, 233–34, 234i
cloning, definition of, 218. *See also* stem cell research, cloning, gene editing
cohabitation, 238
coherence, external, 39
colorblindness, 198
commercialism, 212–13
common grace, 18, 31
communication/media use, 206–10
communitarianism, 179
compassion, 116–21, 117i, 158, 180, 182, 227, 247
compatibility, of romantic partners, 238
competition, business, 213
confidence, 76–77
consequentialist ethics, 35–36, 36i, 39–40
conservation, environmentalism, animal rights
    Bible on, 230–32
    creation and, 229
    definitions of, 228
    and misuse of creation, 232–33
    virtues of, 234
consistency, internal, 39
context, in decision making, 141, 143i
corruption, 93–94
cosmetic surgery, 221
cosmopolitanism, 179–81
courage, 101–5, 104i, 152, 163, 177, 189
covenantal identity, 50
cowardice, 105
created order
    about, 4
    and creational norms, 17

and the Fall, 28–30
and wisdom, 51–52
creation. *See also* conservation, environmentalism, animal rights; created order
  Bible on, 230–32
  ethical issues for, 229
  and ethnic diversity, 199–200
  human care for, 230, 234
  misuse of, 232–33
  virtues for caring for, 234
  and wisdom, 51–52
creational foundations for ethics. *See* ethics, creational foundations of
creational norms, 30i
  definition of, 2, 16–17
  discovering, 18–19
  and laws of creation, 17
  role of, 20–21, 138–39
  wisdom and, 51–53
Creation Mandate, 22, 29, 57, 204, 211, 231, 251, 257
cremation, 224
cruelty, 118
cunningness, 98

D

decisions, method for making ethical, 140i, 143i
  acts, about, 138–39
  agents, about, 140–41
  application of, 143–45
  context, about, 141
  ends, about, 139–40
  questions for, 143i
deontological ethics, 34–35, 39–40, 137
despair, 124–25, 124i
diligence, 101–5, 152, 214
discrimination, 195, 222. *See also* racial discrimination/inequality
disloyalty, 104–5, 104i
disobedience to authority, Christian, 185–90
divorce, 238–41
drug use. *See* addiction
duty, 34–35, 40, 55

E

effort, 9
egoism, ethical, 35
embryonic stem cells, definition of, 217, 220–21i. *See also* stem cell research, cloning, gene editing
emotions, 31
end justifies the means, 35, 98
ends, in decision making, 139–40, 140i, 143i
environmentalism, definition of, 228. *See also* conservation, environmentalism, animal rights
ethical approaches, 33i
  consequentialist, 35–36, 36i, 39–40
  critique of, 39–40
  deontological, 34–35, 39–40

existentialist ethics, 37, 37i, 43, 43i
  virtue ethics, 36–37, 37i, 41–42
ethical egoism, 35
ethical issues. *See* issues, ethical
  righteousness, 92, 92i
ethics, about
  approaches to (*see* ethical approaches)
  biblical worldview themes, 4
  definitions of, 2–3
  relationships of, 3, 3i
ethics, creational foundations of
  basis for, 15
  created order, 16–21
  image of God in man, 21–24
ethics, study of, 5–9
ethnicity, definition of, 195
eugenics, 258–59
euthanasia, 154–59, 157i
evil, 66
exaltation, 56
existentialist ethics, 37, 37i, 43, 43i
exploitation, 212
external coherence, 39
extinct animals, 233i
extortion, 210

F

faith/faithfulness
  application of, 105
  and Christian disobedience to authority, 189
  definition of, 76, 101
  and diligence and courage, 102
  forward looking, 78–79
  vs. hope, 85
  and idolatry, 259
  and marriage, 240, 245
  misapplication of, 103
  object of, 77
  and sexuality, 254
  vice of, 104–5, 104i
the Fall, 28i, 30i, 31i
  and approaches to ethics (*see* ethical approaches)
  and choices, 31–32
  and common grace, 31
  and communication, 208
  and created order, 28–30
  on human nature, 30–31
  medical science and, 220–21
  vices and, 126
falsehoods, 127, 129–30
fear of God, 18–19, 31
fighting, 99–100
first-degree murder, 148
fornication, 242–46
freedom, individual, 43, 49–50
fruit of the Spirit, 115, 116i

for murder, manslaughter, self-defense, 152–53
of organ donation, 227
for racial discrimination/inequality, 200–201
for sexual purity, 245–46, 254
for suicide/euthanasia, 158
for war, 177
virtuousness. *See* Christlikeness
voluntary manslaughter, 148–49
volunteerist perspective, 47

W

war, just, 173–78, 174i
wealth/money, 53–54, 87, 144–45, 184, 204–5
white responsibility, 197–98
wisdom, 3–4, 7, 18–19, 19i, 50–54, 222
workaholism, 104, 104i
worldview, 28i
worldview, biblical, 3–4, 3i, 29
worry, 124–25, 124i, 125i

photo credits

Key: (t) top; (c) center; (b) bottom; (l) left; (r) right

Cover

Pyrosky/E+ via Getty Images

Throughout

(crinkle paper) Phecsone/Shutterstock.com; (crinkle paper) Ton Photographer 4289/Shutterstock.com

Introduction

4 skynesher/E+ via Getty Images; 5 brizmaker/iStockphoto via Getty Images; 6l bigacis/Shutterstock.com; 6r liquidtenerife/iStockphoto via Getty Images; 7 Maryna Patzen/iStockphoto via Getty Images

Chapter 1

13 Hulton Archive/Staff via Getty Images; 14, 25 vadik4444 /Shutterstock.com

Chapter 2

34 Grafissimo/Digital Vision Vectors via Getty Images; 43 Ho Ngoc Binh/Moment RF via Getty Images

Chapter 3

46 IanDagnall Computing/Alamy Stock Photo; 51 Guillem Lopez/ Alamy Stock Photo; 52 Victor Korchenko/Alamy Stock Photo; 54 Krakenimages.com/Shutterstock.com; 55 kate_sept2004/E+ via Getty Images; 57 TommL/E+ via Getty Images; 58 biletskiyevgeniy.com /Shutterstock.com

Chapter 4

63 Alberto Gagliardi/iStockphoto via Getty Images; 66 Historical/Corbis Historical via Getty Images; 68–69 Atid Kiattisaksiri/E+ via Getty Images; 70 Chronicle/Alamy Stock Photo

Chapter 5

75 Matveev Aleksandr/Shutterstock.com; 78 Valdis Skudre/Shutterstock .com; 85 CHAINFOTO24/Shutterstock.com

Chapter 6

94 Draga Saparevska/RooM RF via Getty Images; 95, 110 Floortje/ iStockphoto via Getty Images; 97 Khosrork/iStockphoto via Getty Images; 101 RTRO/Alamy Stock Photo; 103 Prostock-studio /Shutterstock.com

Chapter 7

113 mashabuba/E+ via Getty Images; 120l kieferpix/iStockphoto via Getty Images; 120c Prixel Creative/Shutterstock.com; 120r–21b jacoblund/iStockphoto via Getty Images; 121t SDI Productions/E+ via Getty Images; 128 iShootPhotosLLC/E+ via Getty Images; 130 Rapid Eye Media CC/iStockphoto via Getty Images

Chapter 8

137 Monkey Business Images/Shutterstock.com; 142 cirano83/iStock-photo via Getty Images; 144 Olivier Blondeau/E+ via Getty Images

Chapter 9

152 The Washington Post/Contributor via Getty Images; 154 Ghislain & Marie David de Lossy/The Image Bank via Getty Images; 158 Motortion/Shutterstock.com; 164 Ground Picture/Shutterstock.com

Chapter 10

167 imagedepotpro/E+ viaGetty Images; 170 BERIT ROALD/AFP via Getty Images; 173 3D_generator/iStock/Getty Images Plus via Getty Images; 176 Carl Court/Getty Images News via Getty Images; 181 Michele and Tom Grimm/Alamy Stock Photo

Chapter 11

194 kali9/E+ via Getty Images; 196t Science History Images/Alamy Stock Photo; 196bl Niday Picture Library/Alamy Stock Photo; 196br Tibbut Archive/Alamy Stock Photo; 202 mrs/Moment via Getty Images; 203 Igor Sandra/Alamy Stock Photo; 206l michaeljung/Shutterstock .com; 206r TheVisualsYouNeed/Shutterstock.com; 207 Felix Junker/ EyeEm via Getty Images; 211 tsyhun/Shutterstock.com; 213 fizkes/ Shutterstock.com

Chapter 12

217, 235 luismmolina/iStock/Getty Images Plus via Getty Images; 218 PA Images via Getty Images; 221 Yvonne Hemsey/Hulton Archive via Getty Images; 222 Carlos Fernandez/Moment via Getty Images; 223 PA Images/Alamy; 224 Akarawut/Shutterstock.com; 228–29 Christoph Prokop/Alamy Stock Photo; 230 Mitch Kezar/Design Pics via Getty Images; 231t mustafagi/E+ via Getty Images; 231b Africa Studio/Shutterstock.com; 232 georgeclerk/E+ via Getty Images; 233t Science History Images/Alamy Stock Photo; 233b ~UserGI15633185 /iStock/Getty Images Plus via Getty Images; 234 Peter Summers/Getty Images News via Getty Images

Chapter 13

237, 261 Olga Moreira/Shutterstock.com; 242 ©Kevin Dodge LLC /Tetra images RF via Getty Images; 247 Alessandro Biascioli/iStockphoto via Getty Images; 250 DNY59/iStockphoto via Getty Images; 255 Srdjanns74/iStockphoto via Getty Images; 256 AS photo family /Shutterstock.com; 258 Eddie Gerald/Alamy Stock Photo; 259 monkeybusinessimages/iStockphoto via Getty Images

Back Matter

264 kieferpix/iStockphoto via Getty Images 278-9 Prixel Creative /Shutterstock.com